Yume Kira
Dream
Shoppe

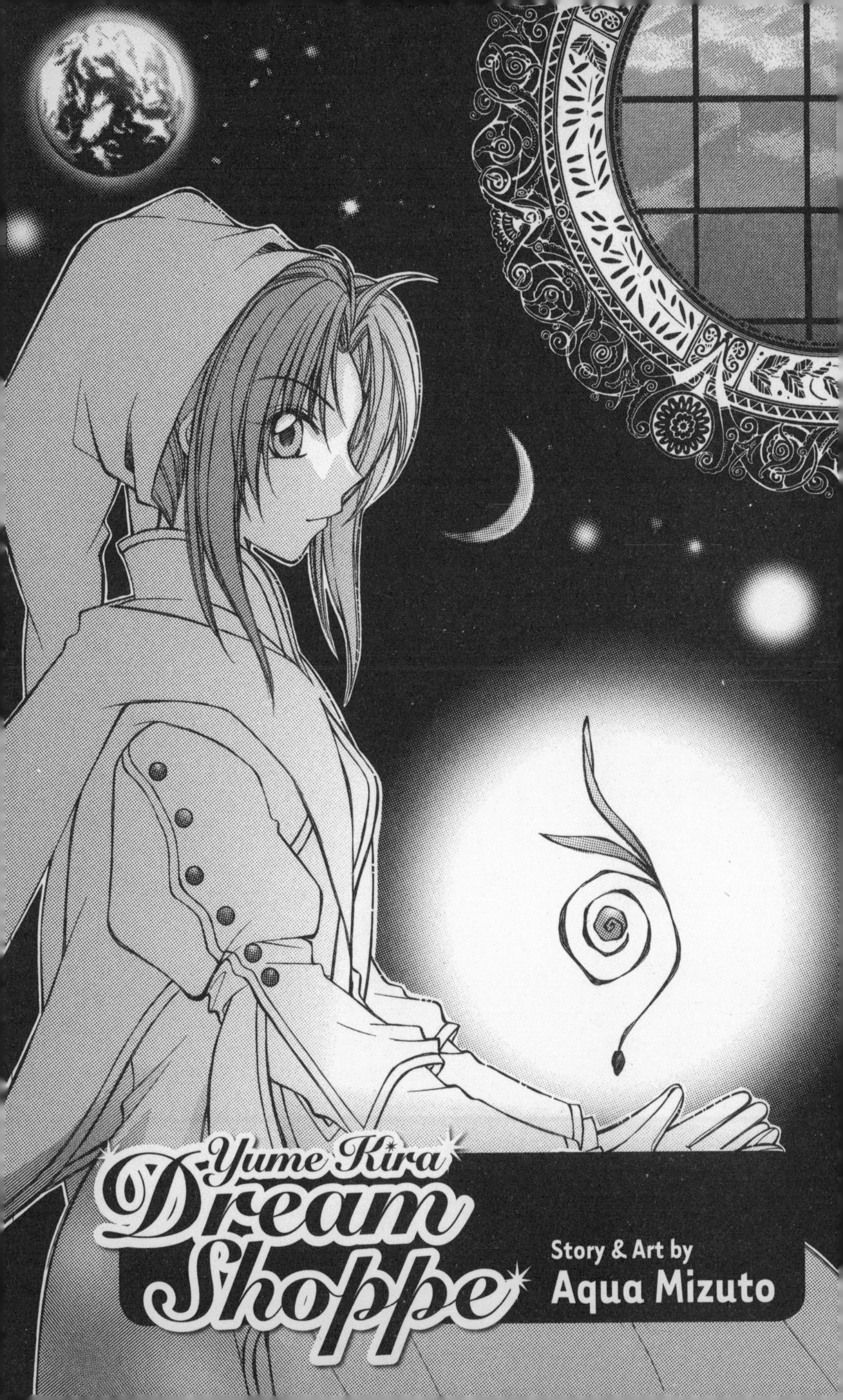
Yume Kira
Dream
Shoppe
Story & Art by
Aqua Mizuto

Yume Kira Dream Shoppe

TABLE OF CONTENTS

The Sound That Brings Blossoms

5

Beyond the Red Eye

47

A Promise to a Grain of Time

89

The Labyrinth Wave of Dreams

127

THE SOUND THAT BRINGS BLOSSOMS

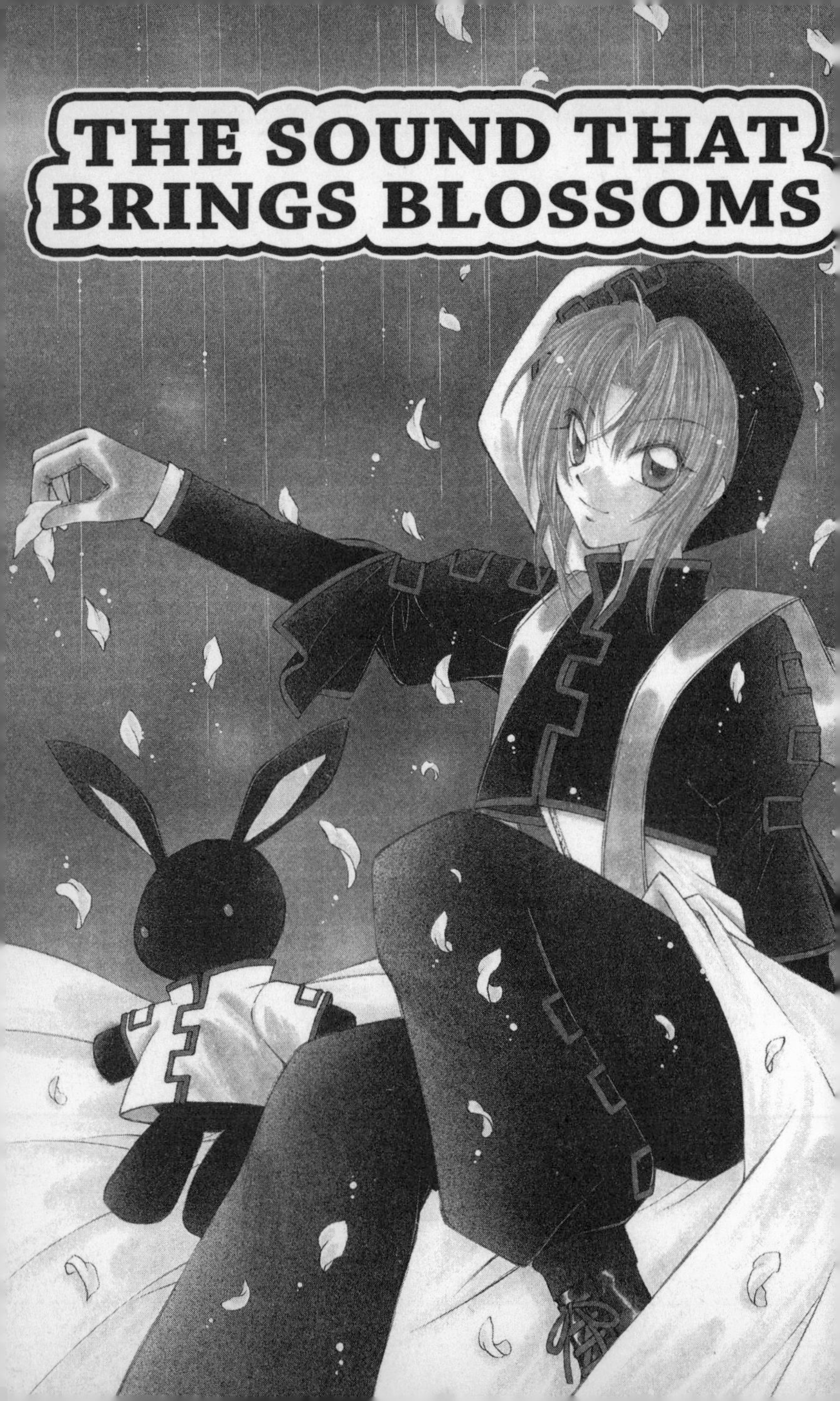

Product No.: **0001**
Product name: **Moon Maiden's Tears**
Quantity: **30 ml**
Directions for use: **Take 10 days before a full moon.**
Place of origin: **The moon**
Effect: **Changes appearance as desired.**

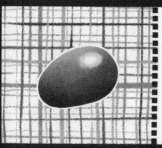

Product No.: **0002**
Product name: **Space Garnet**
Quantity: **1**
Directions for use: **Place on body. (Effective only until Christmas.)**
Place of origin: **Cosmic space**
Effect: **Enables anyone/thing to move and speak freely.**

Product No.: **0003**
Product name: **King's Hourglass**
Quantity: **Immeasurable**
Directions for use: **Think of an incident in the past you want to relive and flip it over.**
Place of origin: **Space-time desert**
Effect: **Allows one to travel back in time.**
Note: **Memories cannot be taken back.**

Product No.: **Not yet for sale**
Product name: **Nightmare candy**
Quantity: **3 (sun, moon & star)**
Directions for use: **Eat before going to bed.**
Place of origin: **Dark Dream Factory**
Effect: **Allows one to enter another's dream in any desired form.**

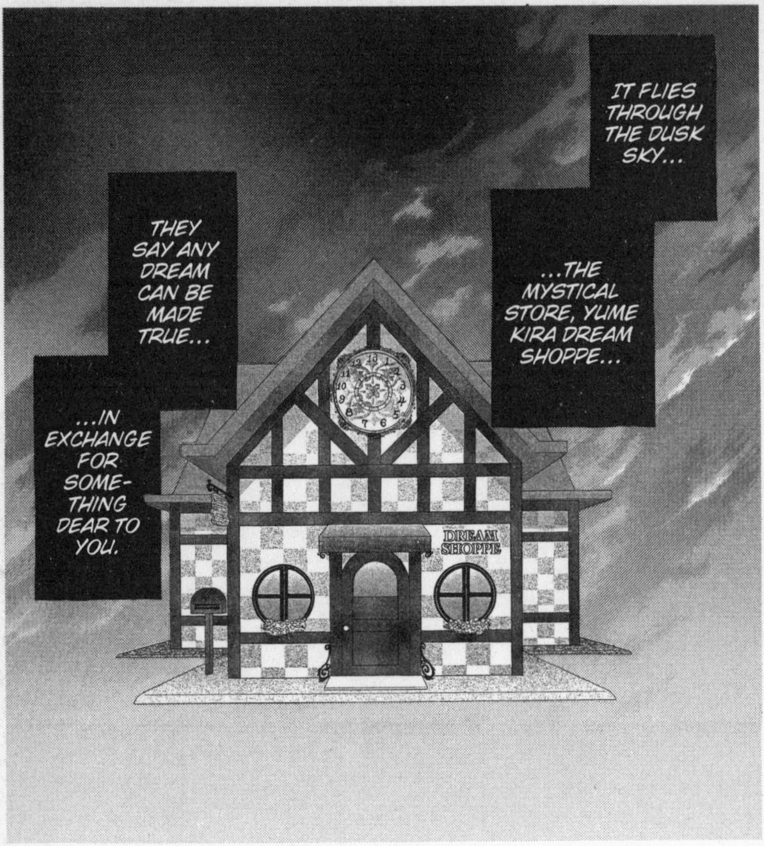
IT FLIES THROUGH THE DUSK SKY...
...THE MYSTICAL STORE, YUME KIRA DREAM SHOPPE...
THEY SAY ANY DREAM CAN BE MADE TRUE...
...IN EXCHANGE FOR SOME-THING DEAR TO YOU.
DREAM SHOPPE

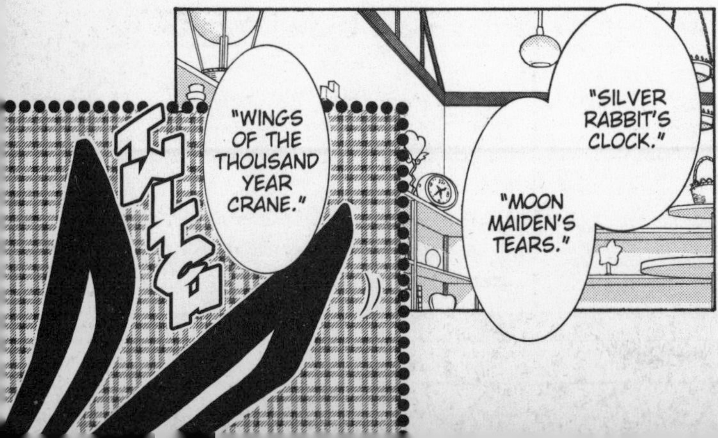
"SILVER RABBIT'S CLOCK."
"MOON MAIDEN'S TEARS."
"WINGS OF THE THOUSAND YEAR CRANE."

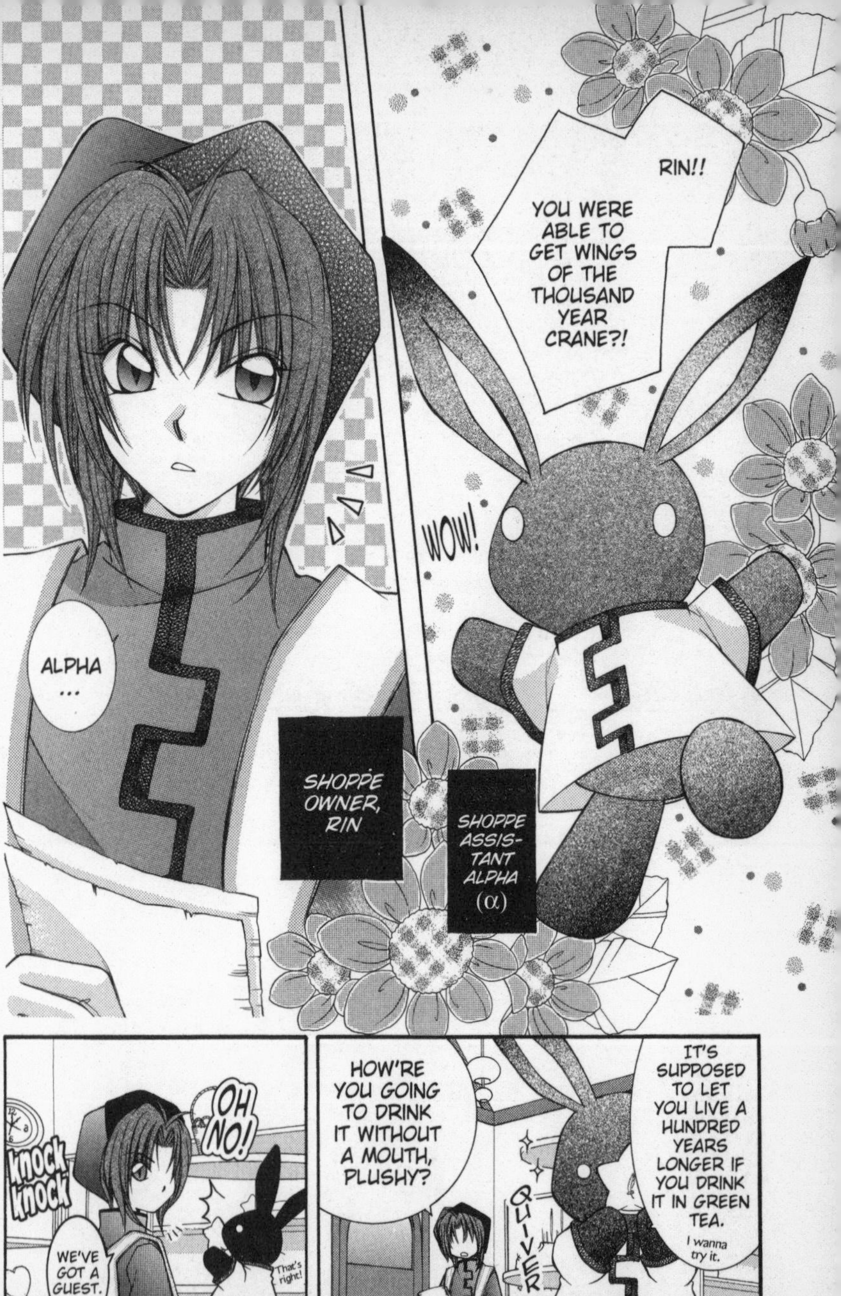
RIN!!
YOU WERE ABLE TO GET WINGS OF THE THOUSAND YEAR CRANE?!
WOW!
SHOPPE ASSISTANT ALPHA (α)
SHOPPE OWNER, RIN
ALPHA ...
IT'S SUPPOSED TO LET YOU LIVE A HUNDRED YEARS LONGER IF YOU DRINK IT IN GREEN TEA.
I wanna try it.
QUIVER
HOW'RE YOU GOING TO DRINK IT WITHOUT A MOUTH, PLUSHY?
OH NO!
knock knock
That's right!
WE'VE GOT A GUEST.

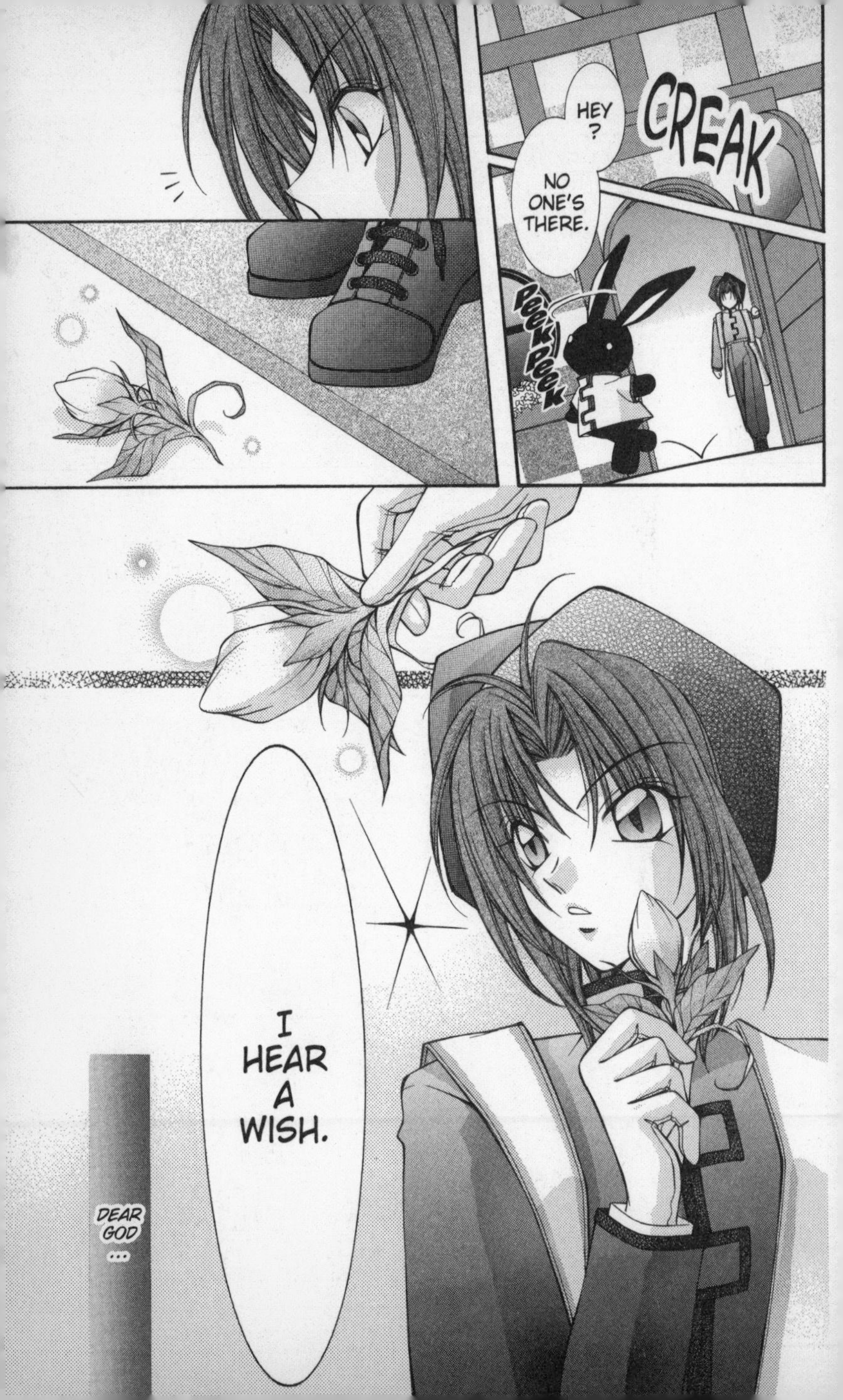
CREAK
HEY? NO ONE'S THERE.
PEEK PEEK
I HEAR A WISH.
DEAR GOD...

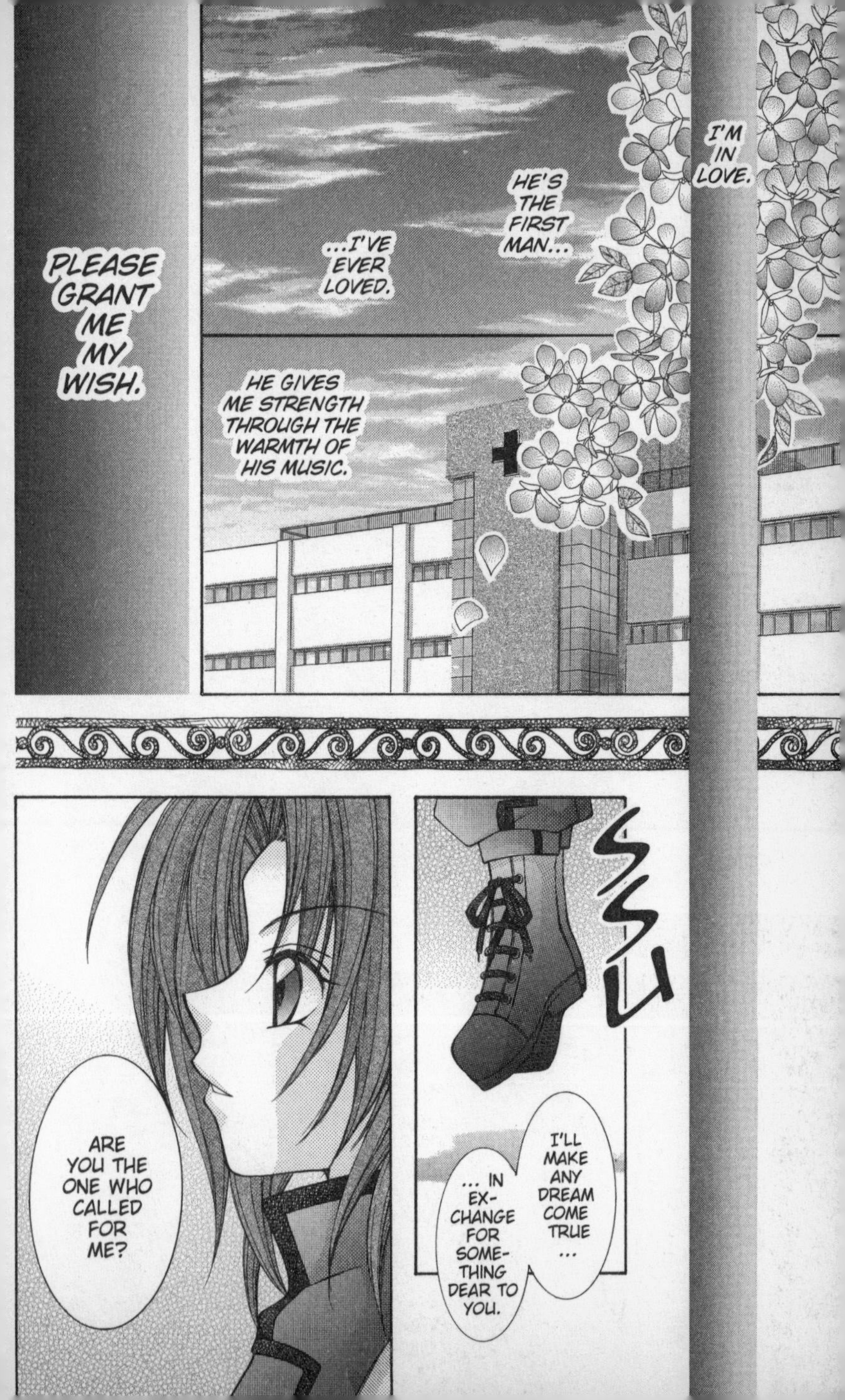
I'M IN LOVE.
HE'S THE FIRST MAN...
...I'VE EVER LOVED.
HE GIVES ME STRENGTH THROUGH THE WARMTH OF HIS MUSIC.
PLEASE GRANT ME MY WISH.
SSU
I'LL MAKE ANY DREAM COME TRUE...
... IN EX-CHANGE FOR SOME-THING DEAR TO YOU.
ARE YOU THE ONE WHO CALLED FOR ME?

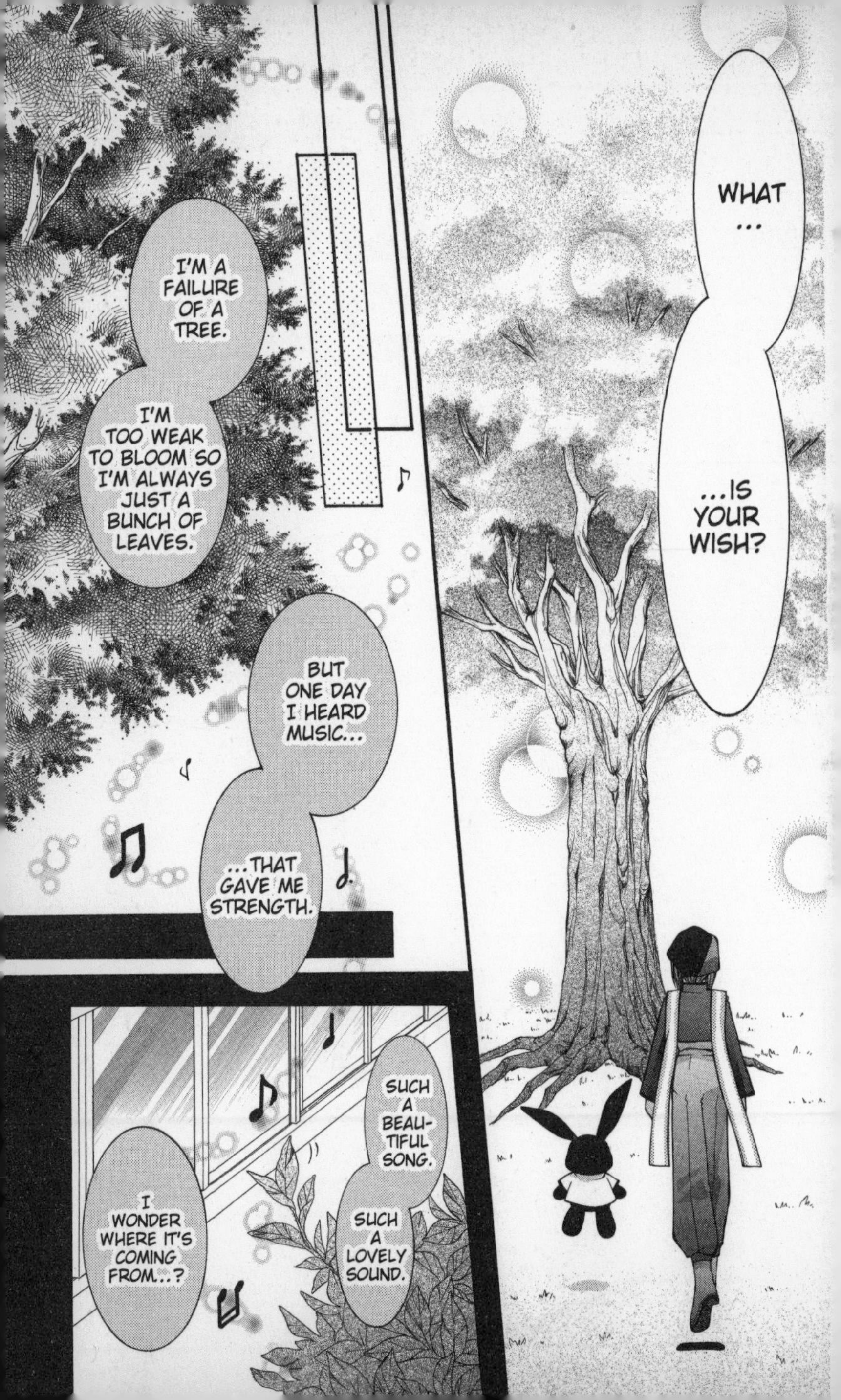
WHAT ...
...IS YOUR WISH?
I'M A FAILURE OF A TREE.
I'M TOO WEAK TO BLOOM SO I'M ALWAYS JUST A BUNCH OF LEAVES.
BUT ONE DAY I HEARD MUSIC...
...THAT GAVE ME STRENGTH.
SUCH A BEAU-TIFUL SONG.
SUCH A LOVELY SOUND.
I WONDER WHERE IT'S COMING FROM...?

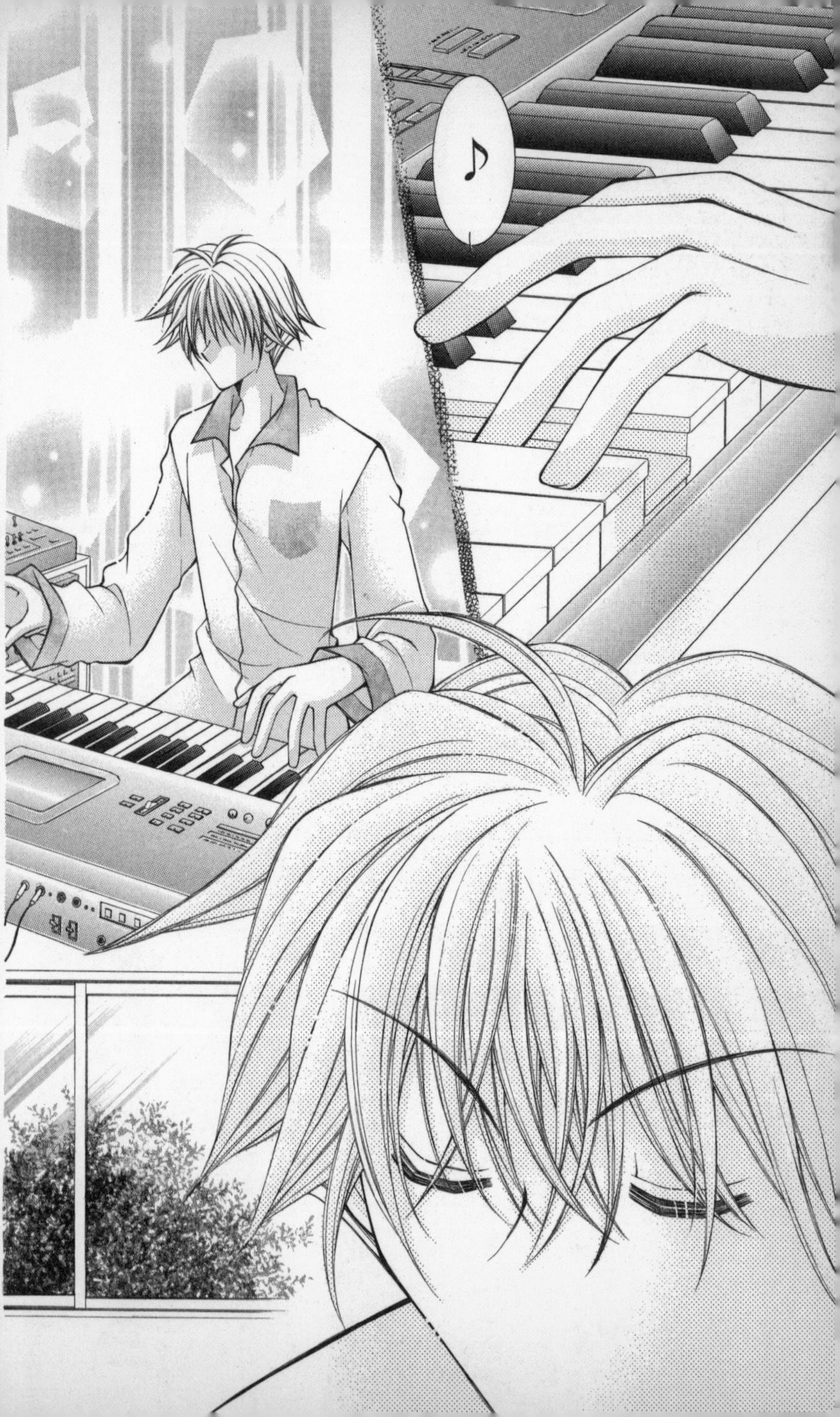
♪

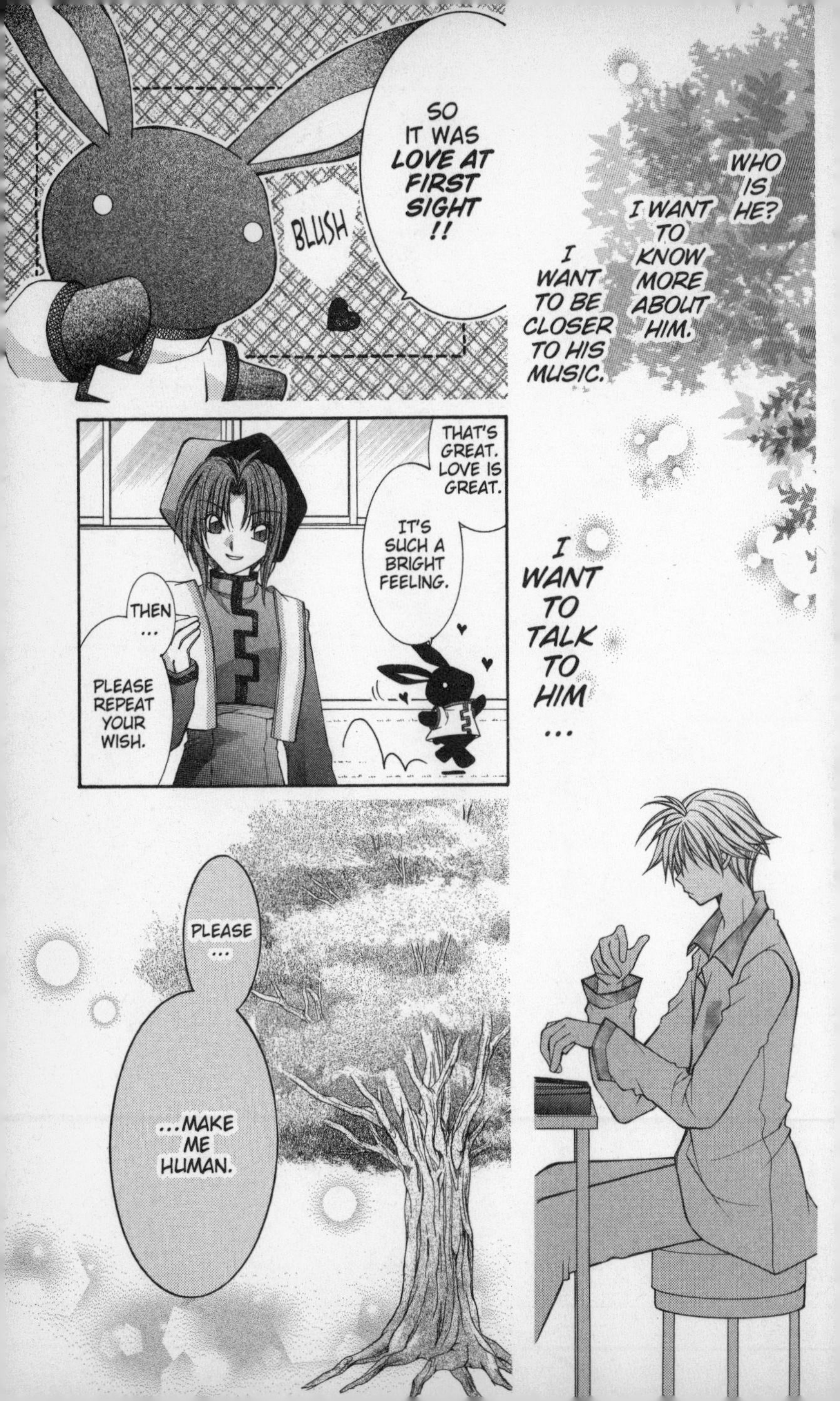
WHO IS HE?
I WANT TO KNOW MORE ABOUT HIM.
I WANT TO BE CLOSER TO HIS MUSIC.
I WANT TO TALK TO HIM...
SO IT WAS LOVE AT FIRST SIGHT!!
BLUSH
THAT'S GREAT. LOVE IS GREAT.
IT'S SUCH A BRIGHT FEELING.
THEN...
PLEASE REPEAT YOUR WISH.
PLEASE...
...MAKE ME HUMAN.

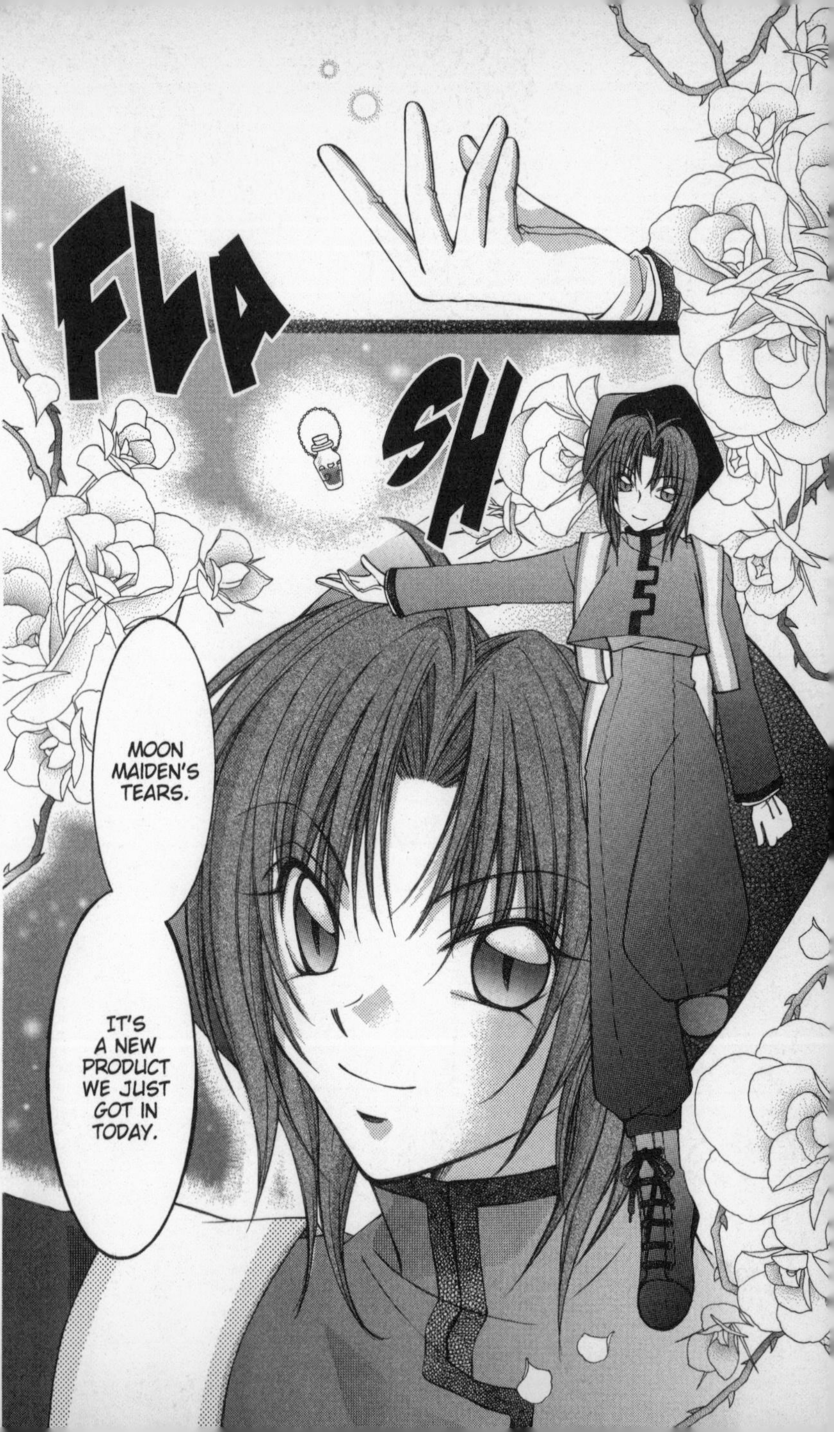
FLASH
MOON MAIDEN'S TEARS.
IT'S A NEW PRODUCT WE JUST GOT IN TODAY.

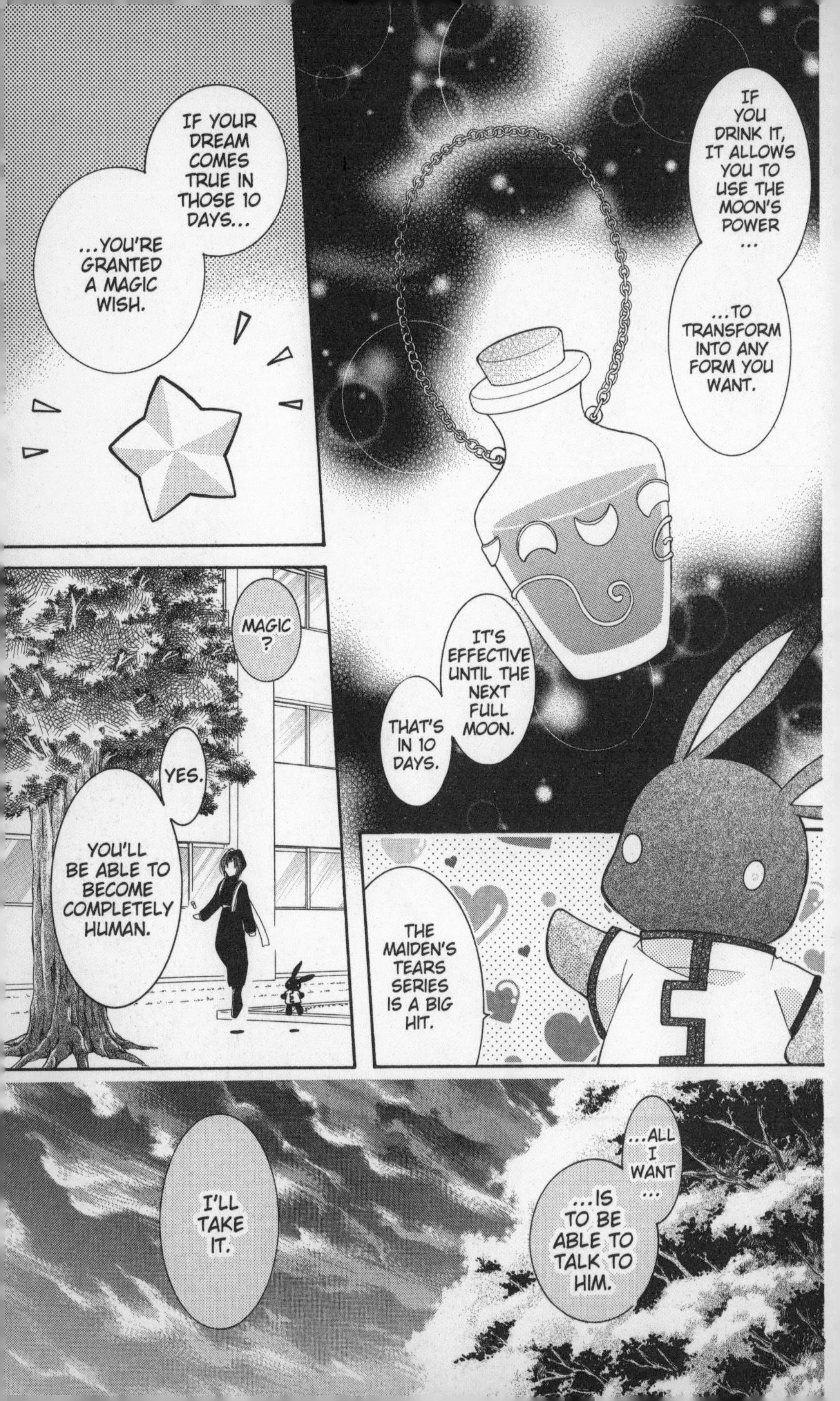
IF YOU DRINK IT, IT ALLOWS YOU TO USE THE MOON'S POWER...
...TO TRANSFORM INTO ANY FORM YOU WANT.
IT'S EFFECTIVE UNTIL THE NEXT FULL MOON.
THAT'S IN 10 DAYS.
IF YOUR DREAM COMES TRUE IN THOSE 10 DAYS...
...YOU'RE GRANTED A MAGIC WISH.
THE MAIDEN'S TEARS SERIES IS A BIG HIT.
MAGIC?
YES.
YOU'LL BE ABLE TO BECOME COMPLETELY HUMAN.
...ALL I WANT...
...IS TO BE ABLE TO TALK TO HIM.
I'LL TAKE IT.

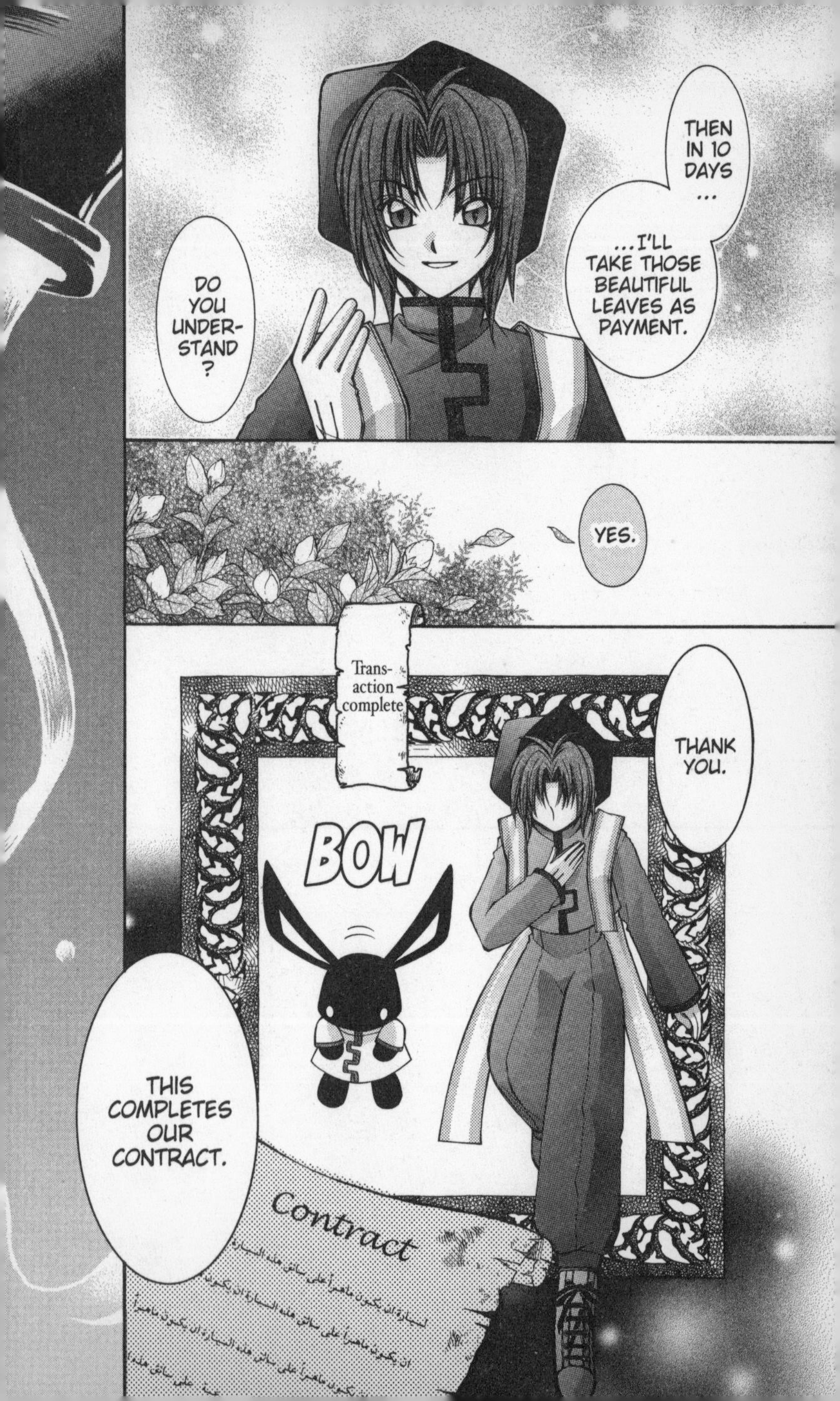
THEN IN 10 DAYS...
...I'LL TAKE THOSE BEAUTIFUL LEAVES AS PAYMENT.
DO YOU UNDER-STAND?
YES.
Trans-action complete
THANK YOU.
BOW
THIS COMPLETES OUR CONTRACT.
Contract

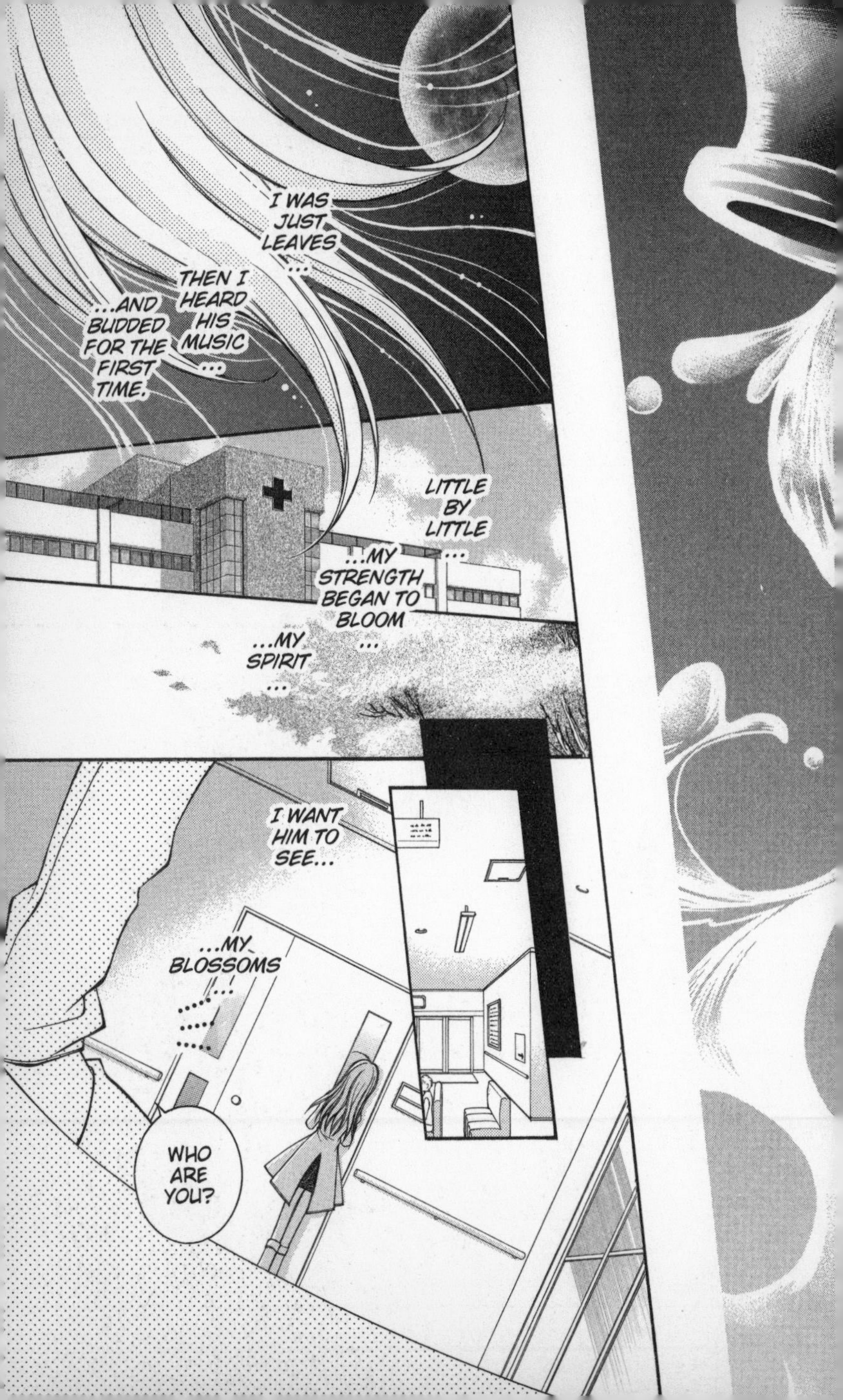
I WAS JUST LEAVES...
THEN I HEARD HIS MUSIC...
...AND BUDDED FOR THE FIRST TIME.
LITTLE BY LITTLE...
...MY STRENGTH BEGAN TO BLOOM...
...MY SPIRIT...
I WANT HIM TO SEE...
...MY BLOSSOMS...
....
WHO ARE YOU?

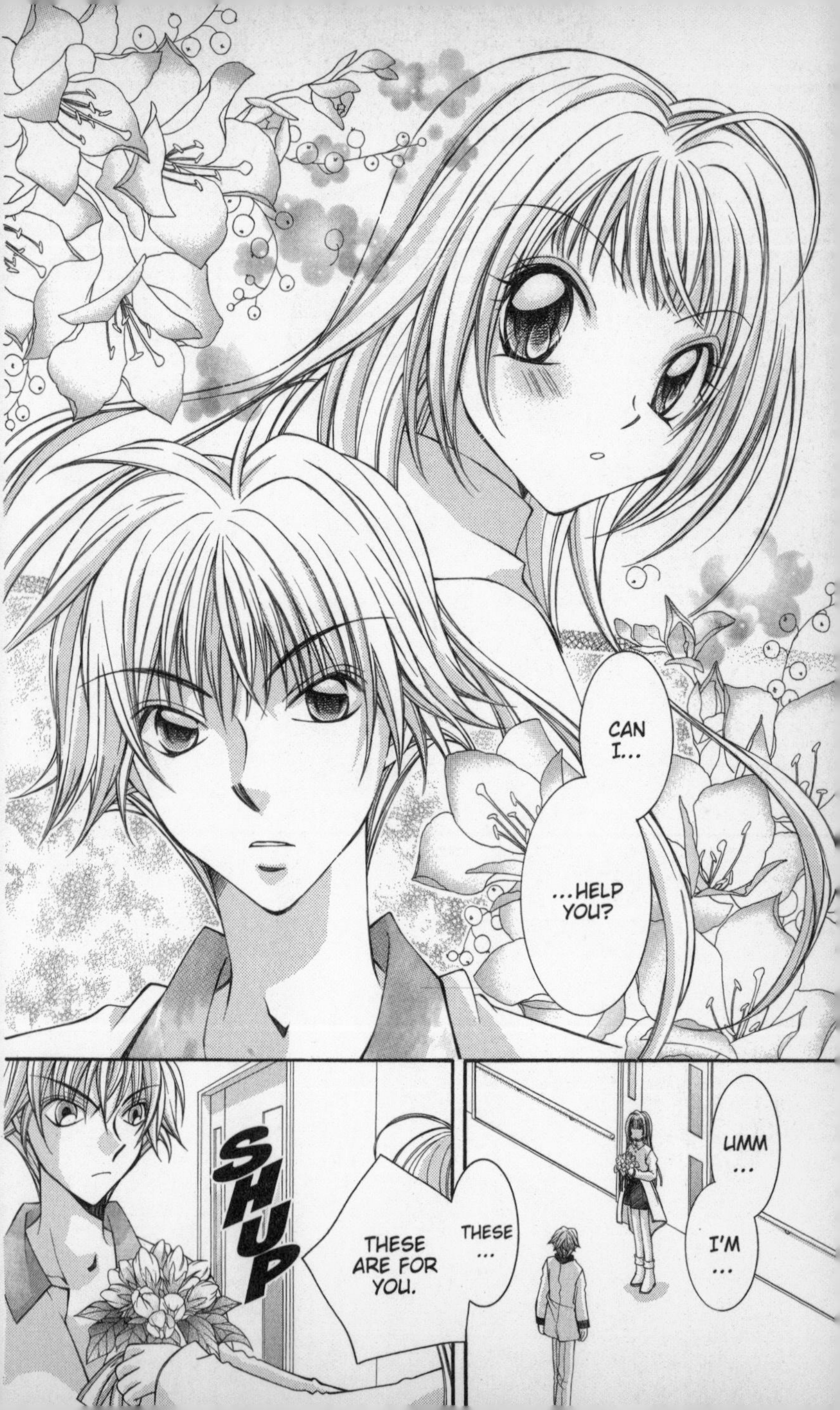
CAN I...
...HELP YOU?
UMM ...
I'M ...
THESE ...
SHUP
THESE ARE FOR YOU.

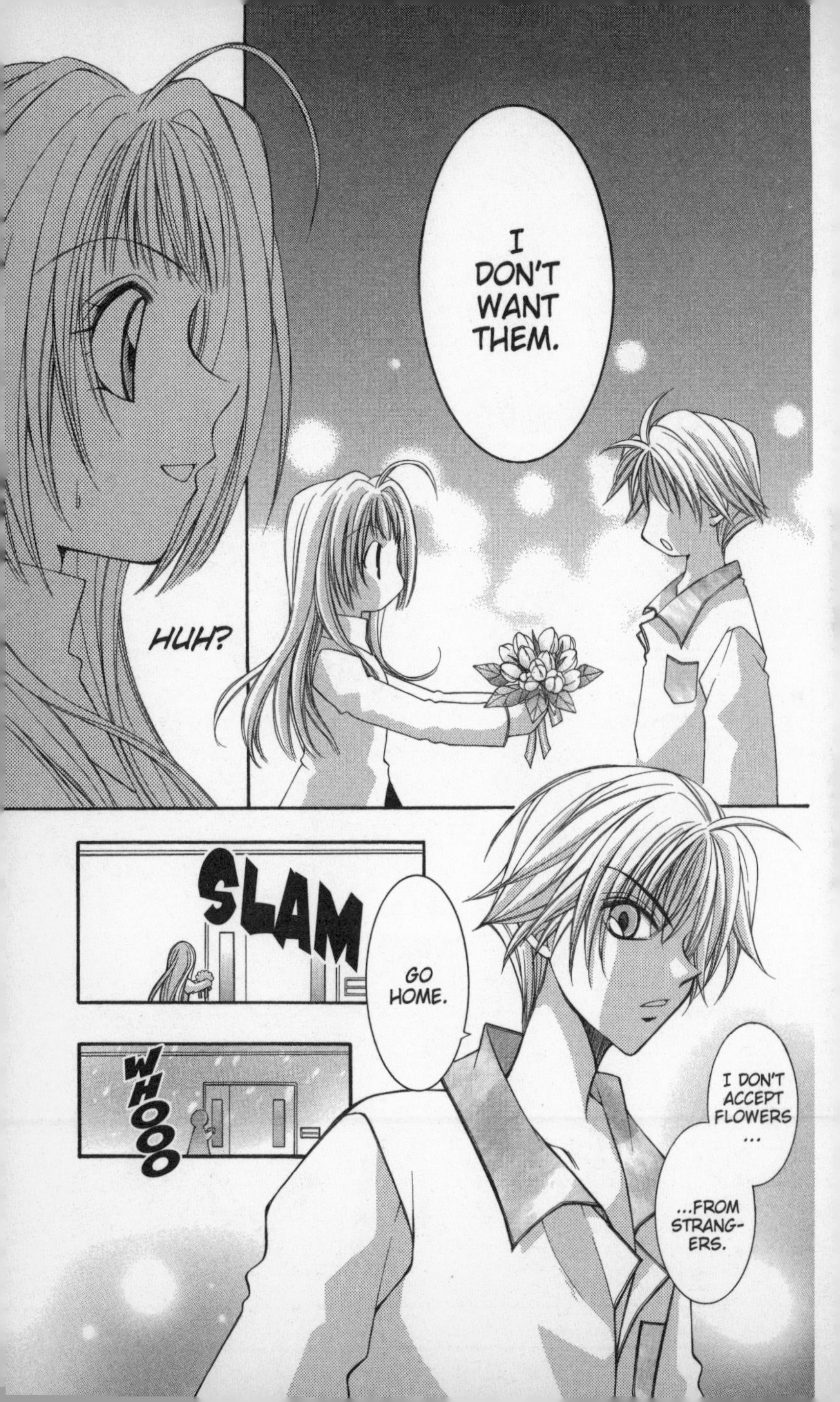
I DON'T WANT THEM.
HUH?
I DON'T ACCEPT FLOWERS...
...FROM STRANGERS.
GO HOME.
SLAM
WHOOO

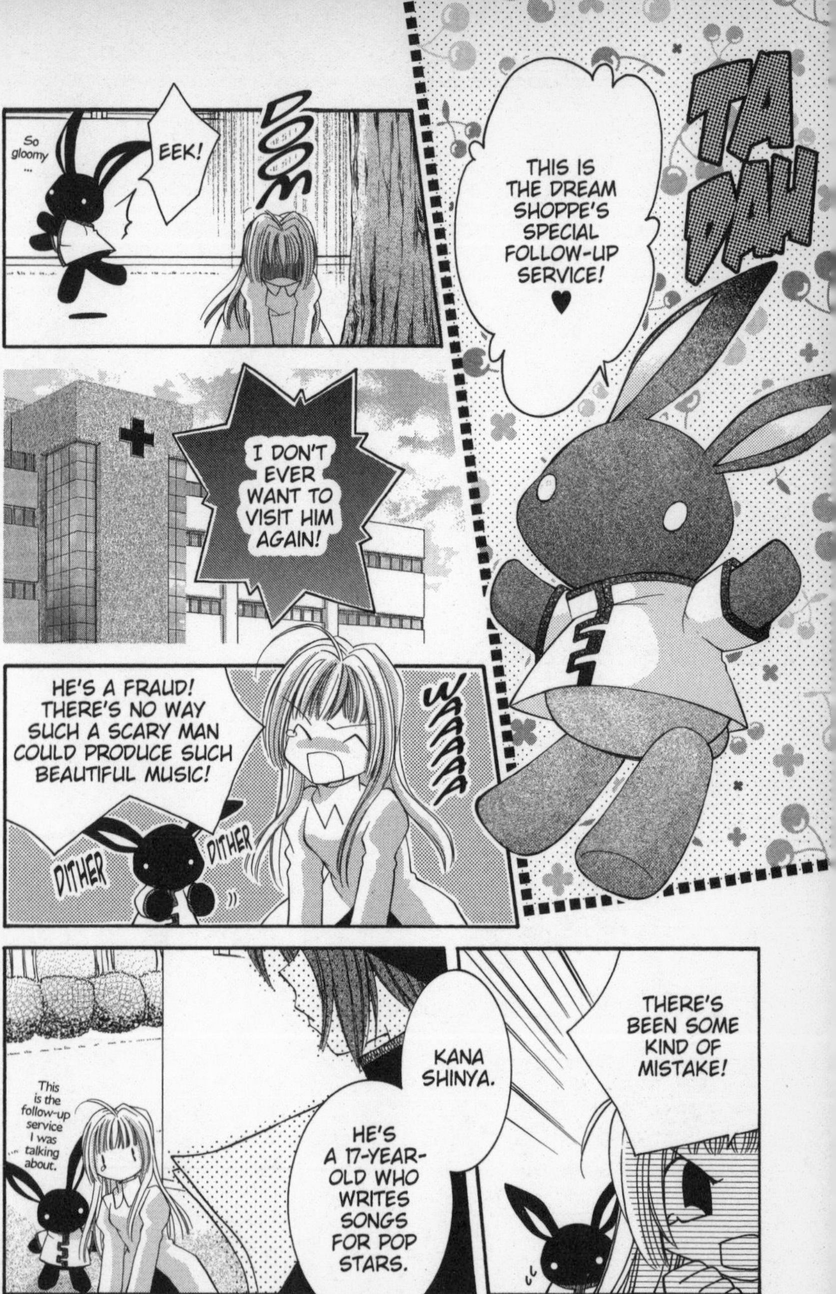
TA DAH
THIS IS THE DREAM SHOPPE'S SPECIAL FOLLOW-UP SERVICE! ♥
DOOM
EEK!
So gloomy...
I DON'T EVER WANT TO VISIT HIM AGAIN!
WAAAAA
HE'S A FRAUD! THERE'S NO WAY SUCH A SCARY MAN COULD PRODUCE SUCH BEAUTIFUL MUSIC!
DITHER
DITHER
THERE'S BEEN SOME KIND OF MISTAKE!
KANA SHINYA.
HE'S A 17-YEAR-OLD WHO WRITES SONGS FOR POP STARS.
This is the follow-up service I was talking about.

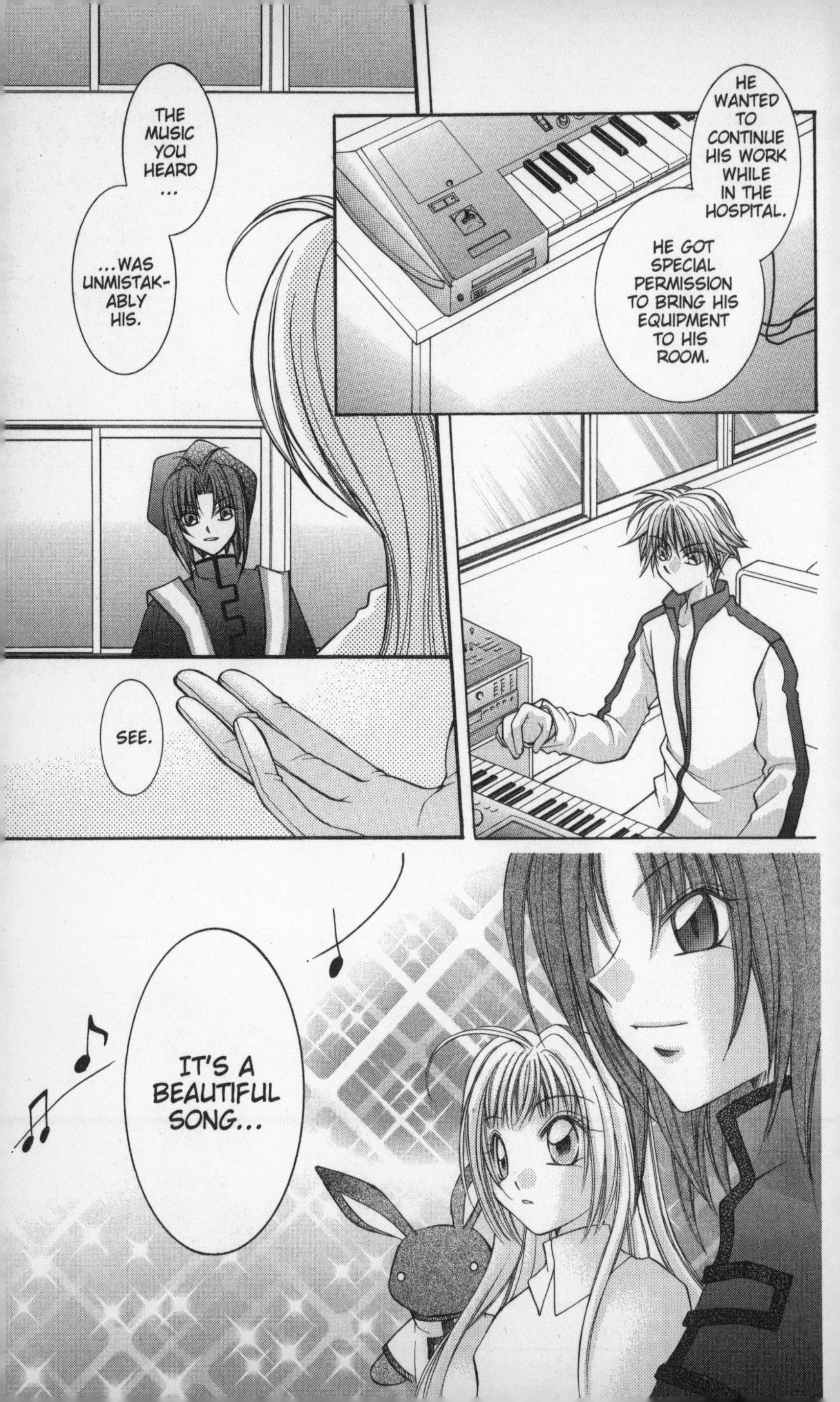
HE WANTED TO CONTINUE HIS WORK WHILE IN THE HOSPITAL.
HE GOT SPECIAL PERMISSION TO BRING HIS EQUIPMENT TO HIS ROOM.
THE MUSIC YOU HEARD ...
...WAS UNMISTAKABLY HIS.
SEE.
IT'S A BEAUTIFUL SONG...

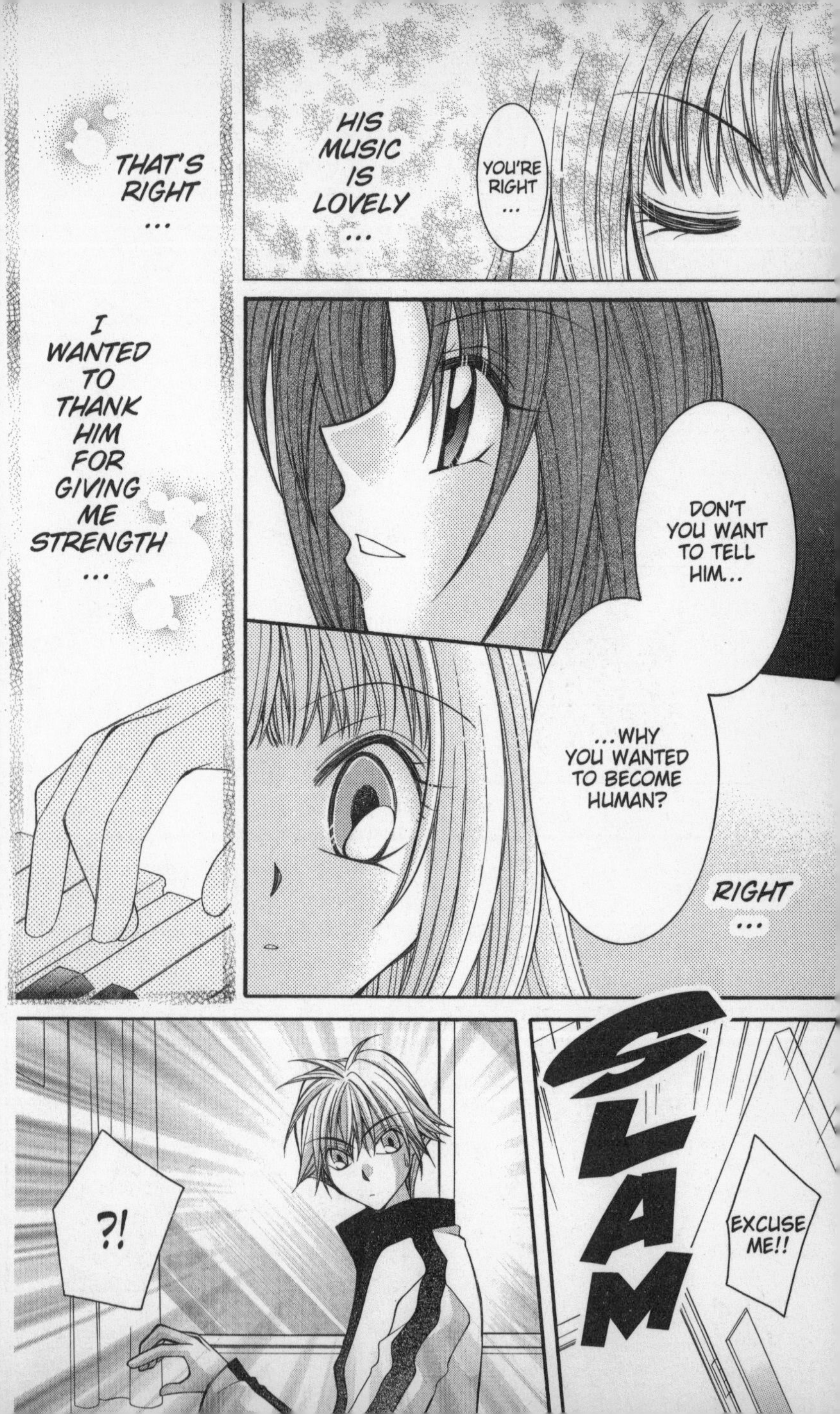
YOU'RE RIGHT ...
HIS MUSIC IS LOVELY ...
DON'T YOU WANT TO TELL HIM...
...WHY YOU WANTED TO BECOME HUMAN?
RIGHT ...
THAT'S RIGHT ...
I WANTED TO THANK HIM FOR GIVING ME STRENGTH ...
SLAM
EXCUSE ME!!
?!

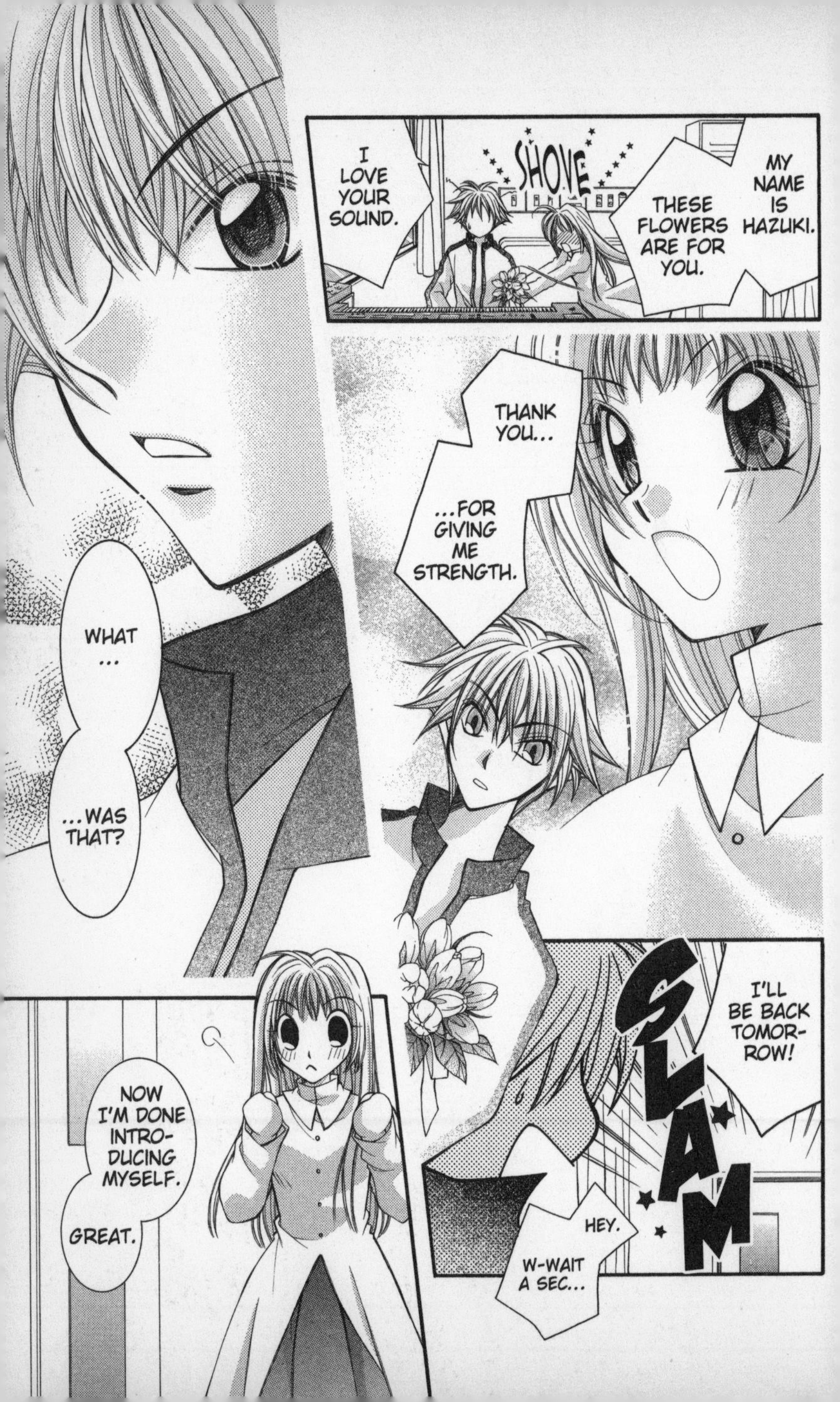

MY NAME IS HAZUKI.
THESE FLOWERS ARE FOR YOU.
SHOVE
I LOVE YOUR SOUND.
THANK YOU...
...FOR GIVING ME STRENGTH.
WHAT...
...WAS THAT?
I'LL BE BACK TOMOR-ROW!
SLAM
HEY.
W-WAIT A SEC...
NOW I'M DONE INTRO-DUCING MYSELF.
GREAT.

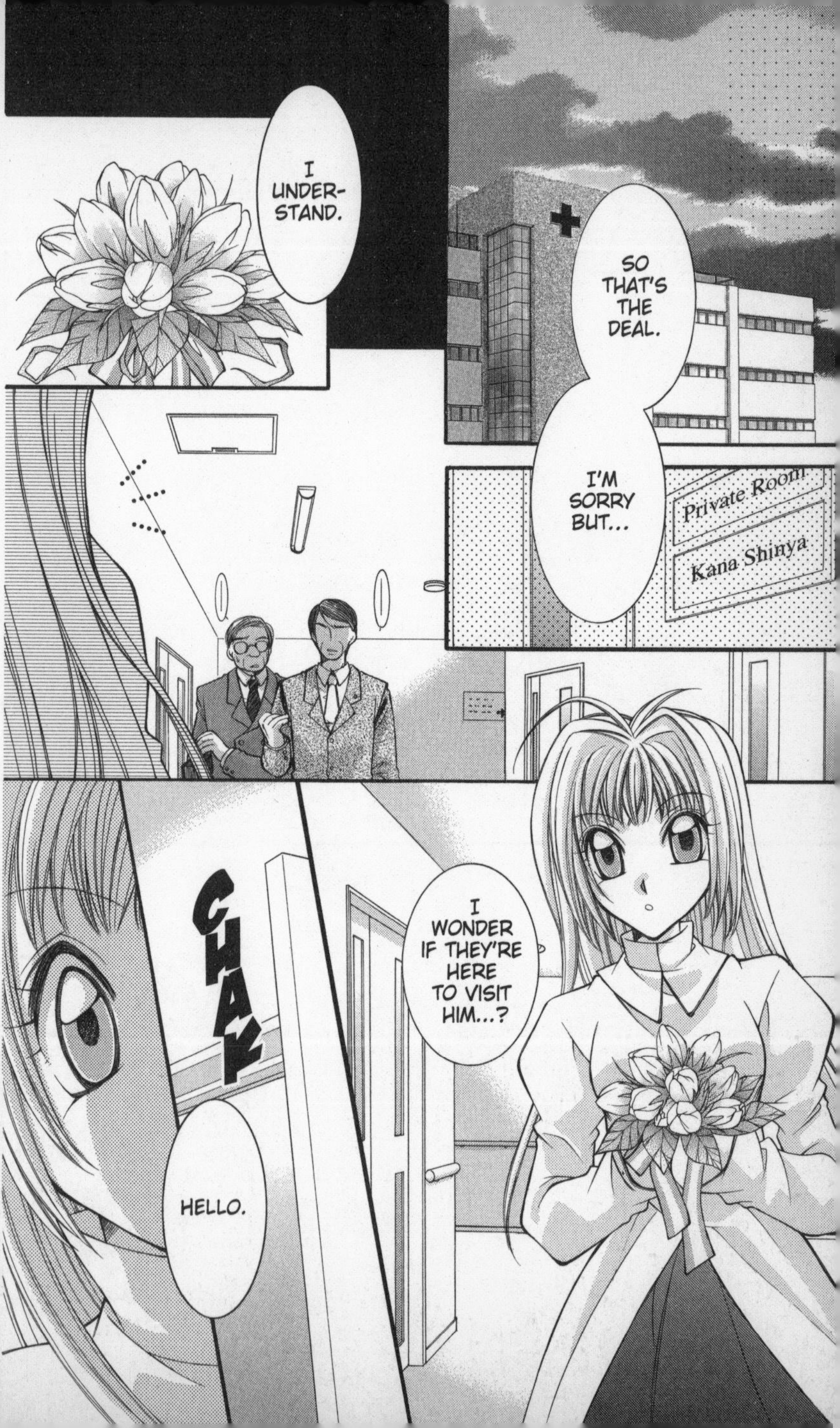
SO THAT'S THE DEAL.
I'M SORRY BUT...
Private Room
Kana Shinya
I UNDERSTAND.
I WONDER IF THEY'RE HERE TO VISIT HIM...?
CHAK
HELLO.

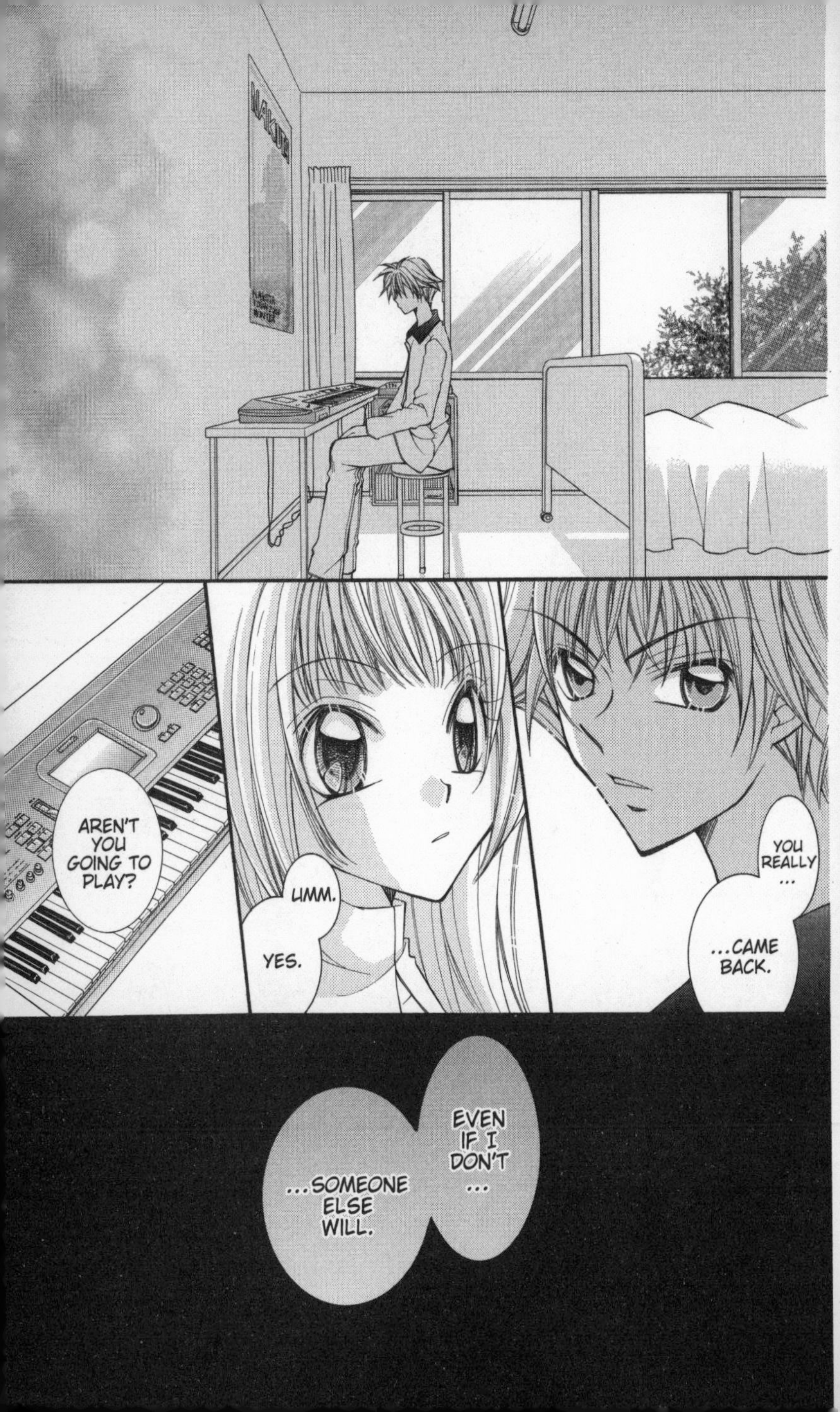
YOU REALLY ...
...CAME BACK.
UMM.
YES.
AREN'T YOU GOING TO PLAY?
EVEN IF I DON'T ...
...SOMEONE ELSE WILL.

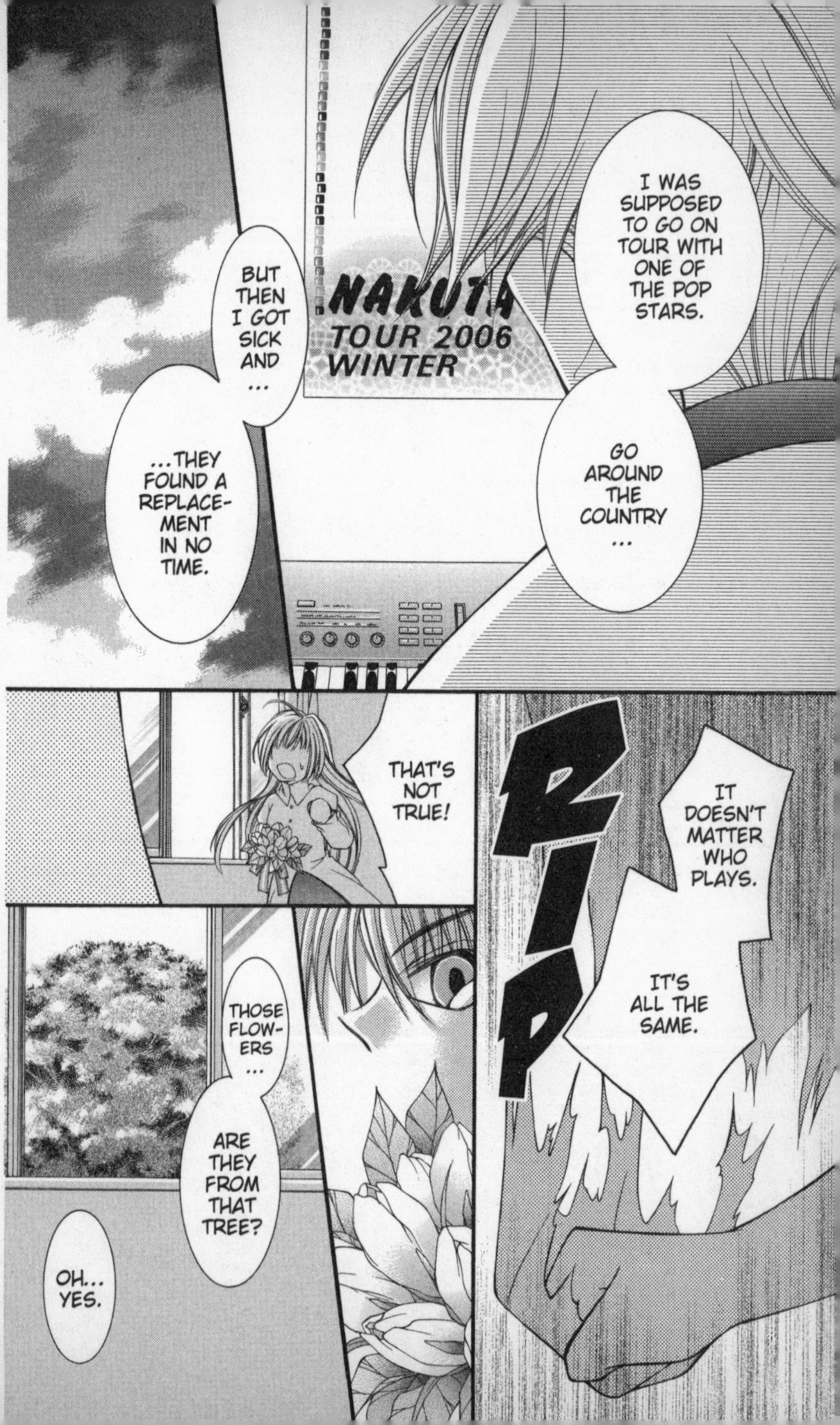
I WAS SUPPOSED TO GO ON TOUR WITH ONE OF THE POP STARS.
GO AROUND THE COUNTRY...
NAKUTA
TOUR 2006 WINTER
BUT THEN I GOT SICK AND...
...THEY FOUND A REPLACEMENT IN NO TIME.
RIP
IT DOESN'T MATTER WHO PLAYS.
IT'S ALL THE SAME.
THAT'S NOT TRUE!
THOSE FLOWERS...
ARE THEY FROM THAT TREE?
OH... YES.

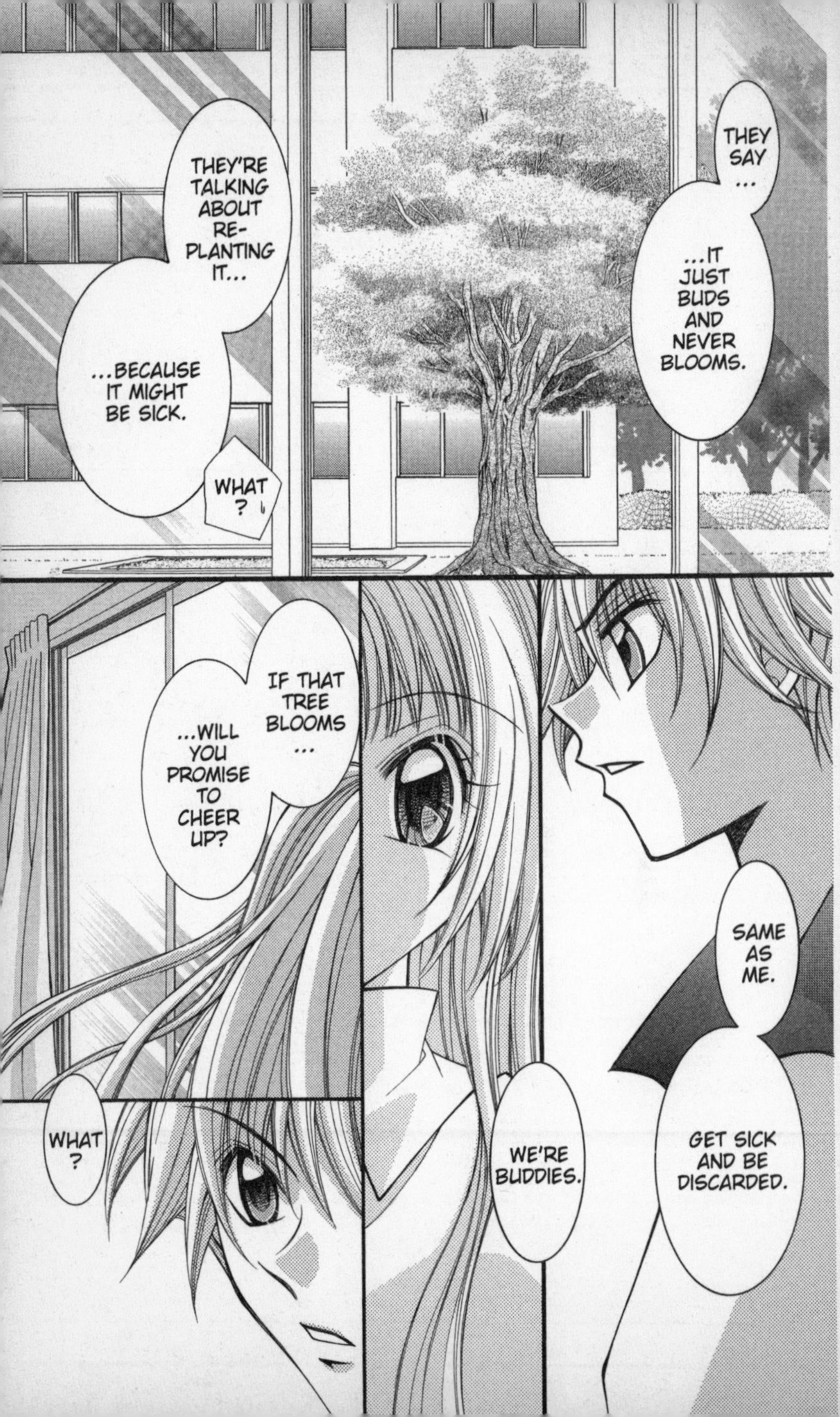
THEY SAY ...
...IT JUST BUDS AND NEVER BLOOMS.
THEY'RE TALKING ABOUT RE-PLANTING IT...
...BECAUSE IT MIGHT BE SICK.
WHAT?
SAME AS ME.
GET SICK AND BE DISCARDED.
WE'RE BUDDIES.
IF THAT TREE BLOOMS ...
...WILL YOU PROMISE TO CHEER UP?
WHAT?

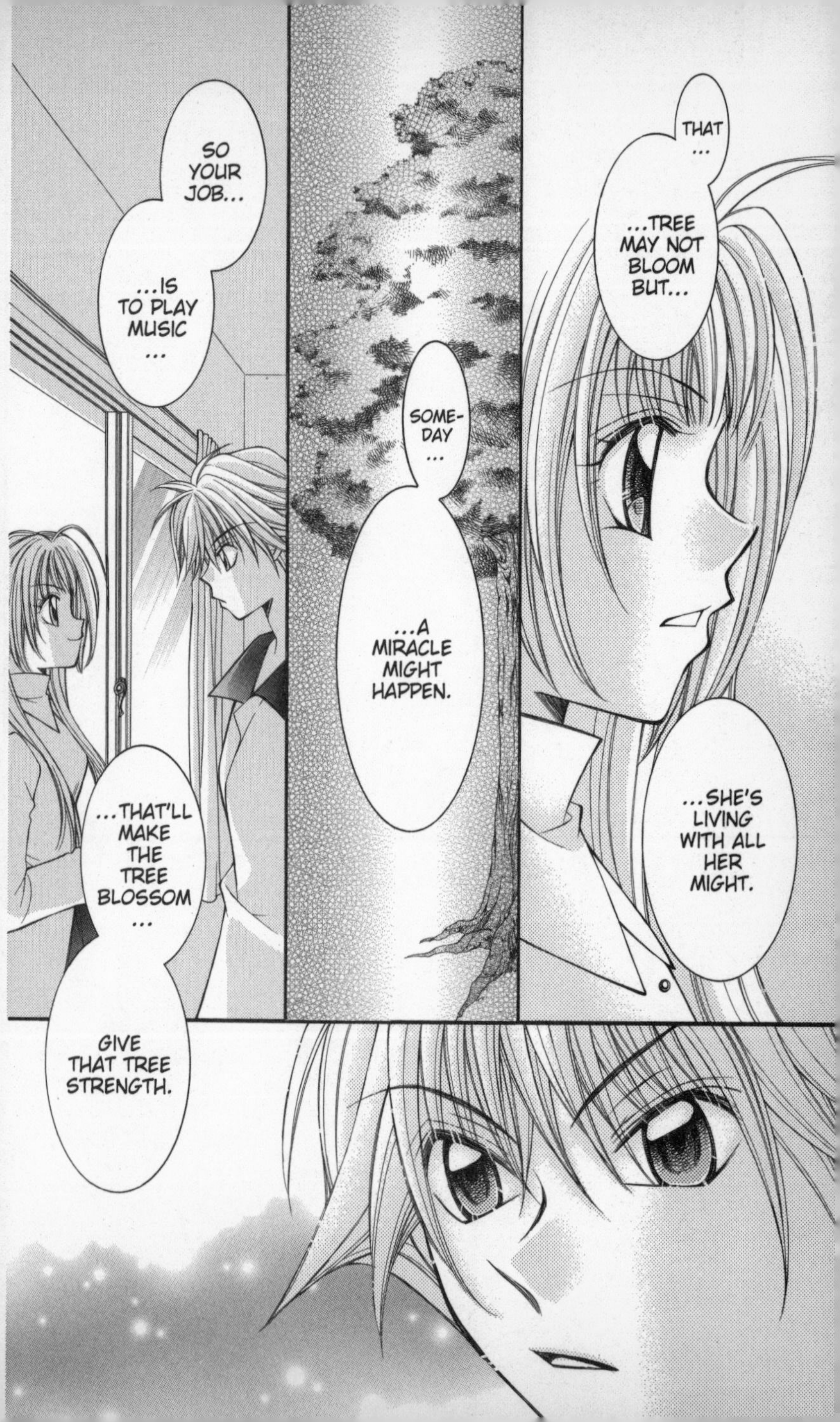
THAT...
...TREE MAY NOT BLOOM BUT...
...SHE'S LIVING WITH ALL HER MIGHT.
SOME-DAY...
...A MIRACLE MIGHT HAPPEN.
SO YOUR JOB...
...IS TO PLAY MUSIC...
...THAT'LL MAKE THE TREE BLOSSOM...
GIVE THAT TREE STRENGTH.

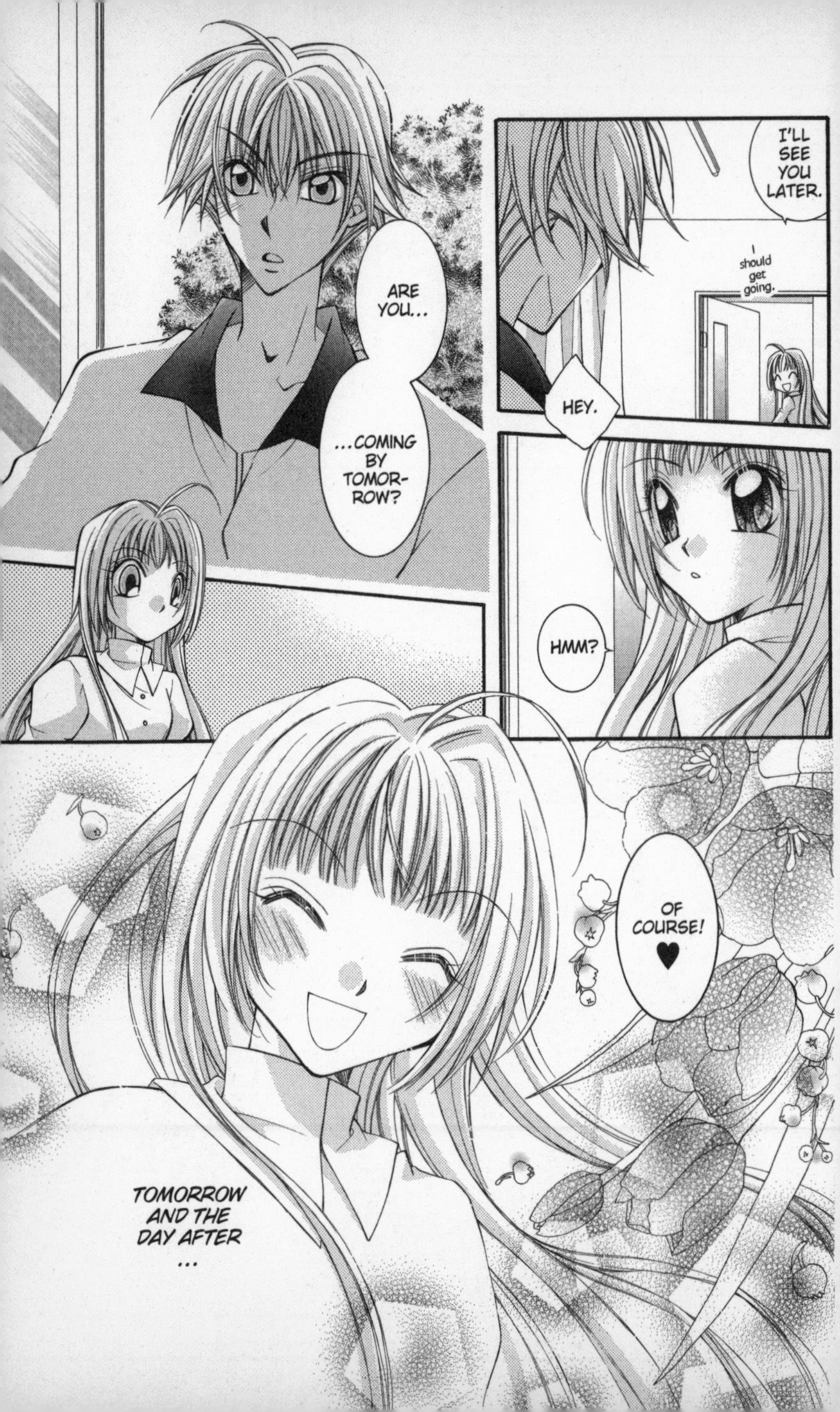
I'LL SEE YOU LATER.
I should get going.
HEY.
HMM?
ARE YOU...
...COMING BY TOMORROW?
OF COURSE! ♥
TOMORROW AND THE DAY AFTER ...

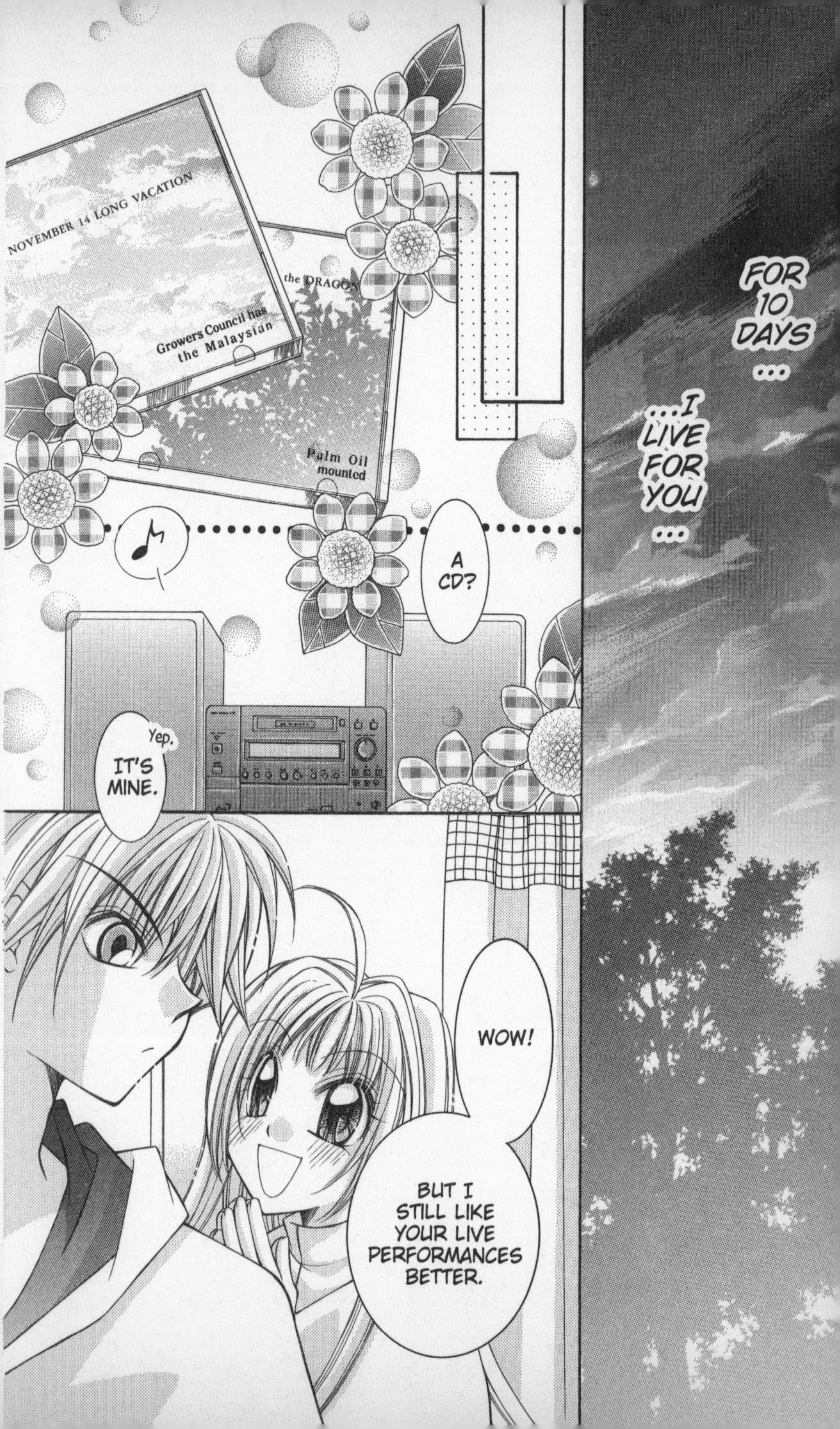
FOR 10 DAYS ...
...I LIVE FOR YOU ...
NOVEMBER 14 LONG VACATION
the DRAGON
Growers Council has the Malaysian
Palm Oil mounted
A CD?
Yep.
IT'S MINE.
WOW!
BUT I STILL LIKE YOUR LIVE PERFORMANCES BETTER.

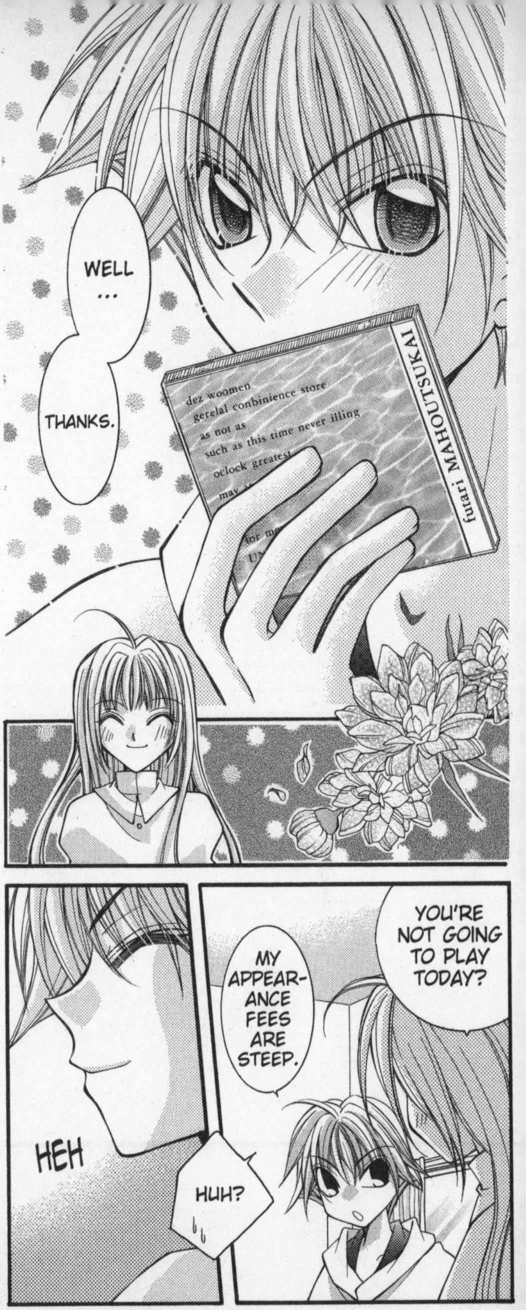
WELL ...
THANKS.
futari MAHOUTSUKAI
dez woomen
gerelal conbinience store
as not as
such as this time never illing
oclock greatest
YOU'RE NOT GOING TO PLAY TODAY?
MY APPEAR-ANCE FEES ARE STEEP.
HUH?
HEH

1

★★★ HELLO.

THIS IS AQUA MIZUTO. I'D LIKE TO EXTEND MY THANKS TO MY FIRST-TIME READERS AS WELL AS TO MY RETURNING AUDIENCE.

YUME KIRA DREAM SHOPPE IS A SERIES MADE UP OF ONE-SHOTS. I HAD ORIGINALLY INTENDED IT TO BE ONLY ONE STORY BUT THE REACTION FROM THE READERS ALLOWED ME TO TURN IT INTO A SERIES. IT EVEN GOT PUBLISHED AS ITS OWN BOOK!

ALTHOUGH IT IS A SERIES, IT'S BEEN A WHILE SINCE I'VE DONE A ONE-SHOT. I ADMIT I'M A LITTLE NERVOUS BUT I'M HAPPY TO BE ABLE TO CREATE SOMETHING THAT CAN BE ENJOYED.

BY THE WAY...THIS FIRST STORY IS SOMETHING I DREW CLOSE TO TWO YEARS AGO...THE DRAWINGS MAY LOOK A LITTLE OLD BUT PLEASE TRY TO IGNORE THAT...

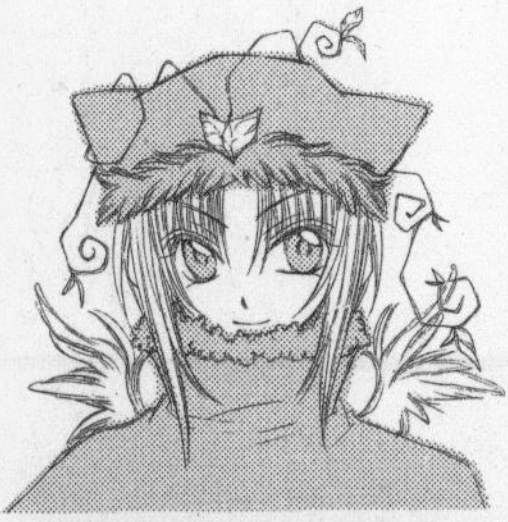

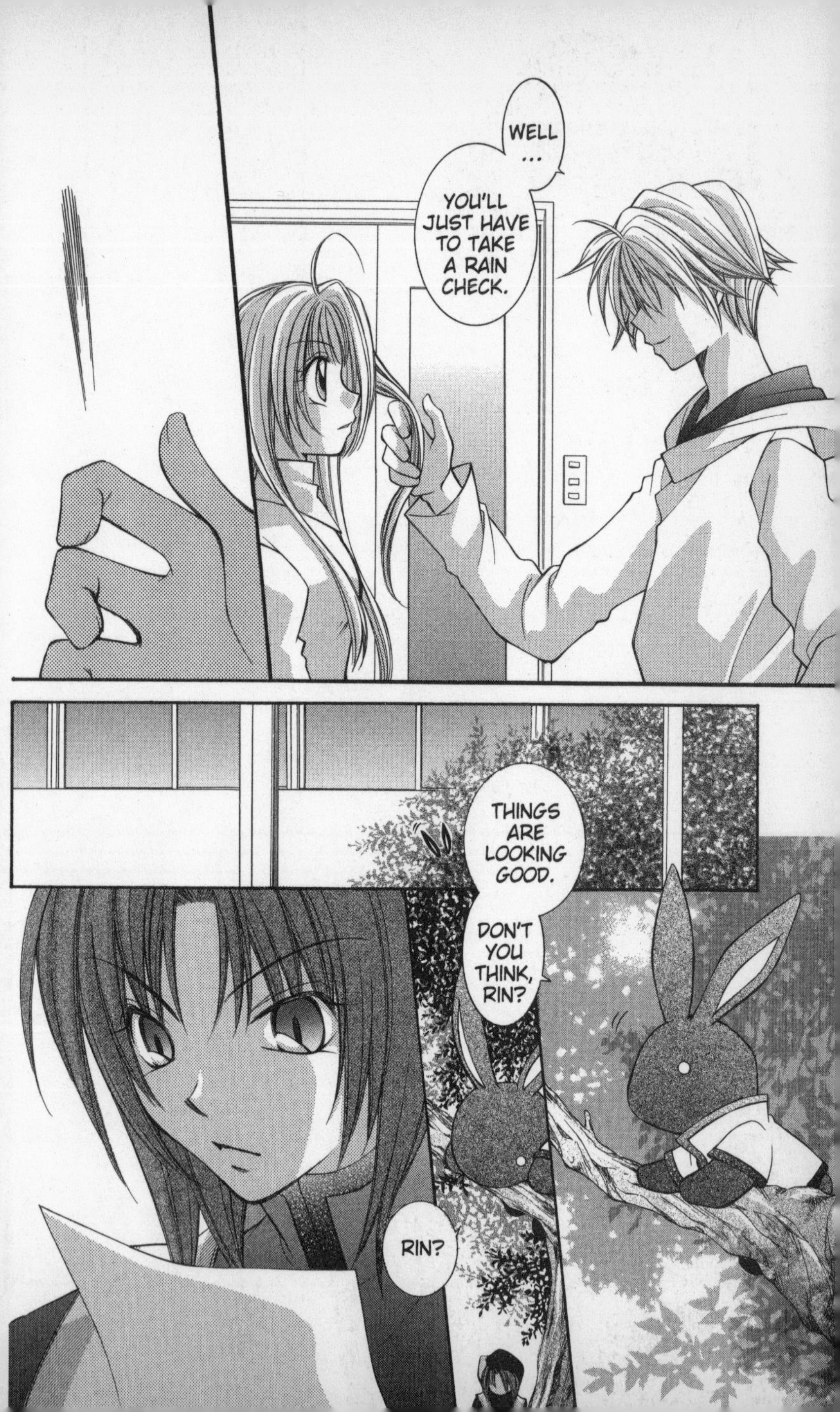
WELL ...
YOU'LL JUST HAVE TO TAKE A RAIN CHECK.
THINGS ARE LOOKING GOOD.
DON'T YOU THINK, RIN?
RIN?

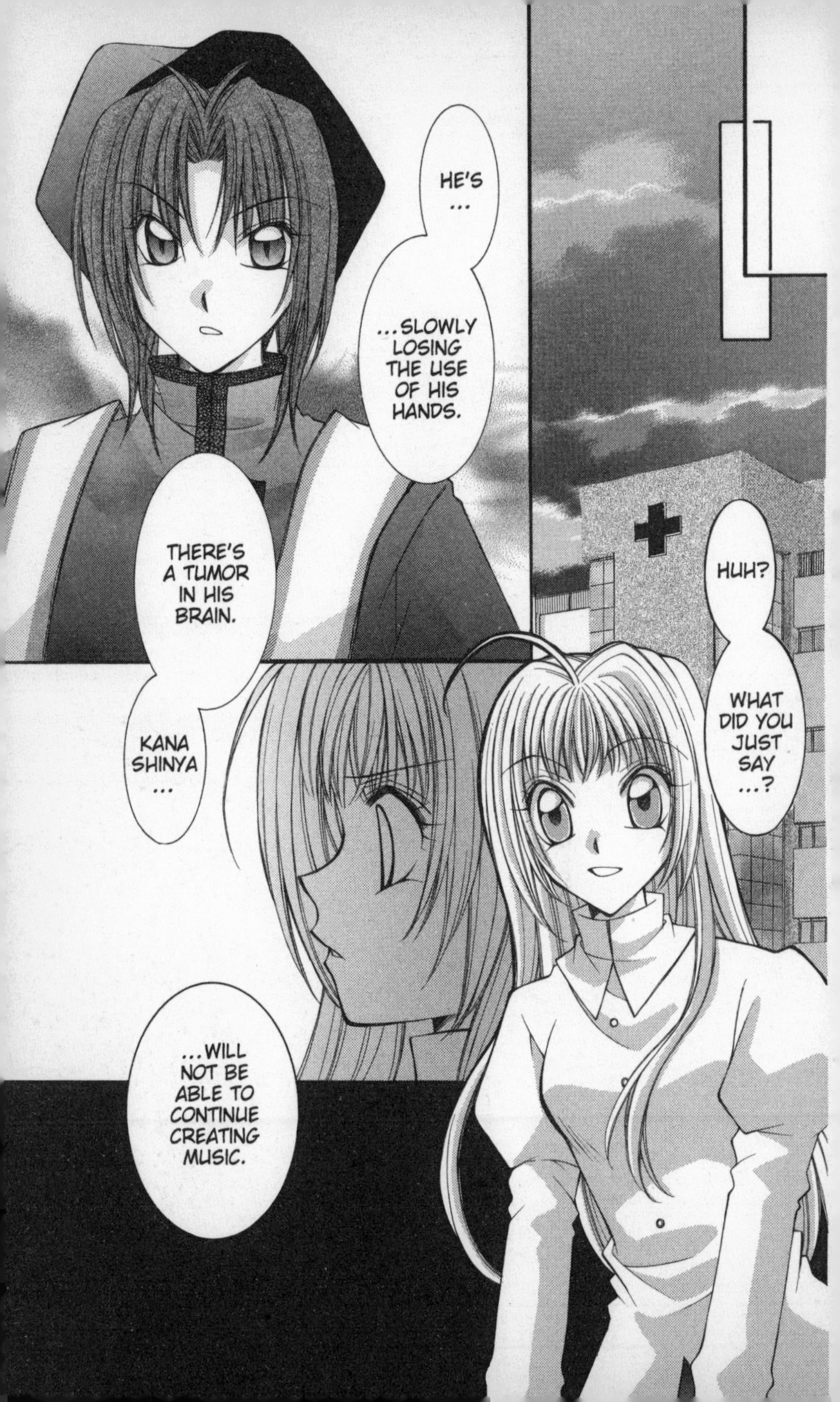
HE'S ...
...SLOWLY LOSING THE USE OF HIS HANDS.
THERE'S A TUMOR IN HIS BRAIN.
HUH?
WHAT DID YOU JUST SAY ...?
KANA SHINYA ...
...WILL NOT BE ABLE TO CONTINUE CREATING MUSIC.

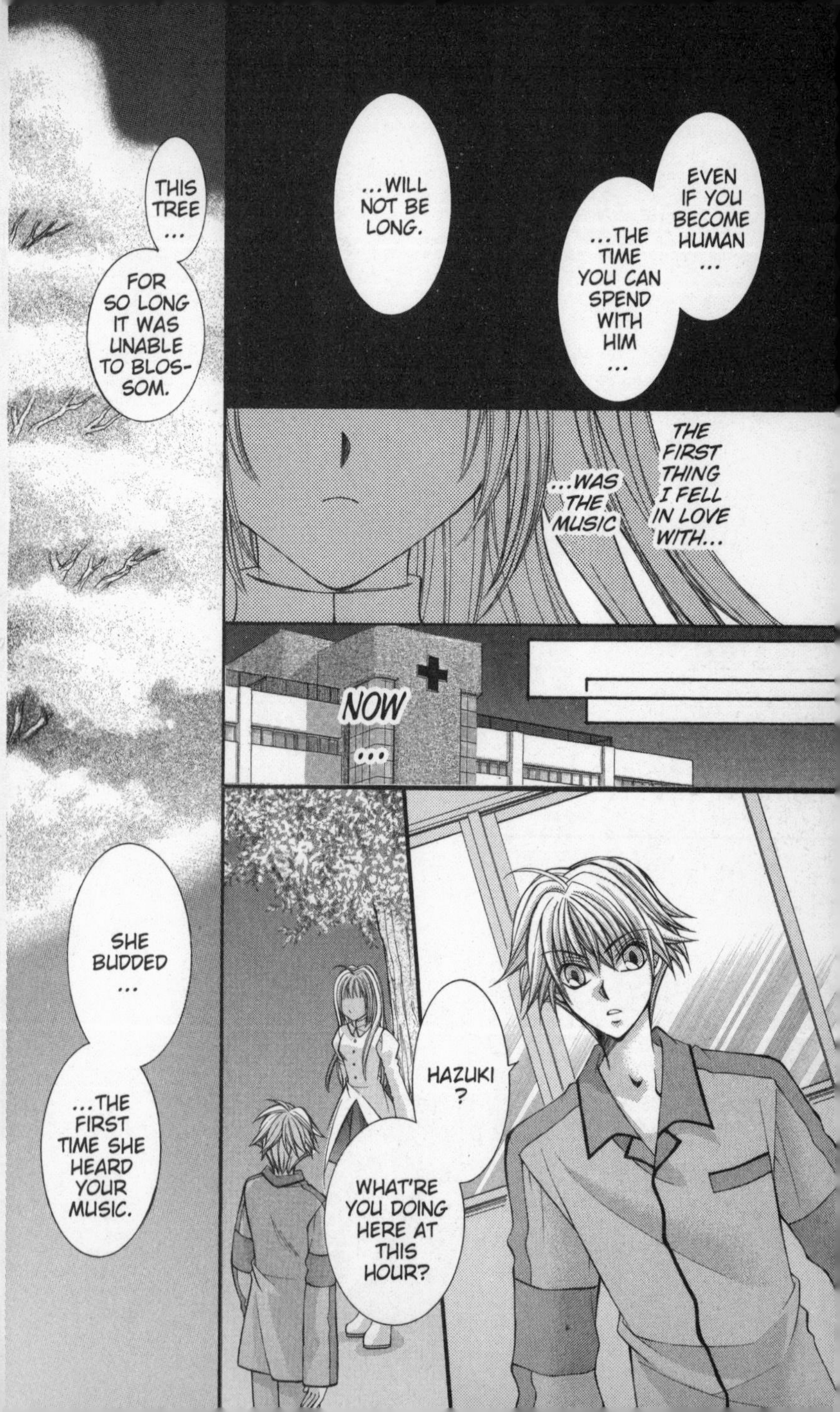

EVEN IF YOU BECOME HUMAN...
...THE TIME YOU CAN SPEND WITH HIM...
...WILL NOT BE LONG.
THE FIRST THING I FELL IN LOVE WITH...
...WAS THE MUSIC
NOW...
HAZUKI?
WHAT'RE YOU DOING HERE AT THIS HOUR?
THIS TREE...
FOR SO LONG IT WAS UNABLE TO BLOSSOM.
SHE BUDDED...
...THE FIRST TIME SHE HEARD YOUR MUSIC.

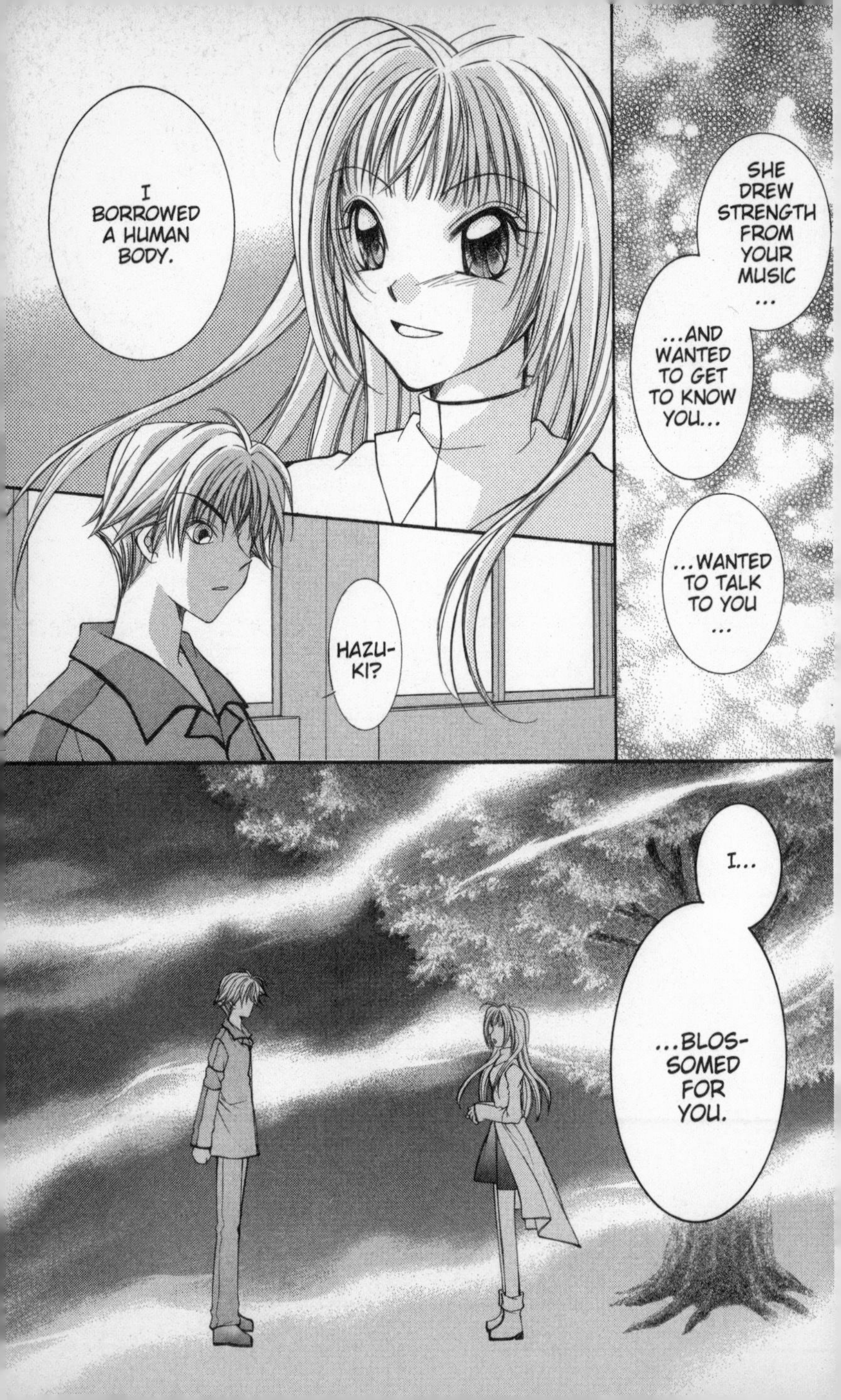
SHE DREW STRENGTH FROM YOUR MUSIC...
...AND WANTED TO GET TO KNOW YOU...
...WANTED TO TALK TO YOU...
I BORROWED A HUMAN BODY.
HAZU-KI?
I...
...BLOS-SOMED FOR YOU.

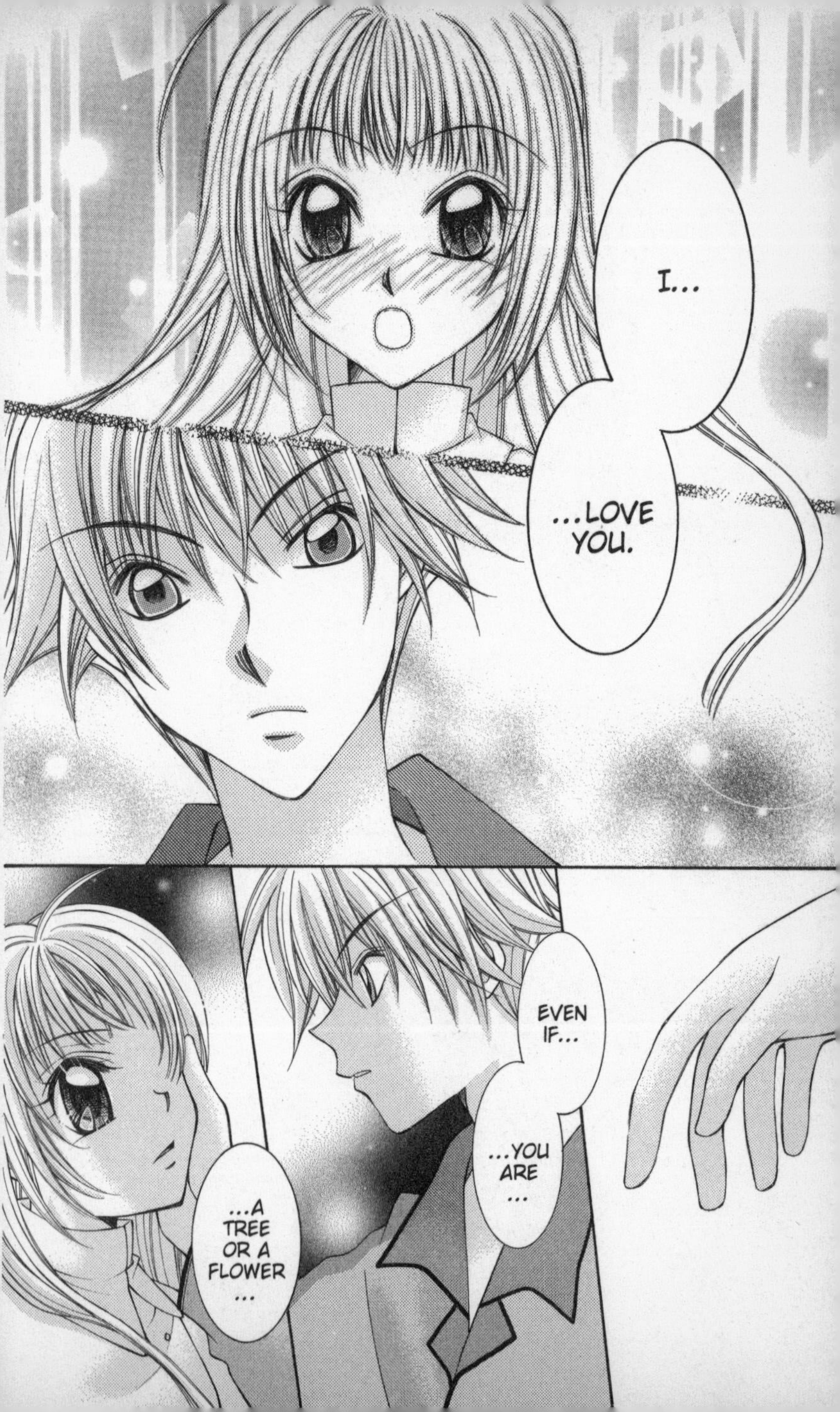
I...
...LOVE YOU.
EVEN IF...
...YOU ARE ...
...A TREE OR A FLOWER ...

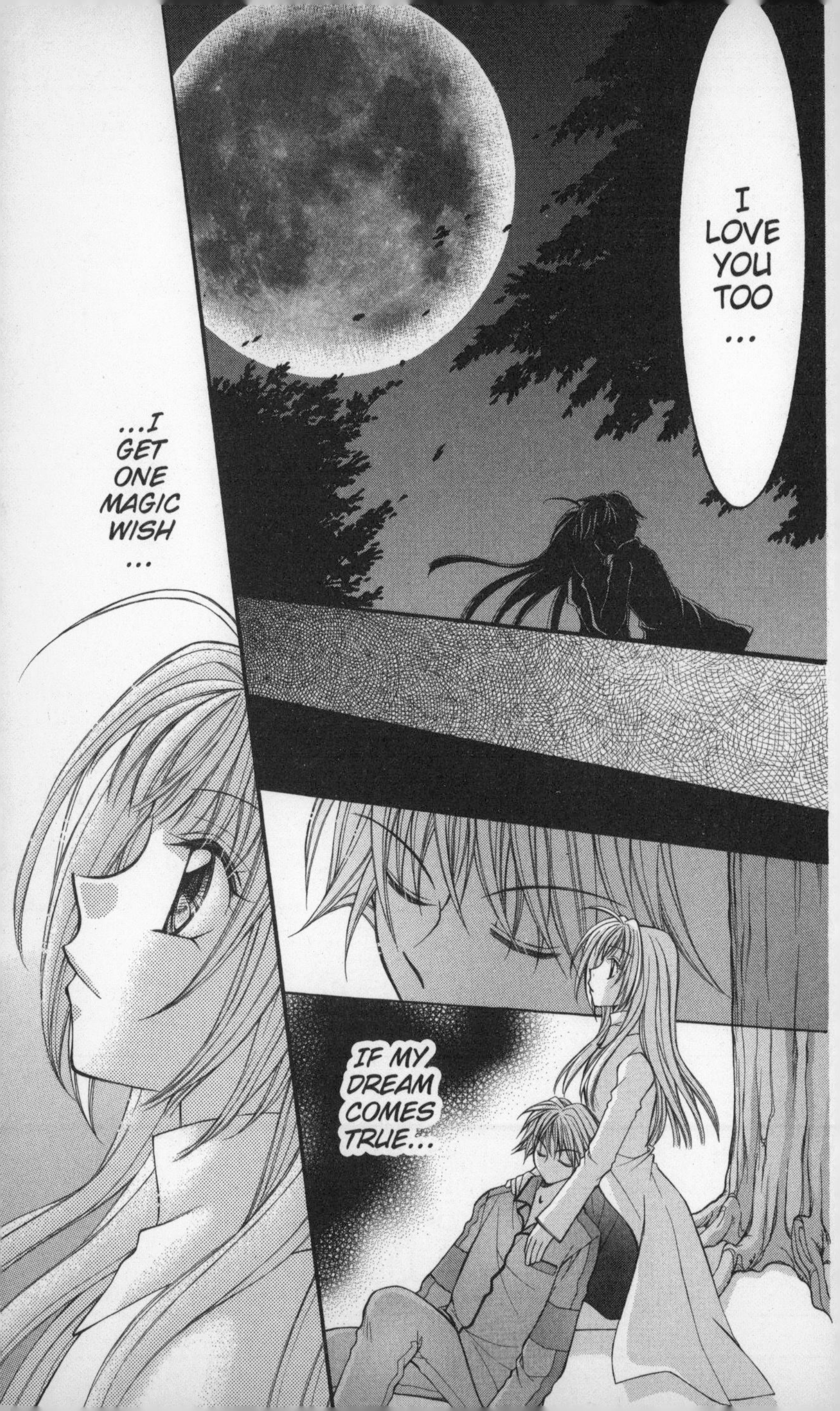
I LOVE YOU TOO...
IF MY DREAM COMES TRUE...
...I GET ONE MAGIC WISH...

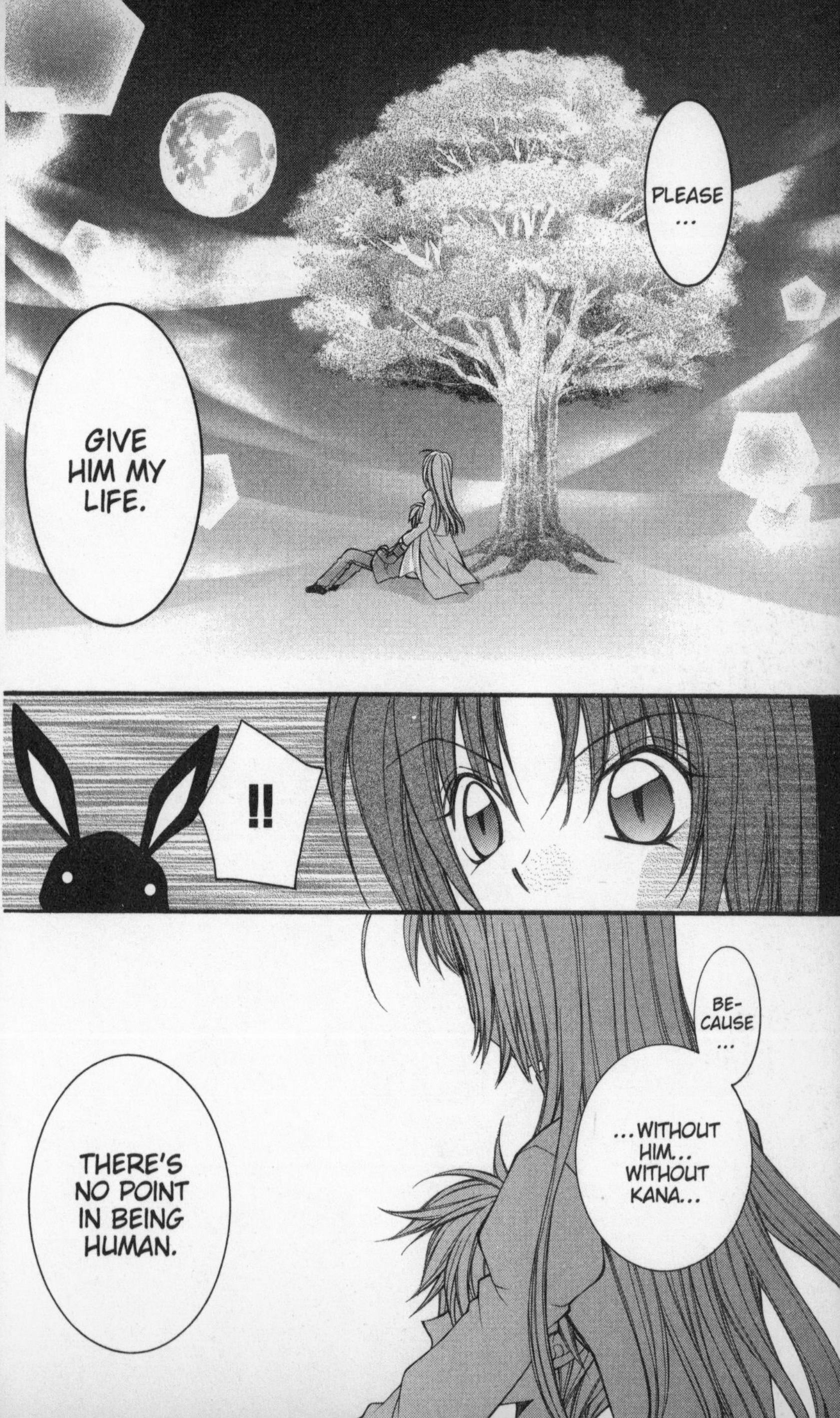
PLEASE ...
GIVE HIM MY LIFE.
!!
BE-CAUSE ...
...WITHOUT HIM... WITHOUT KANA...
THERE'S NO POINT IN BEING HUMAN.

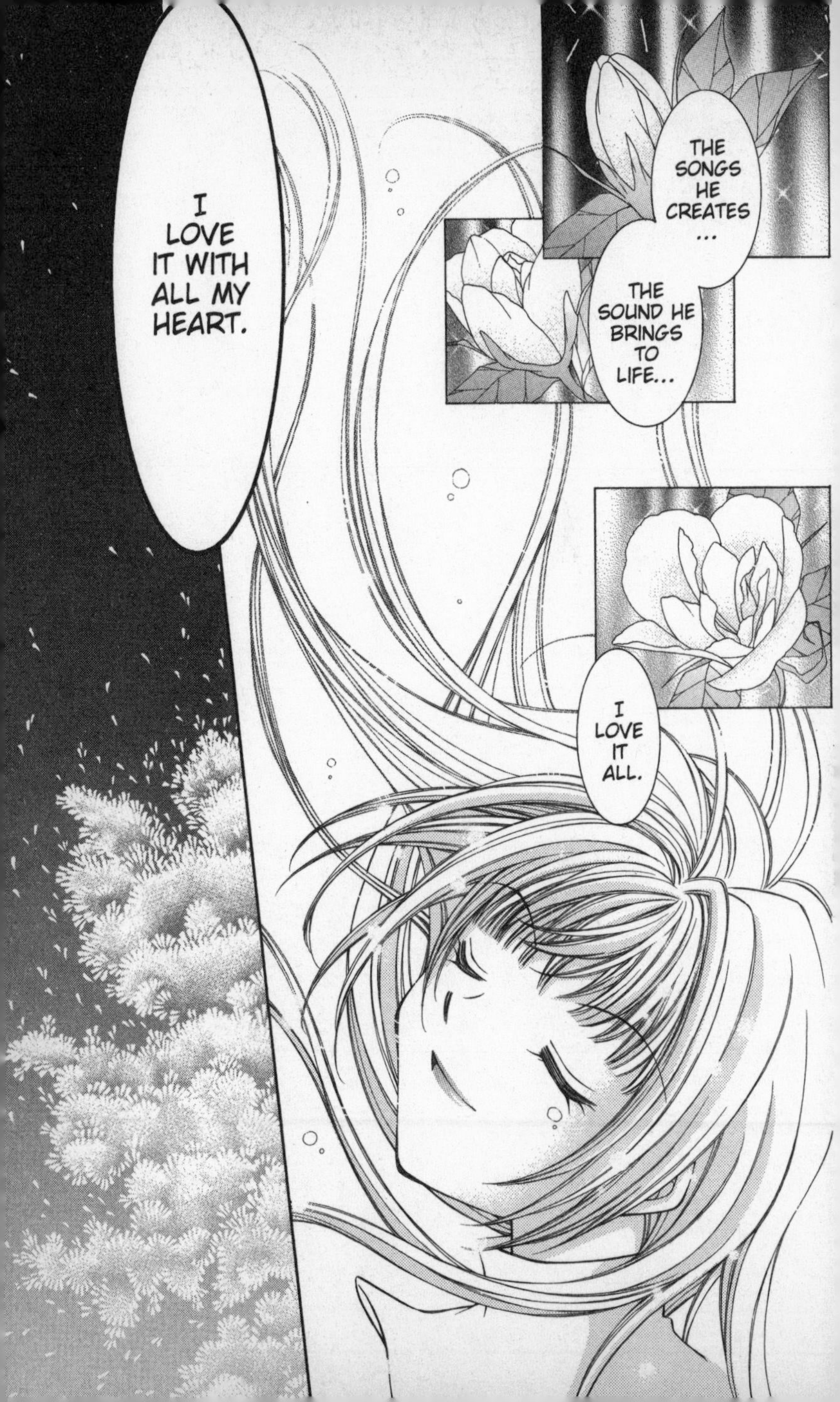
THE SONGS HE CREATES...
THE SOUND HE BRINGS TO LIFE...
I LOVE IT ALL.
I LOVE IT WITH ALL MY HEART.

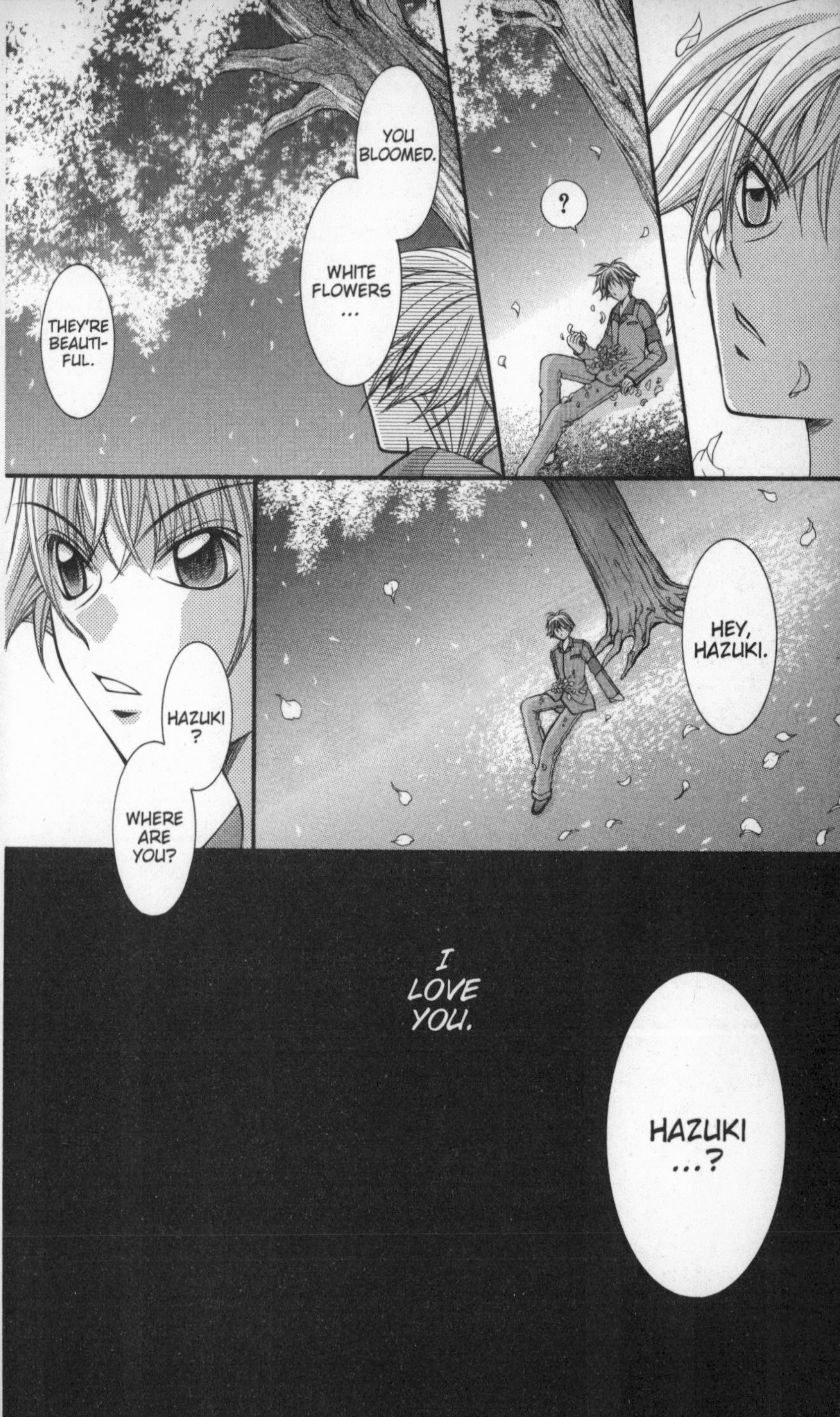
?
YOU BLOOMED.
WHITE FLOWERS ...
THEY'RE BEAUTI-FUL.
HEY, HAZUKI.
HAZUKI ?
WHERE ARE YOU?
I LOVE YOU.
HAZUKI ...?

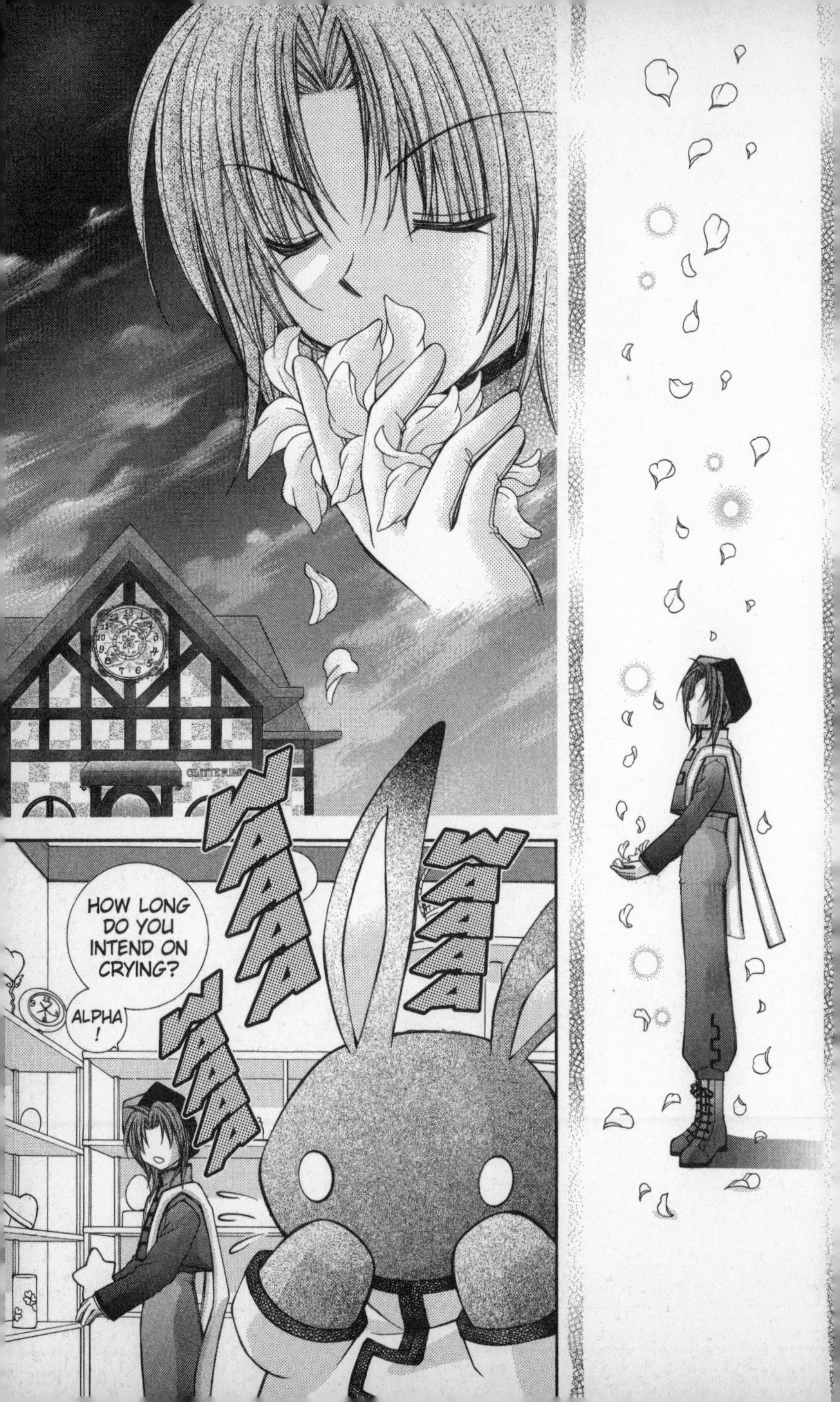
HOW LONG DO YOU INTEND ON CRYING?
ALPHA!

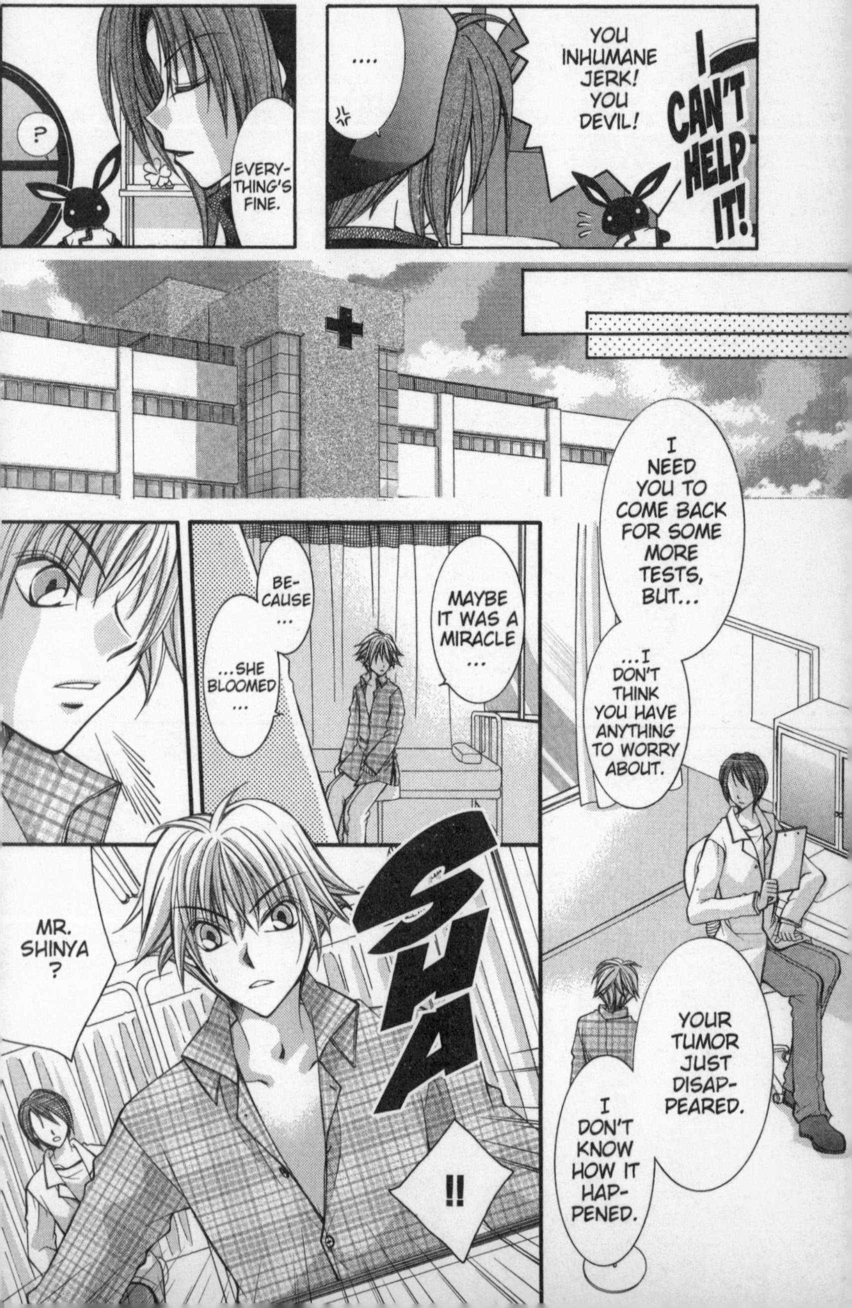
I CAN'T HELP IT!
YOU INHUMANE JERK! YOU DEVIL!
....
EVERYTHING'S FINE.
?
I NEED YOU TO COME BACK FOR SOME MORE TESTS, BUT...
...I DON'T THINK YOU HAVE ANYTHING TO WORRY ABOUT.
YOUR TUMOR JUST DISAPPEARED.
I DON'T KNOW HOW IT HAPPENED.
MAYBE IT WAS A MIRACLE ...
BECAUSE ...
...SHE BLOOMED ...
SHA
!!
MR. SHINYA ?

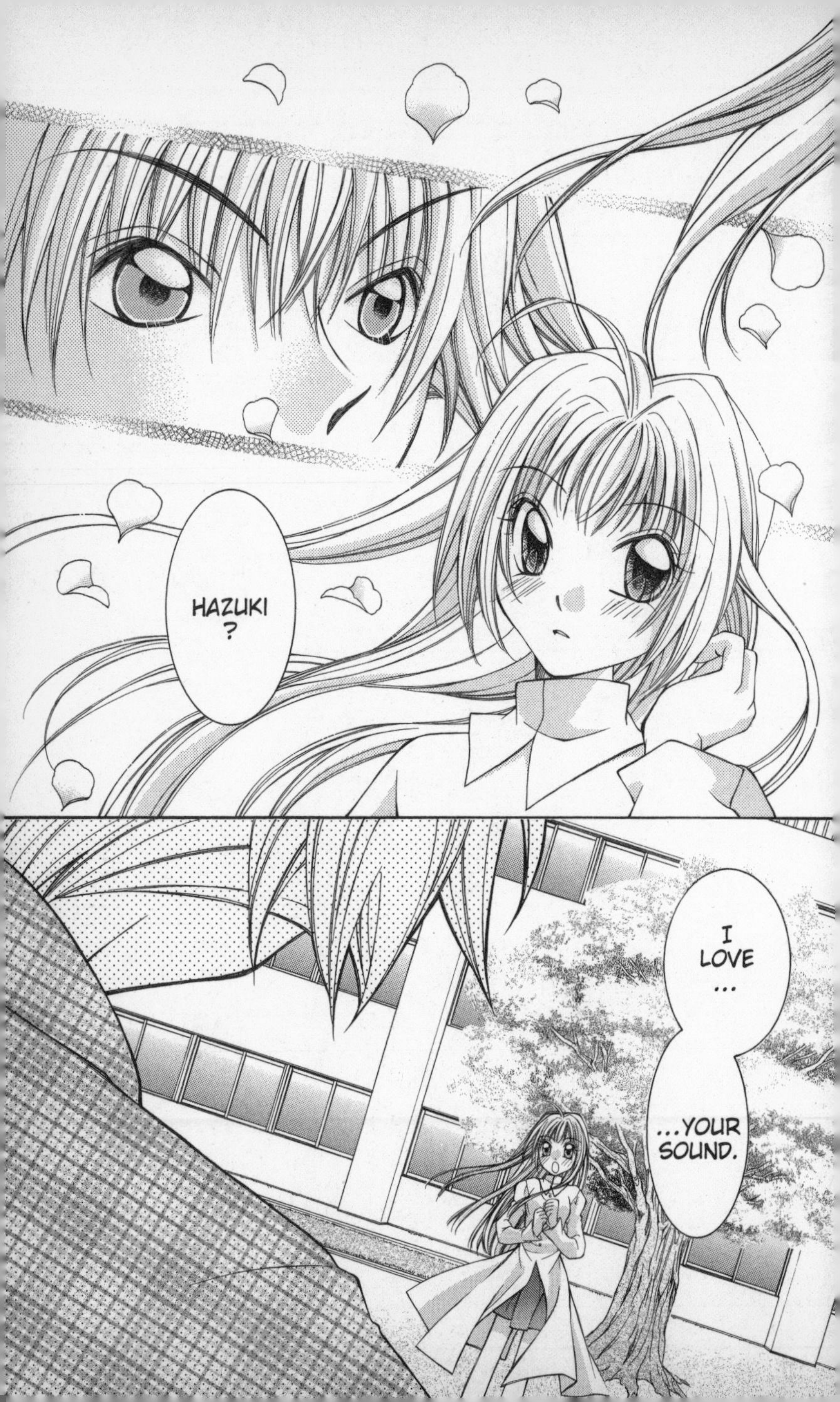
HAZUKI ?
I LOVE ...
...YOUR SOUND.

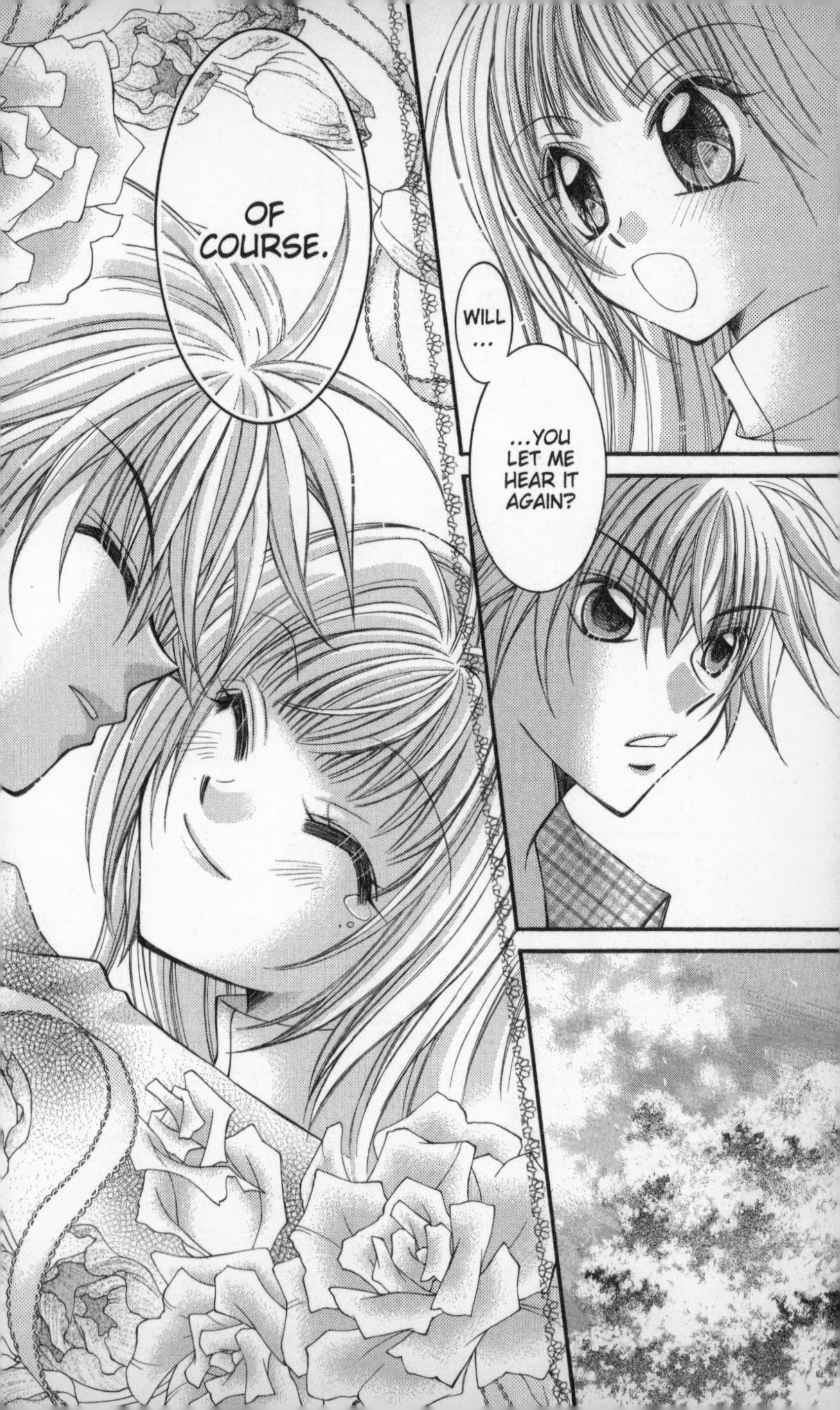
WILL ...
...YOU LET ME HEAR IT AGAIN?
OF COURSE.

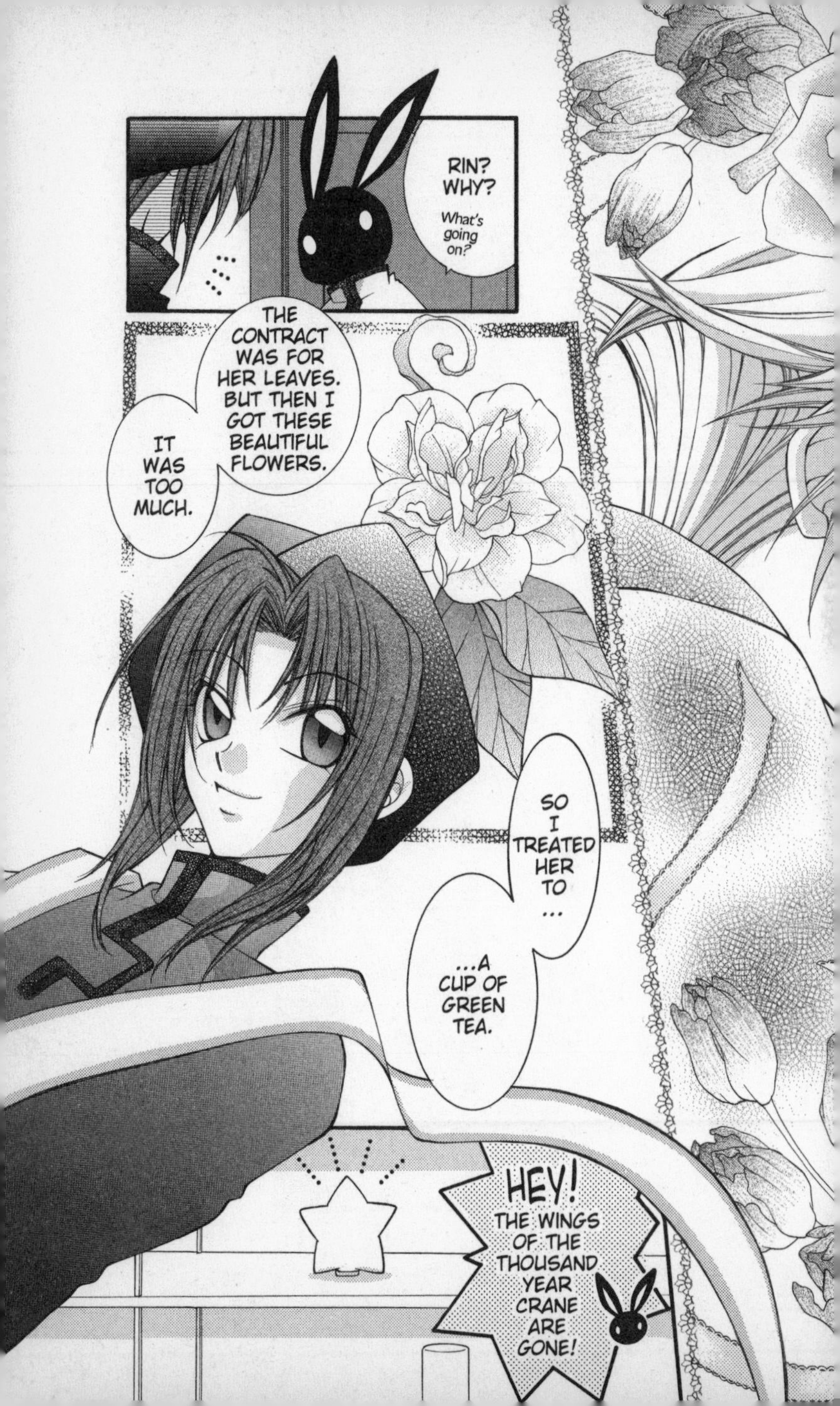
RIN? WHY?
What's going on?
...
THE CONTRACT WAS FOR HER LEAVES. BUT THEN I GOT THESE BEAUTIFUL FLOWERS.
IT WAS TOO MUCH.
SO I TREATED HER TO ...
...A CUP OF GREEN TEA.
HEY! THE WINGS OF THE THOUSAND YEAR CRANE ARE GONE!

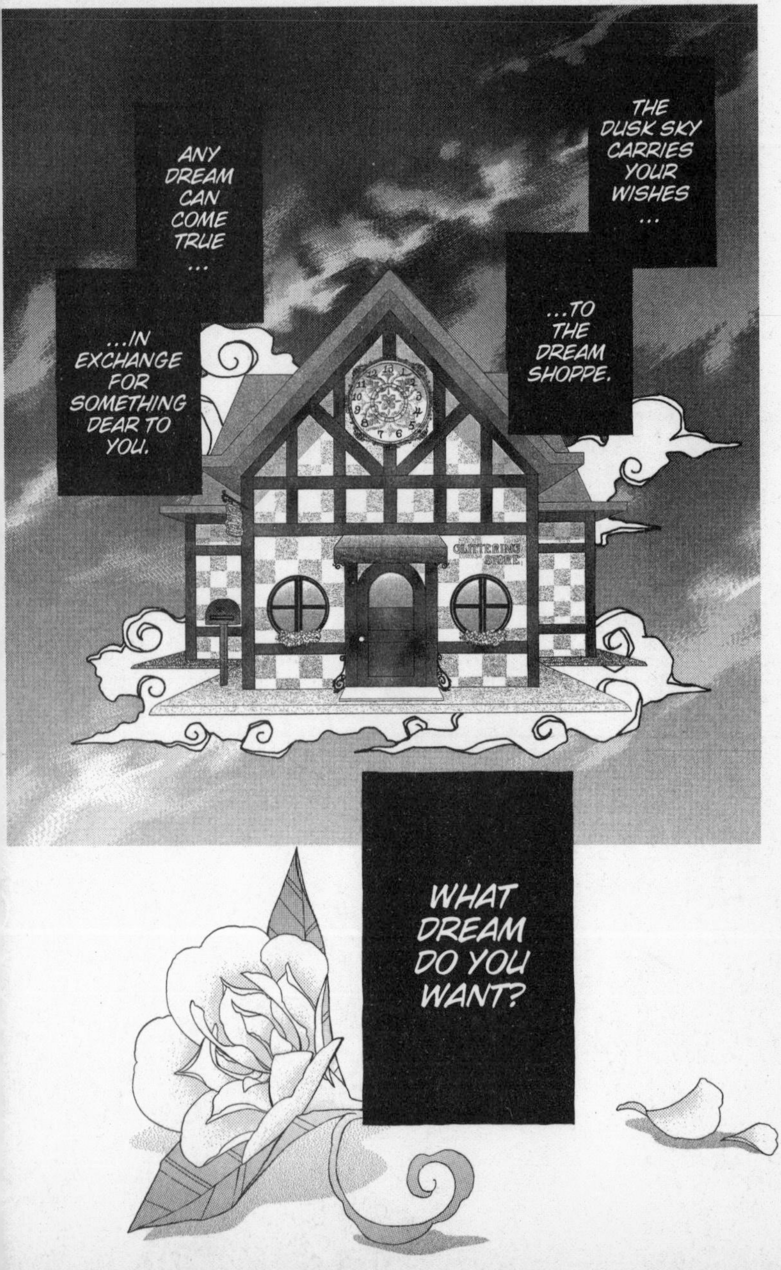
THE DUSK SKY CARRIES YOUR WISHES...
...TO THE DREAM SHOPPE.
ANY DREAM CAN COME TRUE...
...IN EXCHANGE FOR SOMETHING DEAR TO YOU.
GLITTERING STORE
WHAT DREAM DO YOU WANT?

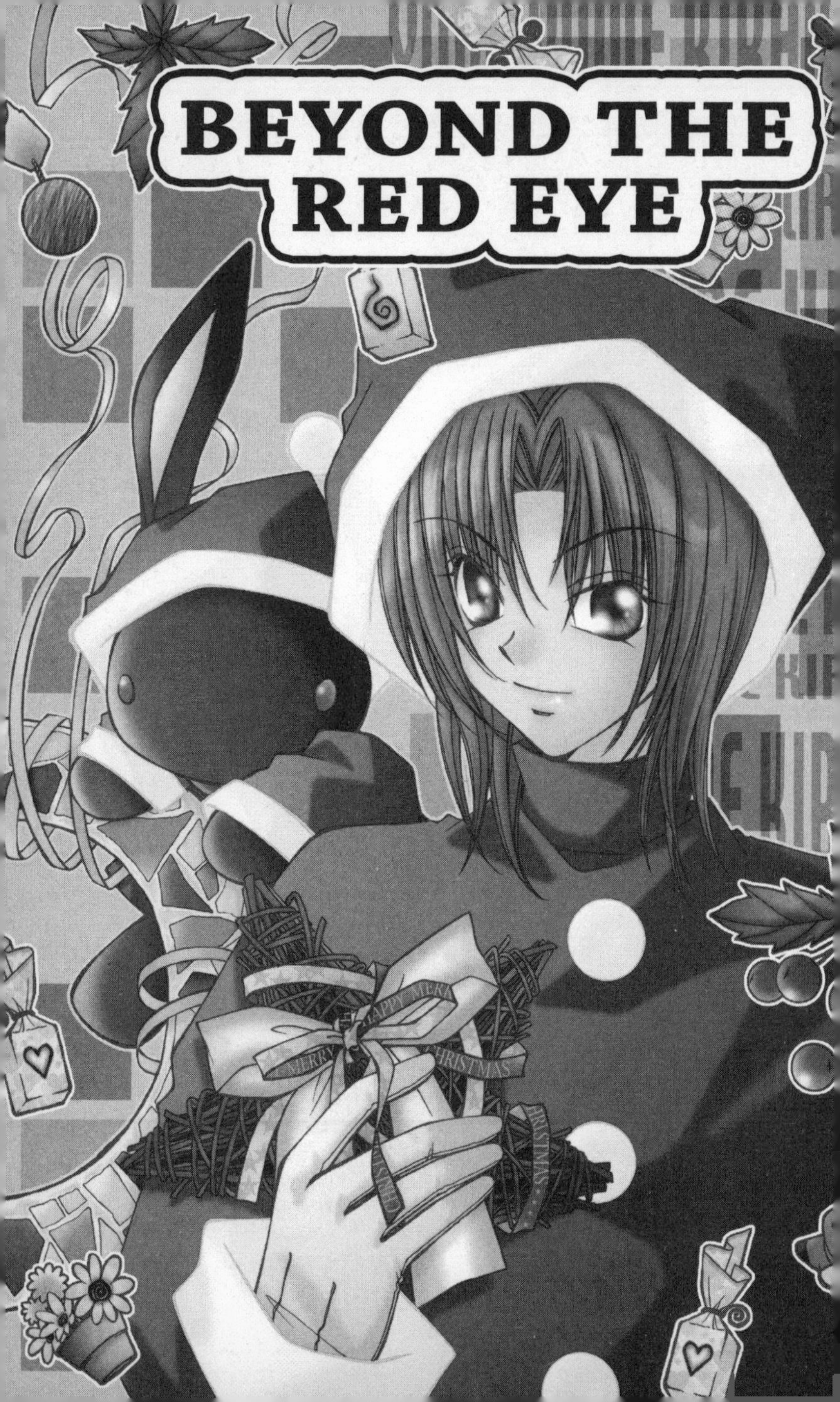
BEYOND THE RED EYE
MERRY
CHRISTMAS

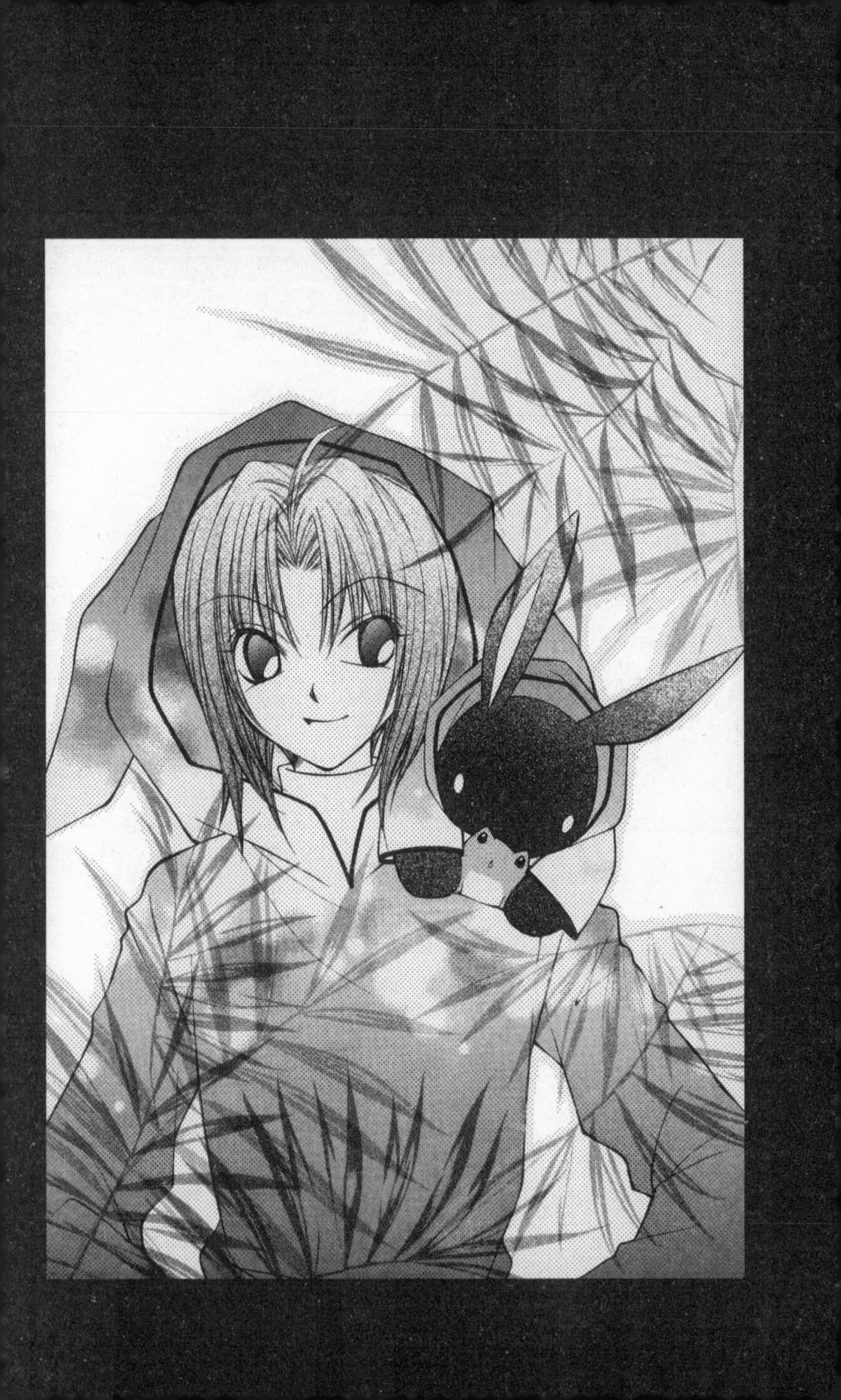

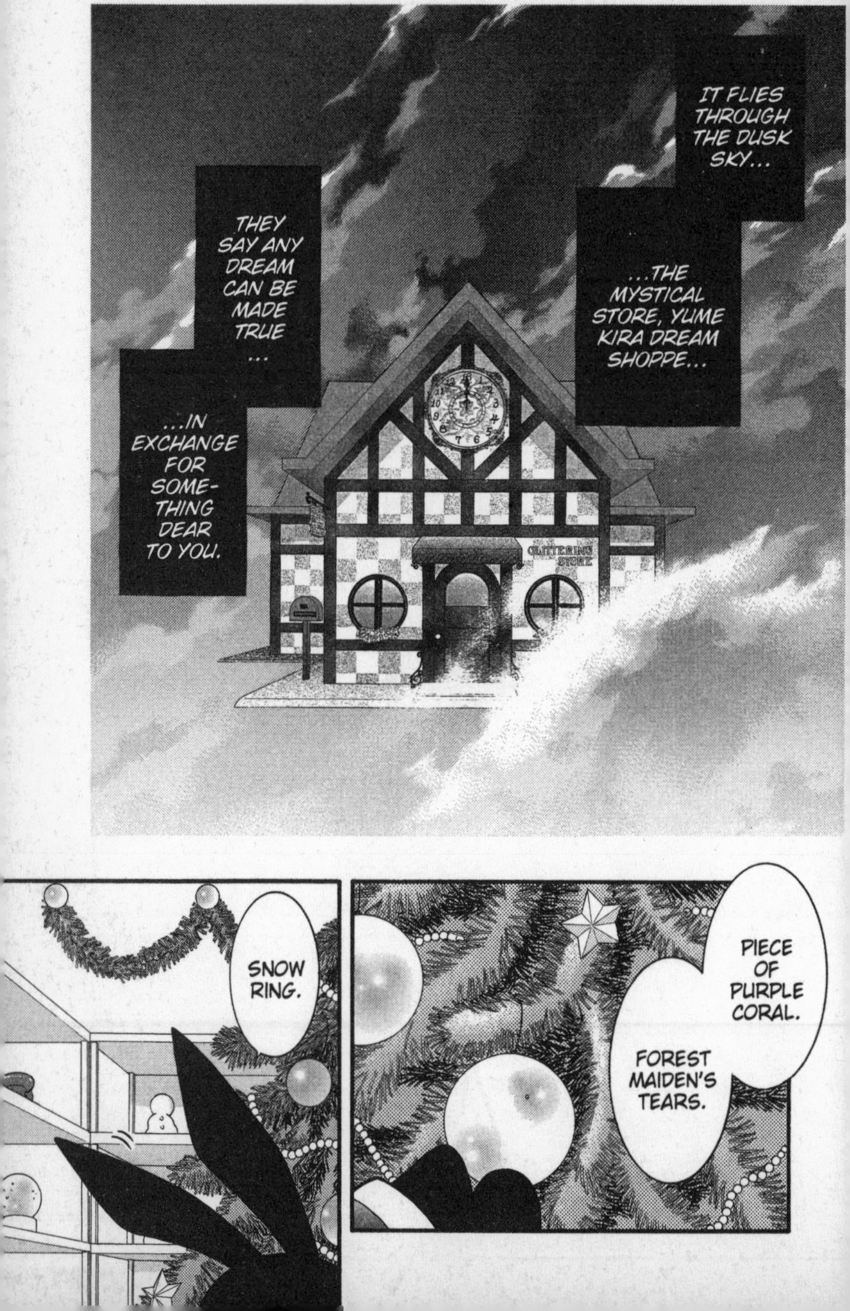
IT FLIES THROUGH THE DUSK SKY...
...THE MYSTICAL STORE, YUME KIRA DREAM SHOPPE...
THEY SAY ANY DREAM CAN BE MADE TRUE...
...IN EXCHANGE FOR SOME-THING DEAR TO YOU.
GLITTERING STORE
PIECE OF PURPLE CORAL.
FOREST MAIDEN'S TEARS.
SNOW RING.

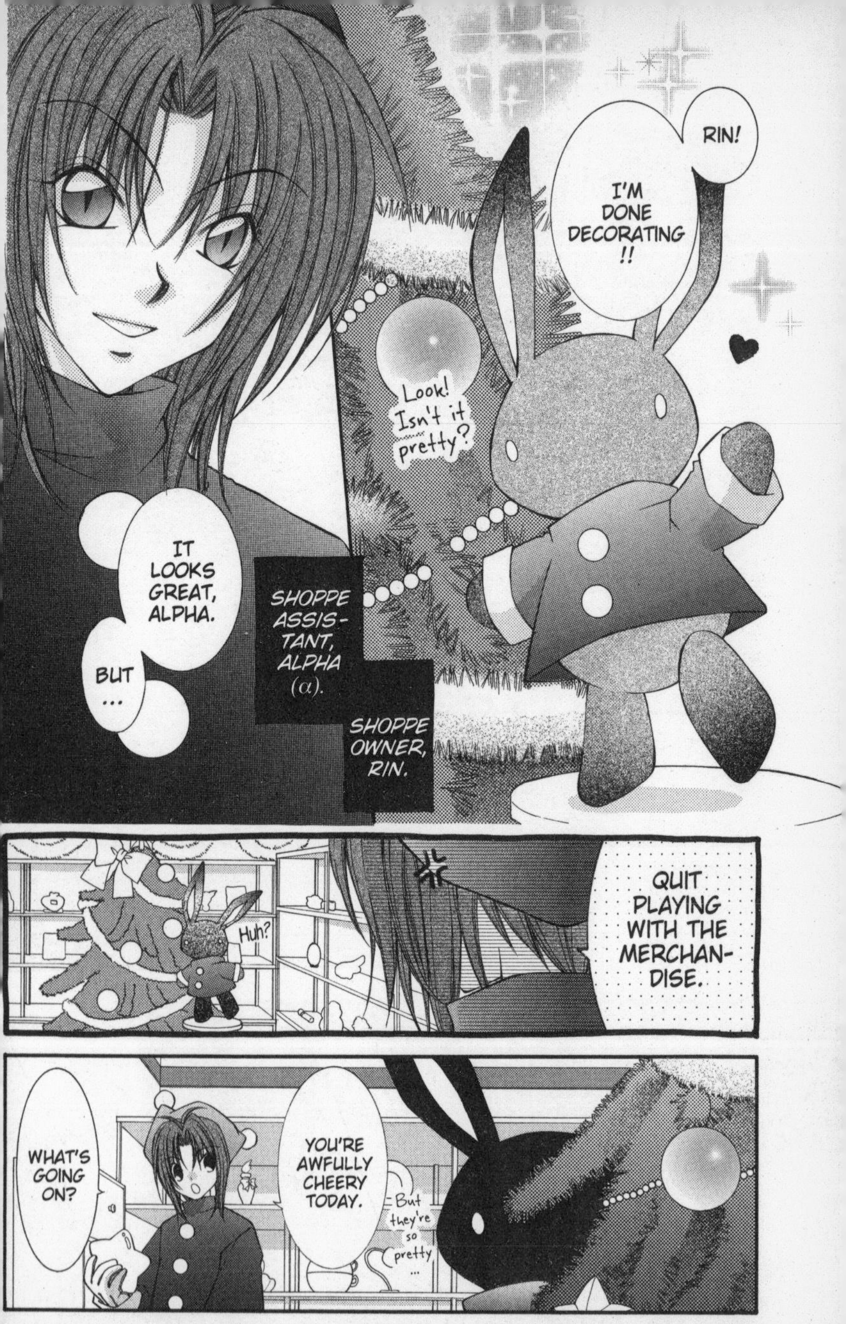
RIN!
I'M DONE DECORATING !!
Look! Isn't it pretty?
SHOPPE OWNER, RIN.
SHOPPE ASSIS-TANT, ALPHA (α).
IT LOOKS GREAT, ALPHA.
BUT ...
QUIT PLAYING WITH THE MERCHAN-DISE.
Huh?
But they're so pretty ...
YOU'RE AWFULLY CHEERY TODAY.
WHAT'S GOING ON?

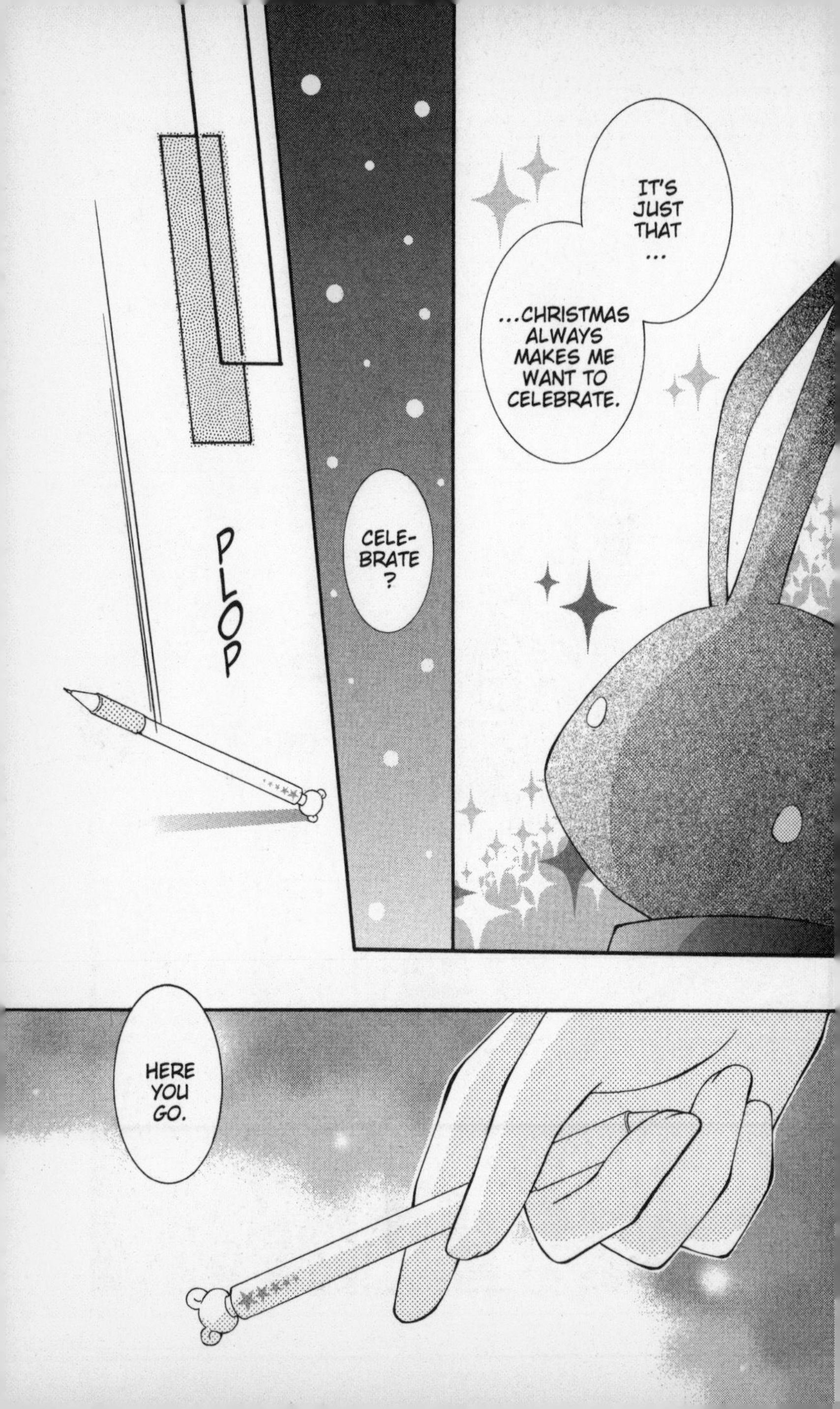

IT'S JUST THAT ...
...CHRISTMAS ALWAYS MAKES ME WANT TO CELEBRATE.
CELE-BRATE?
PLOP
HERE YOU GO.

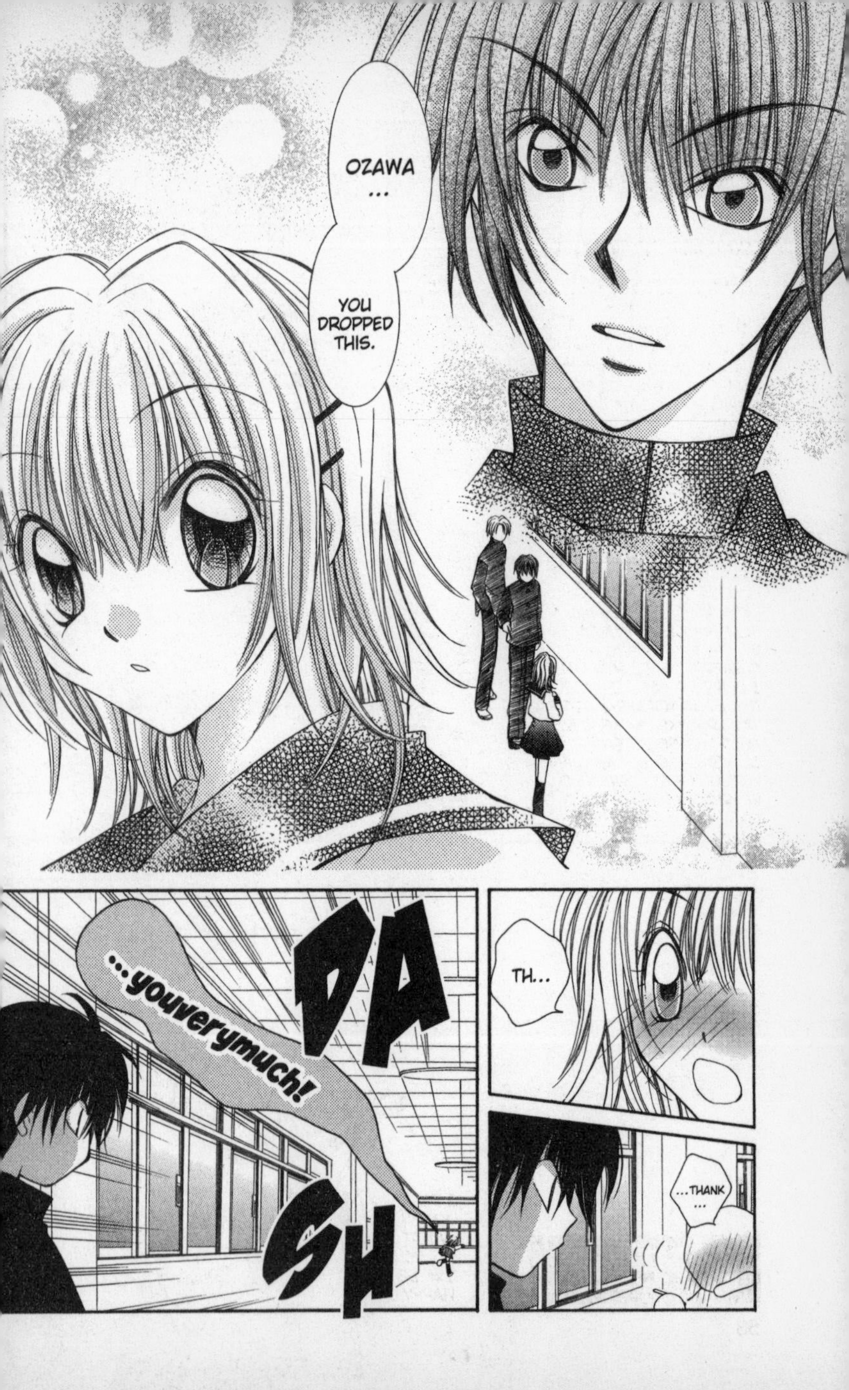
OZAWA ...
YOU DROPPED THIS.
TH...
...THANK ...
...youverymuch!
DASH

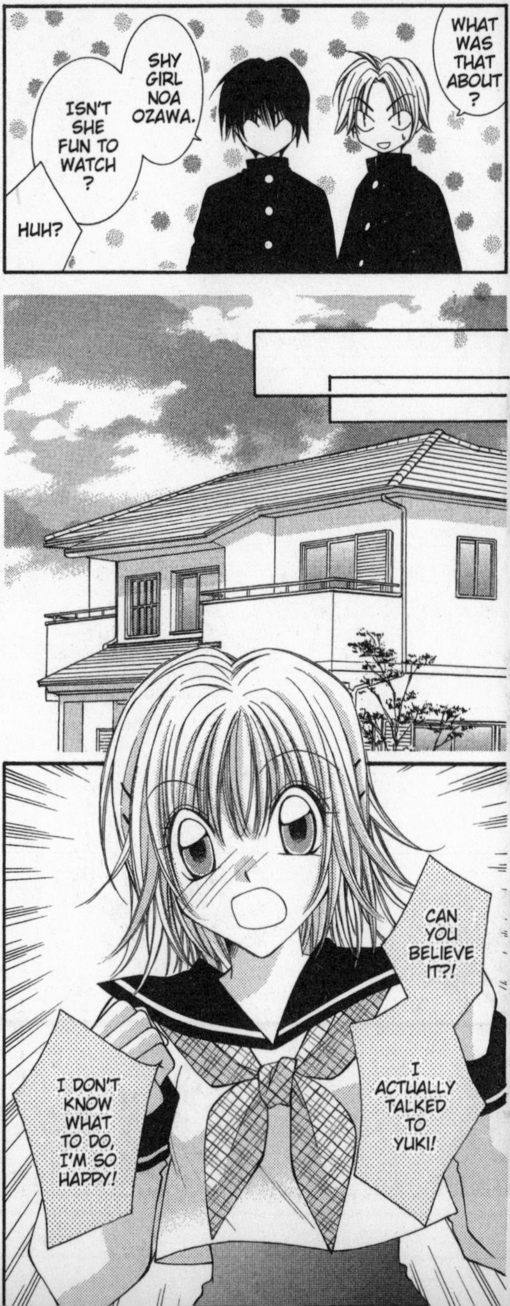
WHAT WAS THAT ABOUT?
SHY GIRL NOA OZAWA.
ISN'T SHE FUN TO WATCH?
HUH?
CAN YOU BELIEVE IT?!
I ACTUALLY TALKED TO YUKI!
I DON'T KNOW WHAT TO DO, I'M SO HAPPY!

2

★★★ CONGRATS!

...THAT IS...*YUME KIRA DREAM SHOPPE* IS ACTUALLY MY 21ST MANGA. I DIDN'T HAVE TIME TO CELEBRATE, BUT I'M EXCITED ABOUT HAVING GOT TO WHERE I AM. (MY ORIGINAL THOUGHT WAS TO CELEBRATE FOR THE 21ST MANGA SINCE I WAS UNABLE TO DO IT FOR MY 20TH?)

I'VE RECEIVED LETTERS FROM PEOPLE WHO SAY THAT THEY HAVE ALL MY MANGA. I'M HONORED. JUST HAVING ONE READ IS A REAL PLEASURE, SO TO HAVE PEOPLE WHO'VE READ THEM ALL?!! I'VE CLEARED THE 20 MARK AND I HOPE TO GET TO THE 30 MANGA BENCHMARK! NOTHING WOULD MAKE ME HAPPIER THAN HAVING MY FANS CONTINUE TO BUY MY MANGA. FOR THOSE READERS WHO ARE READING MY WORK FOR THE FIRST TIME NOW...IF YOU HAVE SOME TIME, PLEASE TRY CHECKING OUT SOME OF MY OTHER MANGA. SOME OF THEM HAVE CONNECTING ELEMENTS.

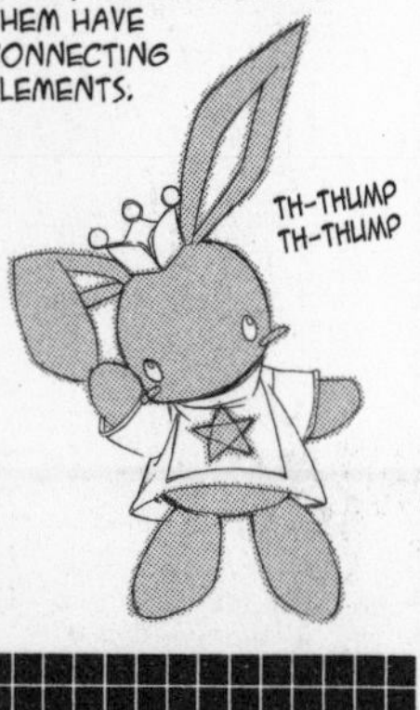
TH-THUMP
TH-THUMP

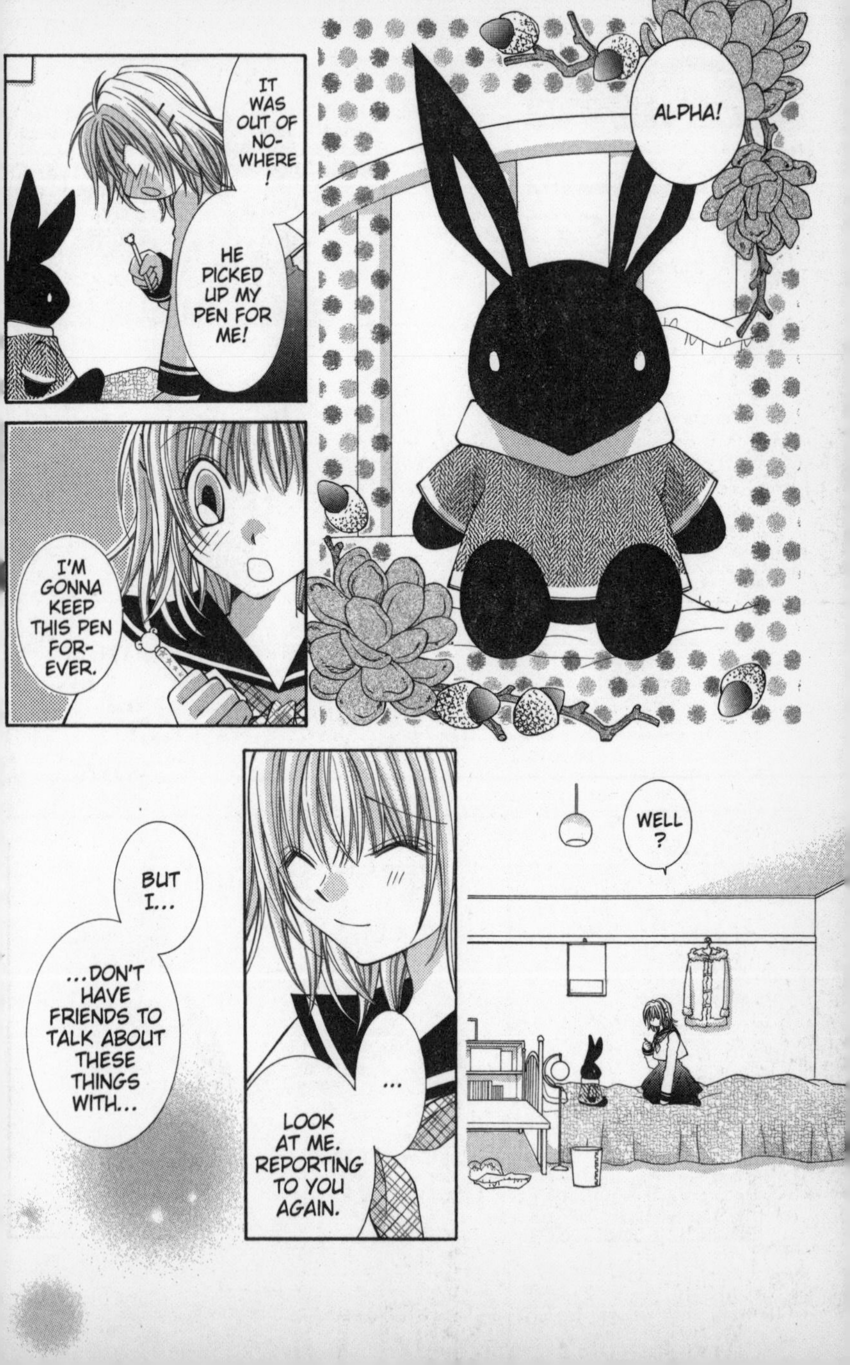
ALPHA!
IT WAS OUT OF NO-WHERE!
HE PICKED UP MY PEN FOR ME!
I'M GONNA KEEP THIS PEN FOR-EVER.
WELL?
...
LOOK AT ME. REPORTING TO YOU AGAIN.
BUT I...
...DON'T HAVE FRIENDS TO TALK ABOUT THESE THINGS WITH...

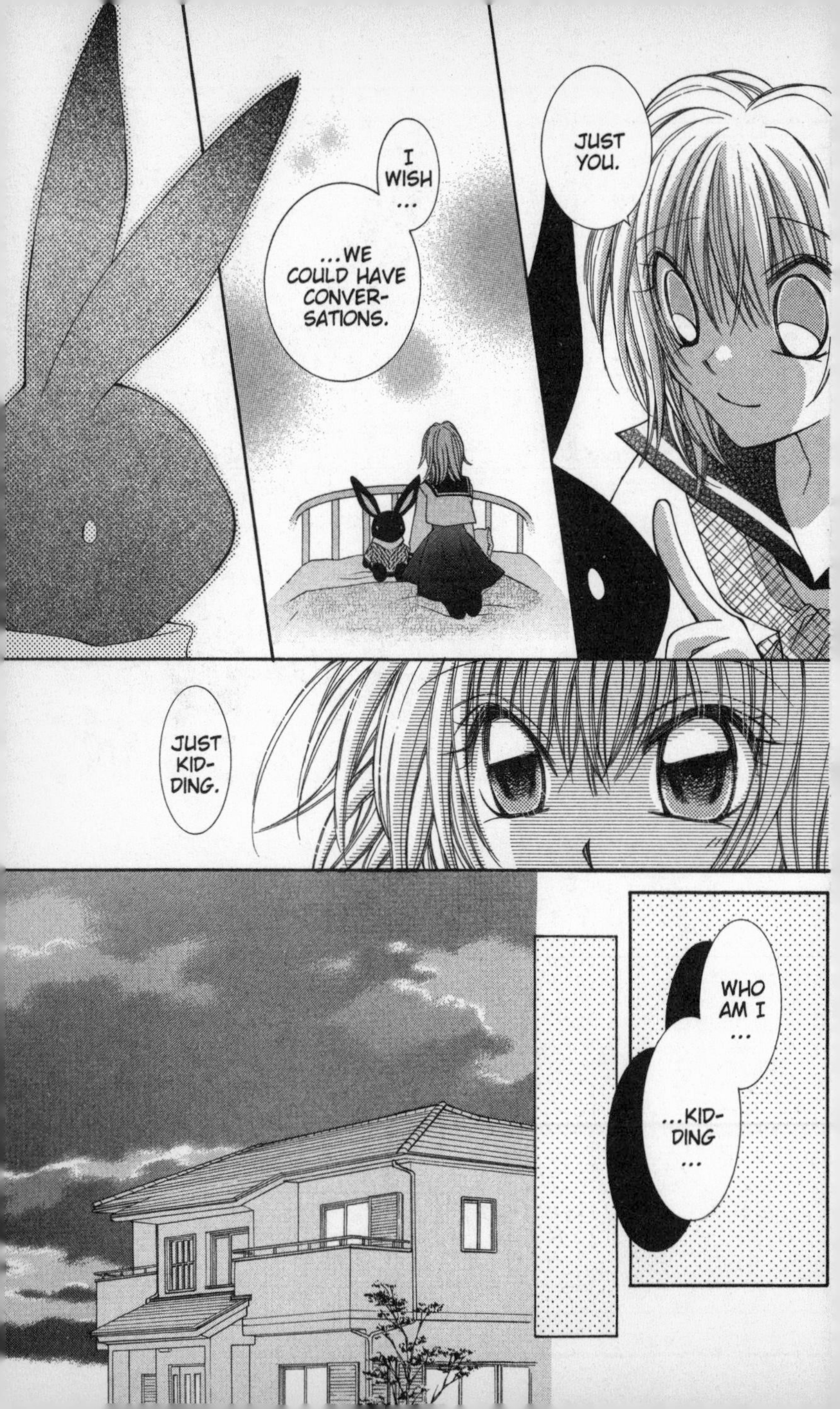
JUST YOU.
I WISH ...
...WE COULD HAVE CONVER-SATIONS.
JUST KID-DING.
WHO AM I ...
...KID-DING ...

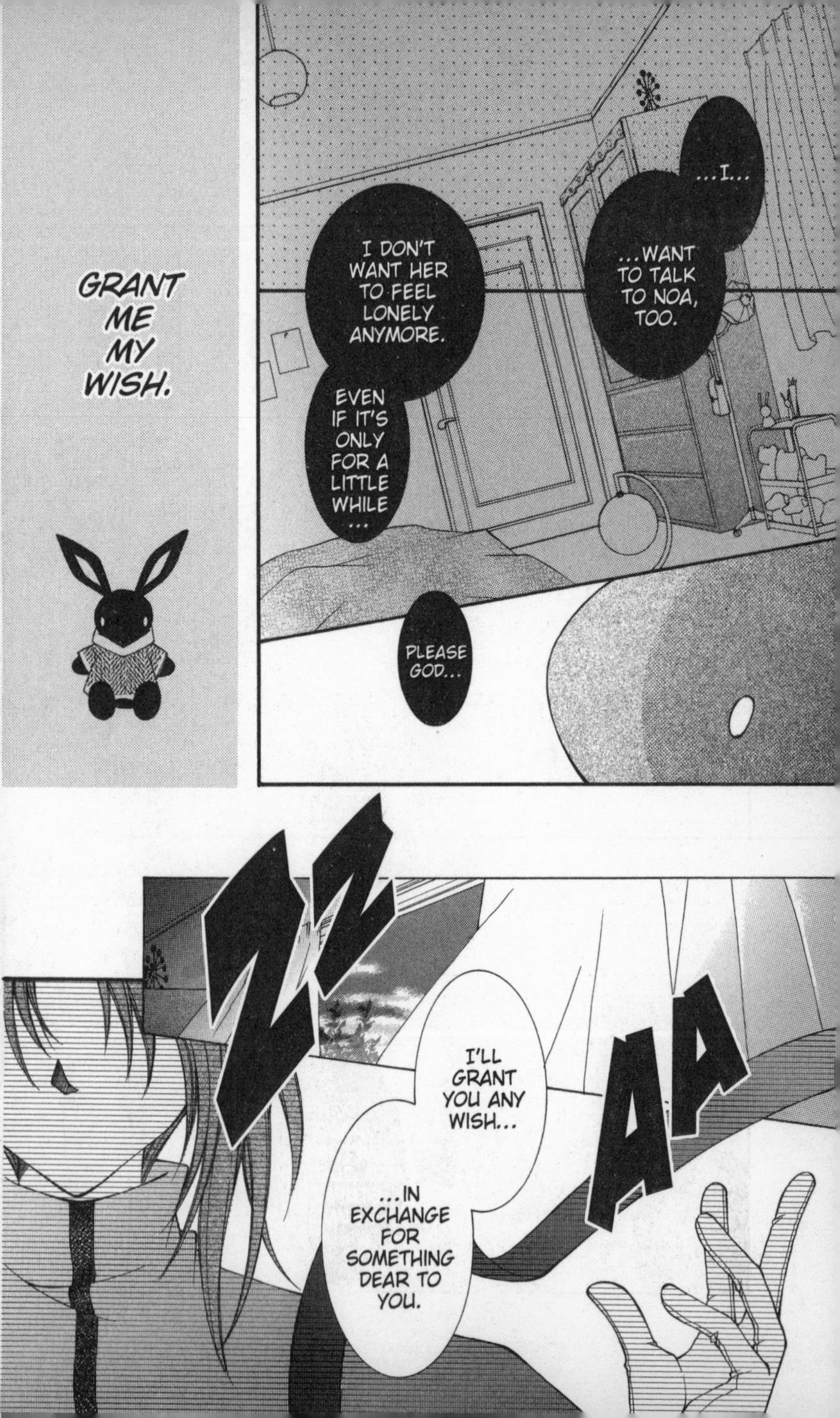

...I...
...WANT TO TALK TO NOA, TOO.
I DON'T WANT HER TO FEEL LONELY ANYMORE.
EVEN IF IT'S ONLY FOR A LITTLE WHILE...
PLEASE GOD...
GRANT ME MY WISH.
ZZAA
I'LL GRANT YOU ANY WISH...
...IN EXCHANGE FOR SOMETHING DEAR TO YOU.

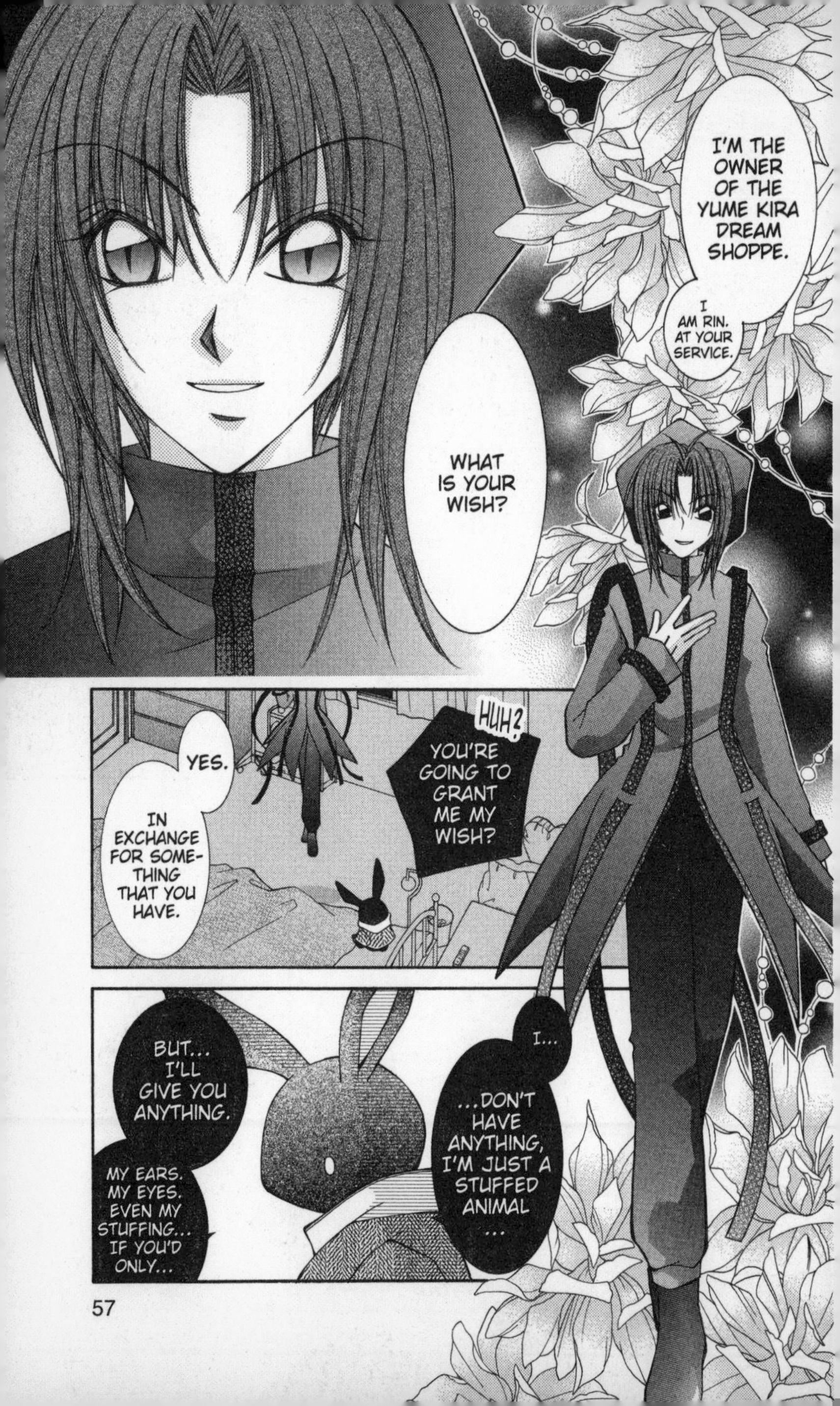
I'M THE OWNER OF THE YUME KIRA DREAM SHOPPE.
I AM RIN. AT YOUR SERVICE.
WHAT IS YOUR WISH?
HUH?
YOU'RE GOING TO GRANT ME MY WISH?
YES.
IN EXCHANGE FOR SOME-THING THAT YOU HAVE.
I...
...DON'T HAVE ANYTHING, I'M JUST A STUFFED ANIMAL...
BUT... I'LL GIVE YOU ANYTHING.
MY EARS. MY EYES. EVEN MY STUFFING... IF YOU'D ONLY...

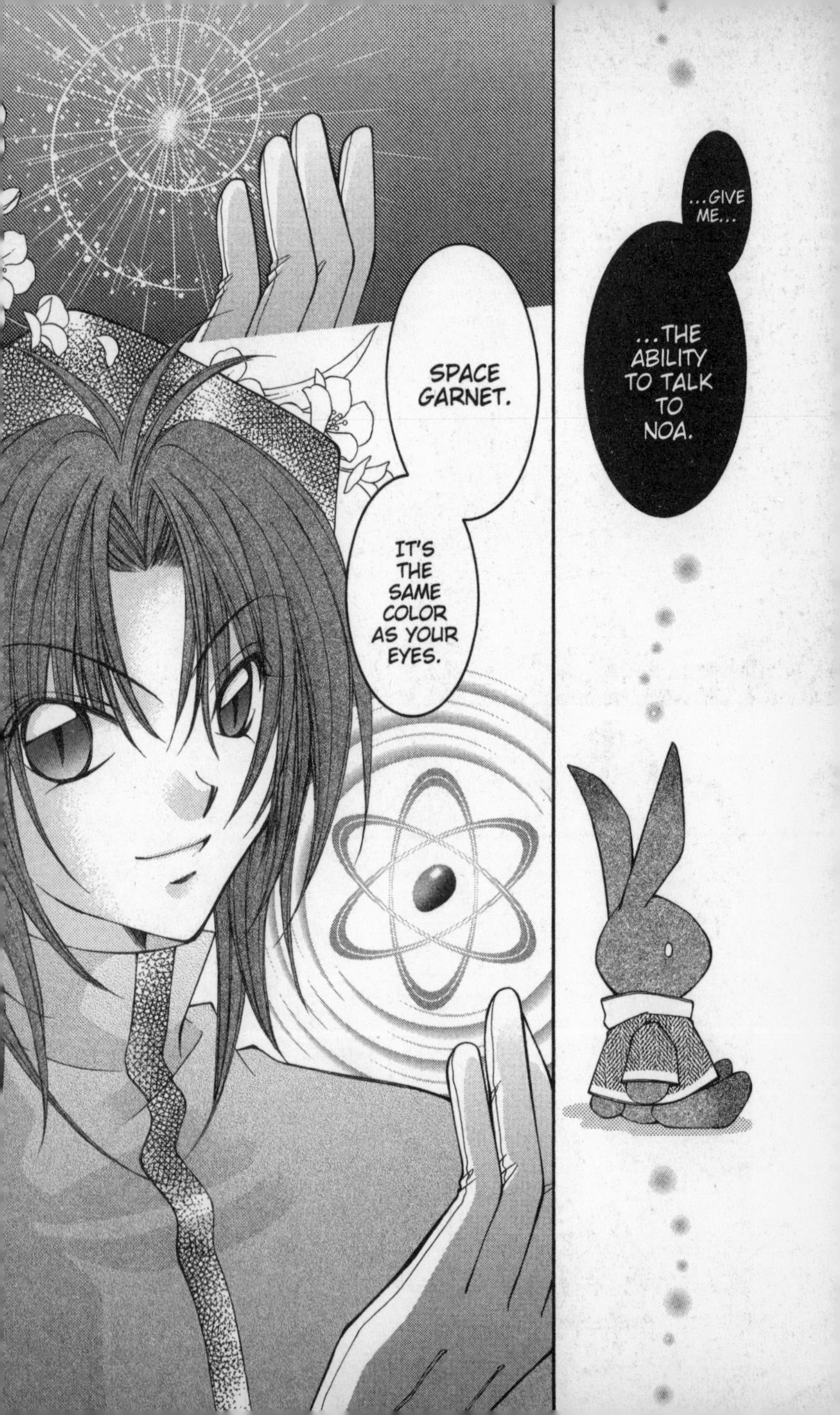
...GIVE ME...
...THE ABILITY TO TALK TO NOA.
SPACE GARNET.
IT'S THE SAME COLOR AS YOUR EYES.

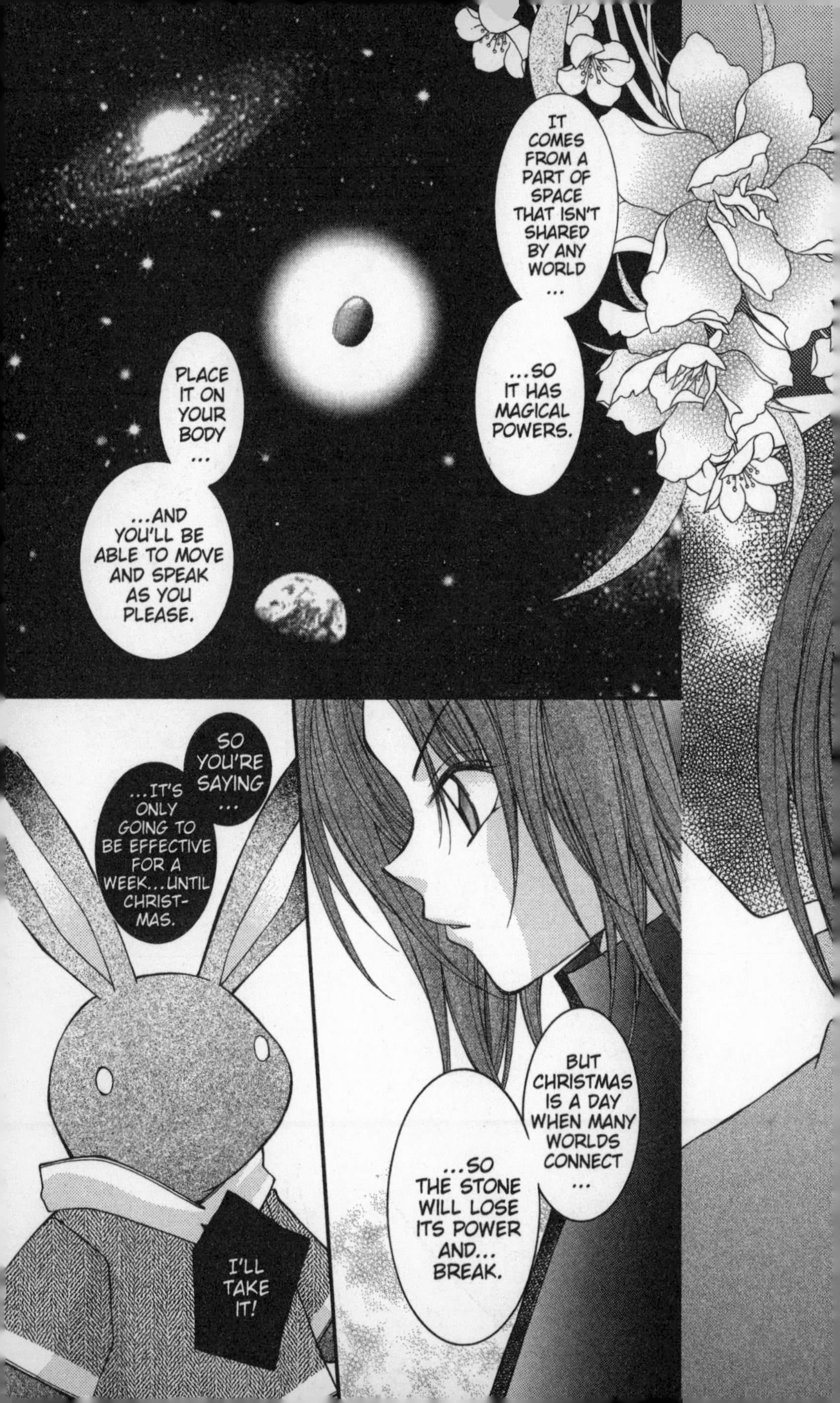
IT COMES FROM A PART OF SPACE THAT ISN'T SHARED BY ANY WORLD...
...SO IT HAS MAGICAL POWERS.
PLACE IT ON YOUR BODY...
...AND YOU'LL BE ABLE TO MOVE AND SPEAK AS YOU PLEASE.
BUT CHRISTMAS IS A DAY WHEN MANY WORLDS CONNECT...
...SO THE STONE WILL LOSE ITS POWER AND... BREAK.
SO YOU'RE SAYING...
...IT'S ONLY GOING TO BE EFFECTIVE FOR A WEEK...UNTIL CHRIST-MAS.
I'LL TAKE IT!

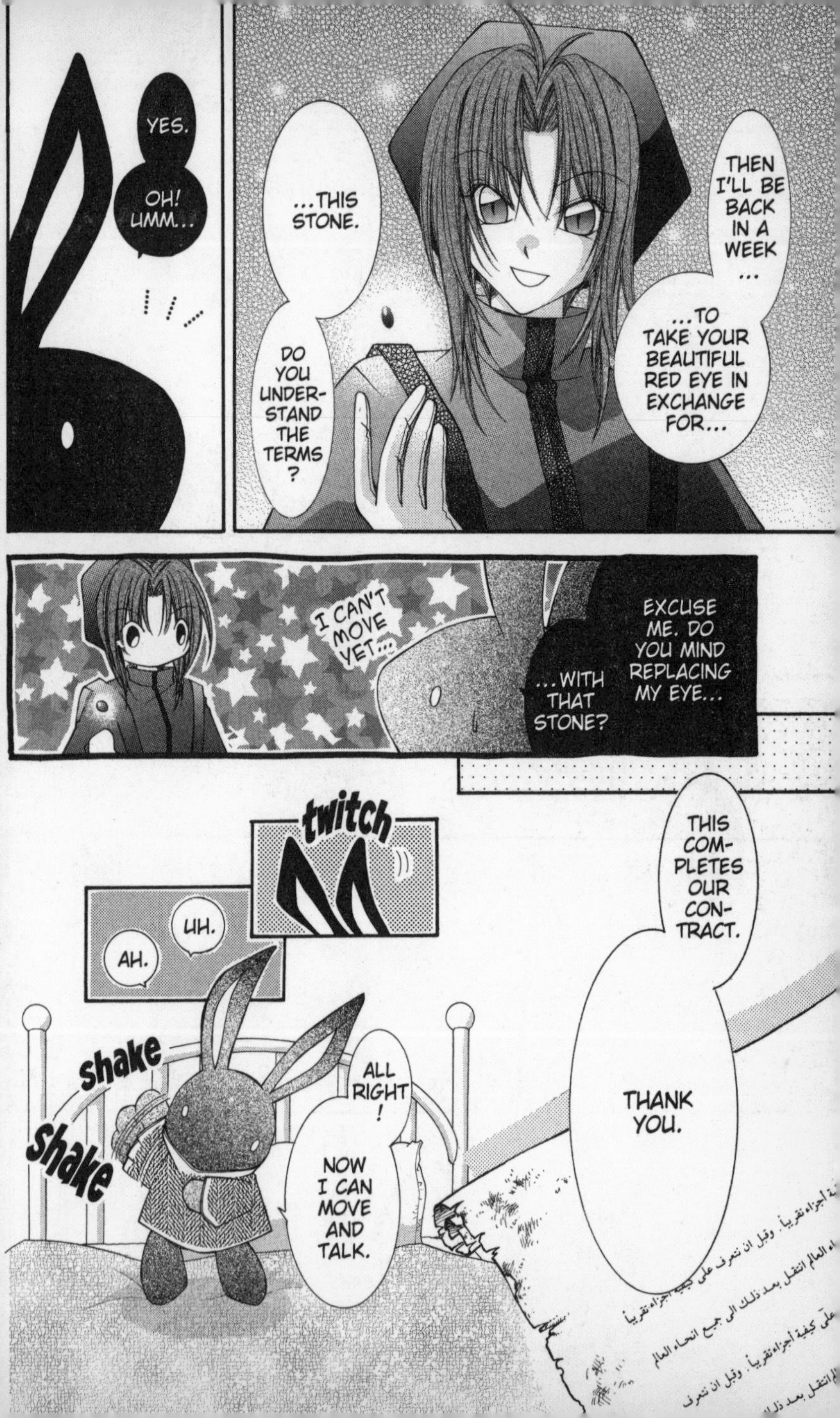
THEN I'LL BE BACK IN A WEEK...
...TO TAKE YOUR BEAUTIFUL RED EYE IN EXCHANGE FOR...
...THIS STONE.
DO YOU UNDER-STAND THE TERMS?
YES.
OH! UMM...
EXCUSE ME. DO YOU MIND REPLACING MY EYE...
...WITH THAT STONE?
I CAN'T MOVE YET...
THIS COM-PLETES OUR CON-TRACT.
THANK YOU.
twitch
UH.
AH.
ALL RIGHT!
NOW I CAN MOVE AND TALK.
shake
shake

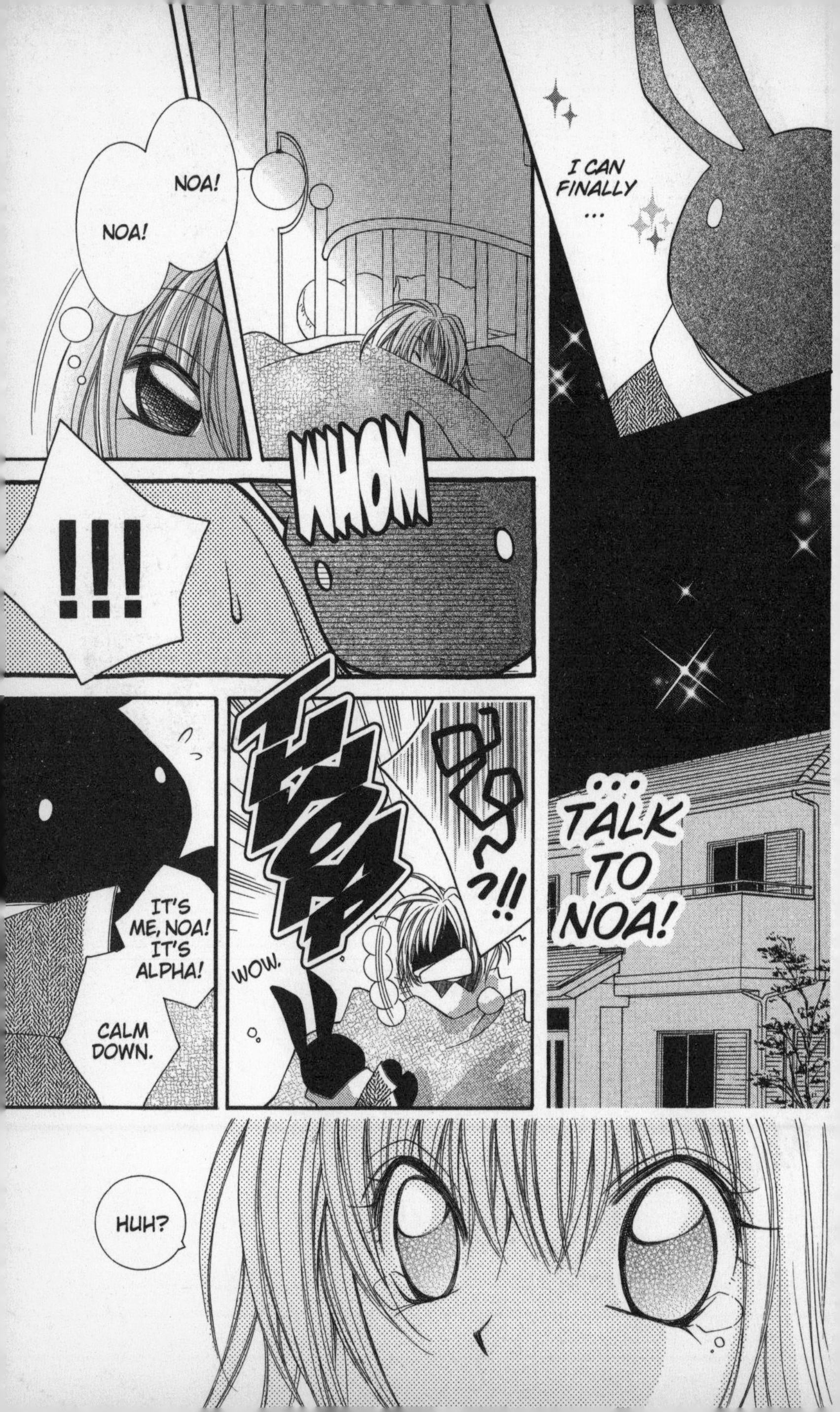
I CAN FINALLY ...
... TALK TO NOA!
NOA!
NOA!
WHOM
!!!
WOW.
IT'S ME, NOA! IT'S ALPHA!
CALM DOWN.
HUH?

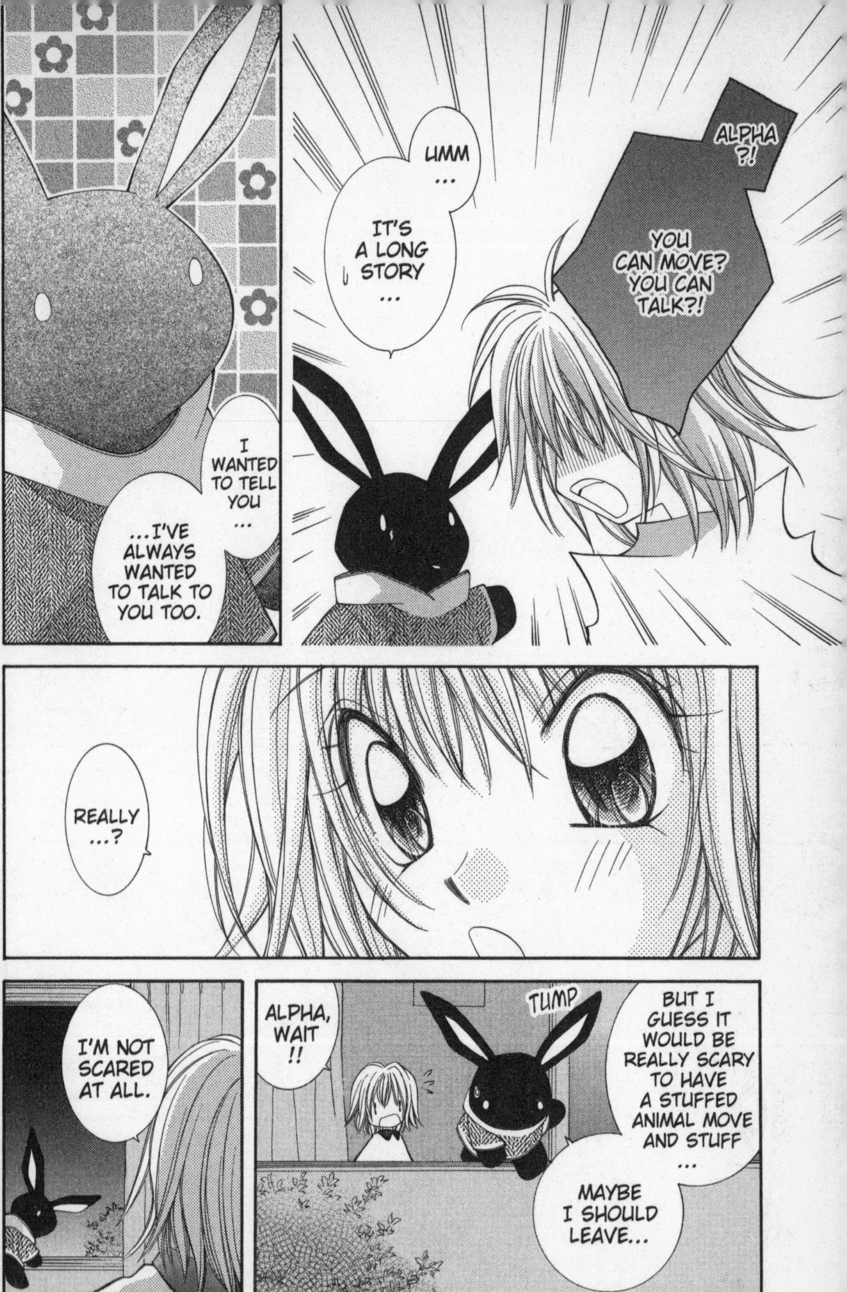
ALPHA ?!
YOU CAN MOVE? YOU CAN TALK?!
UMM ...
IT'S A LONG STORY ...
I WANTED TO TELL YOU ...
...I'VE ALWAYS WANTED TO TALK TO YOU TOO.
REALLY ...?
BUT I GUESS IT WOULD BE REALLY SCARY TO HAVE A STUFFED ANIMAL MOVE AND STUFF ...
TUMP
MAYBE I SHOULD LEAVE...
ALPHA, WAIT !!
I'M NOT SCARED AT ALL.

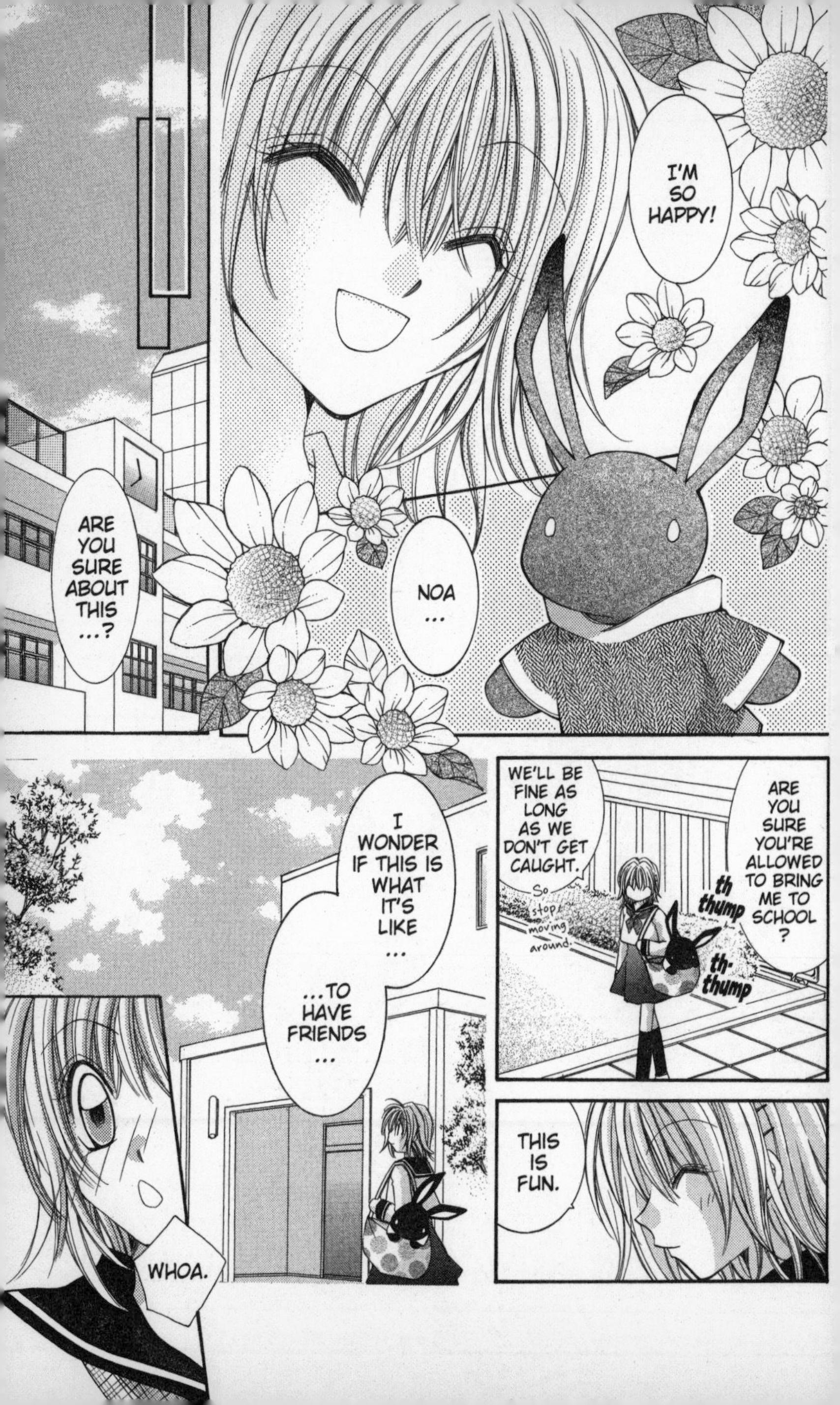

I'M SO HAPPY!
NOA ...
ARE YOU SURE ABOUT THIS ...?
ARE YOU SURE YOU'RE ALLOWED TO BRING ME TO SCHOOL ?
th thump
th-thump
WE'LL BE FINE AS LONG AS WE DON'T GET CAUGHT.
So stop moving around.
THIS IS FUN.
I WONDER IF THIS IS WHAT IT'S LIKE ...
...TO HAVE FRIENDS ...
WHOA.

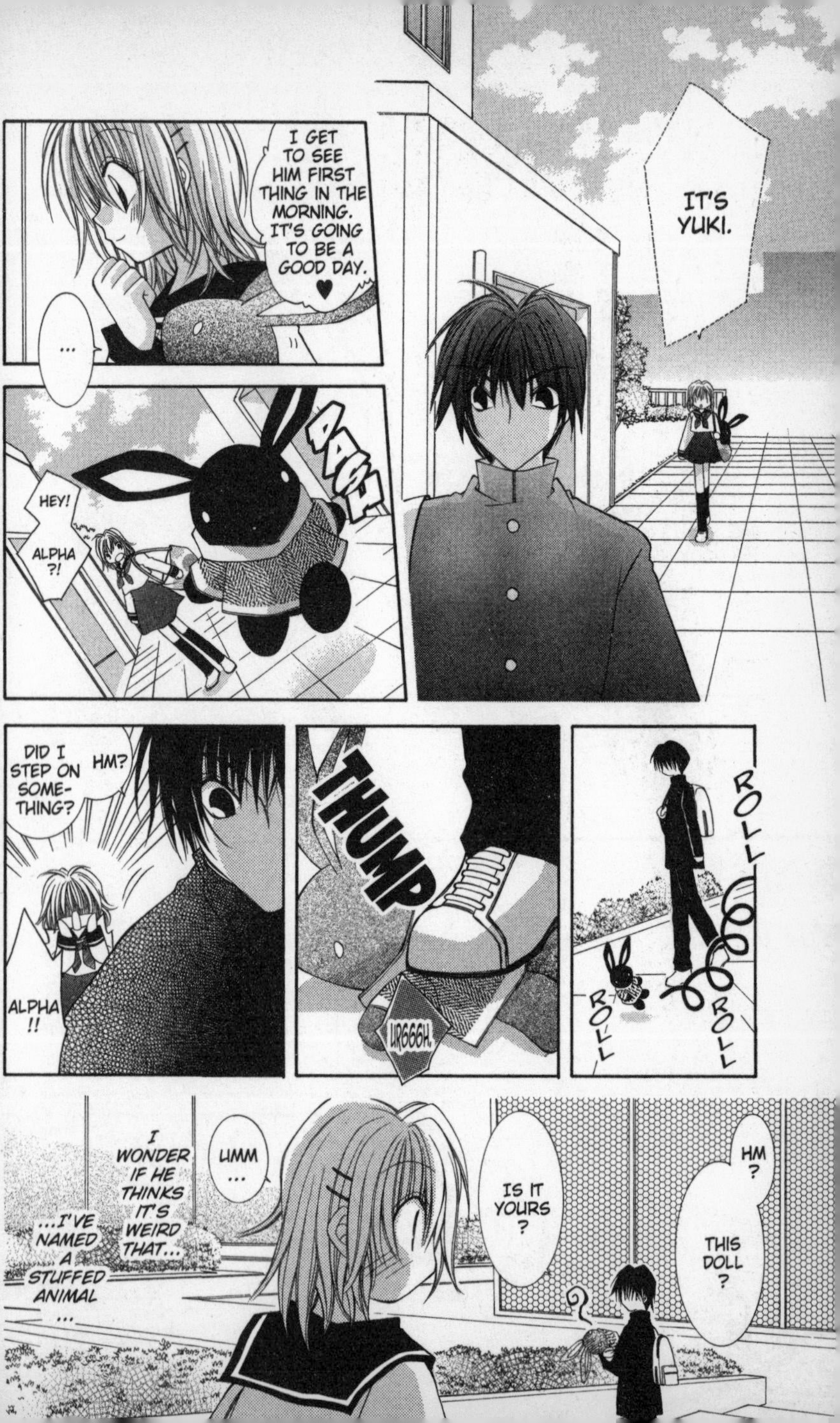
IT'S YUKI.
I GET TO SEE HIM FIRST THING IN THE MORNING. IT'S GOING TO BE A GOOD DAY. ♥
...
DASH
HEY!
ALPHA?!
ROLL
ROLL
ROLL
THUMP
URGGGH.
HM?
DID I STEP ON SOMETHING?
ALPHA!!
HM? THIS DOLL?
IS IT YOURS?
UMM...
I WONDER IF HE THINKS IT'S WEIRD THAT...
...I'VE NAMED A STUFFED ANIMAL...

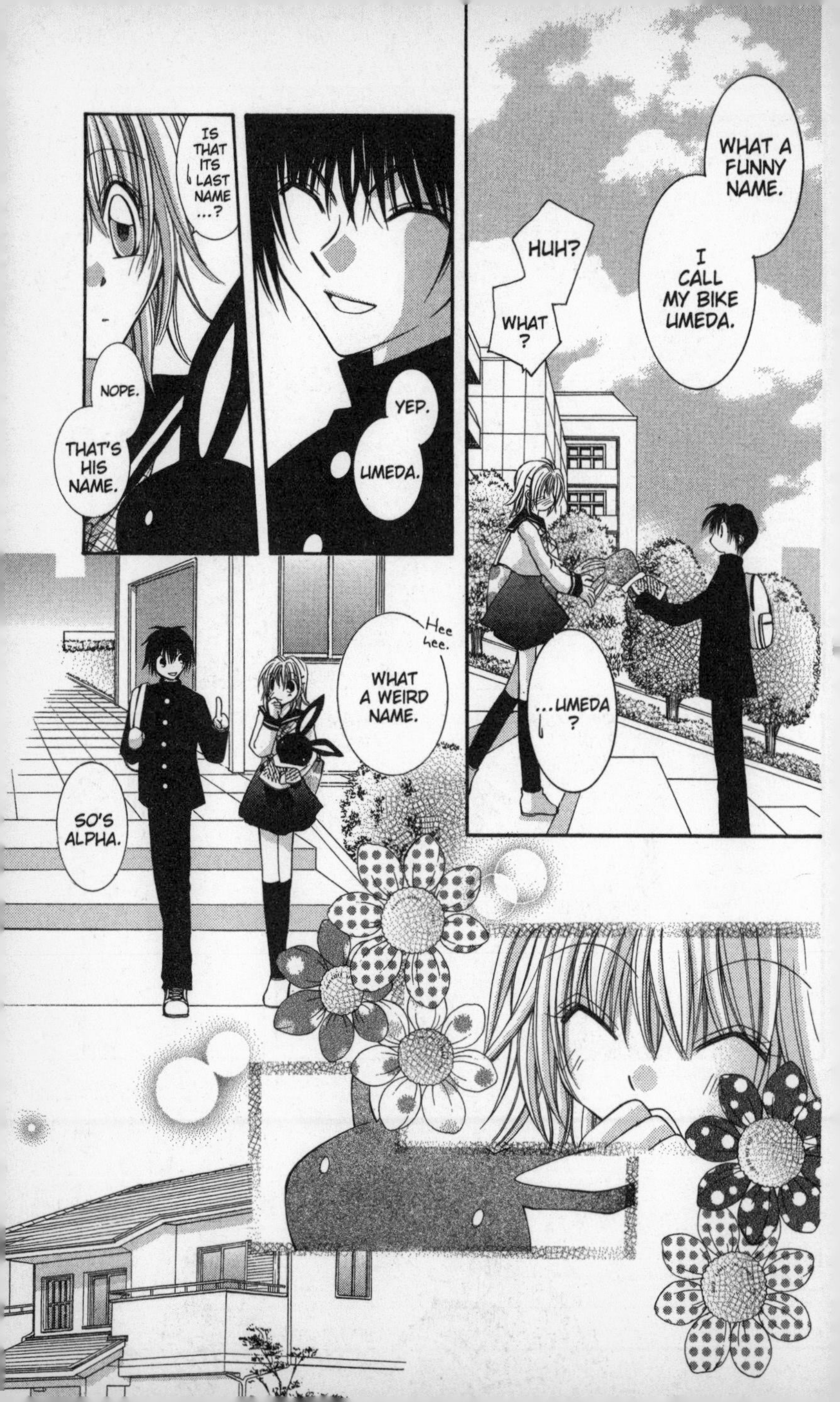
WHAT A FUNNY NAME.
I CALL MY BIKE UMEDA.
HUH?
WHAT?
...UMEDA?
YEP.
UMEDA.
IS THAT ITS LAST NAME ...?
NOPE.
THAT'S HIS NAME.
Hee hee.
WHAT A WEIRD NAME.
SO'S ALPHA.

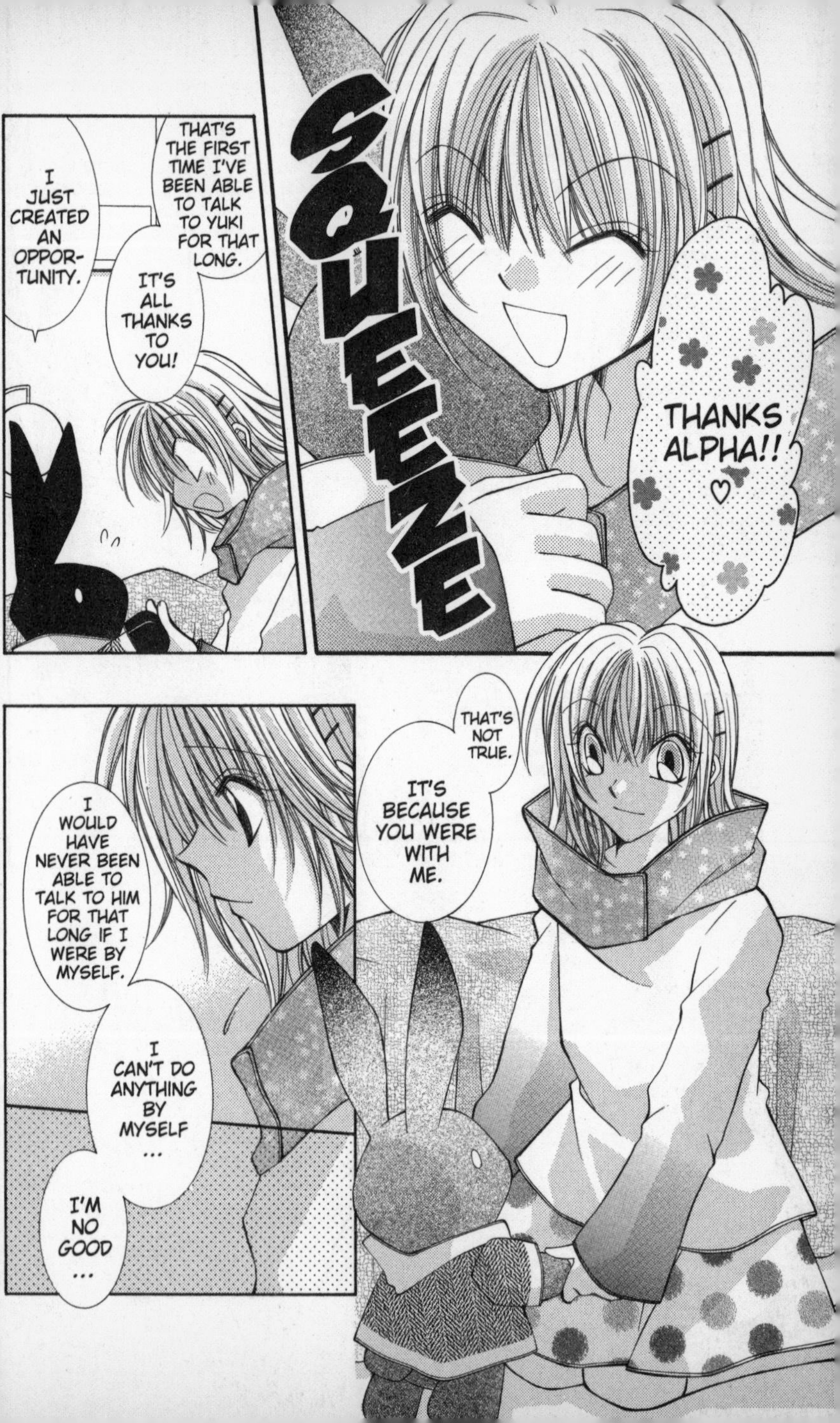
SQUEEZE
THANKS ALPHA!! ♡
THAT'S THE FIRST TIME I'VE BEEN ABLE TO TALK TO YUKI FOR THAT LONG.
IT'S ALL THANKS TO YOU!
I JUST CREATED AN OPPOR-TUNITY.
THAT'S NOT TRUE.
IT'S BECAUSE YOU WERE WITH ME.
I WOULD HAVE NEVER BEEN ABLE TO TALK TO HIM FOR THAT LONG IF I WERE BY MYSELF.
I CAN'T DO ANYTHING BY MYSELF ...
I'M NO GOOD ...

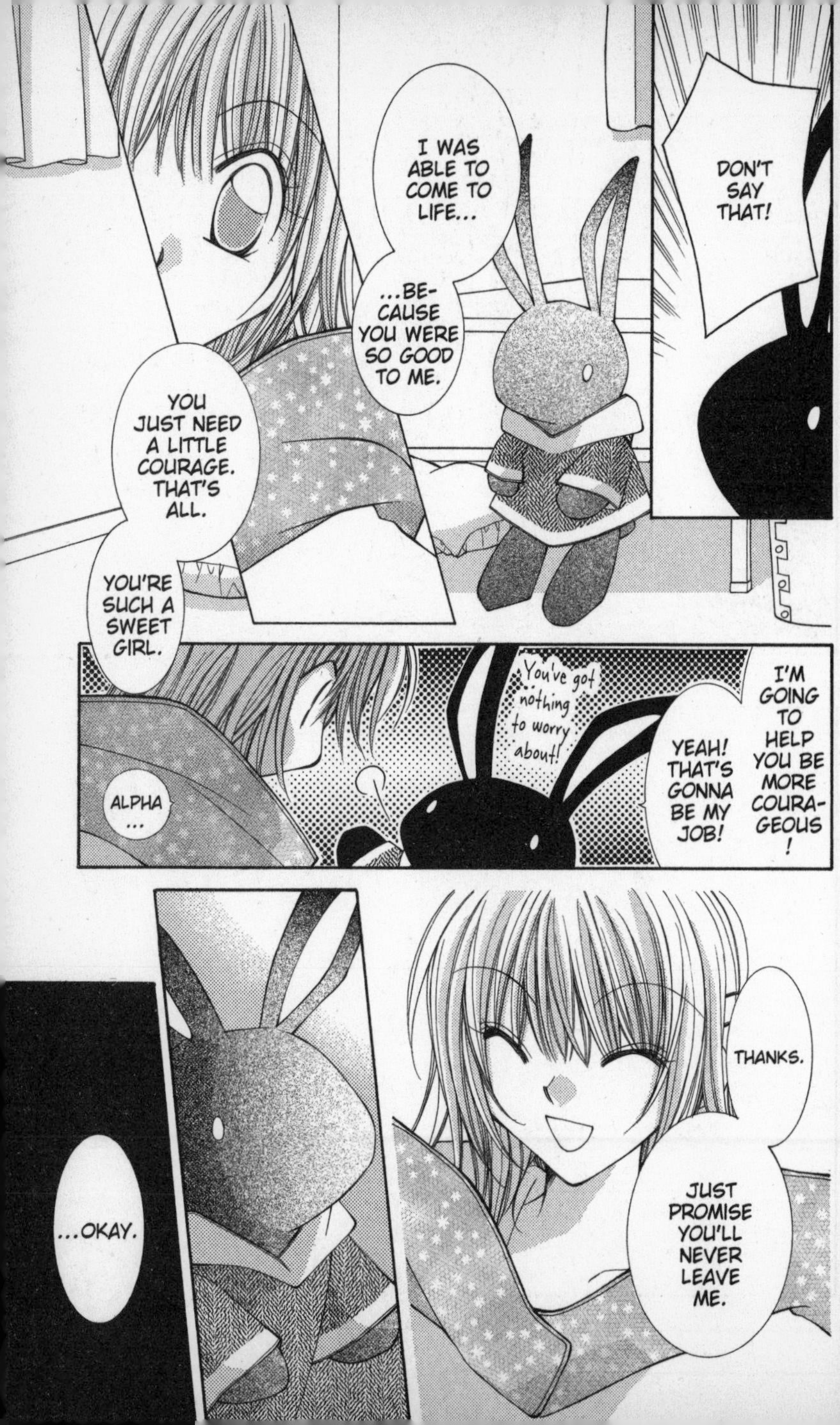
DON'T SAY THAT!
I WAS ABLE TO COME TO LIFE...
...BE-CAUSE YOU WERE SO GOOD TO ME.
YOU JUST NEED A LITTLE COURAGE. THAT'S ALL.
YOU'RE SUCH A SWEET GIRL.
I'M GOING TO HELP YOU BE MORE COURA-GEOUS!
YEAH! THAT'S GONNA BE MY JOB!
You've got nothing to worry about!
ALPHA...
THANKS.
JUST PROMISE YOU'LL NEVER LEAVE ME.
...OKAY.

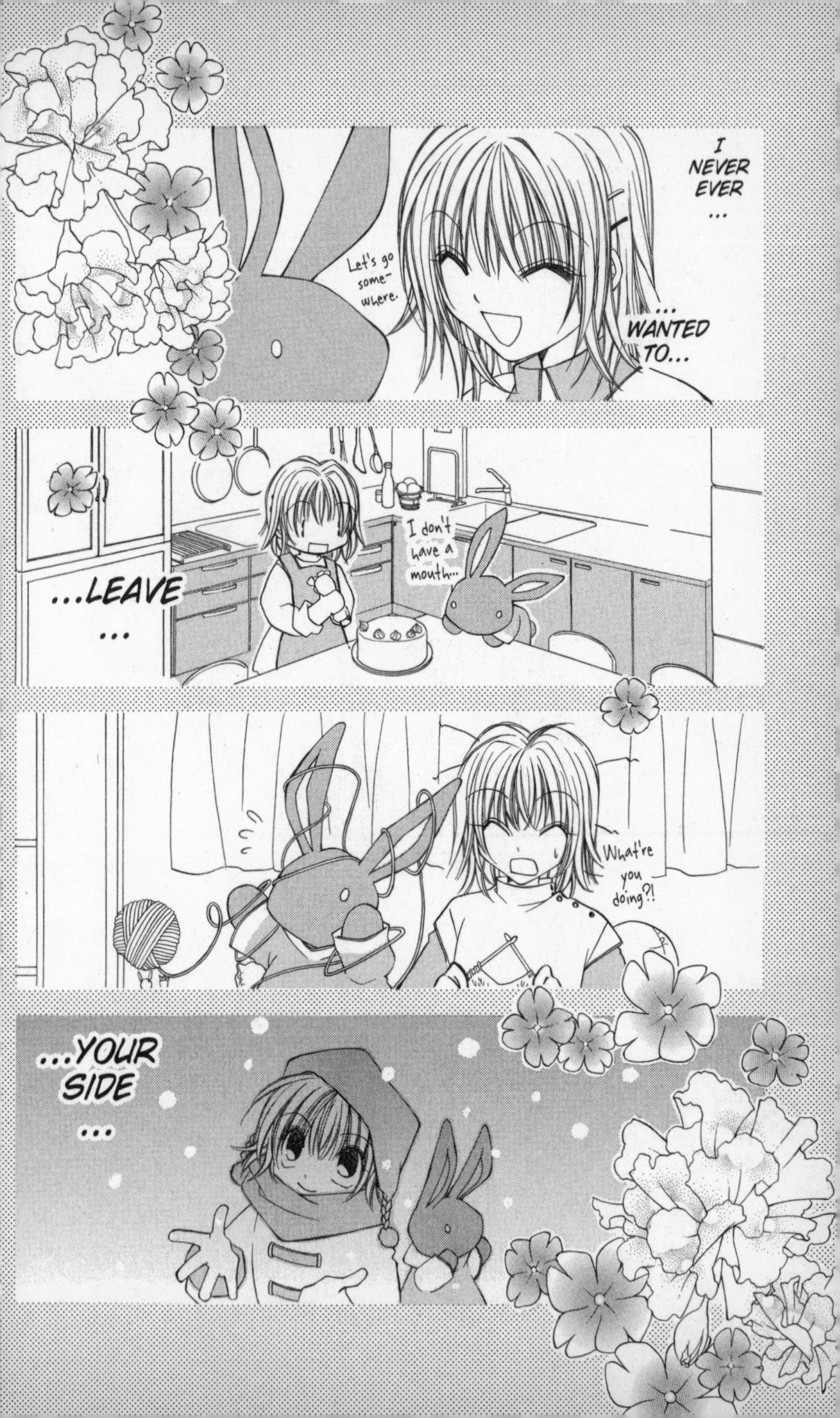
I NEVER EVER ...
Let's go some-where.
... WANTED TO...
I don't have a mouth...
...LEAVE ...
What're you doing?!
...YOUR SIDE ...

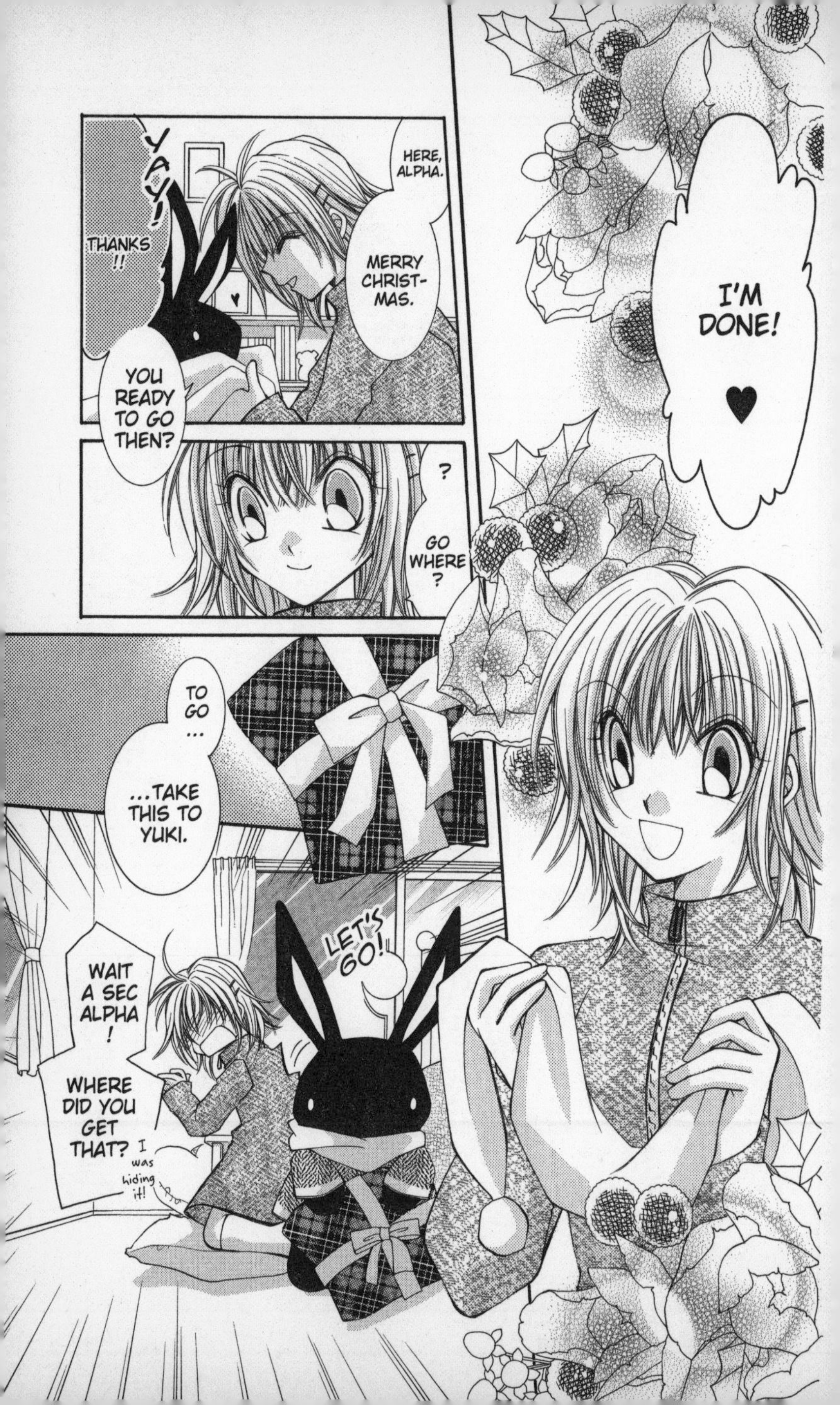

I'M DONE! ♥
HERE, ALPHA.
MERRY CHRIST-MAS.
YAY!
THANKS!!
YOU READY TO GO THEN?
?
GO WHERE?
TO GO...
...TAKE THIS TO YUKI.
LET'S GO!
WAIT A SEC ALPHA!
WHERE DID YOU GET THAT?
I was hiding it!

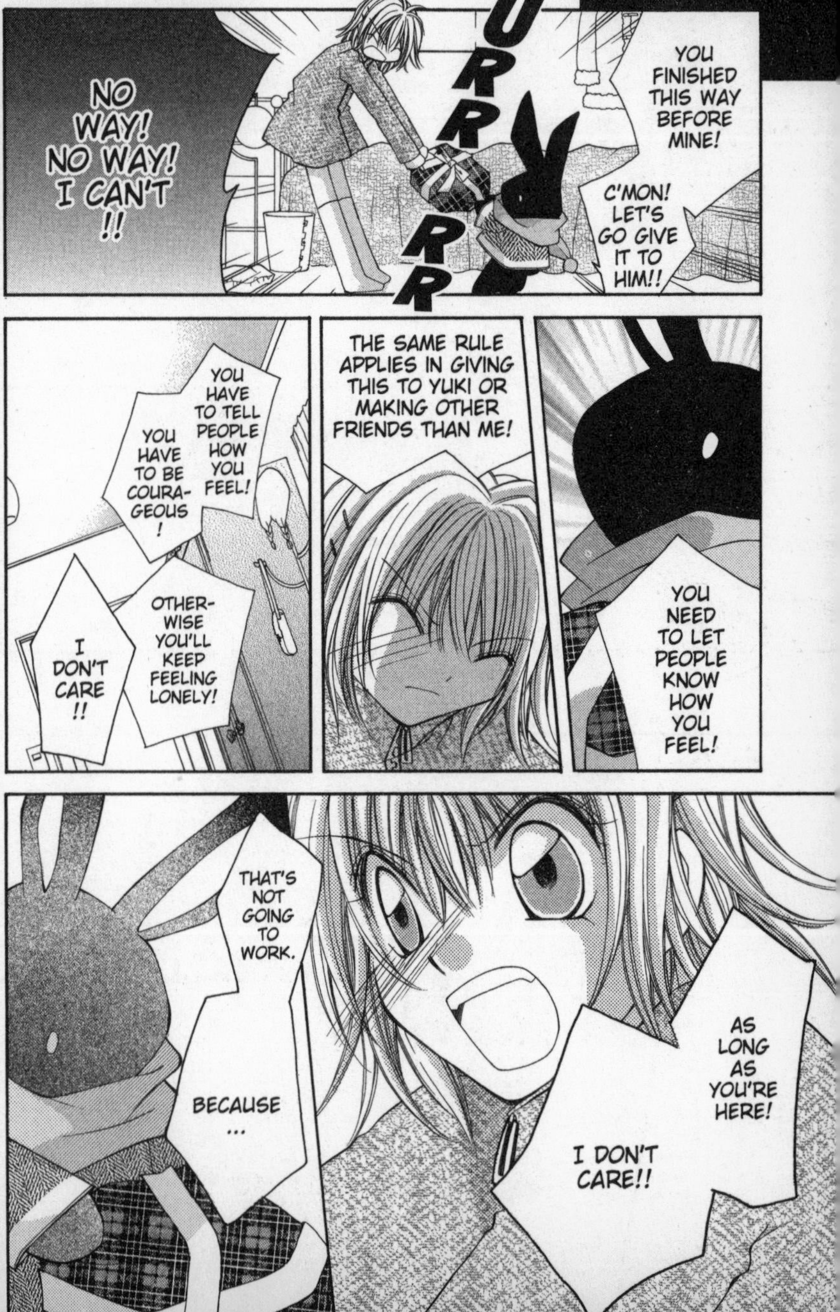
YOU FINISHED THIS WAY BEFORE MINE!
C'MON! LET'S GO GIVE IT TO HIM!!
URRRR
NO WAY! NO WAY! I CAN'T!!
YOU NEED TO LET PEOPLE KNOW HOW YOU FEEL!
THE SAME RULE APPLIES IN GIVING THIS TO YUKI OR MAKING OTHER FRIENDS THAN ME!
YOU HAVE TO TELL PEOPLE HOW YOU FEEL!
YOU HAVE TO BE COURA-GEOUS!
OTHER-WISE YOU'LL KEEP FEELING LONELY!
I DON'T CARE!!
AS LONG AS YOU'RE HERE!
I DON'T CARE!!
THAT'S NOT GOING TO WORK.
BECAUSE...

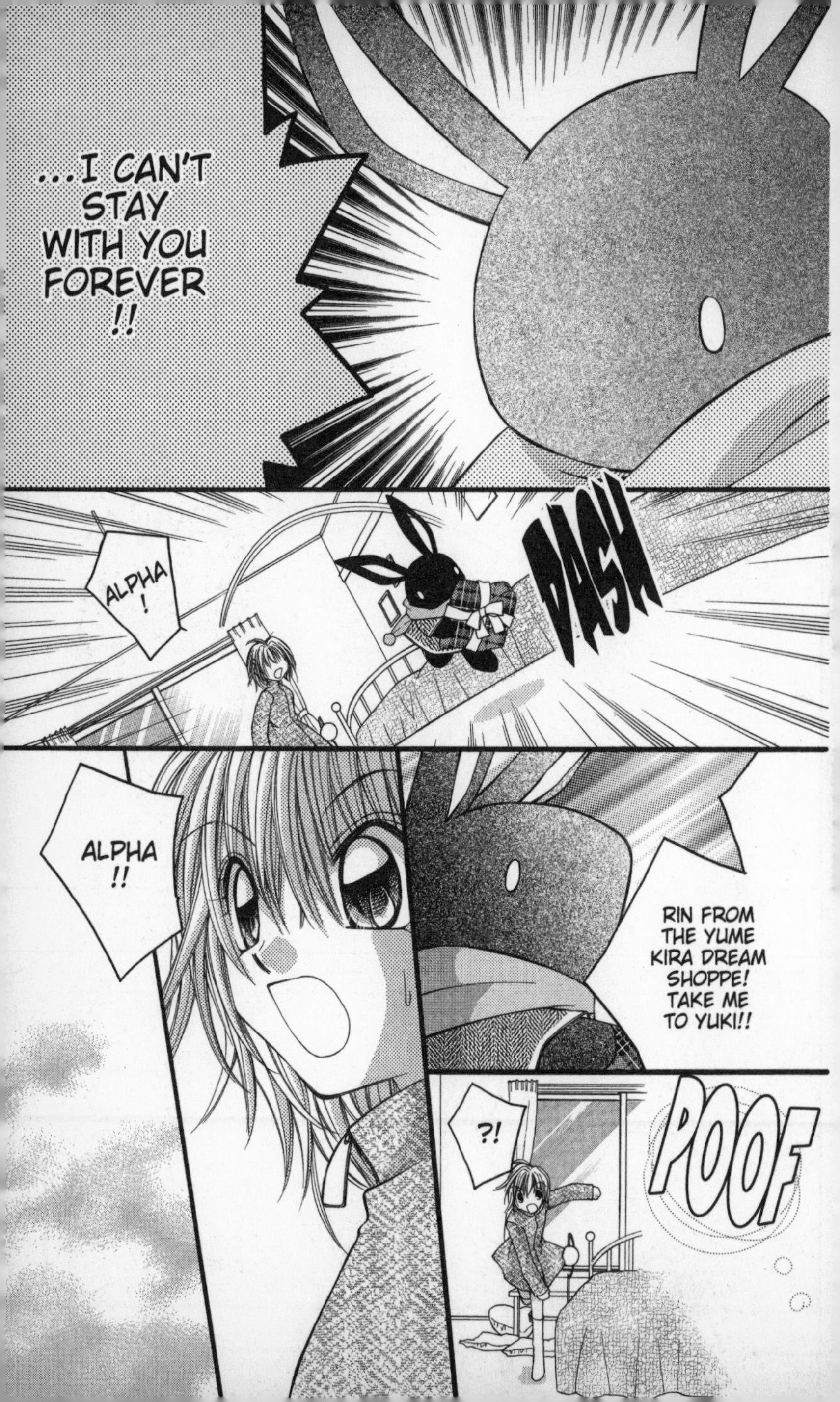
...I CAN'T STAY WITH YOU FOREVER !!
DASH
ALPHA !
RIN FROM THE YUME KIRA DREAM SHOPPE! TAKE ME TO YUKI!!
ALPHA !!
POOF
?!

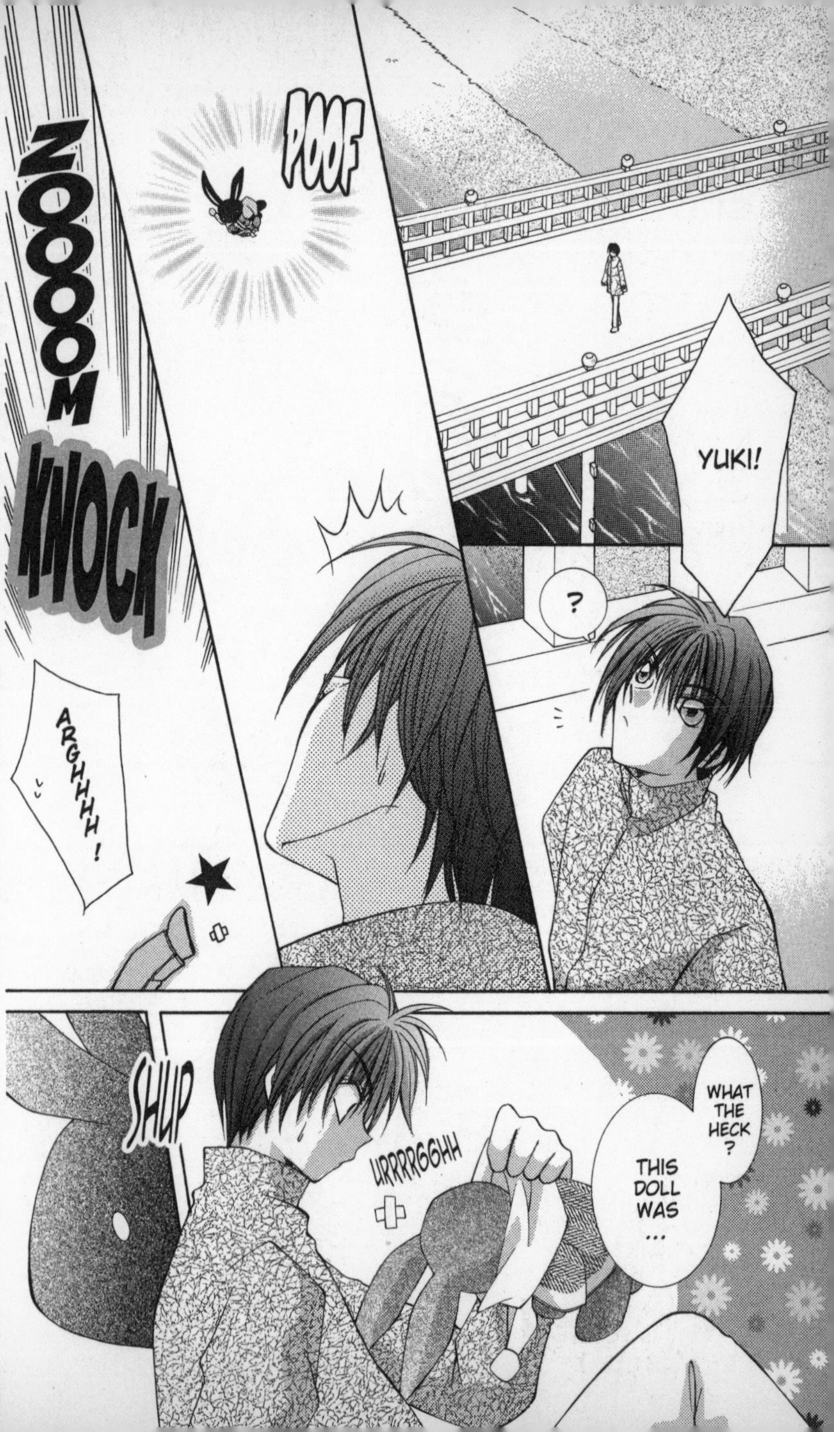
YUKI!
?
POOF
ZOOOOOM
KNOCK
ARGHHHH!
WHAT THE HECK?
THIS DOLL WAS ...
SHUP
URRRRGGHH

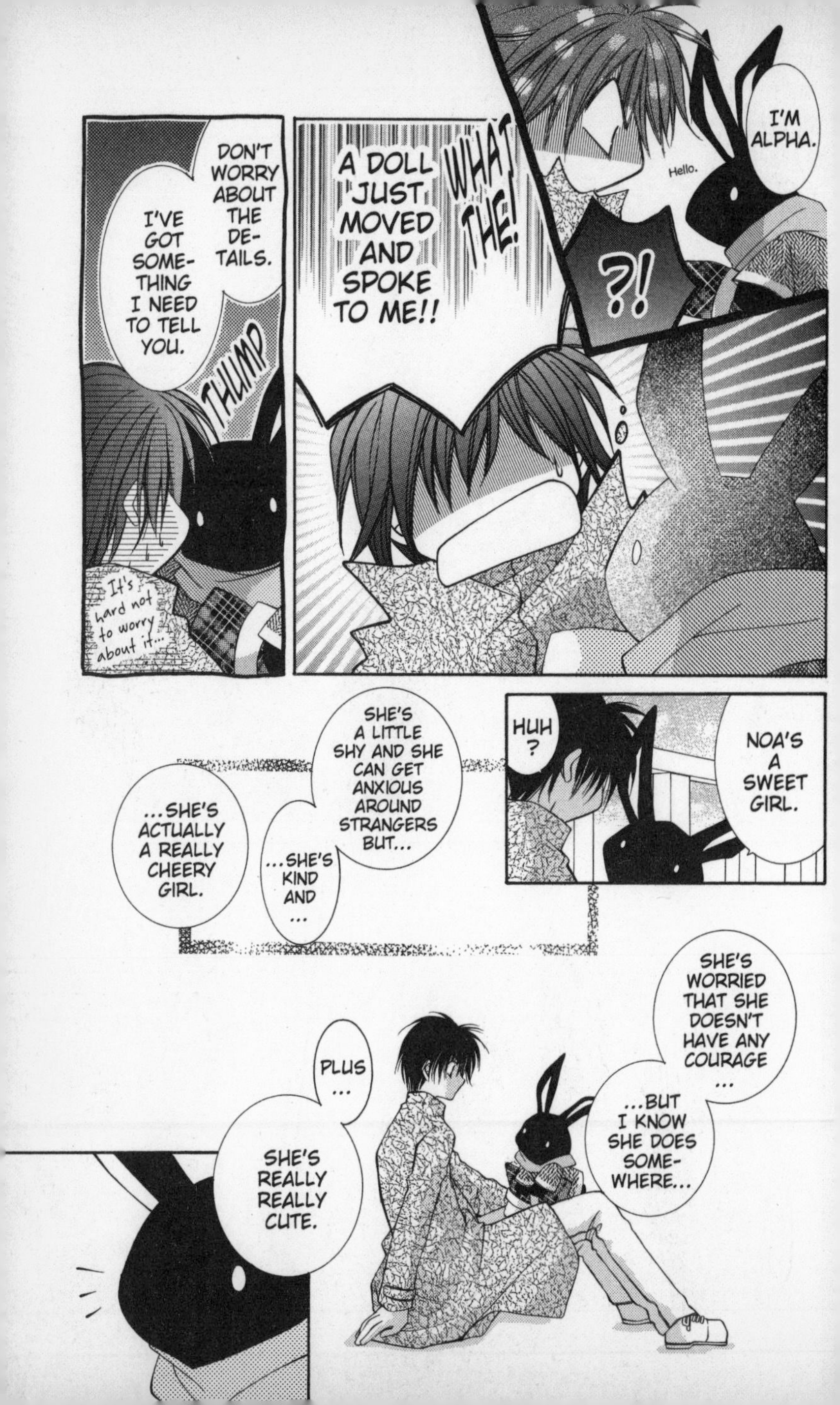
I'M ALPHA.
Hello.
?!
WHAT THE!
A DOLL JUST MOVED AND SPOKE TO ME!!
DON'T WORRY ABOUT THE DE-TAILS.
I'VE GOT SOME-THING I NEED TO TELL YOU.
THUMP
It's hard not to worry about it...
NOA'S A SWEET GIRL.
HUH?
SHE'S A LITTLE SHY AND SHE CAN GET ANXIOUS AROUND STRANGERS BUT...
...SHE'S KIND AND ...
...SHE'S ACTUALLY A REALLY CHEERY GIRL.
SHE'S WORRIED THAT SHE DOESN'T HAVE ANY COURAGE ...
...BUT I KNOW SHE DOES SOME-WHERE...
PLUS ...
SHE'S REALLY REALLY CUTE.

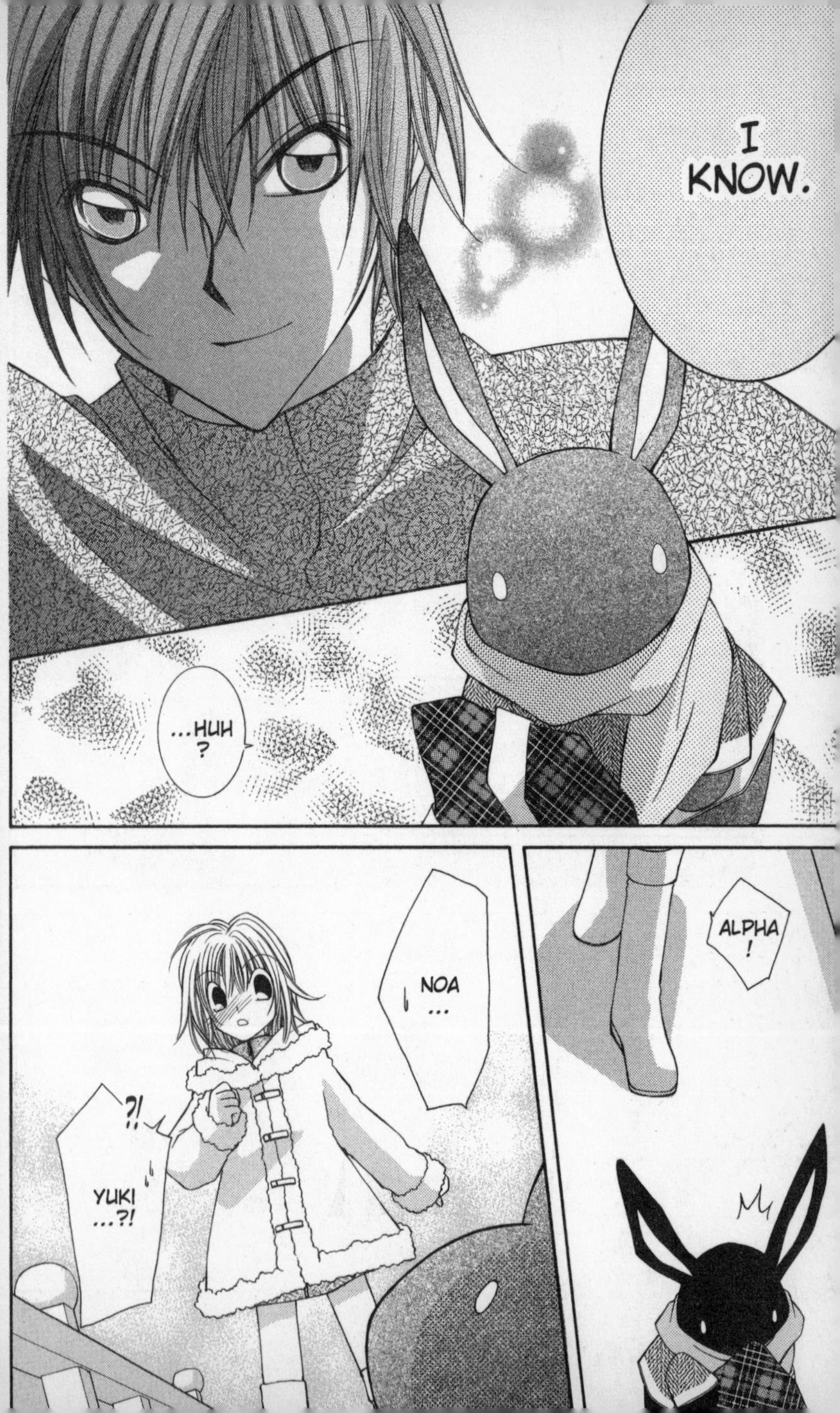
I KNOW.
...HUH?
ALPHA!
NOA...
?! YUKI...?!

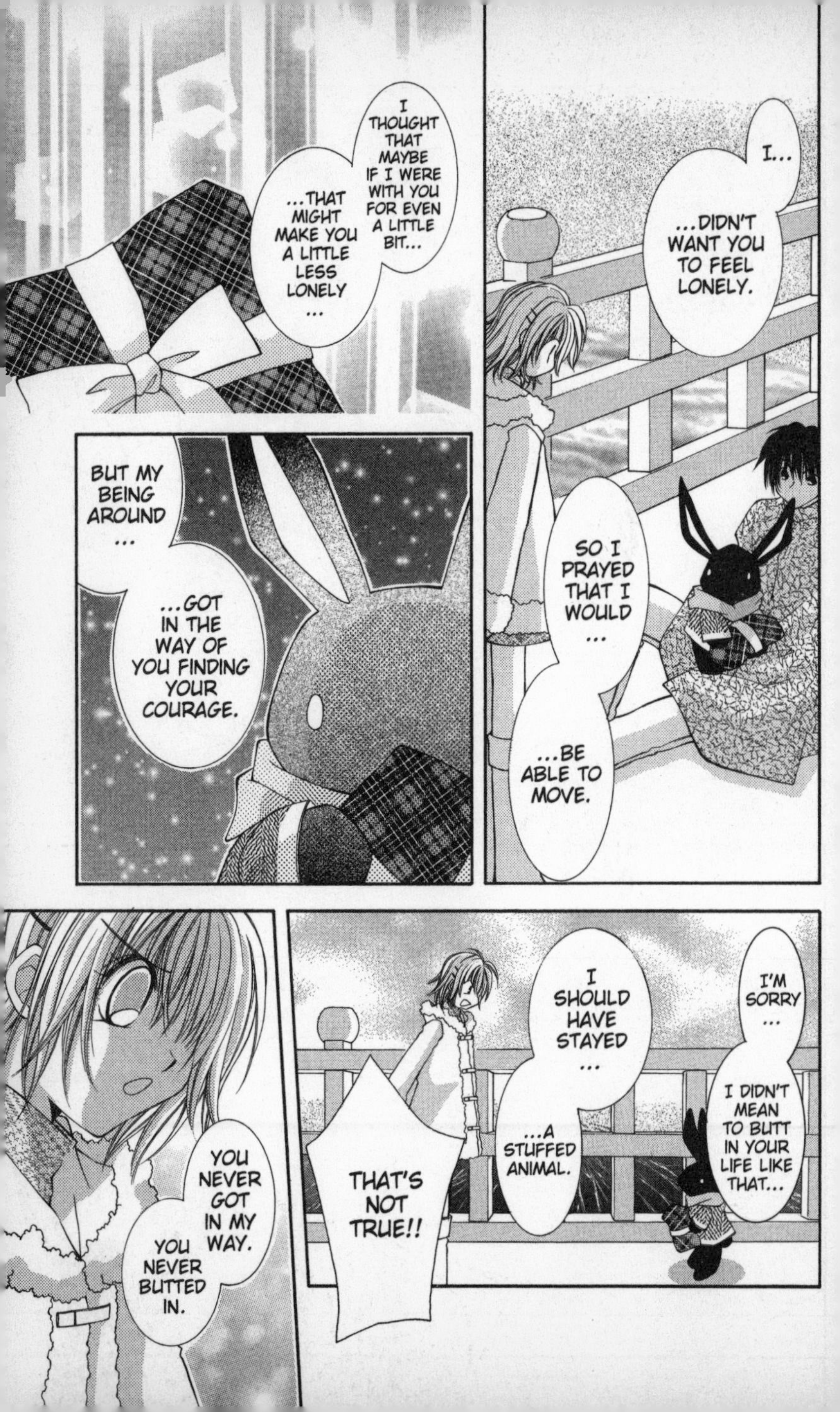

I...
...DIDN'T WANT YOU TO FEEL LONELY.
SO I PRAYED THAT I WOULD...
...BE ABLE TO MOVE.
I THOUGHT THAT MAYBE IF I WERE WITH YOU FOR EVEN A LITTLE BIT...
...THAT MIGHT MAKE YOU A LITTLE LESS LONELY...
BUT MY BEING AROUND...
...GOT IN THE WAY OF YOU FINDING YOUR COURAGE.
I'M SORRY...
I DIDN'T MEAN TO BUTT IN YOUR LIFE LIKE THAT...
I SHOULD HAVE STAYED...
...A STUFFED ANIMAL.
THAT'S NOT TRUE!!
YOU NEVER GOT IN MY WAY.
YOU NEVER BUTTED IN.

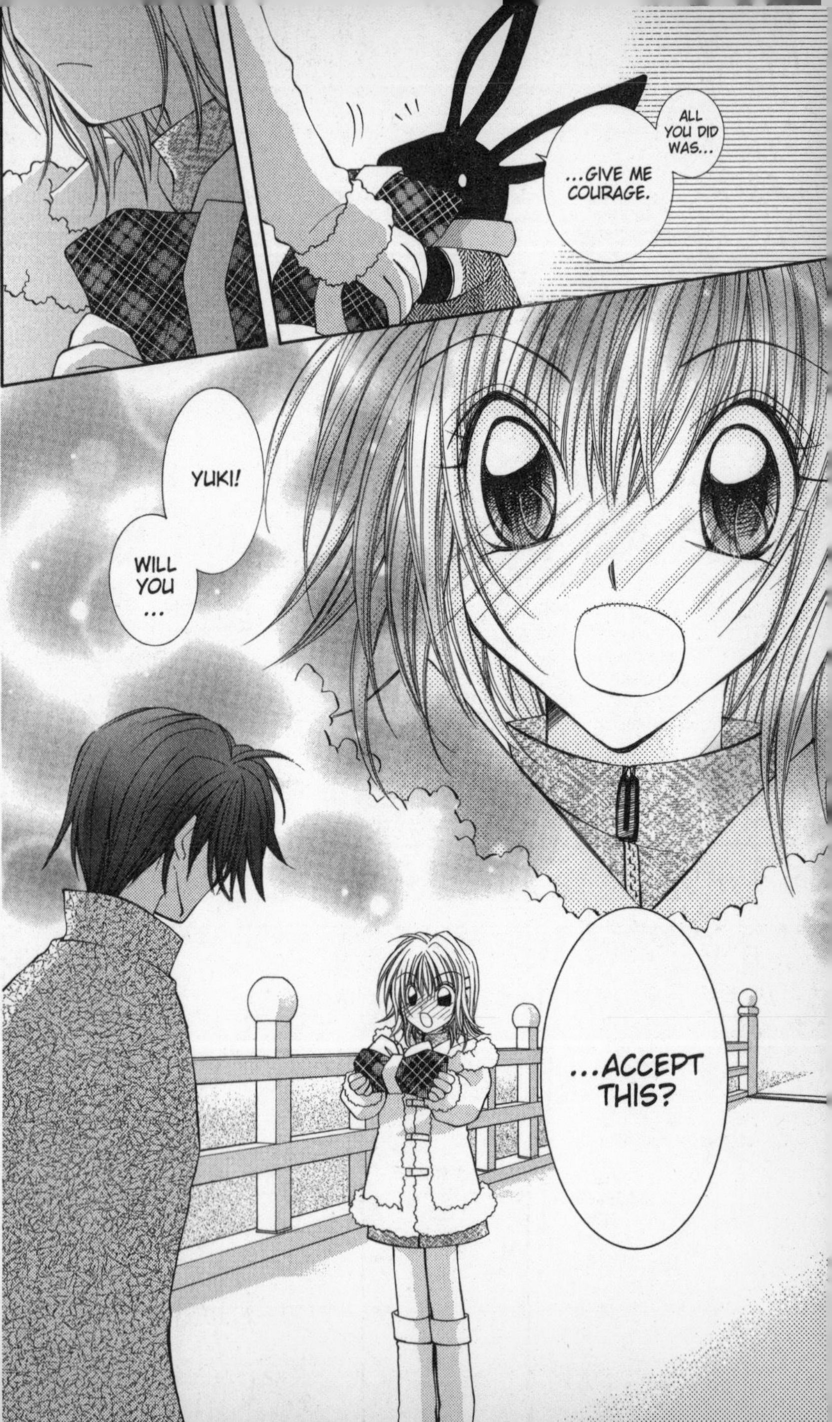
ALL YOU DID WAS...
...GIVE ME COURAGE.
YUKI!
WILL YOU ...
...ACCEPT THIS?

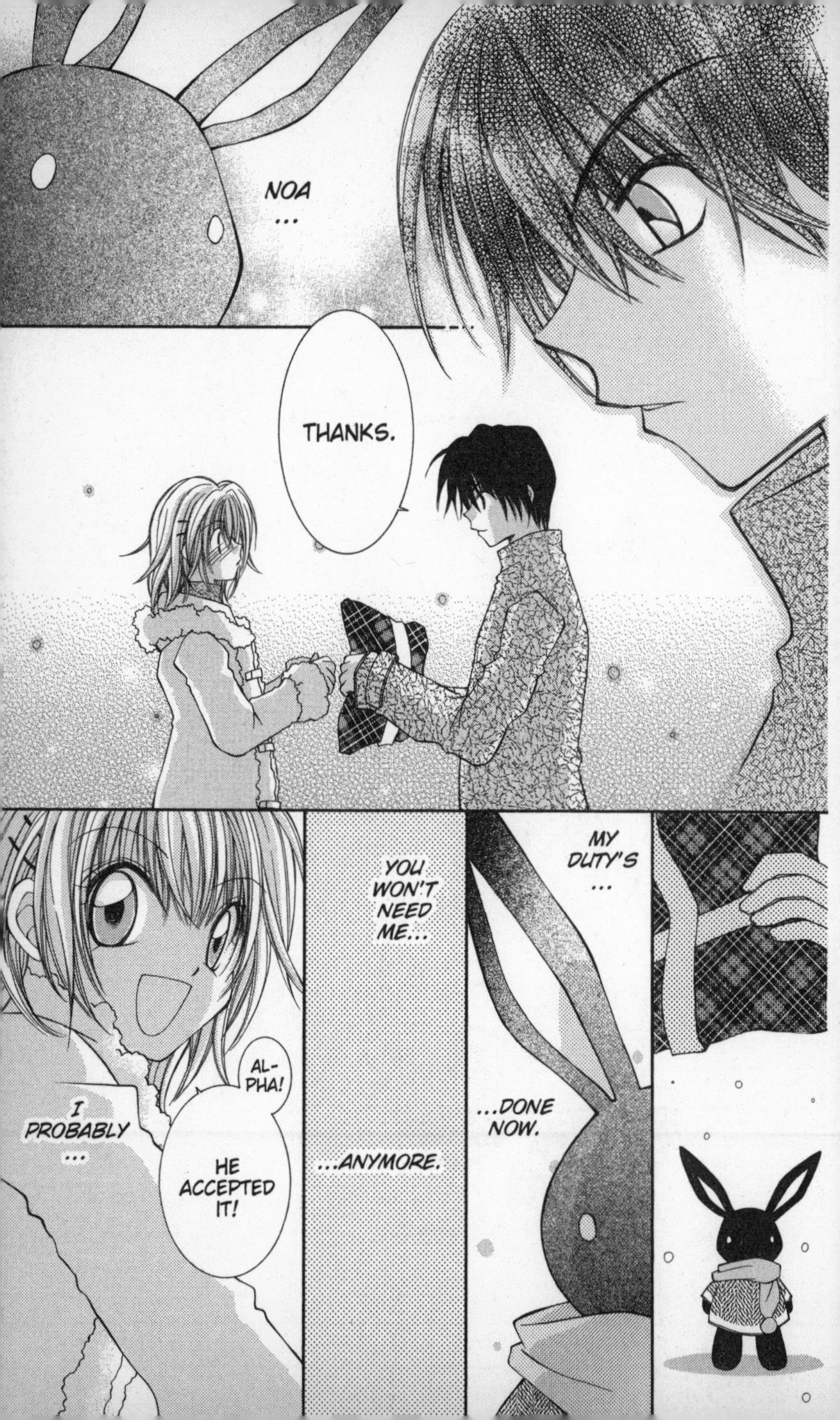
NOA ...
THANKS.
MY DUTY'S ...
...DONE NOW.
YOU WON'T NEED ME...
...ANYMORE.
AL-PHA!
HE ACCEPTED IT!
I PROBABLY ...

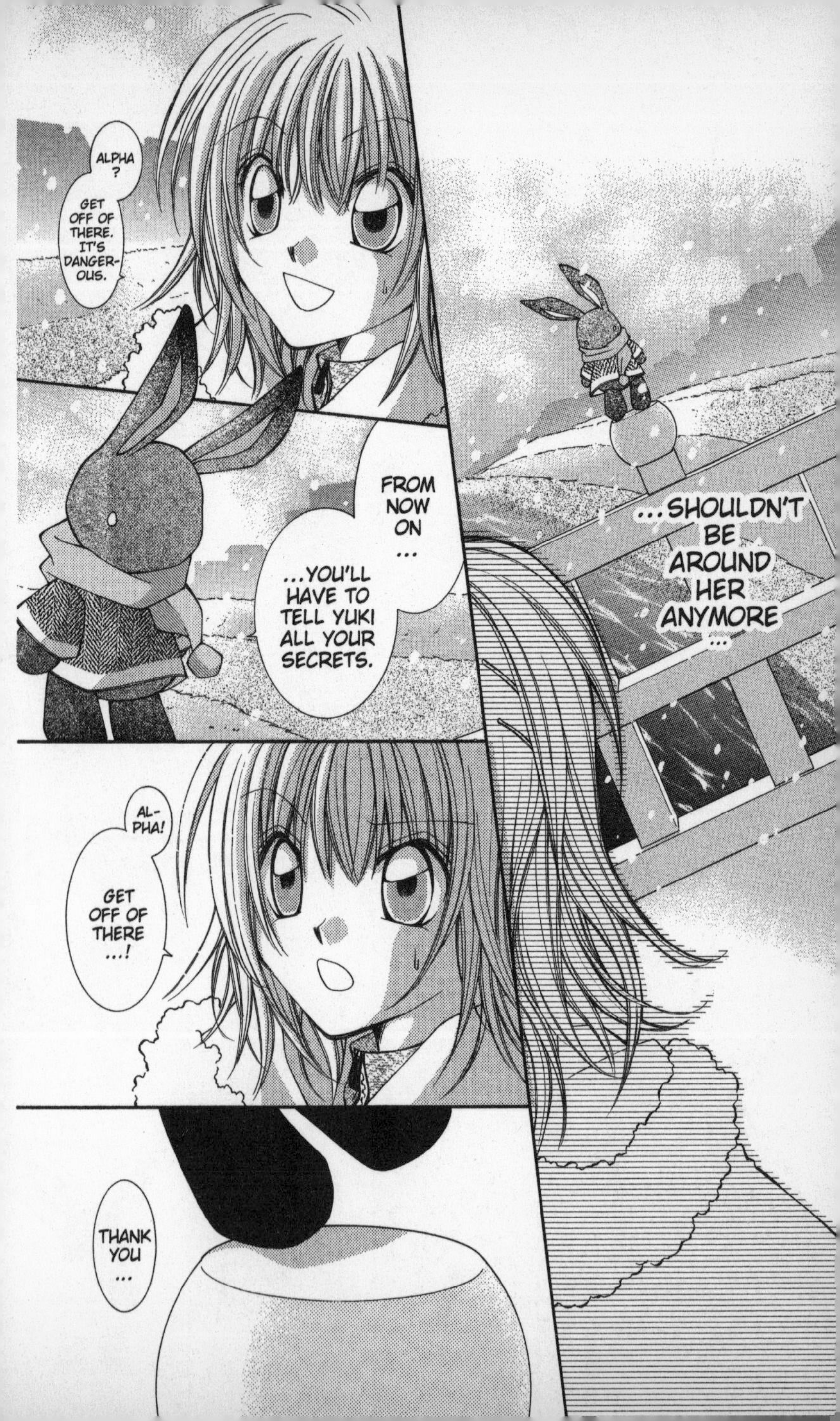
ALPHA?
GET OFF OF THERE. IT'S DANGER-OUS.
FROM NOW ON ...
...YOU'LL HAVE TO TELL YUKI ALL YOUR SECRETS.
...SHOULDN'T BE AROUND HER ANYMORE ...
AL-PHA!
GET OFF OF THERE ...!
THANK YOU ...

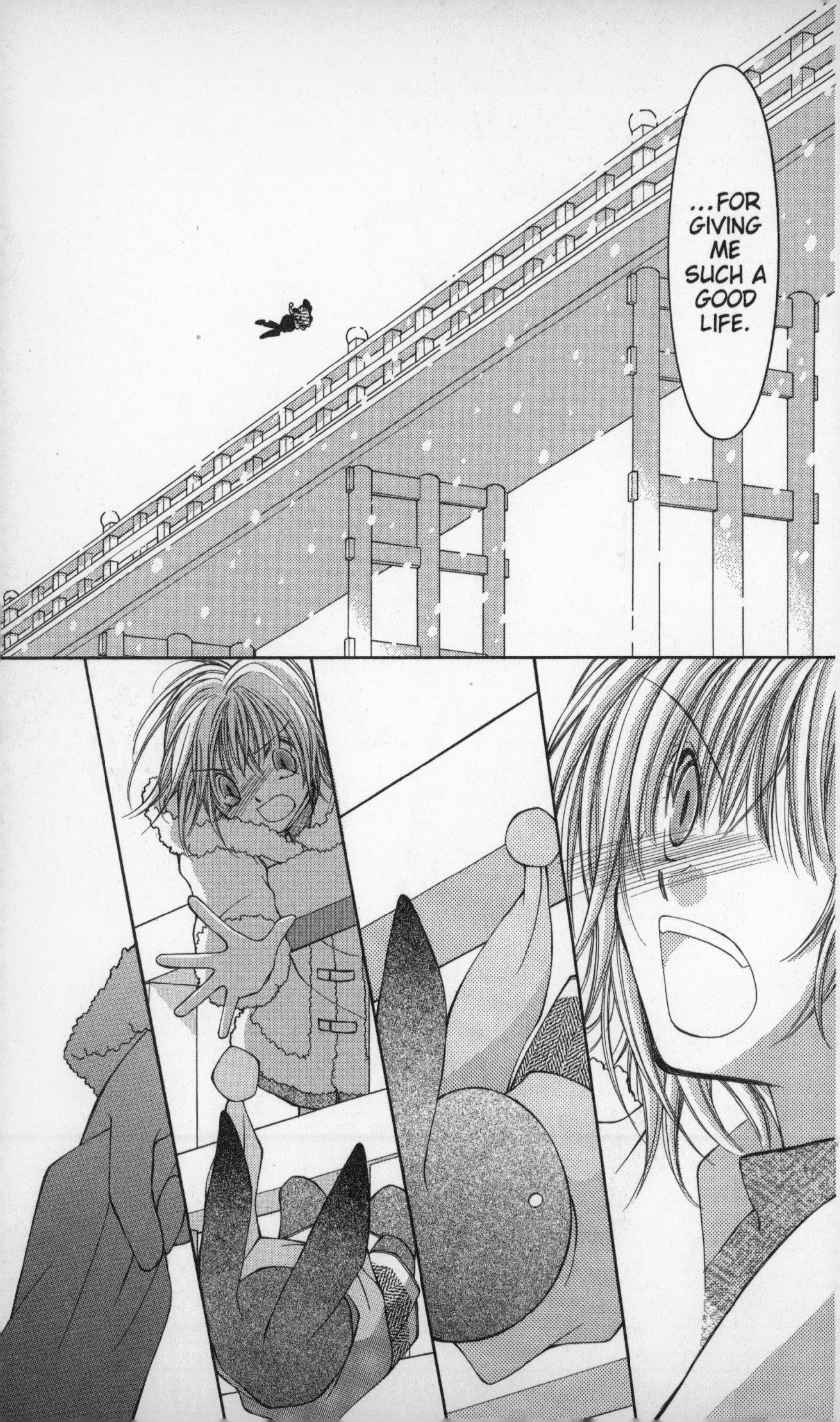
...FOR GIVING ME SUCH A GOOD LIFE.

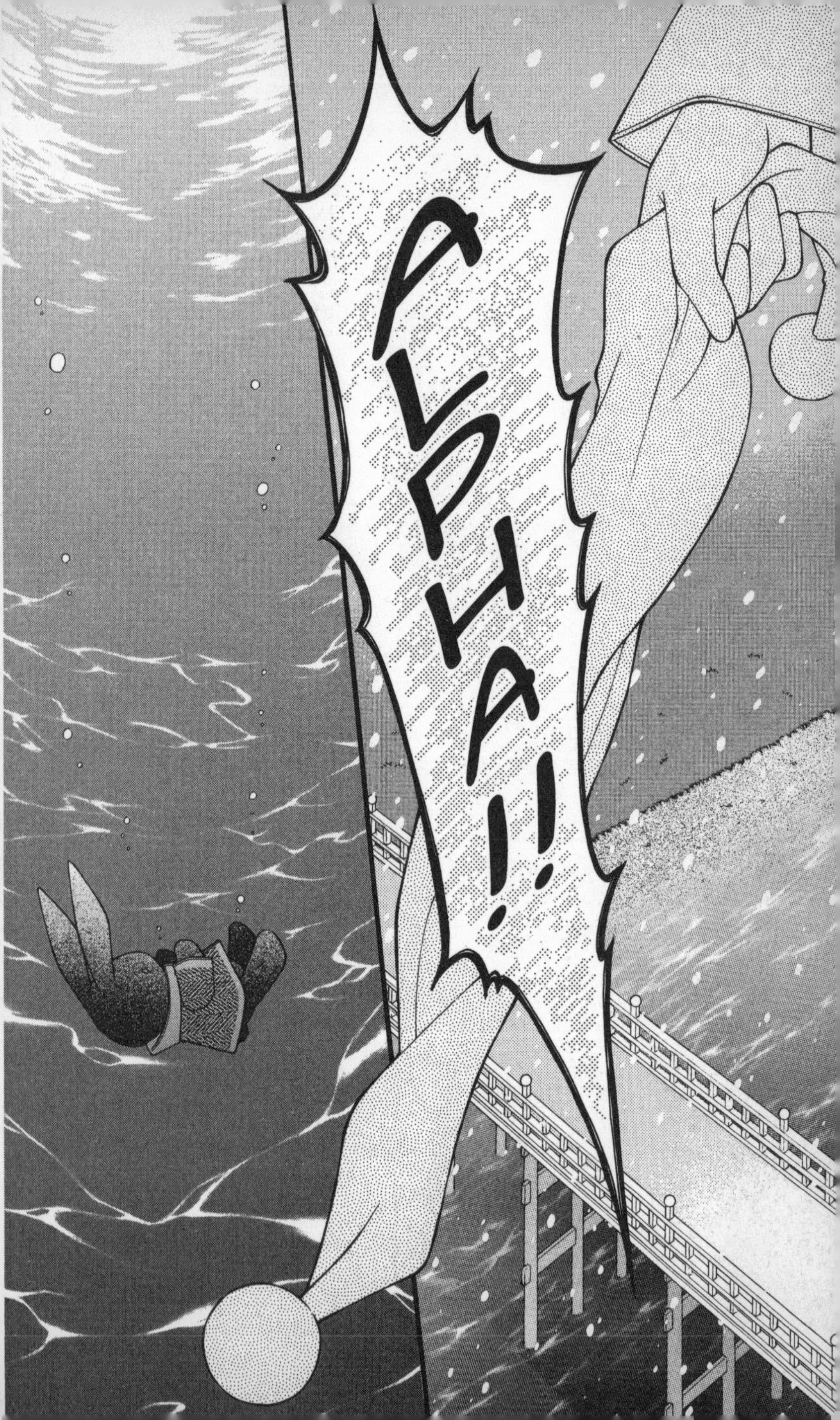
AAHHH!!

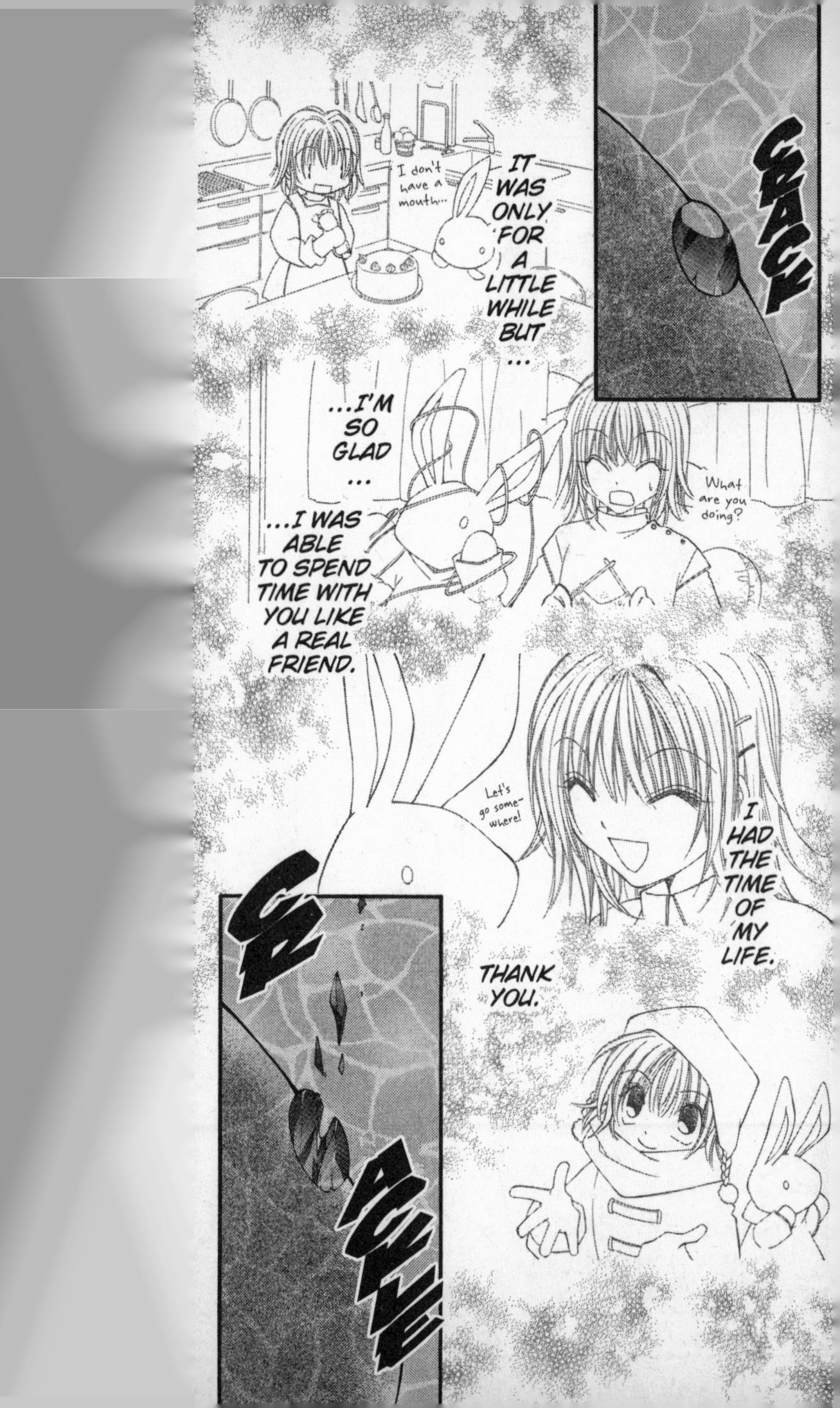
CRACK
IT WAS ONLY FOR A LITTLE WHILE BUT...
I don't have a mouth...
...I'M SO GLAD...
What are you doing?
...I WAS ABLE TO SPEND TIME WITH YOU LIKE A REAL FRIEND.
Let's go somewhere!
I HAD THE TIME OF MY LIFE.
THANK YOU.
CRACKLE

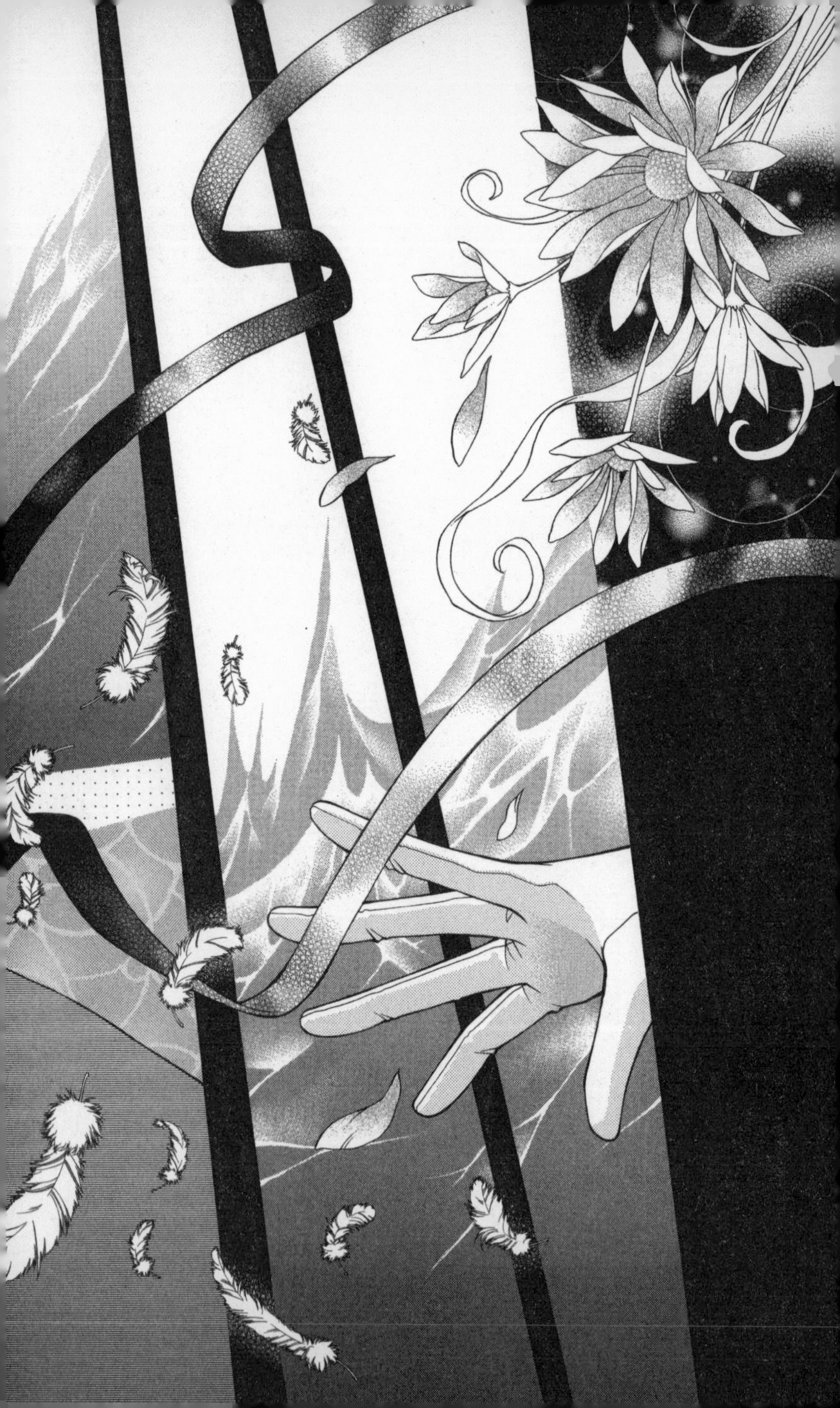

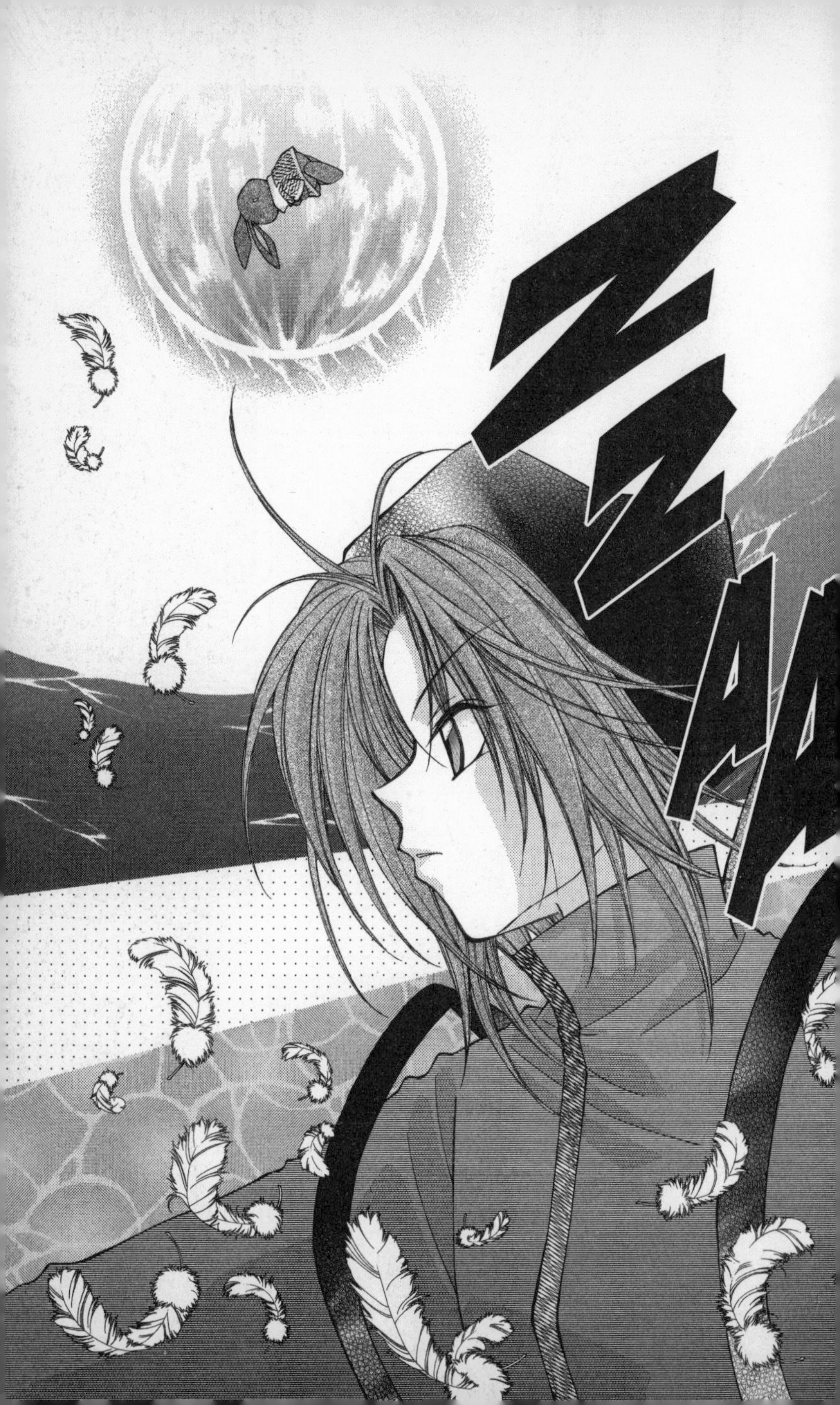
ZZAA

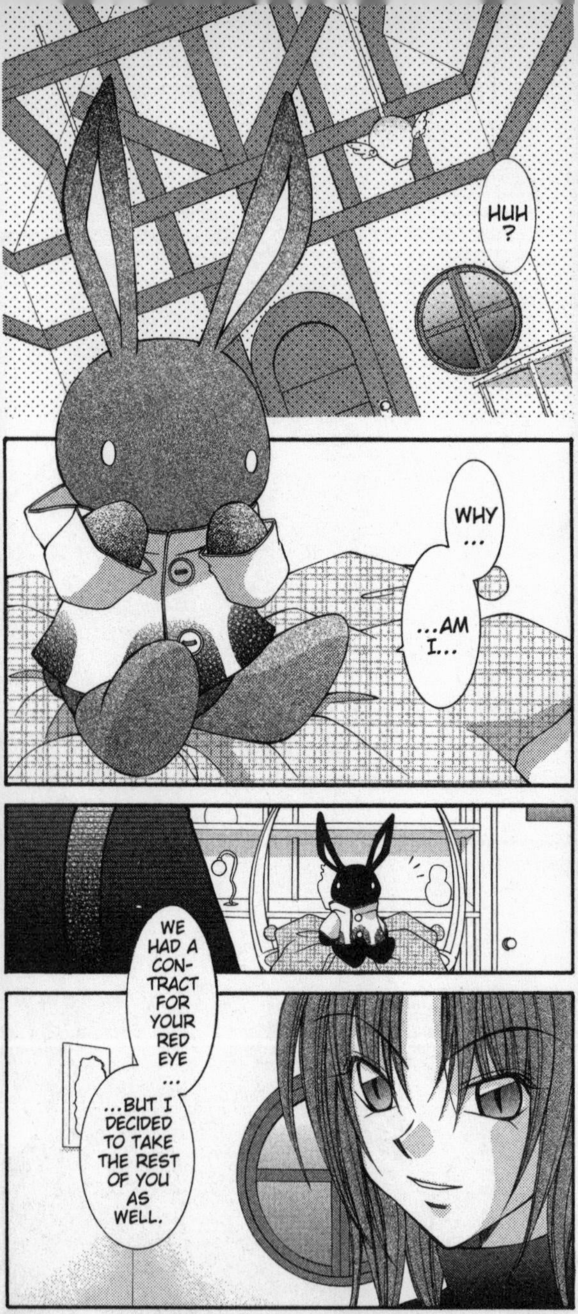
HUH?
WHY...
...AM I...
WE HAD A CONTRACT FOR YOUR RED EYE...
...BUT I DECIDED TO TAKE THE REST OF YOU AS WELL.

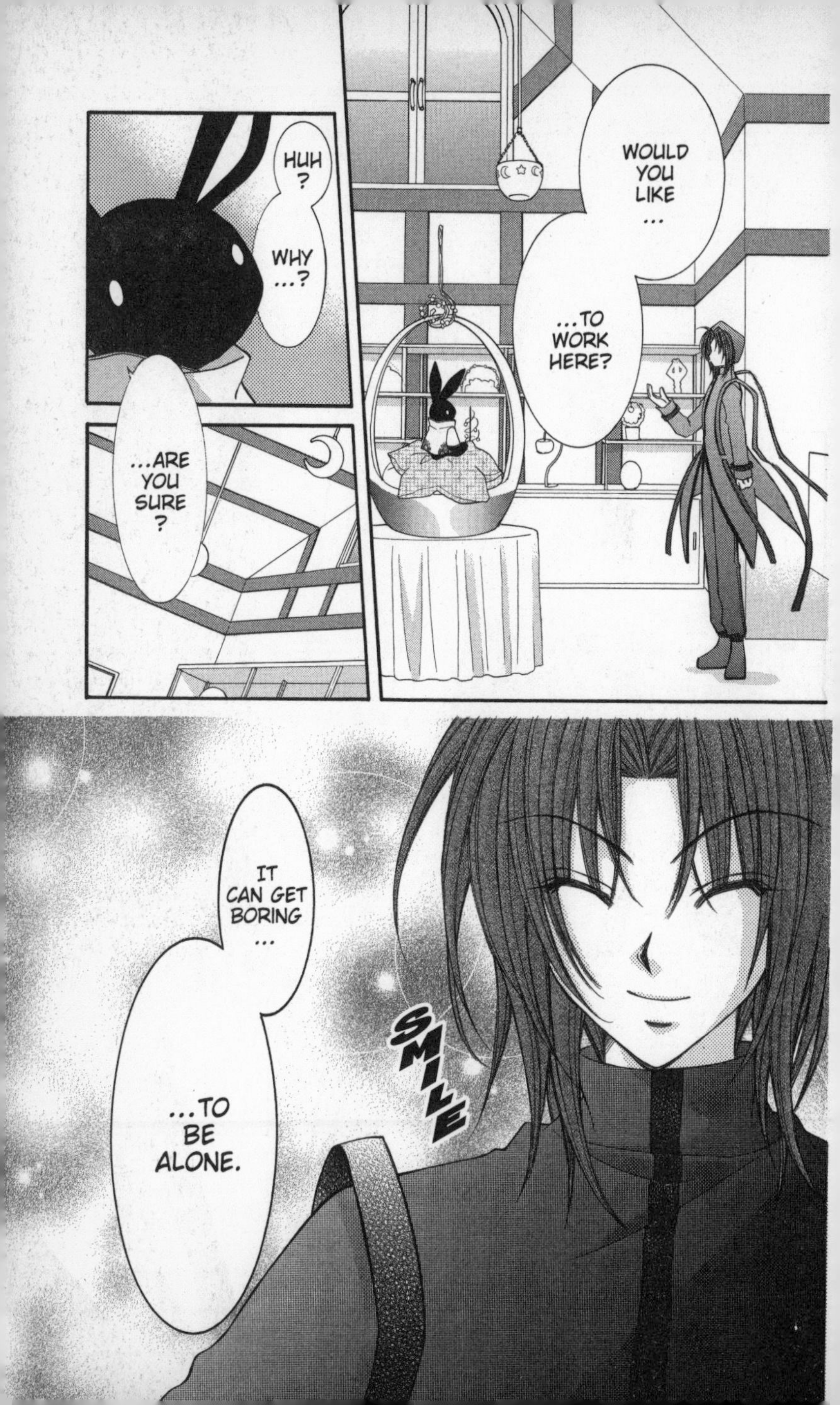
WOULD YOU LIKE ...
...TO WORK HERE?
HUH? WHY...?
...ARE YOU SURE?
IT CAN GET BORING ...
SMILE
...TO BE ALONE.

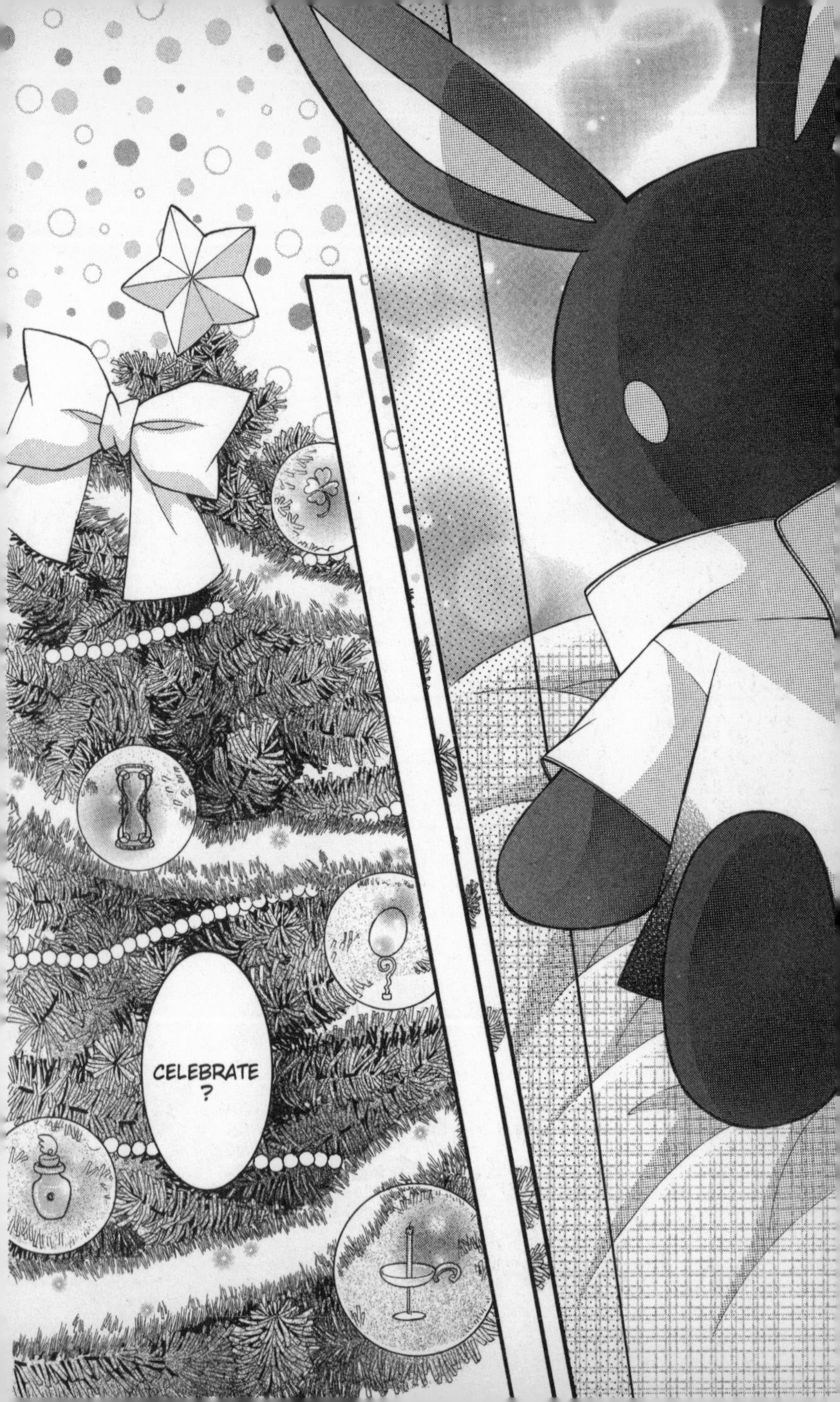
CELEBRATE?

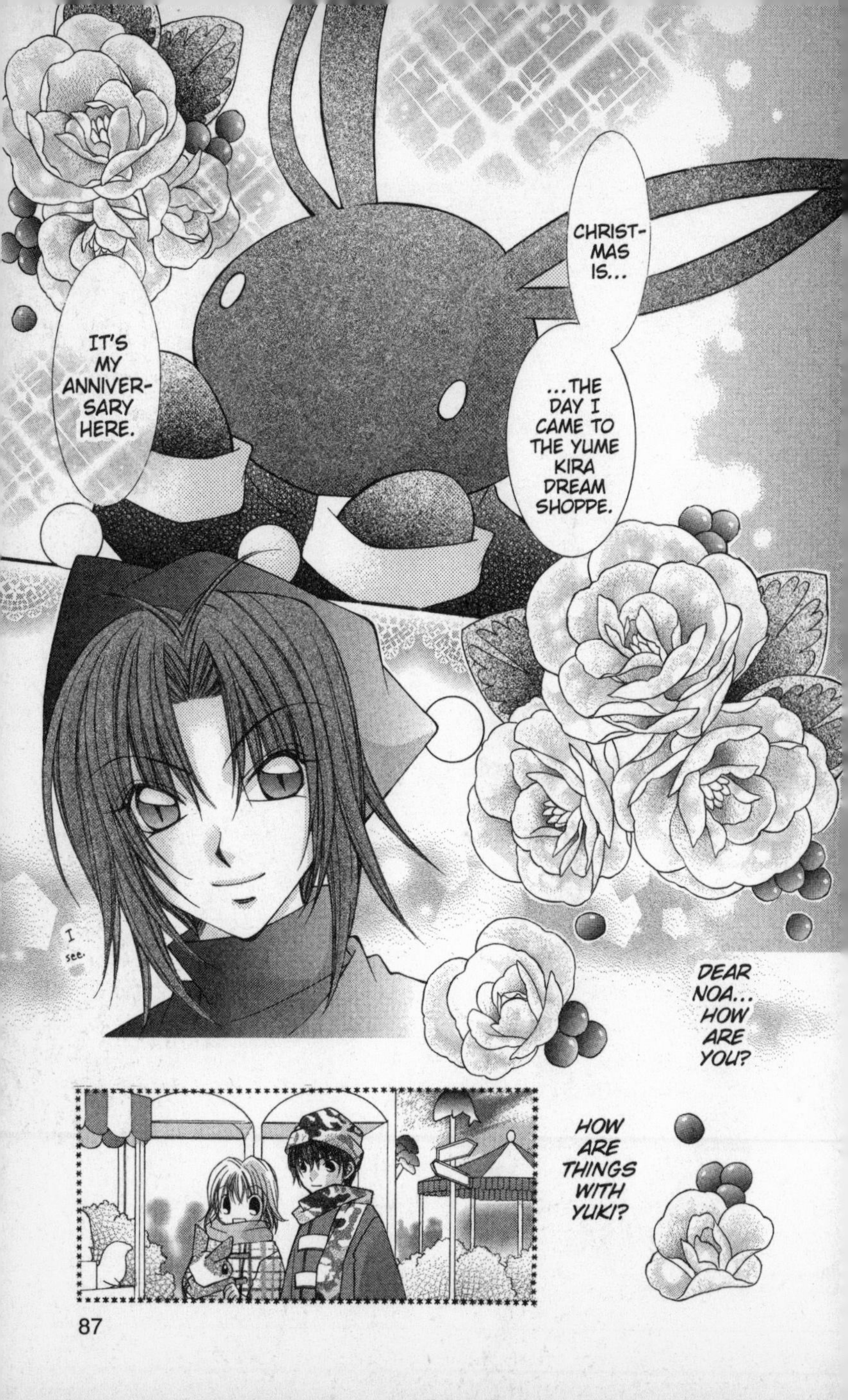
CHRISTMAS IS...
...THE DAY I CAME TO THE YUME KIRA DREAM SHOPPE.
IT'S MY ANNIVERSARY HERE.
I see.
DEAR NOA... HOW ARE YOU?
HOW ARE THINGS WITH YUKI?

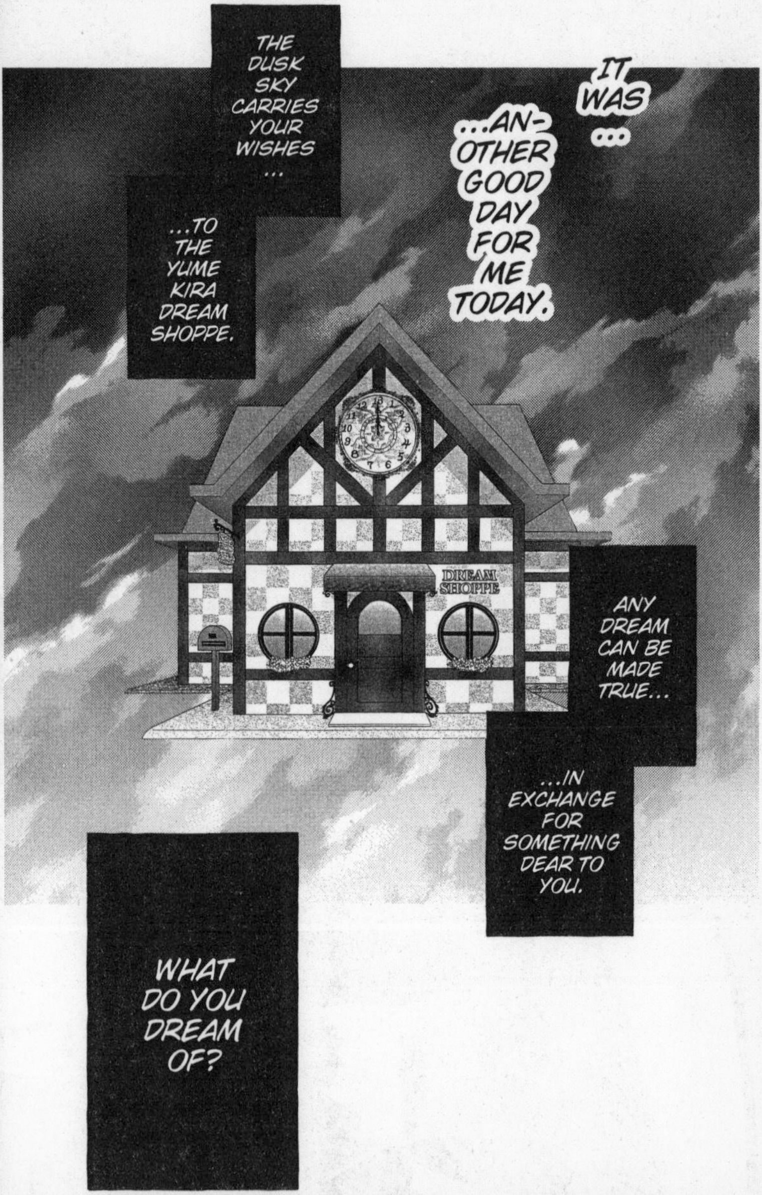
IT WAS...
...AN-OTHER GOOD DAY FOR ME TODAY.
THE DUSK SKY CARRIES YOUR WISHES...
...TO THE YUME KIRA DREAM SHOPPE.
DREAM SHOPPE
ANY DREAM CAN BE MADE TRUE...
...IN EXCHANGE FOR SOMETHING DEAR TO YOU.
WHAT DO YOU DREAM OF?

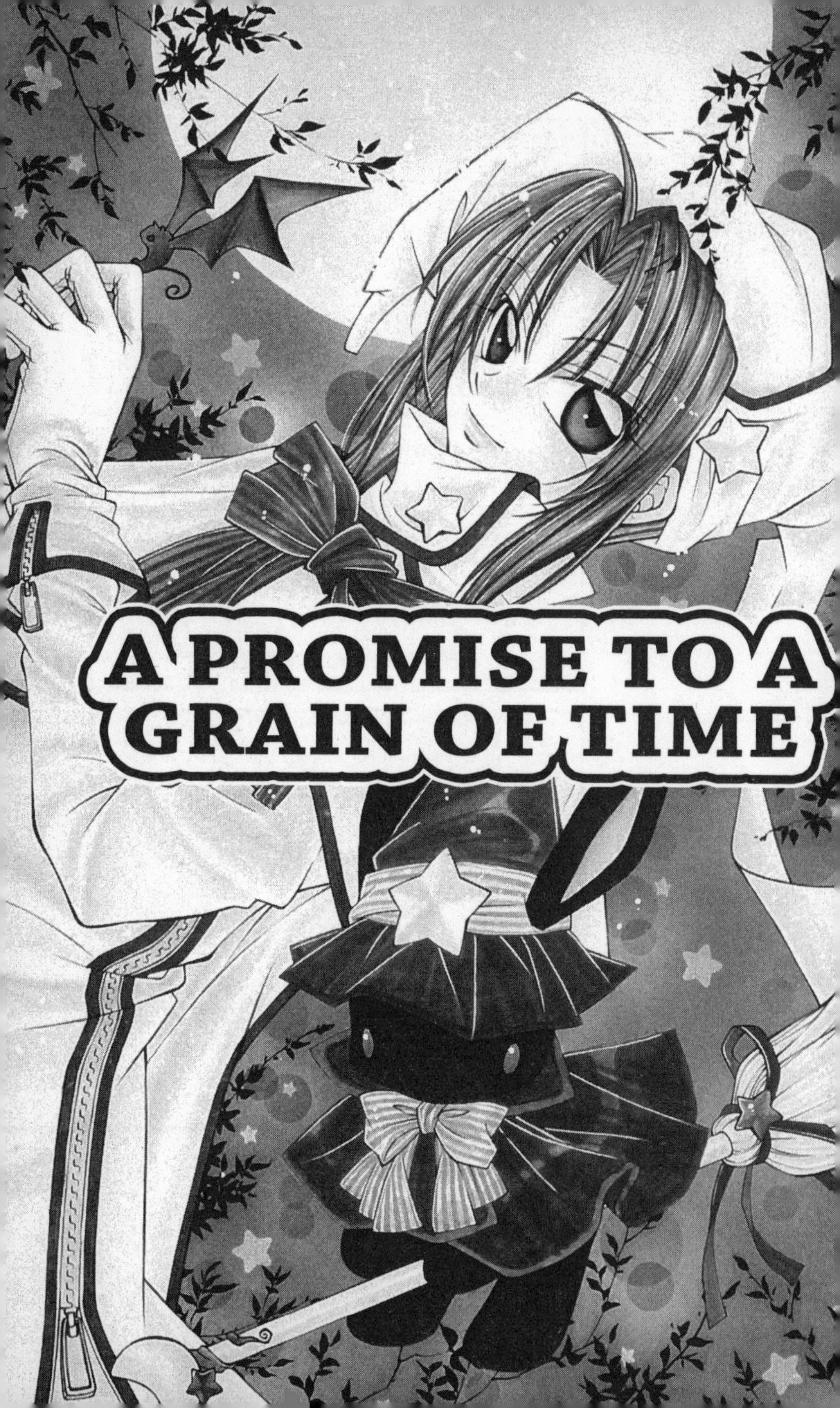
A PROMISE TO A GRAIN OF TIME

Alpha's Job

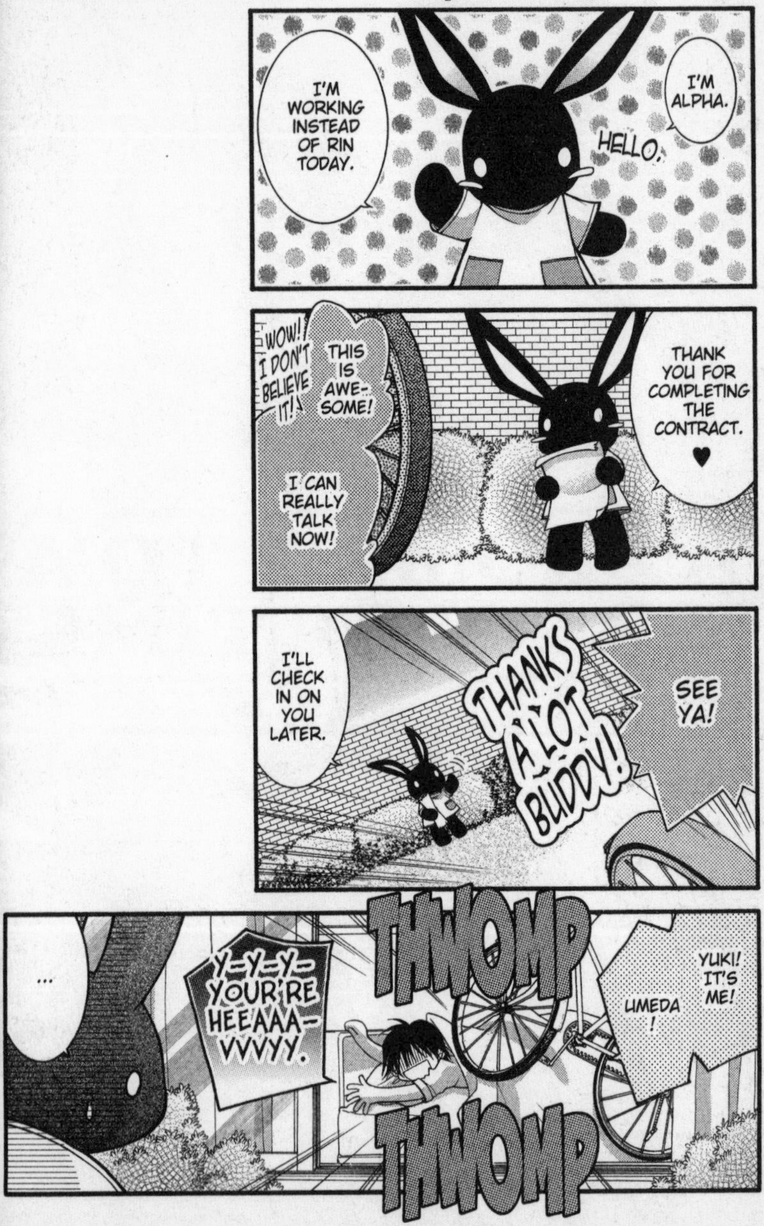
I'M ALPHA.
HELLO.
I'M WORKING INSTEAD OF RIN TODAY.
THANK YOU FOR COMPLETING THE CONTRACT. ♥
THIS IS AWE-SOME!
WOW! I DON'T BELIEVE IT!
I CAN REALLY TALK NOW!
SEE YA!
THANKS A LOT BUDDY!
I'LL CHECK IN ON YOU LATER.
YUKI! IT'S ME!
UMEDA!
THWOMP
Y-Y-Y-YOUR'RE HEEAAA-VVVYY.
THWOMP
...

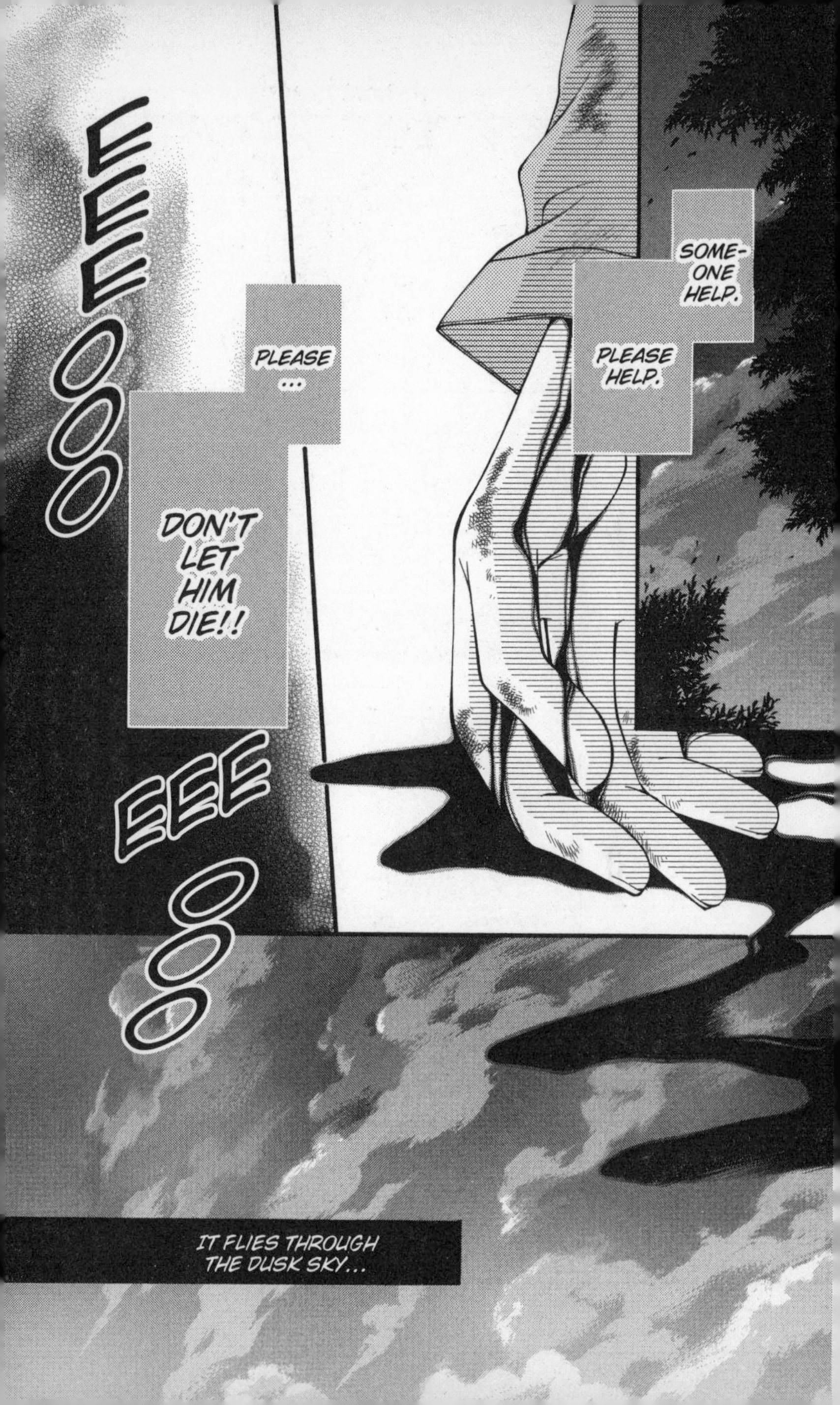
SOME-ONE HELP.
PLEASE HELP.
PLEASE ...
DON'T LET HIM DIE!!
EEEEOOOO
EEEOOO
IT FLIES THROUGH THE DUSK SKY...

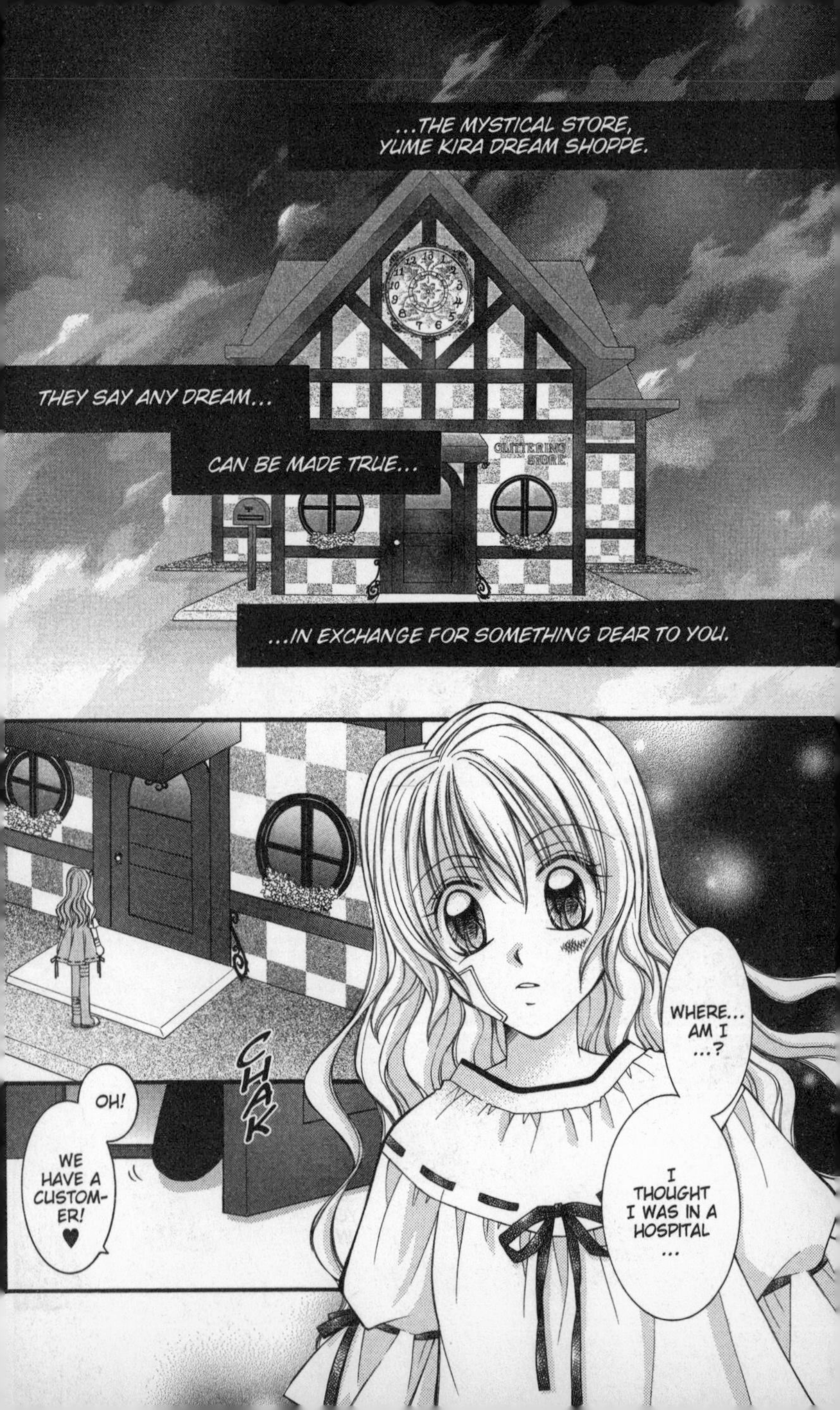
...THE MYSTICAL STORE, YUME KIRA DREAM SHOPPE.
THEY SAY ANY DREAM...
CAN BE MADE TRUE...
GLITTERING STORE
...IN EXCHANGE FOR SOMETHING DEAR TO YOU.
WHERE... AM I ...?
I THOUGHT I WAS IN A HOSPITAL ...
CHAK
OH!
WE HAVE A CUSTOMER! ♥

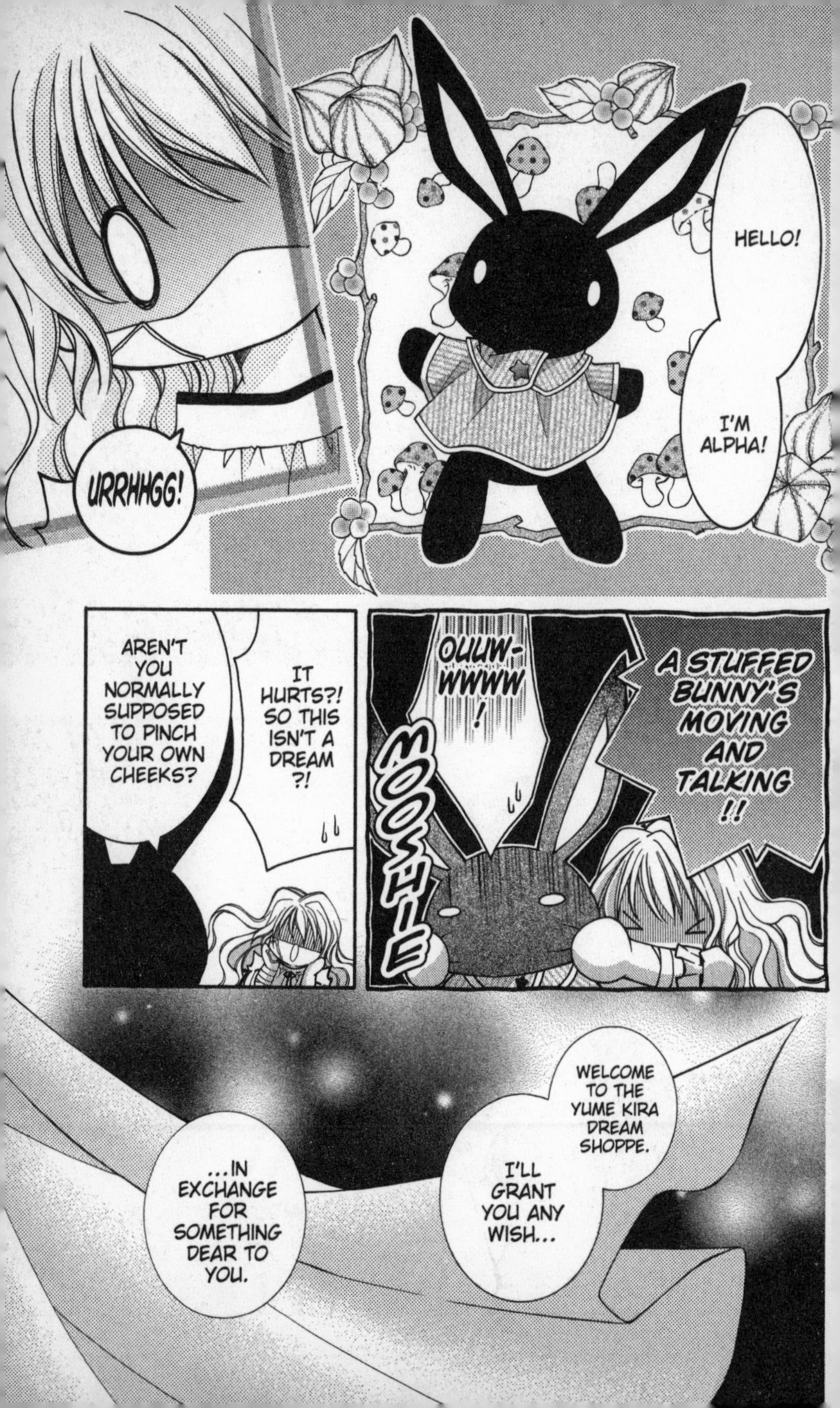
HELLO!
I'M ALPHA!
URRHHGG!
A STUFFED BUNNY'S MOVING AND TALKING!!
OUUW-WWWW!
MOOSHIE
IT HURTS?! SO THIS ISN'T A DREAM?!
AREN'T YOU NORMALLY SUPPOSED TO PINCH YOUR OWN CHEEKS?
WELCOME TO THE YUME KIRA DREAM SHOPPE.
I'LL GRANT YOU ANY WISH...
...IN EXCHANGE FOR SOMETHING DEAR TO YOU.

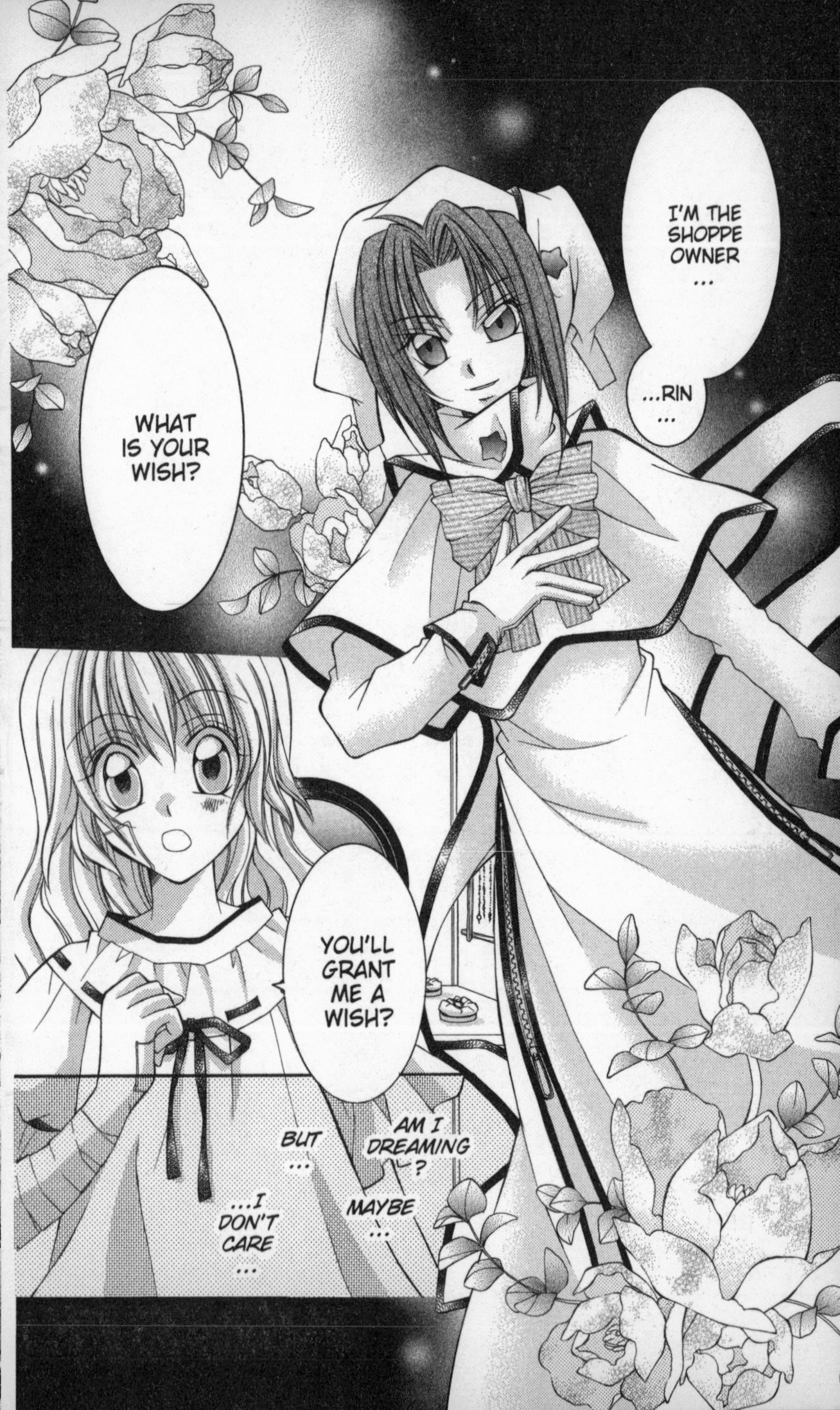
I'M THE SHOPPE OWNER ...
...RIN ...
WHAT IS YOUR WISH?
YOU'LL GRANT ME A WISH?
AM I DREAMING ?
BUT ...
MAYBE ...
...I DON'T CARE ...

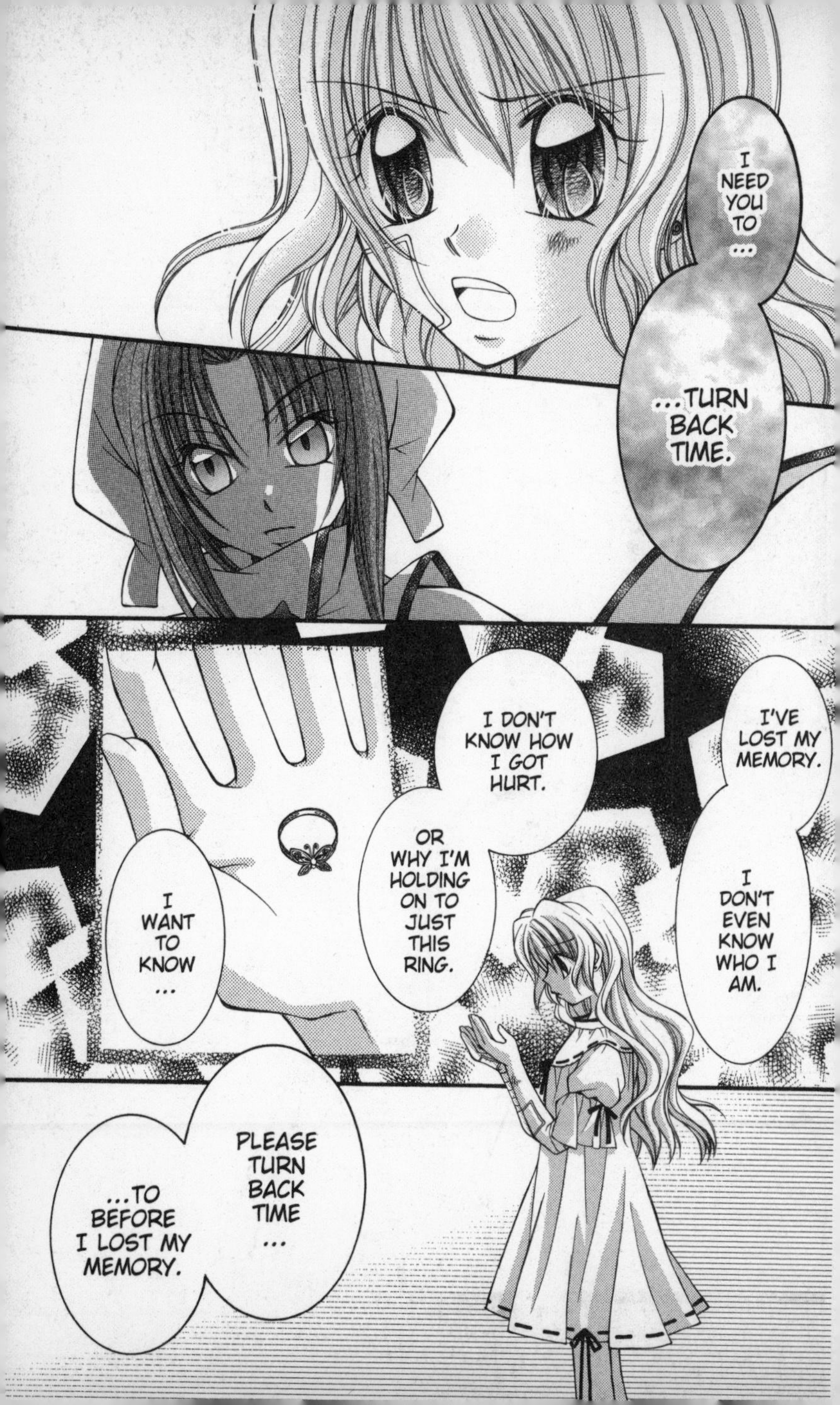
I NEED YOU TO ...
...TURN BACK TIME.
I'VE LOST MY MEMORY.
I DON'T EVEN KNOW WHO I AM.
I DON'T KNOW HOW I GOT HURT.
OR WHY I'M HOLDING ON TO JUST THIS RING.
I WANT TO KNOW ...
PLEASE TURN BACK TIME ...
...TO BEFORE I LOST MY MEMORY.

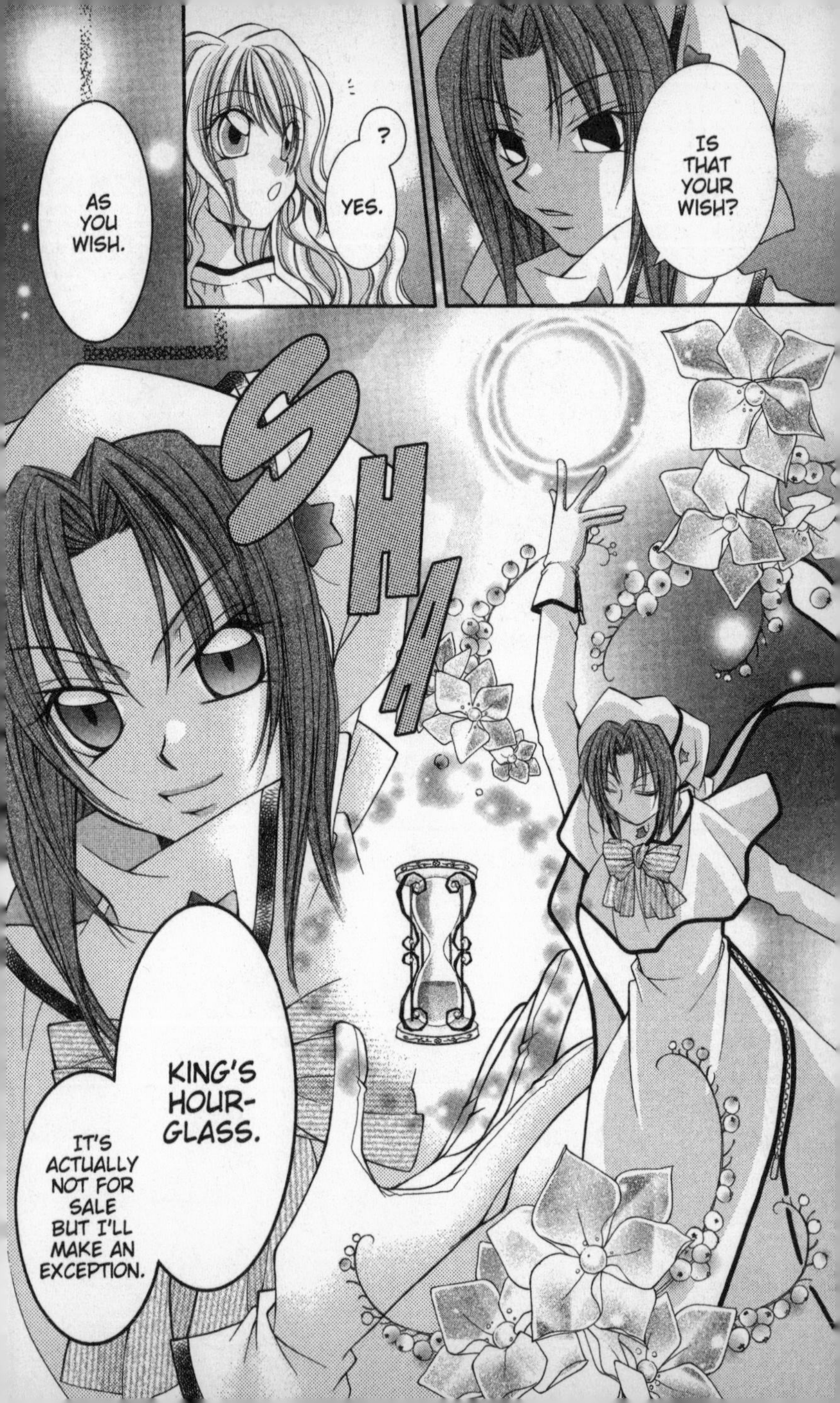
IS THAT YOUR WISH?
?
YES.
AS YOU WISH.
SHA
KING'S HOUR-GLASS.
IT'S ACTUALLY NOT FOR SALE BUT I'LL MAKE AN EXCEPTION.

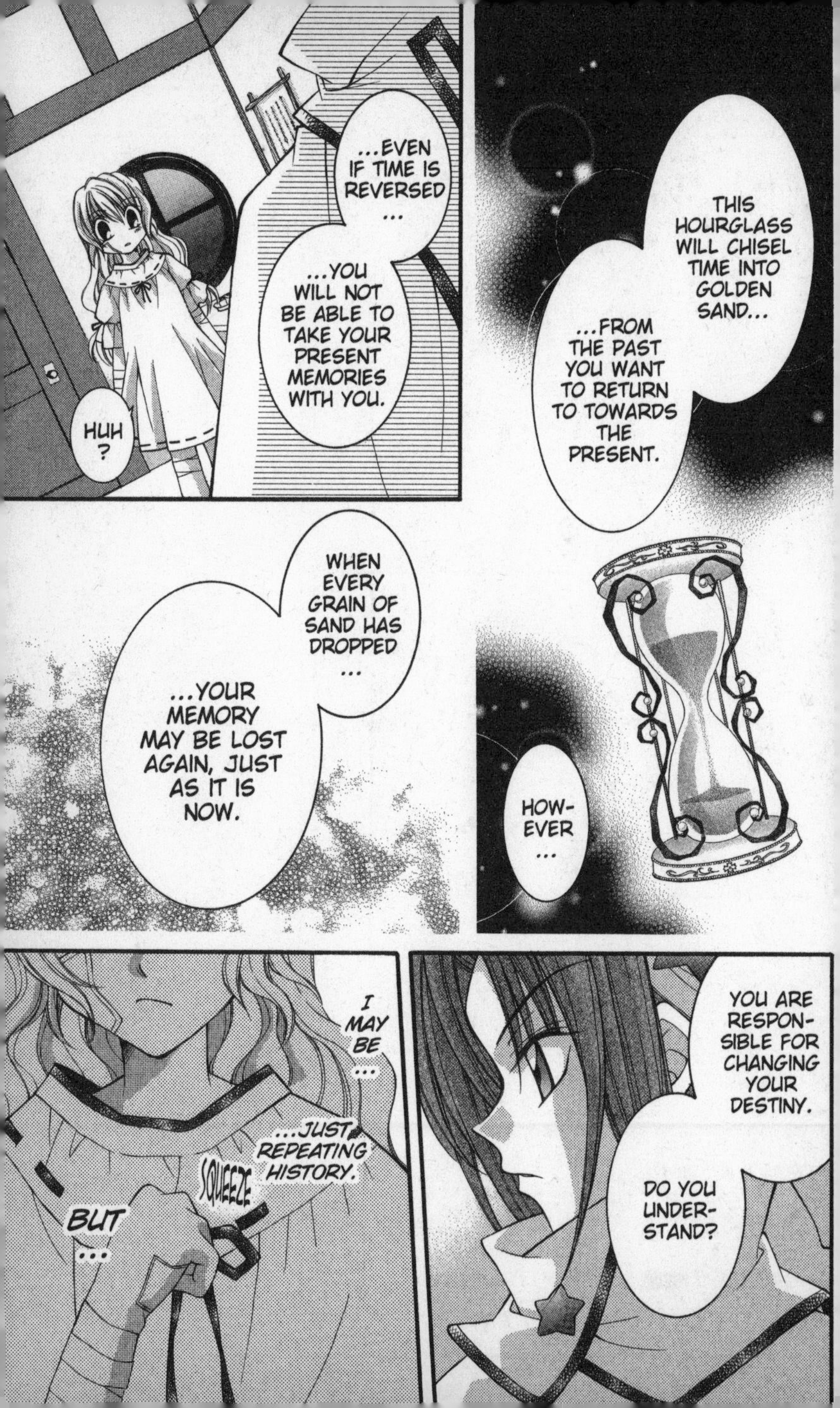
THIS HOURGLASS WILL CHISEL TIME INTO GOLDEN SAND...
...FROM THE PAST YOU WANT TO RETURN TO TOWARDS THE PRESENT.
...EVEN IF TIME IS REVERSED...
...YOU WILL NOT BE ABLE TO TAKE YOUR PRESENT MEMORIES WITH YOU.
HUH?
HOW-EVER...
WHEN EVERY GRAIN OF SAND HAS DROPPED...
...YOUR MEMORY MAY BE LOST AGAIN, JUST AS IT IS NOW.
YOU ARE RESPON-SIBLE FOR CHANGING YOUR DESTINY.
DO YOU UNDER-STAND?
I MAY BE...
...JUST REPEATING HISTORY.
SQUEEZE
BUT...

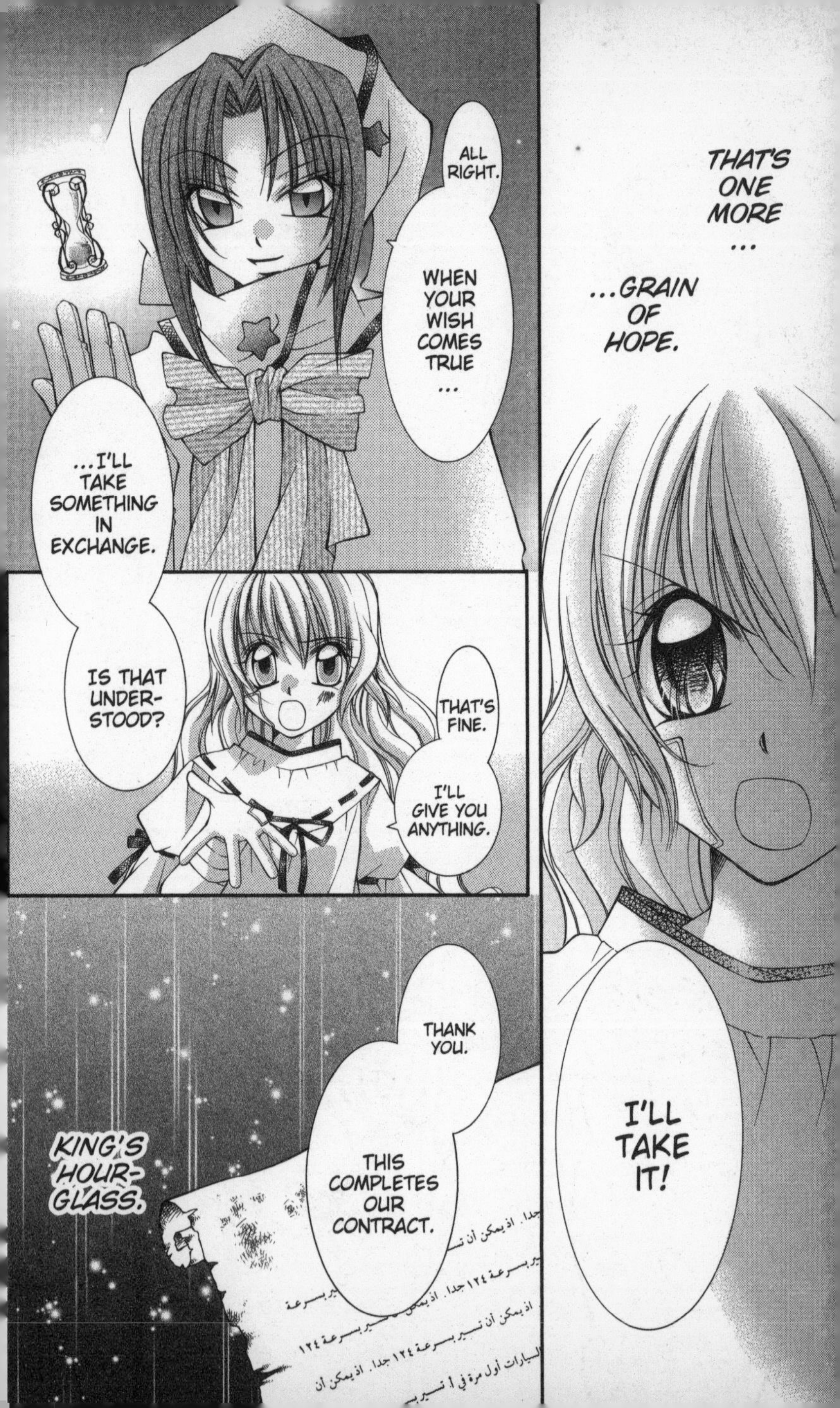
THAT'S ONE MORE ...
...GRAIN OF HOPE.
I'LL TAKE IT!
ALL RIGHT.
WHEN YOUR WISH COMES TRUE ...
...I'LL TAKE SOMETHING IN EXCHANGE.
IS THAT UNDER-STOOD?
THAT'S FINE.
I'LL GIVE YOU ANYTHING.
THANK YOU.
THIS COMPLETES OUR CONTRACT.
KING'S HOUR-GLASS.

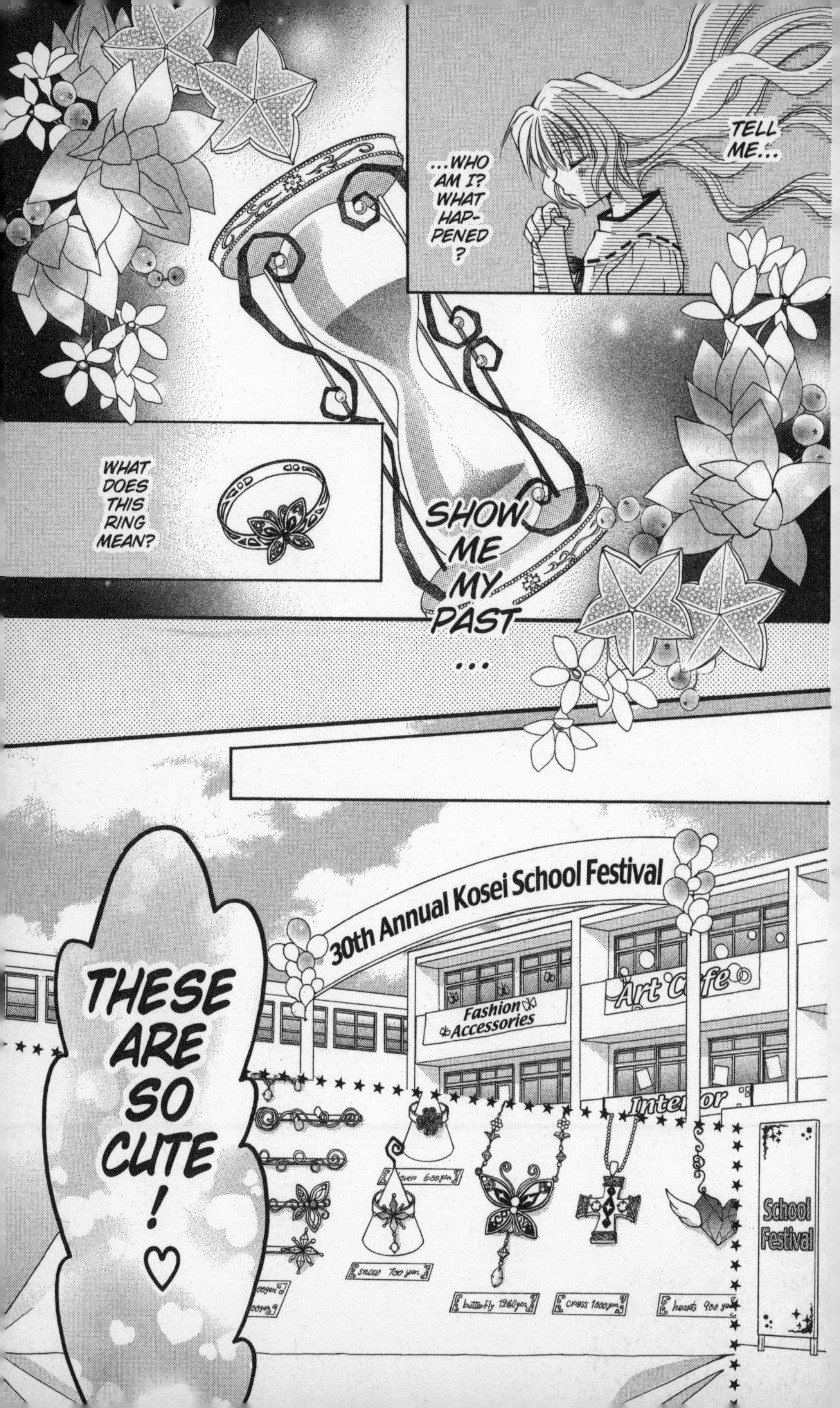
TELL ME...
...WHO AM I? WHAT HAP-PENED?
WHAT DOES THIS RING MEAN?
SHOW ME MY PAST...
30th Annual Kosei School Festival
Art Cafe
Fashion Accessories
School Festival
snow 700 yen
butterfly 1260 yen
cross 1800 yen
THESE ARE SO CUTE! ♡

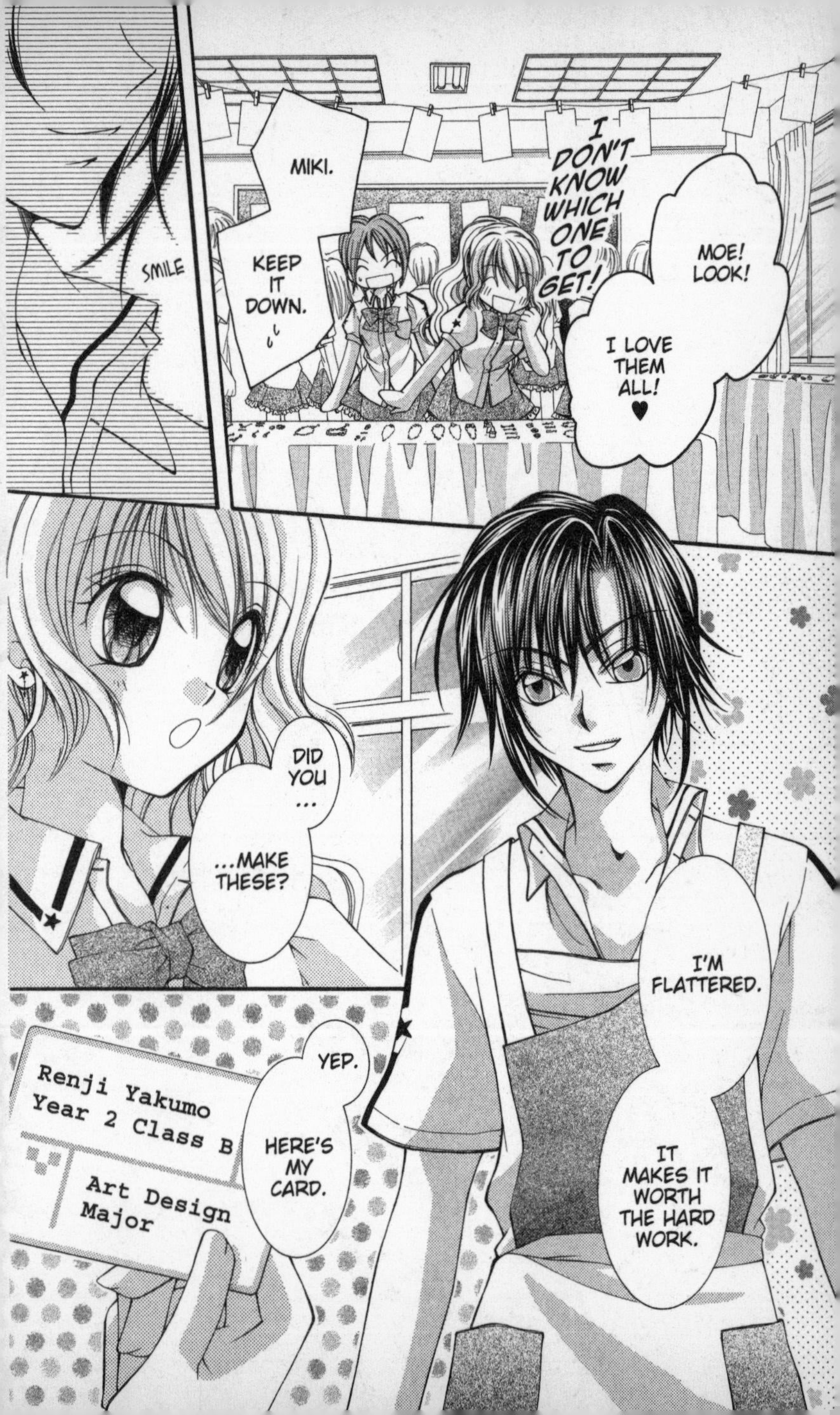
I DON'T KNOW WHICH ONE TO GET!
MOE! LOOK!
I LOVE THEM ALL! ♥
MIKI.
KEEP IT DOWN.
SMILE
I'M FLATTERED.
IT MAKES IT WORTH THE HARD WORK.
DID YOU ...
...MAKE THESE?
YEP.
HERE'S MY CARD.
Renji Yakumo
Year 2 Class B
Art Design
Major

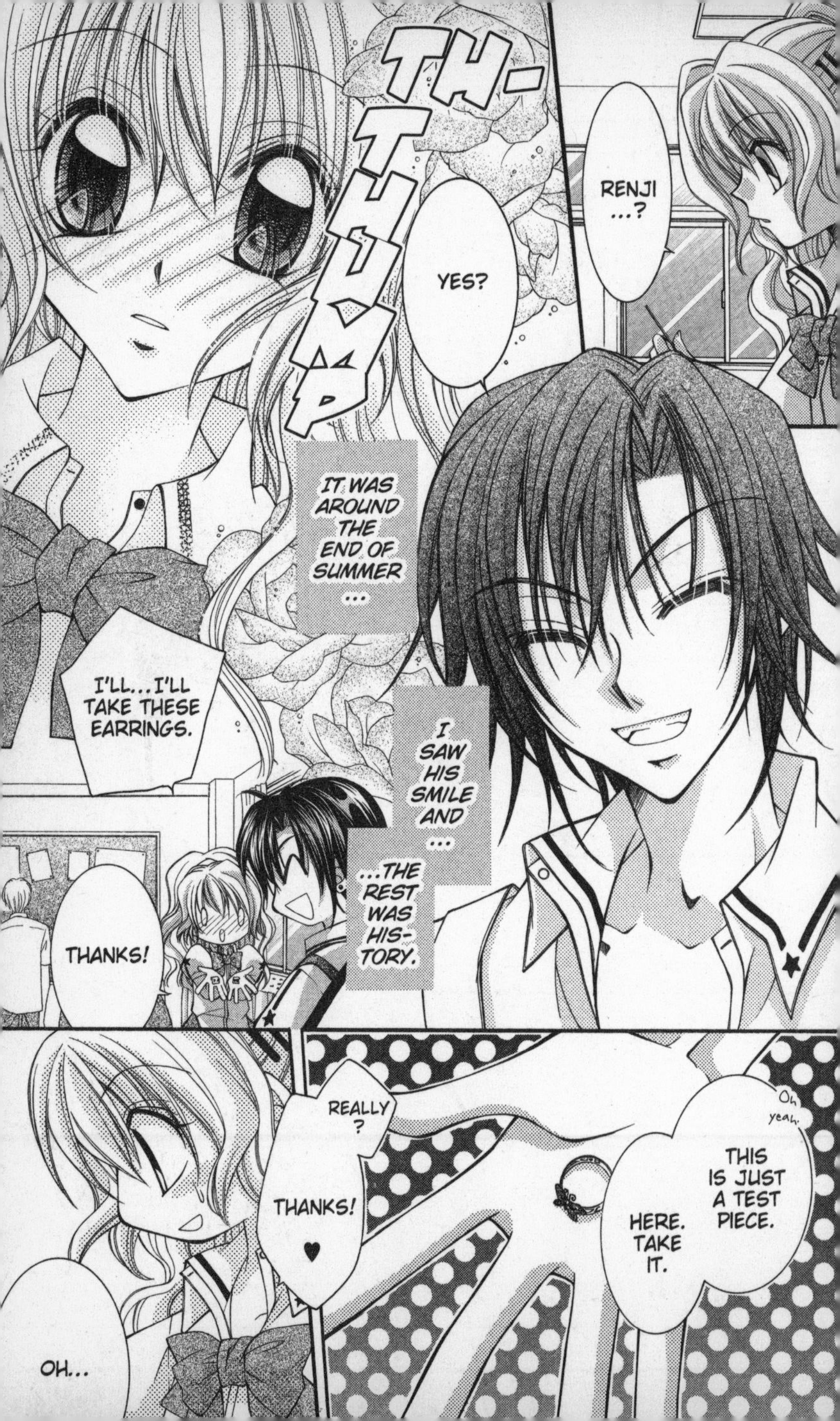
RENJI...?
YES?
TH-THUMP
IT WAS AROUND THE END OF SUMMER...
I SAW HIS SMILE AND...
...THE REST WAS HISTORY.
I'LL...I'LL TAKE THESE EARRINGS.
THANKS!
Oh yeah.
THIS IS JUST A TEST PIECE.
HERE. TAKE IT.
REALLY?
THANKS! ♥
OH...

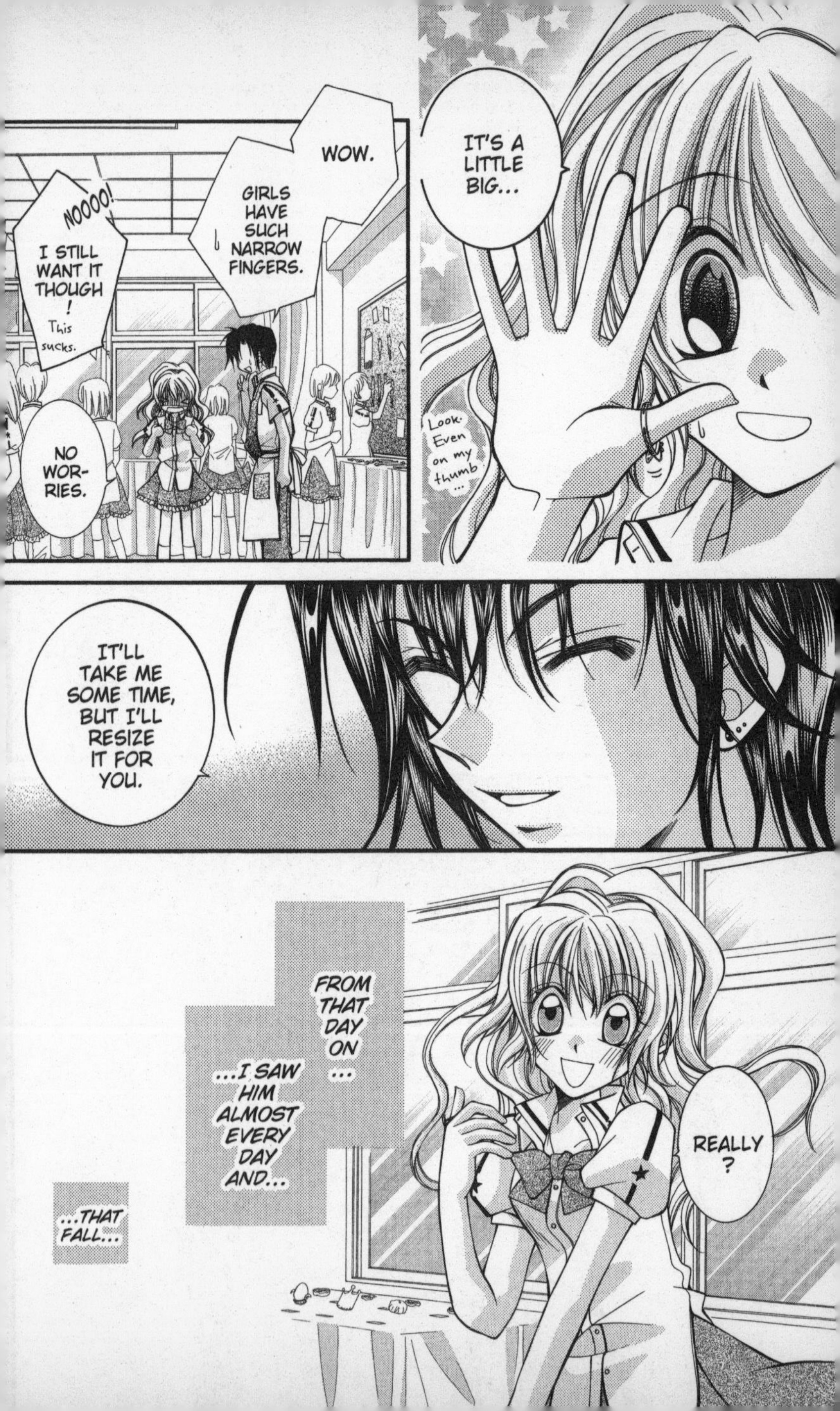
IT'S A LITTLE BIG...
Look. Even on my thumb...
WOW.
GIRLS HAVE SUCH NARROW FINGERS.
NOOOO!
I STILL WANT IT THOUGH!
This sucks.
NO WOR-RIES.
IT'LL TAKE ME SOME TIME, BUT I'LL RESIZE IT FOR YOU.
REALLY?
FROM THAT DAY ON...
...I SAW HIM ALMOST EVERY DAY AND...
...THAT FALL...

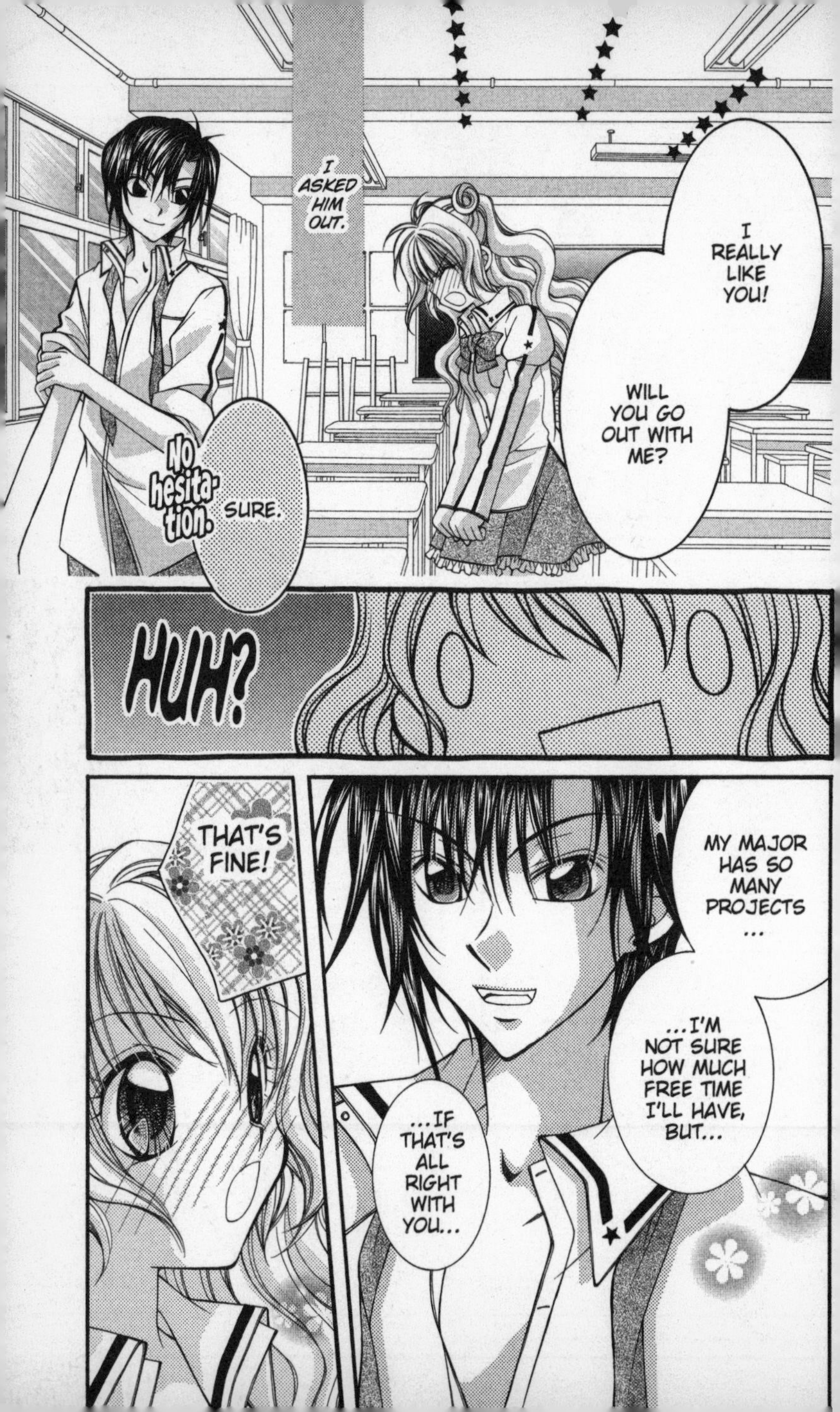
I REALLY LIKE YOU!
WILL YOU GO OUT WITH ME?
I ASKED HIM OUT.
SURE.
No hesitation.
HUH?
MY MAJOR HAS SO MANY PROJECTS...
...I'M NOT SURE HOW MUCH FREE TIME I'LL HAVE, BUT...
...IF THAT'S ALL RIGHT WITH YOU...
THAT'S FINE!

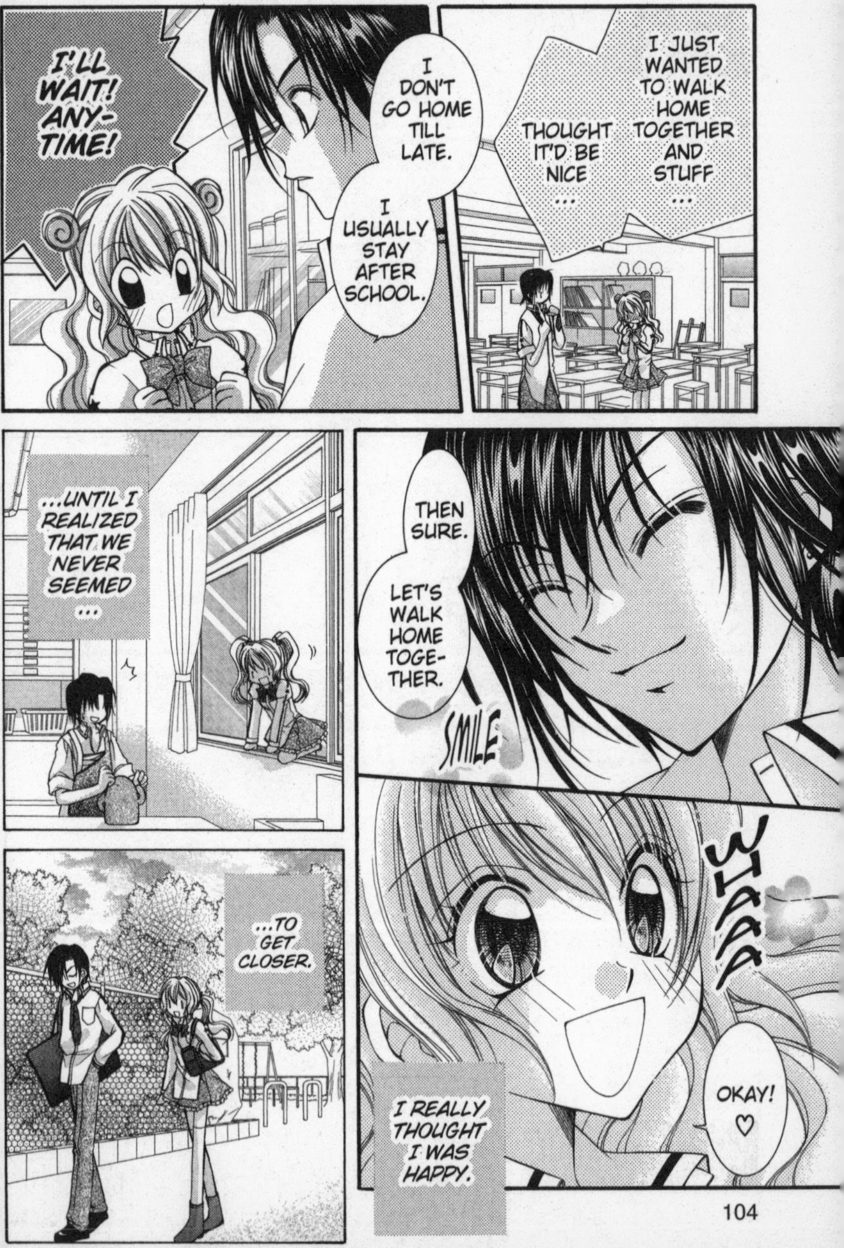
I JUST WANTED TO WALK HOME TOGETHER AND STUFF ...
THOUGHT IT'D BE NICE ...
I DON'T GO HOME TILL LATE.
I USUALLY STAY AFTER SCHOOL.
I'LL WAIT! ANY-TIME!
THEN SURE.
LET'S WALK HOME TOGE-THER.
SMILE
WHAAA
OKAY! ♡
I REALLY THOUGHT I WAS HAPPY.
...UNTIL I REALIZED THAT WE NEVER SEEMED ...
...TO GET CLOSER.

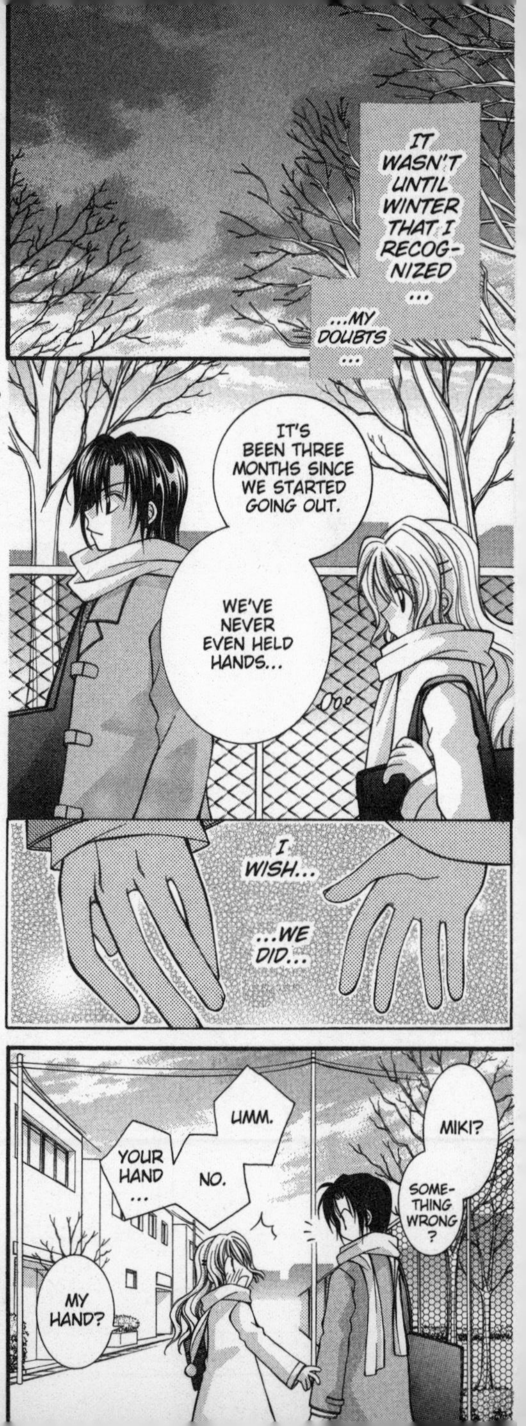
IT WASN'T UNTIL WINTER THAT I RECOGNIZED...
...MY DOUBTS...
IT'S BEEN THREE MONTHS SINCE WE STARTED GOING OUT.
WE'VE NEVER EVEN HELD HANDS...
I WISH...
...WE DID...
MIKI?
SOMETHING WRONG?
UMM.
YOUR HAND...
NO.
MY HAND?

3

★★★ SPECIAL THANKS

I'M STILL A TOTAL HANDFUL. THANK YOU SO MUCH TO ALL MY ASSISTANTS. THERE WERE A LOT OF CORRECTIONS THAT THEY SO GRACIOUSLY WORKED ON FOR ME. I'M WRITING THIS AS THEY'RE PASSED OUT IN THE NEXT ROOM. THE BUZZ WORD AROUND HERE THESE DAYS IS "GAN-HI." THE KANJI FOR IT LITERALLY MEANS "EYE FATIGUE." IT'S BEEN A COMMON PROBLEM HERE LATELY. (LOL)

I'VE ALSO GOT A NEW EDITOR STARTING THE FOURTH STORY IN YUME KIRA. IT'S GOOD TO BE WORKING WITH YOU. *BOWS*

AND TO THOSE READERS WHO'VE READ THIS UP TO THIS POINT, THANK YOU SO VERY MUCH! I'LL KEEP WORKING HARD AS LONG AS I HAVE AN AUDIENCE! I'M COUNTING ON YOUR CONTINUED SUPPORT!

JUNE, 2005 AQUA MIZUNO

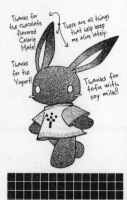

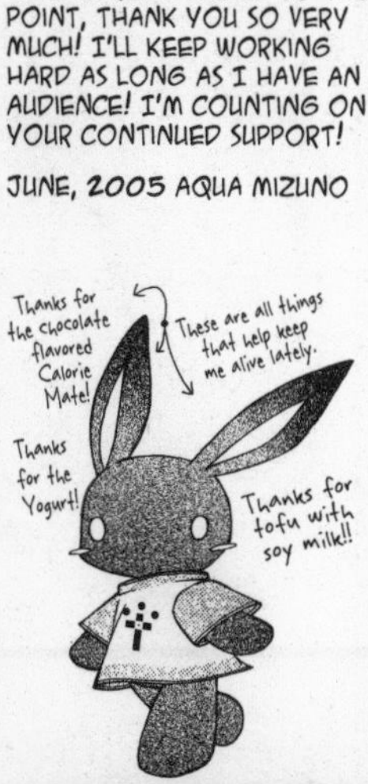
Thanks for the chocolate flavored Calorie Mate!
These are all things that help keep me alive lately.
Thanks for the Yogurt!
Thanks for tofu with soy milk!!

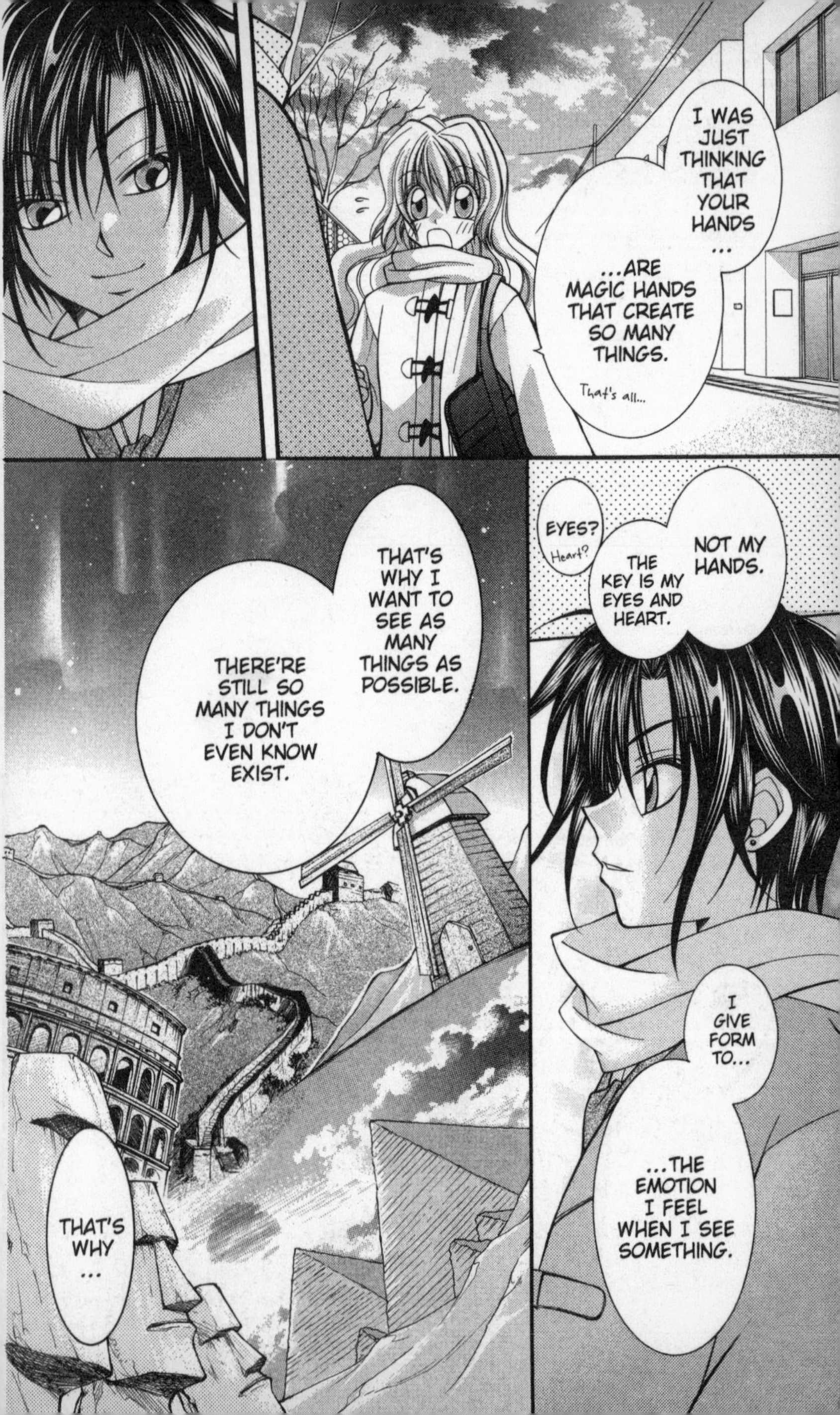
I WAS JUST THINKING THAT YOUR HANDS...
...ARE MAGIC HANDS THAT CREATE SO MANY THINGS.
That's all...
NOT MY HANDS.
THE KEY IS MY EYES AND HEART.
EYES?
Heart?
I GIVE FORM TO...
...THE EMOTION I FEEL WHEN I SEE SOMETHING.
THAT'S WHY I WANT TO SEE AS MANY THINGS AS POSSIBLE.
THERE'RE STILL SO MANY THINGS I DON'T EVEN KNOW EXIST.
THAT'S WHY...

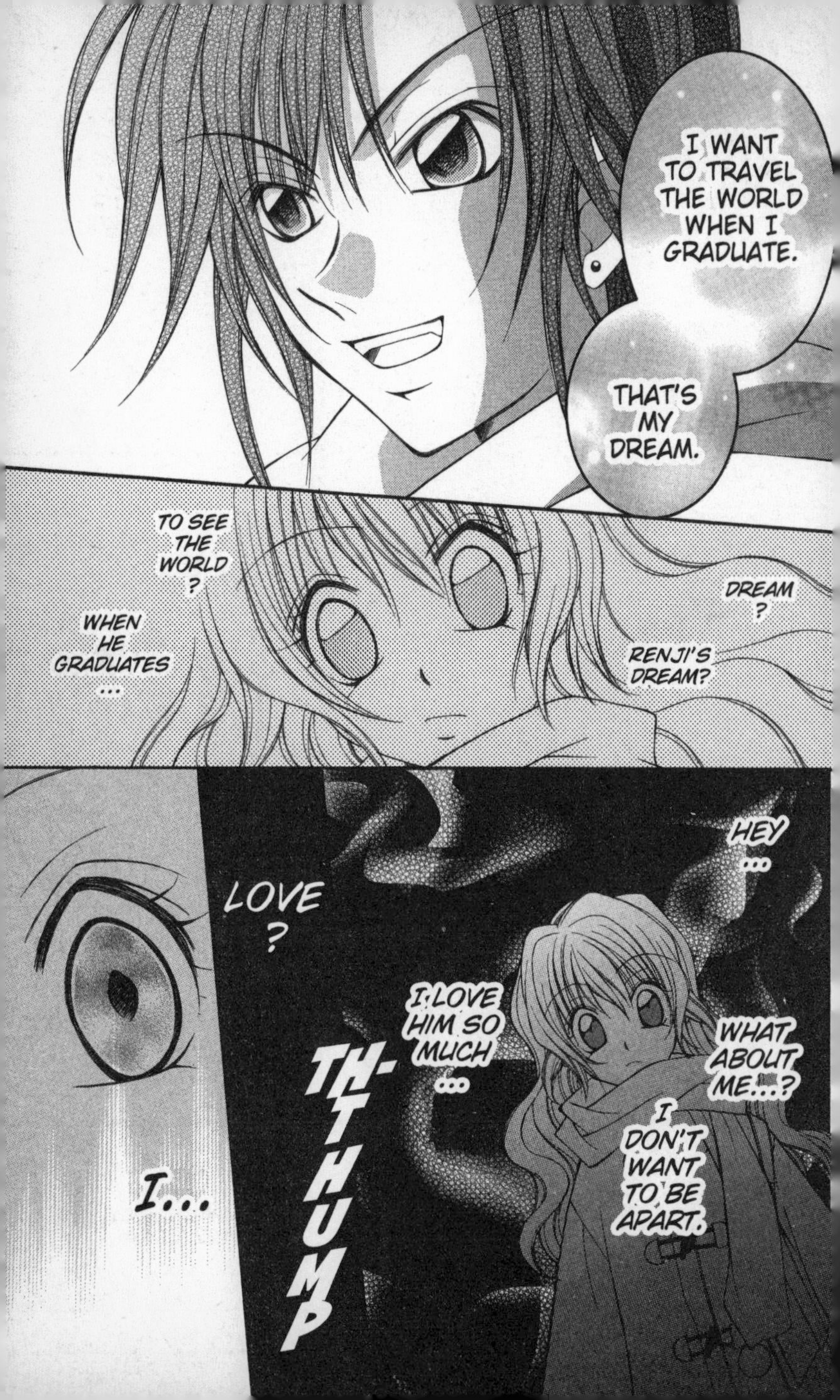
I WANT TO TRAVEL THE WORLD WHEN I GRADUATE.
THAT'S MY DREAM.
DREAM?
RENJI'S DREAM?
TO SEE THE WORLD?
WHEN HE GRADUATES...
HEY...
WHAT ABOUT ME...?
I DON'T WANT TO BE APART.
I LOVE HIM SO MUCH...
LOVE?
TH-THUMP
I...

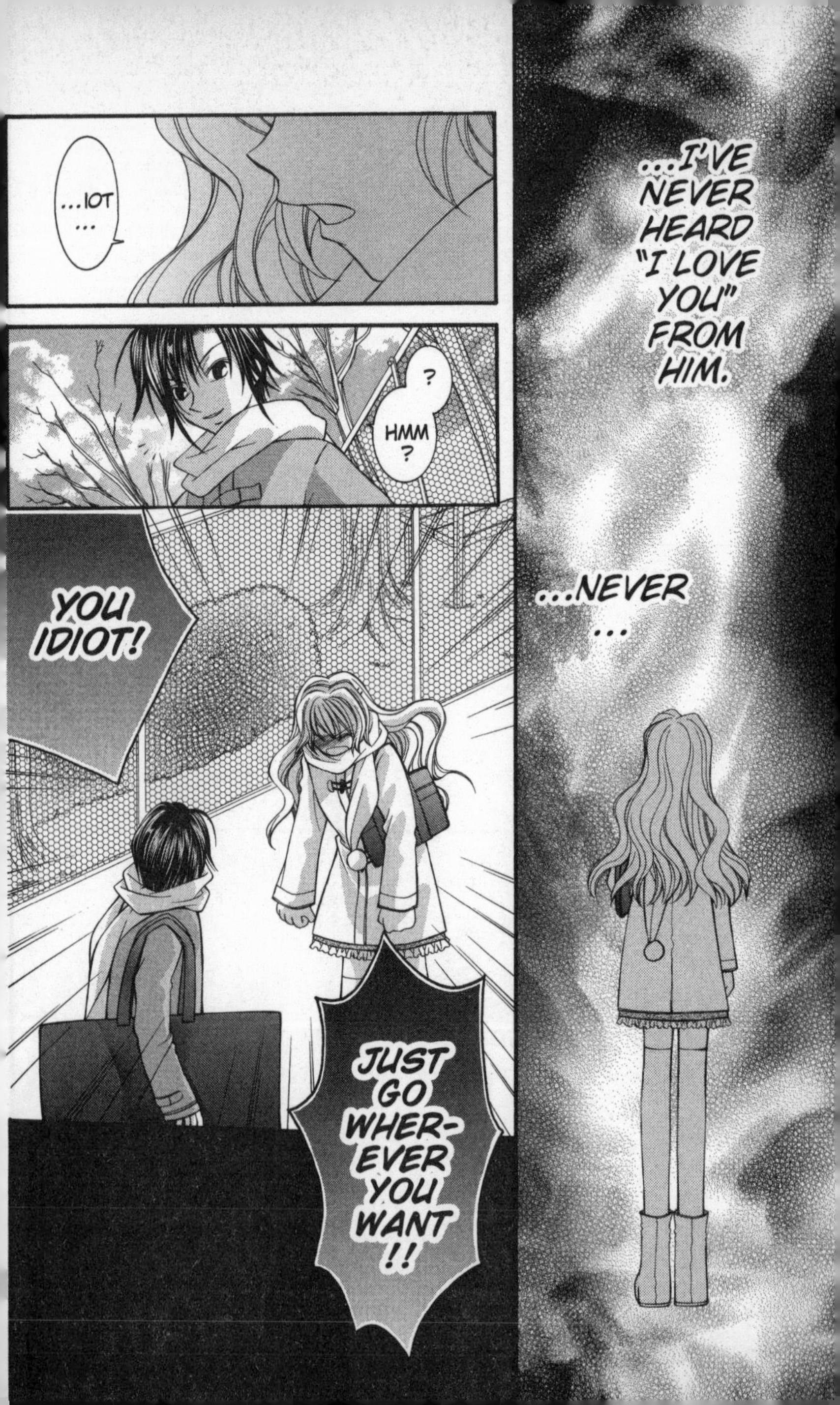
...I'VE NEVER HEARD "I LOVE YOU" FROM HIM.
...NEVER ...
...IOT ...
?
HMM ?
YOU IDIOT!
JUST GO WHER-EVER YOU WANT !!

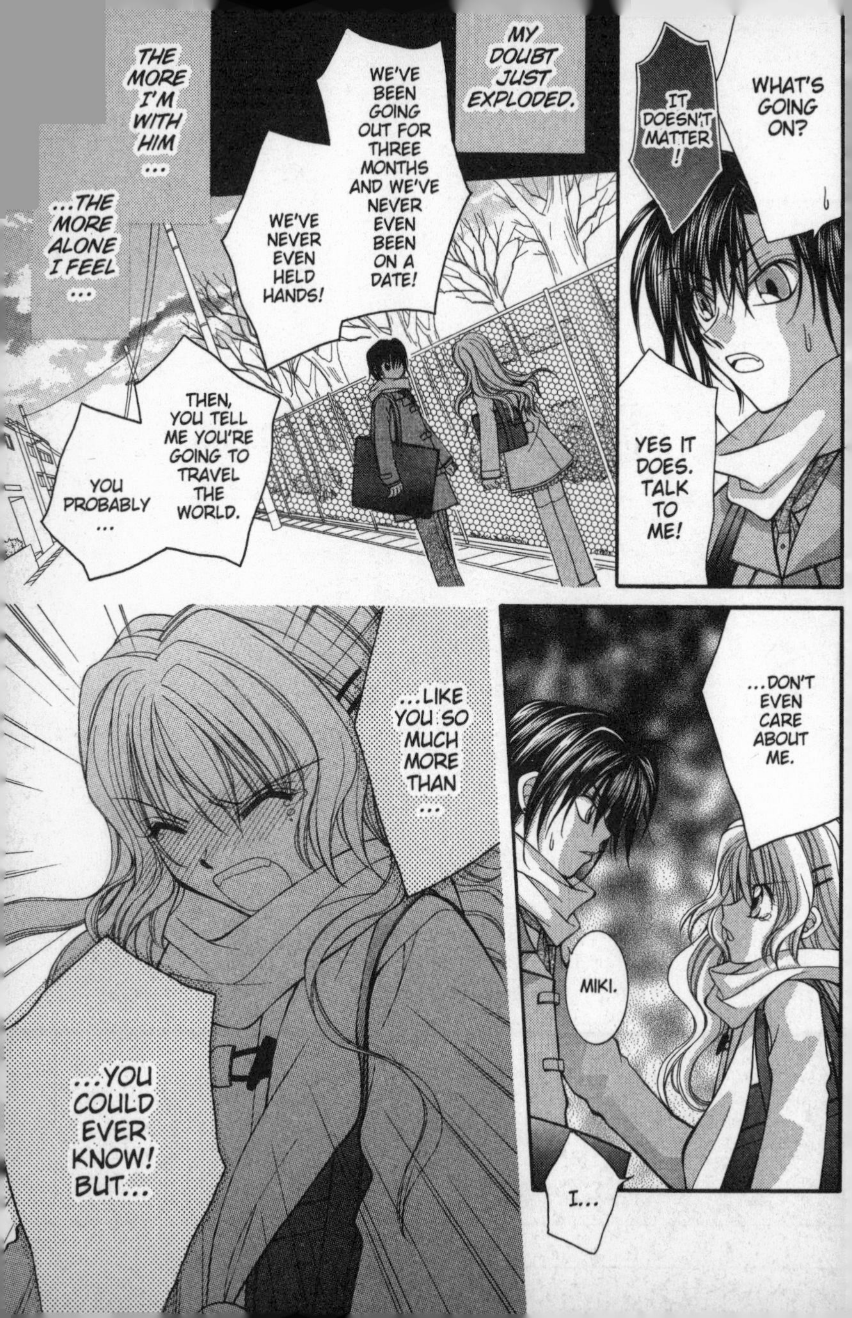
WHAT'S GOING ON?
IT DOESN'T MATTER!
YES IT DOES. TALK TO ME!
MY DOUBT JUST EXPLODED.
WE'VE BEEN GOING OUT FOR THREE MONTHS AND WE'VE NEVER EVEN BEEN ON A DATE!
WE'VE NEVER EVEN HELD HANDS!
THE MORE I'M WITH HIM...
...THE MORE ALONE I FEEL...
THEN, YOU TELL ME YOU'RE GOING TO TRAVEL THE WORLD.
YOU PROBABLY...
...DON'T EVEN CARE ABOUT ME.
MIKI.
I...
...LIKE YOU SO MUCH MORE THAN...
...YOU COULD EVER KNOW! BUT...

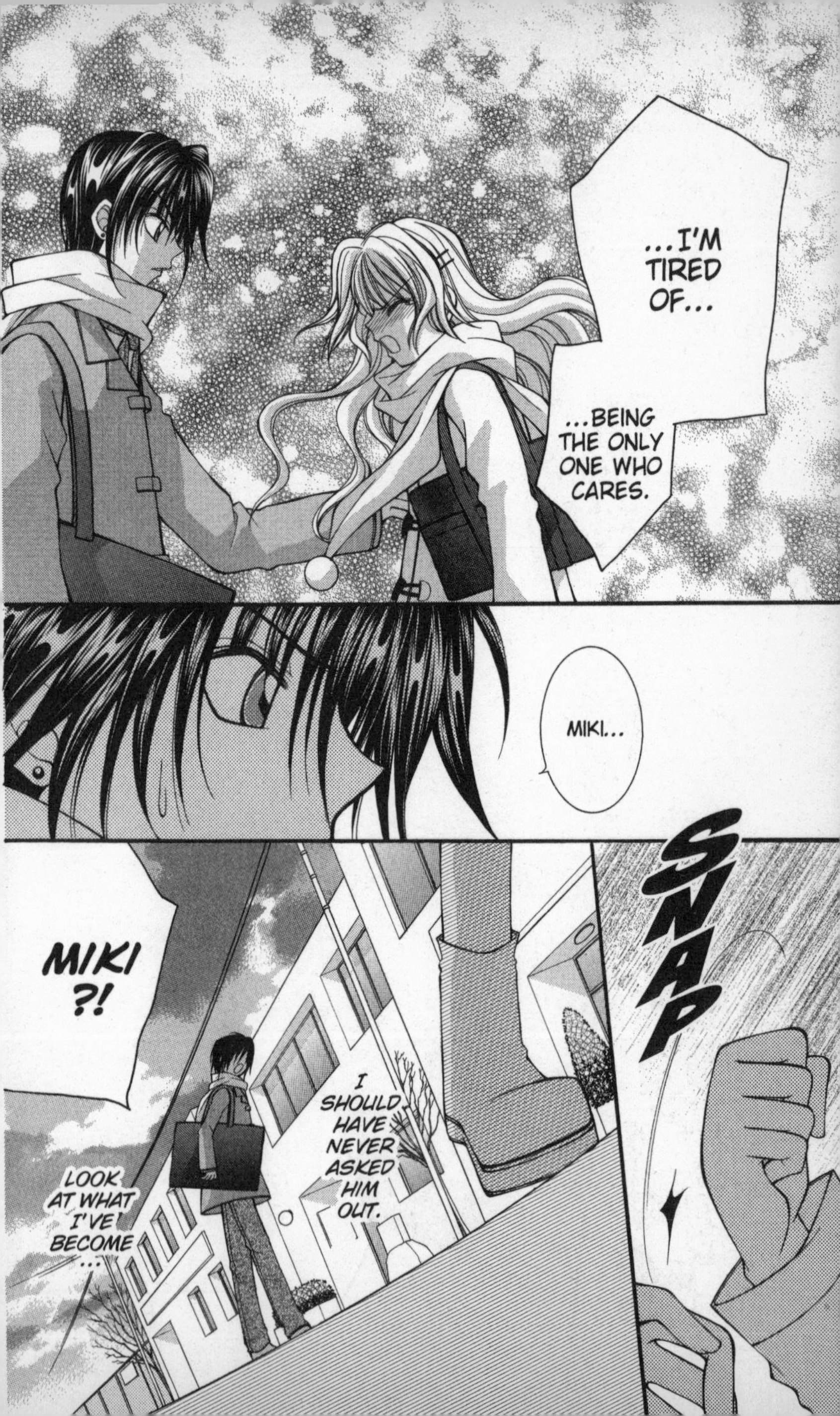
...I'M TIRED OF...
...BEING THE ONLY ONE WHO CARES.
MIKI...
SNAP
MIKI ?!
I SHOULD HAVE NEVER ASKED HIM OUT.
LOOK AT WHAT I'VE BECOME ...

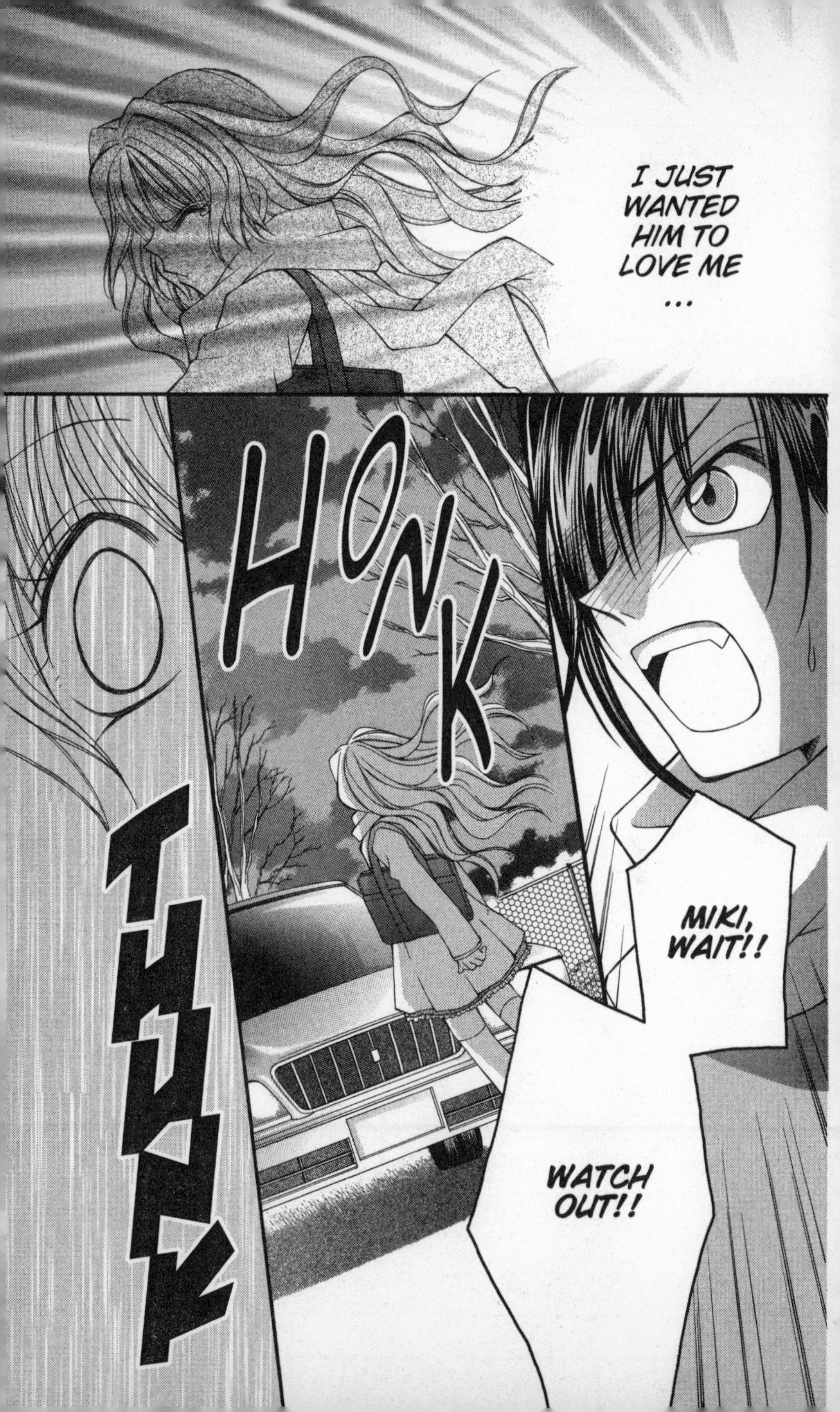
I JUST WANTED HIM TO LOVE ME ...
MIKI, WAIT!!
WATCH OUT!!
HONK

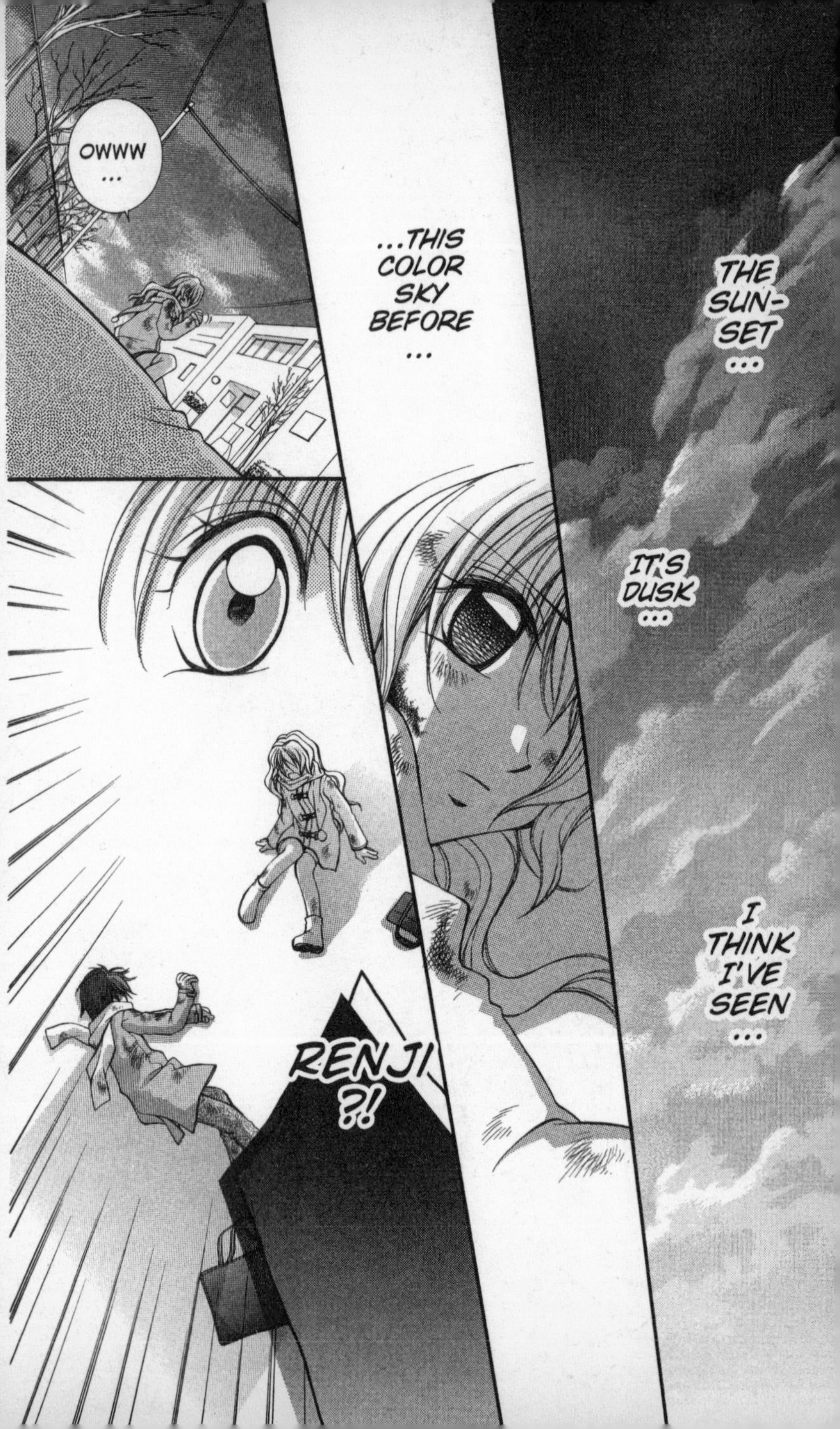
THE SUN-SET ...
IT'S DUSK ...
I THINK I'VE SEEN ...
...THIS COLOR SKY BEFORE ...
OWWW ...
RENJI ?!

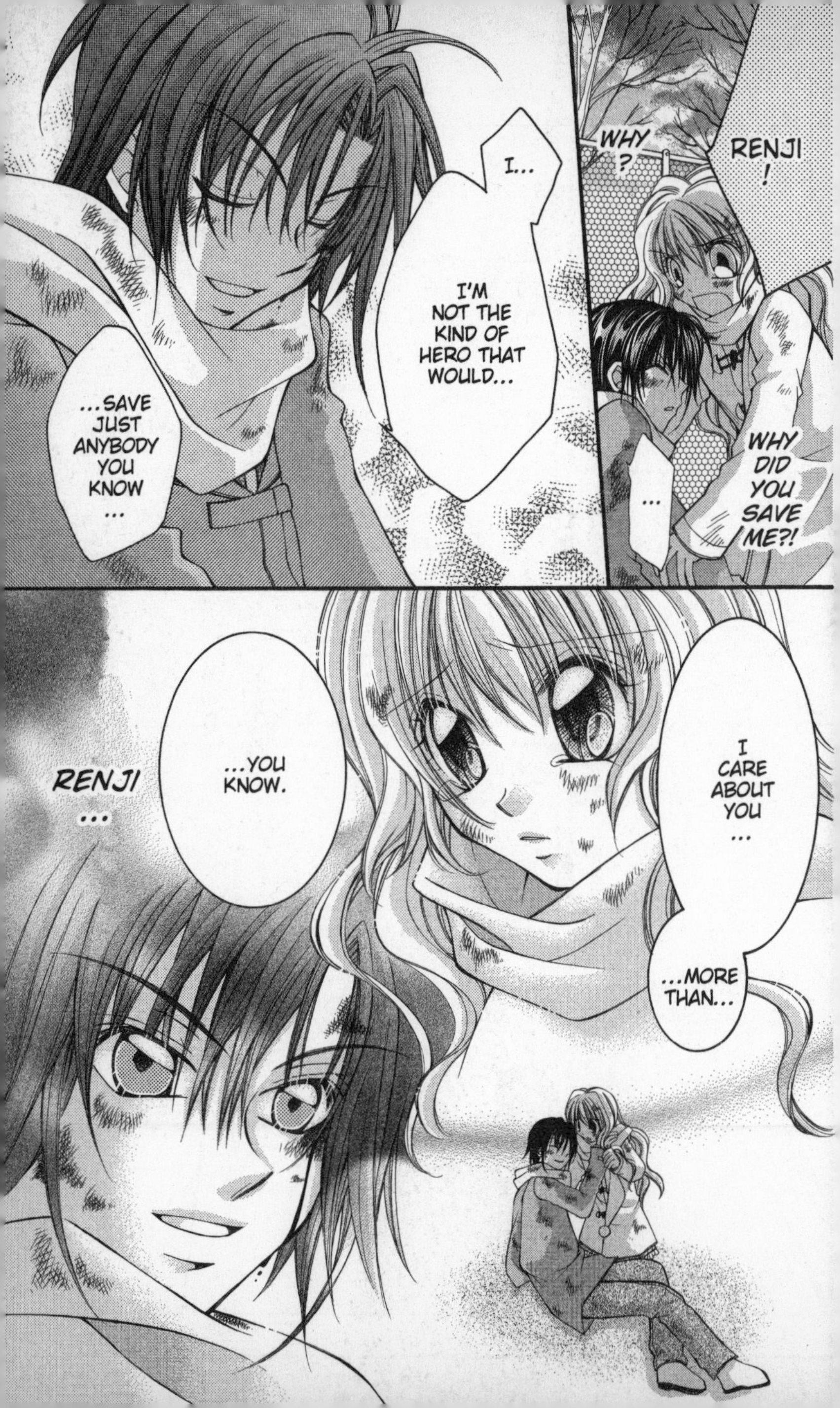
RENJI!
WHY?
WHY DID YOU SAVE ME?!
...
I...
I'M NOT THE KIND OF HERO THAT WOULD...
...SAVE JUST ANYBODY YOU KNOW...
I CARE ABOUT YOU...
...MORE THAN...
...YOU KNOW.
RENJI...

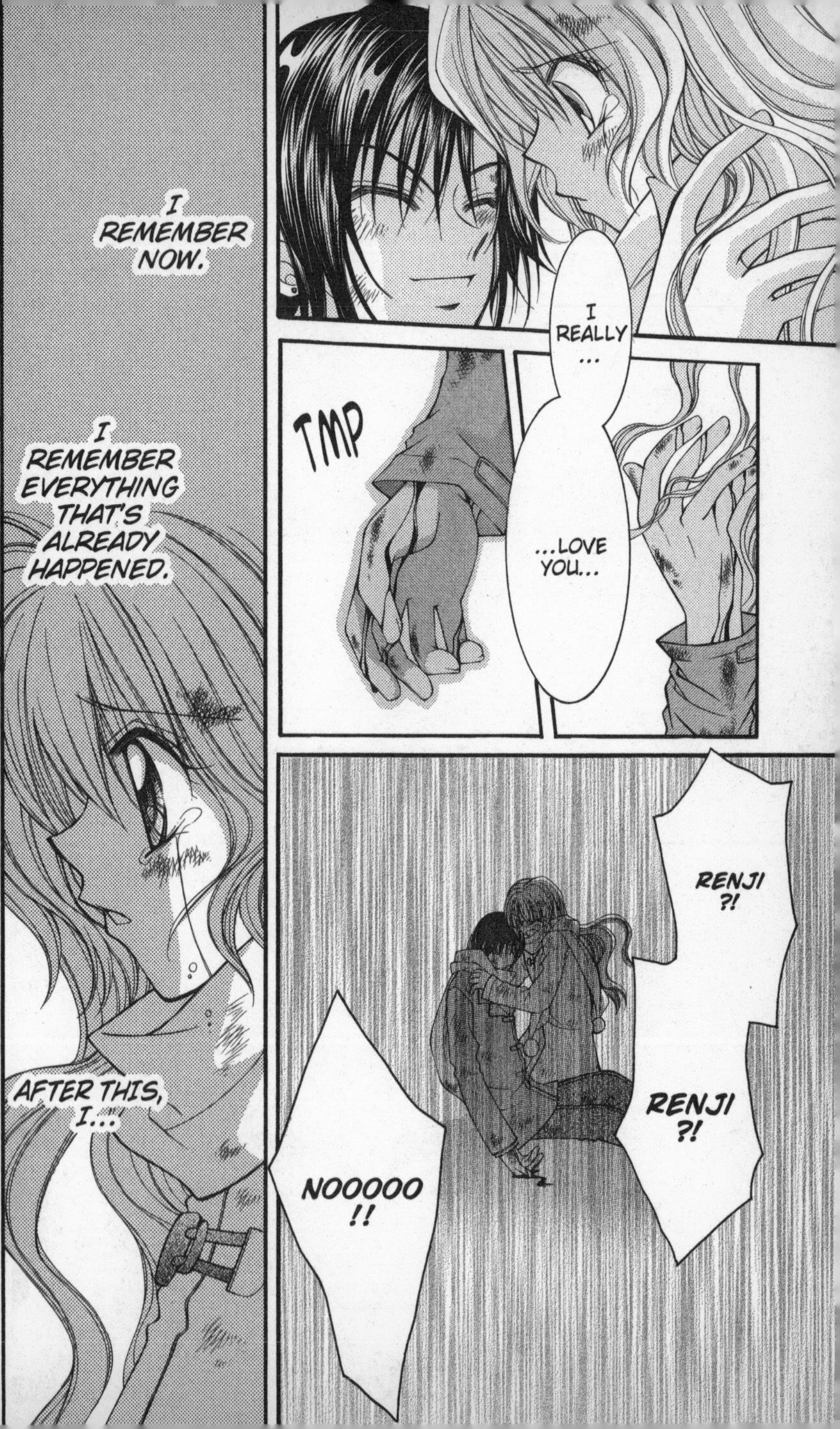
I REALLY...
...LOVE YOU...
TMP
RENJI?!
RENJI?!
NOOOOO!!
I REMEMBER NOW.
I REMEMBER EVERYTHING THAT'S ALREADY HAPPENED.
AFTER THIS, I...

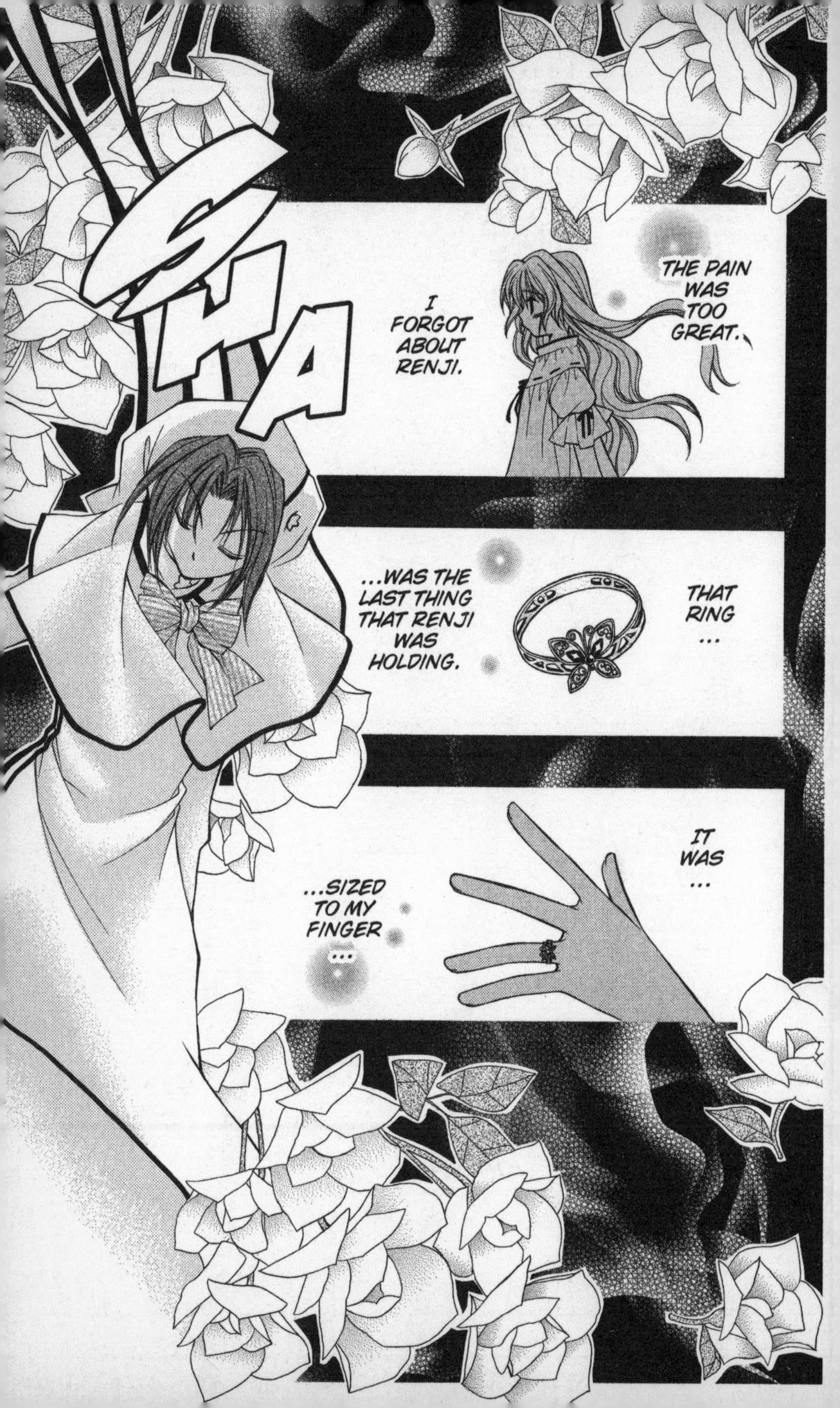
THE PAIN WAS TOO GREAT.
I FORGOT ABOUT RENJI.
SHA
THAT RING ...
...WAS THE LAST THING THAT RENJI WAS HOLDING.
IT WAS ...
...SIZED TO MY FINGER ...

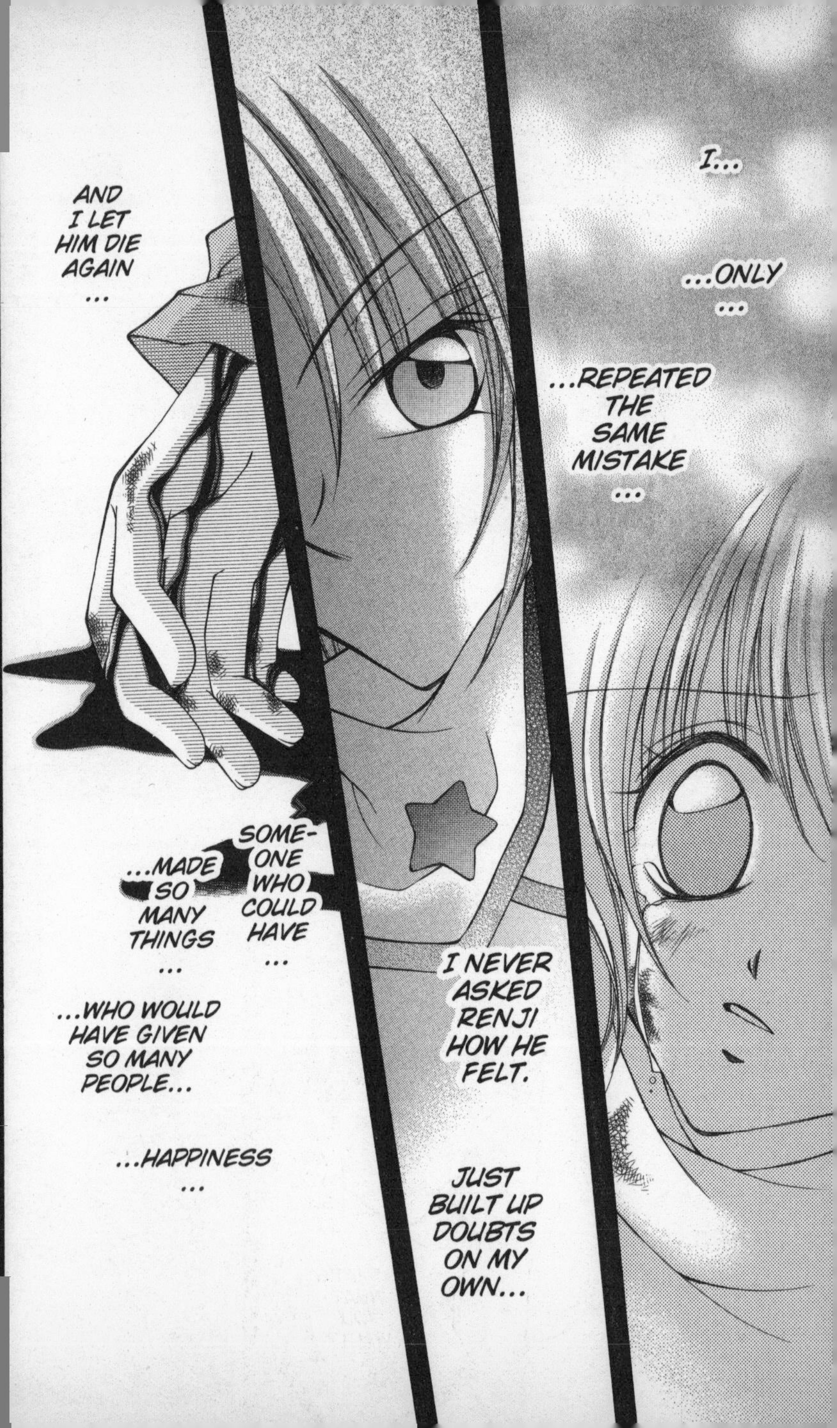
I...
...ONLY ...
...REPEATED THE SAME MISTAKE ...
I NEVER ASKED RENJI HOW HE FELT.
JUST BUILT UP DOUBTS ON MY OWN...
AND I LET HIM DIE AGAIN ...
SOME-ONE WHO COULD HAVE ...
...MADE SO MANY THINGS ...
...WHO WOULD HAVE GIVEN SO MANY PEOPLE...
...HAPPINESS ...

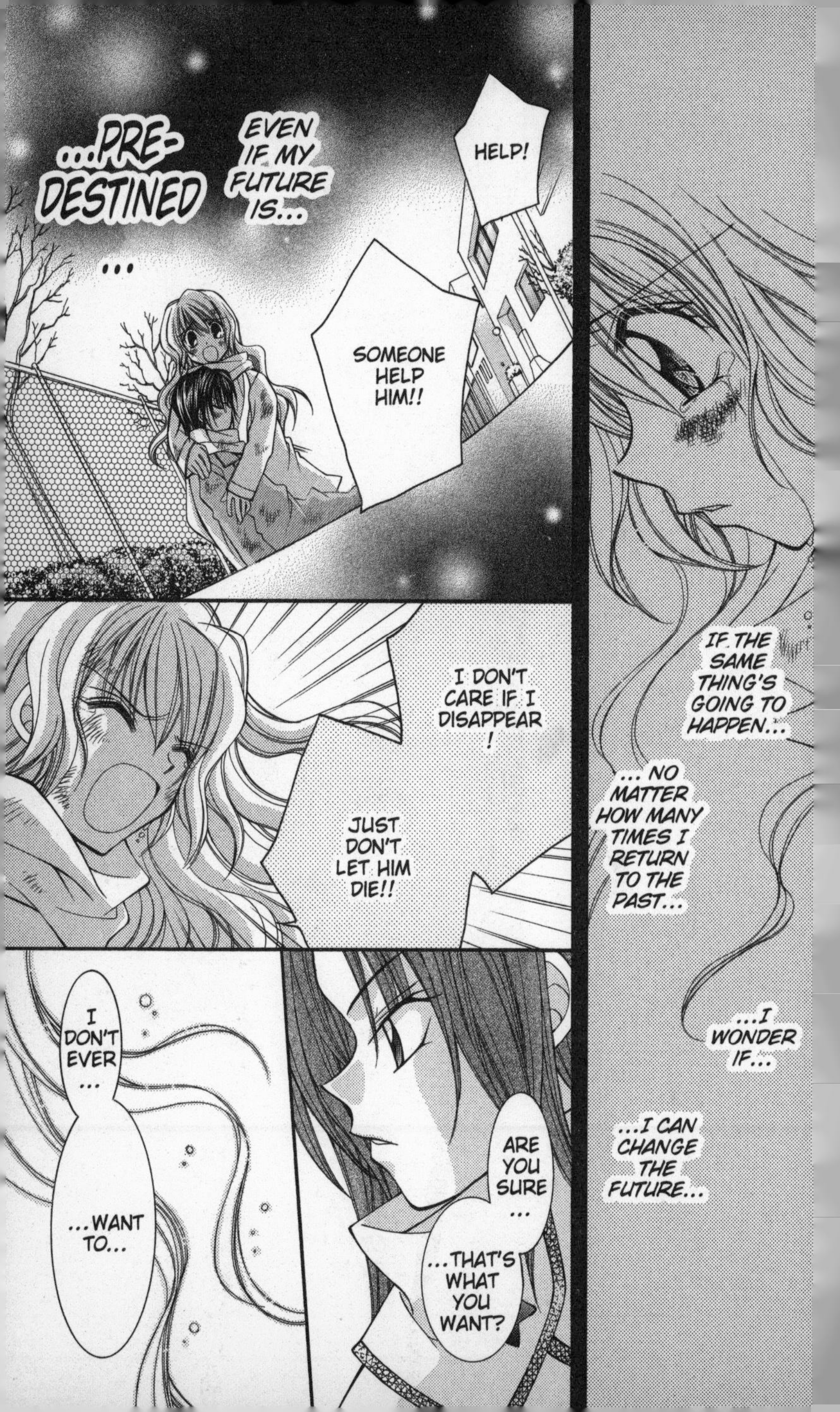
IF THE SAME THING'S GOING TO HAPPEN...
... NO MATTER HOW MANY TIMES I RETURN TO THE PAST...
...I WONDER IF...
...I CAN CHANGE THE FUTURE...
HELP!
EVEN IF MY FUTURE IS...
...PRE-DESTINED
...
SOMEONE HELP HIM!!
I DON'T CARE IF I DISAPPEAR!
JUST DON'T LET HIM DIE!!
ARE YOU SURE...
...THAT'S WHAT YOU WANT?
I DON'T EVER...
...WANT TO...

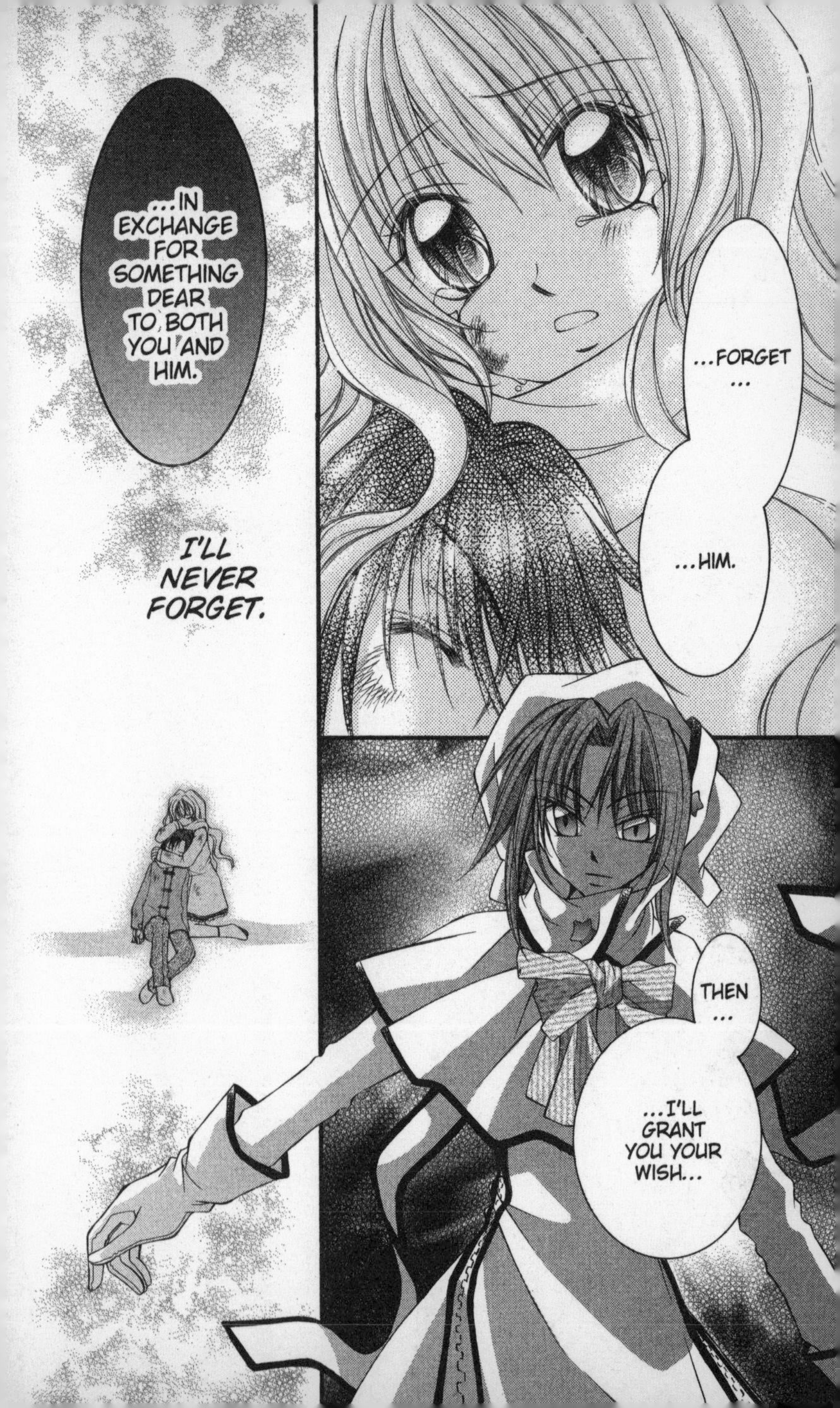
...FORGET ...
...HIM.
THEN ...
...I'LL GRANT YOU YOUR WISH...
...IN EXCHANGE FOR SOMETHING DEAR TO BOTH YOU AND HIM.
I'LL NEVER FORGET.

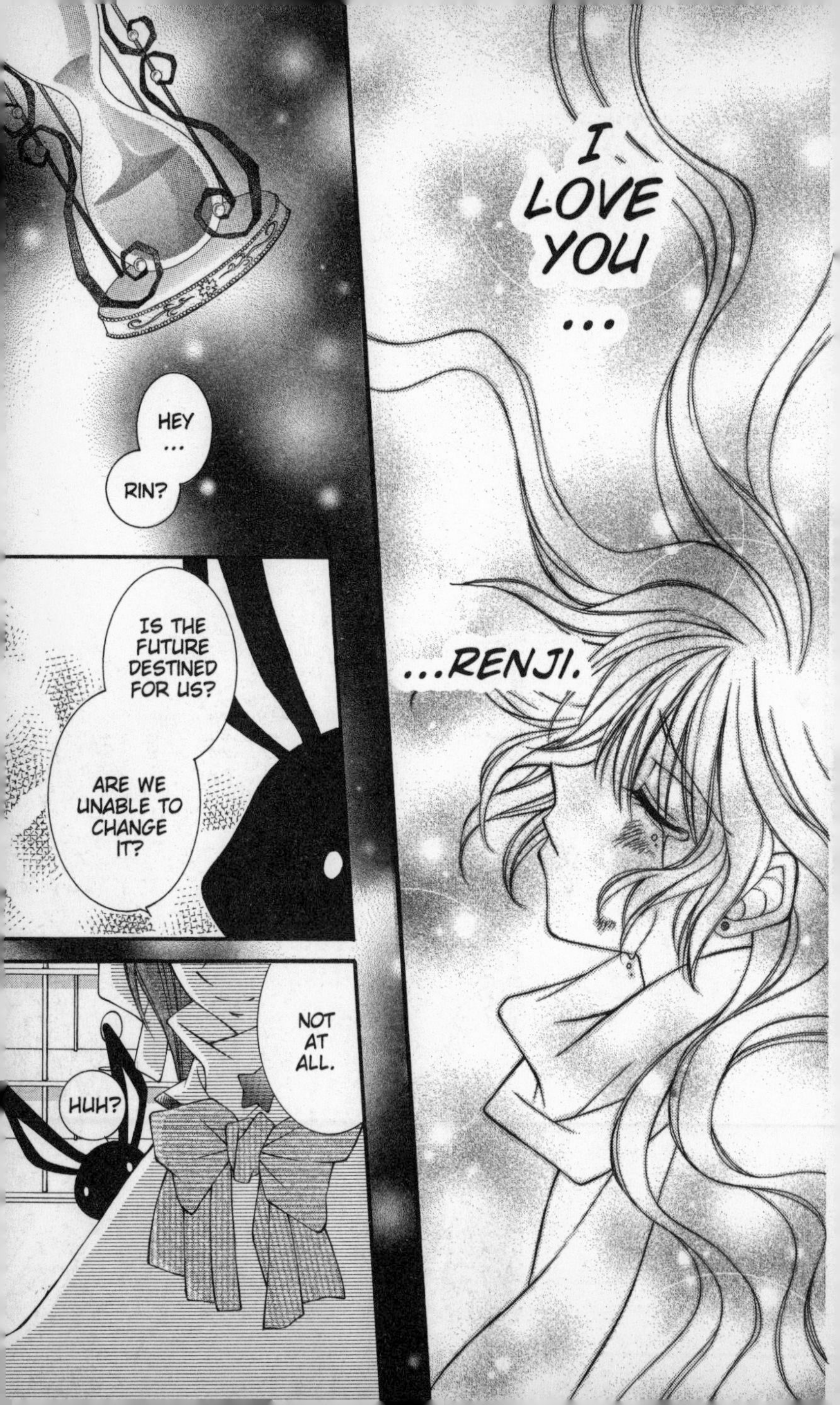
I LOVE YOU ...
...RENJI.
HEY ... RIN?
IS THE FUTURE DESTINED FOR US?
ARE WE UNABLE TO CHANGE IT?
NOT AT ALL.
HUH?

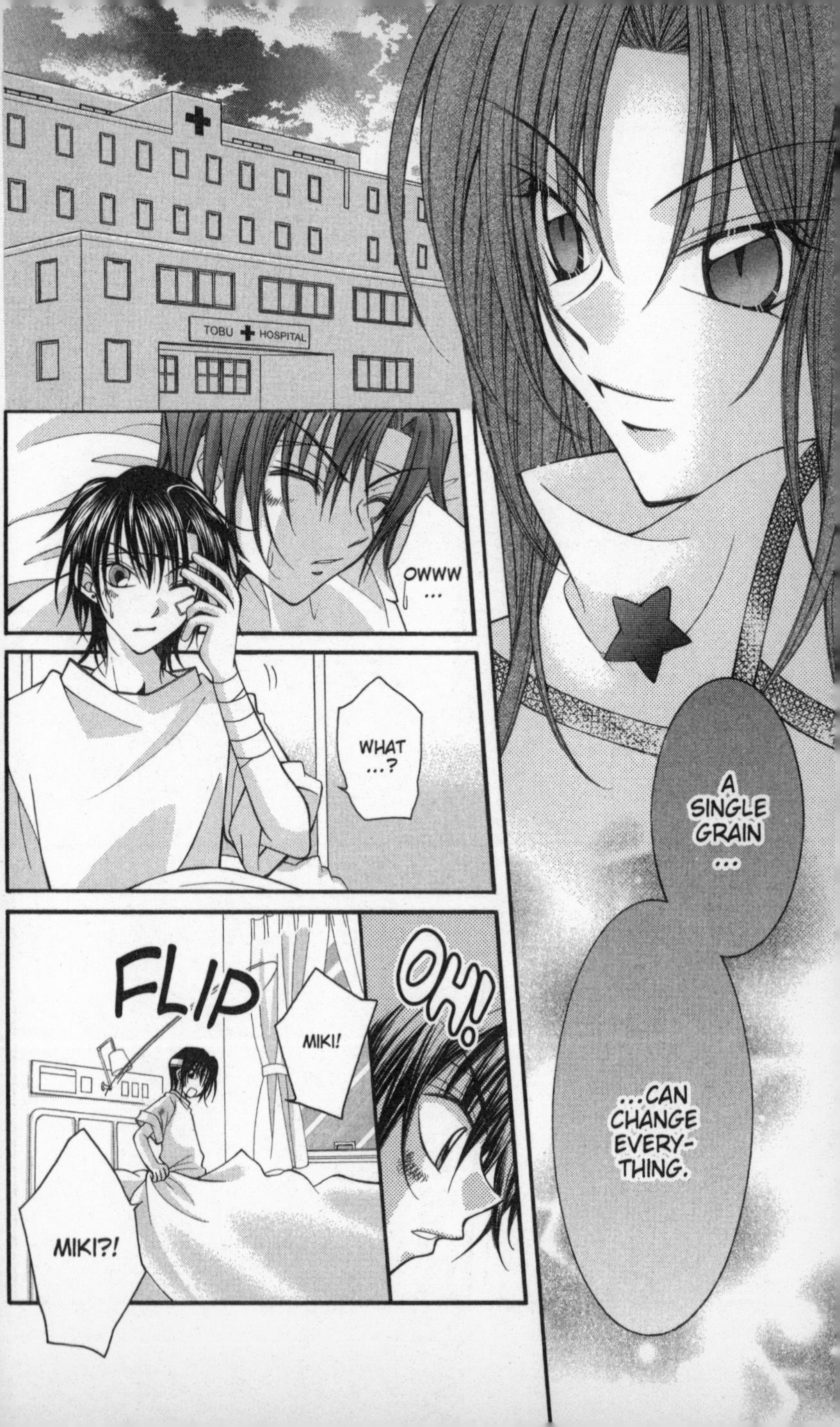
A SINGLE GRAIN ...
...CAN CHANGE EVERY-THING.
TOBU HOSPITAL
OWWW ...
WHAT ...?
OH!
MIKI!
FLIP
MIKI?!

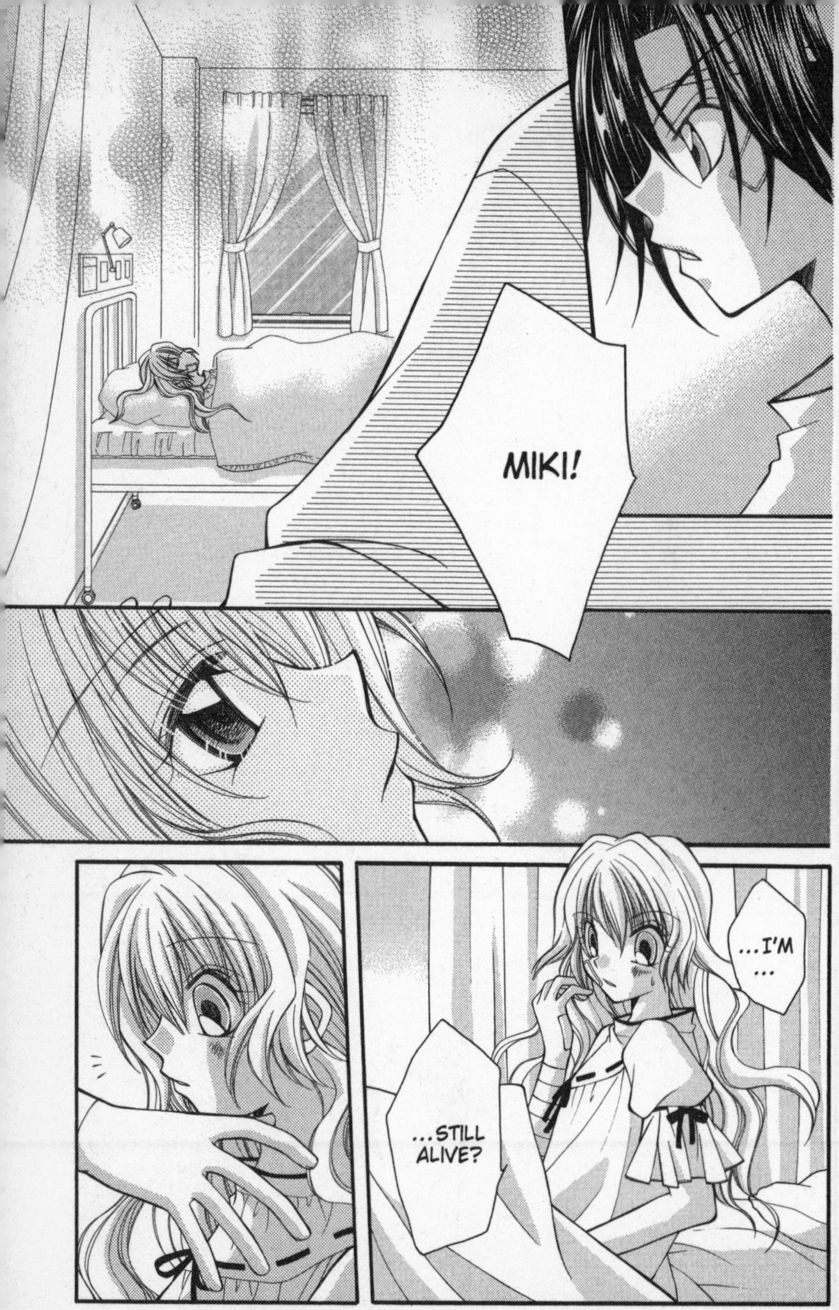
MIKI!
...I'M ...
...STILL ALIVE?

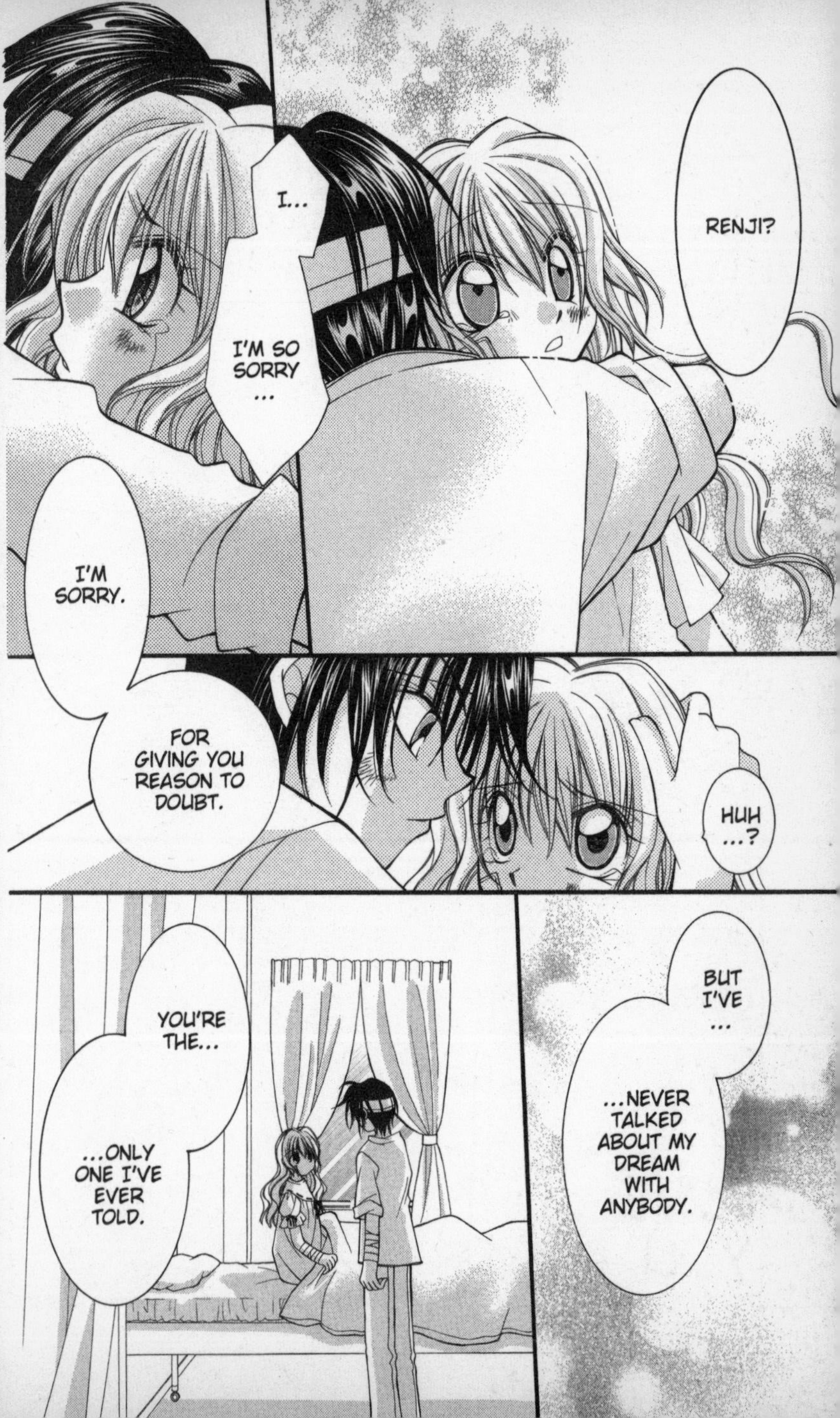
RENJI?
I...
I'M SO SORRY ...
I'M SORRY.
FOR GIVING YOU REASON TO DOUBT.
HUH ...?
BUT I'VE ...
...NEVER TALKED ABOUT MY DREAM WITH ANYBODY.
YOU'RE THE...
...ONLY ONE I'VE EVER TOLD.

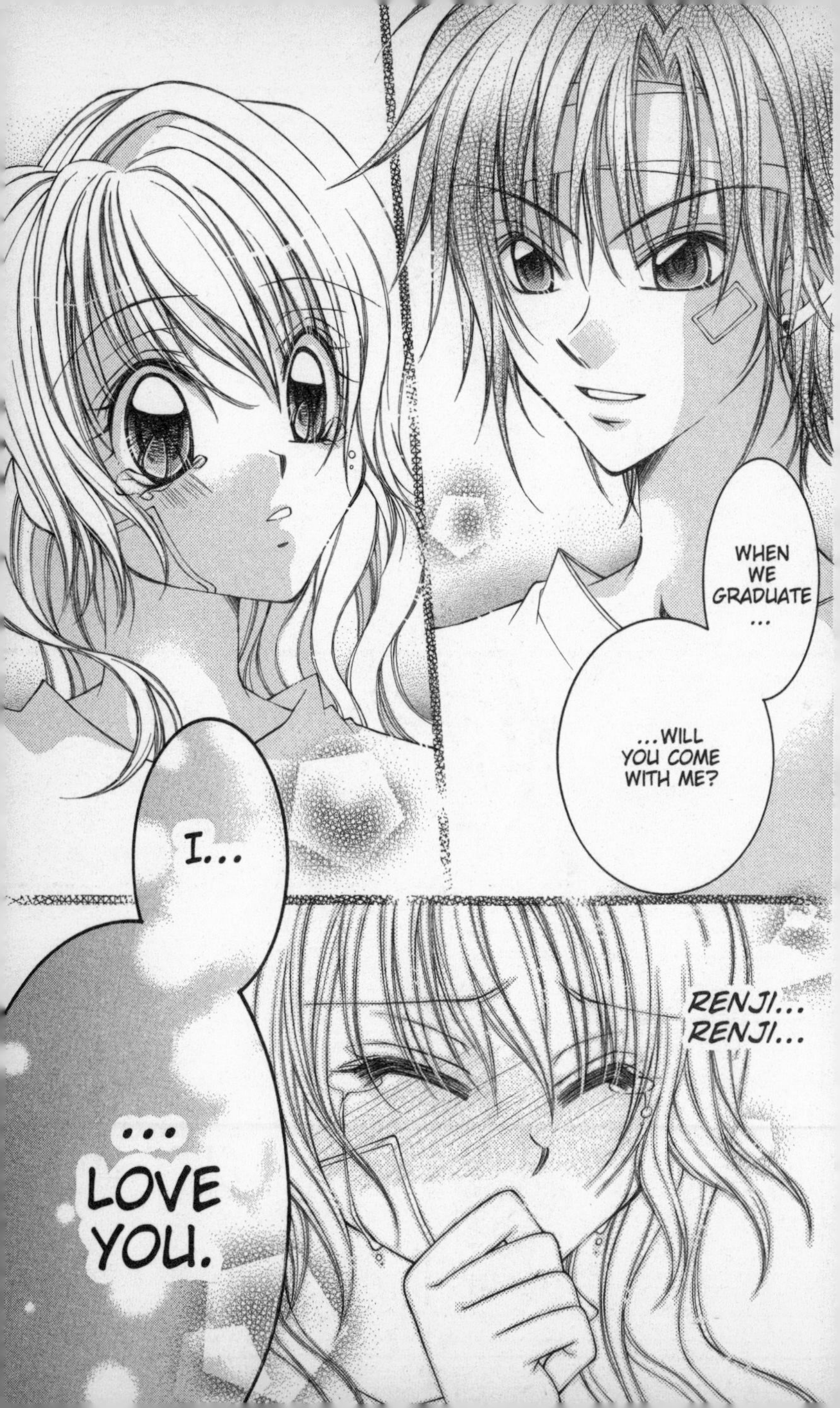
WHEN WE GRADUATE...
...WILL YOU COME WITH ME?
I...
RENJI... RENJI...
...LOVE YOU.

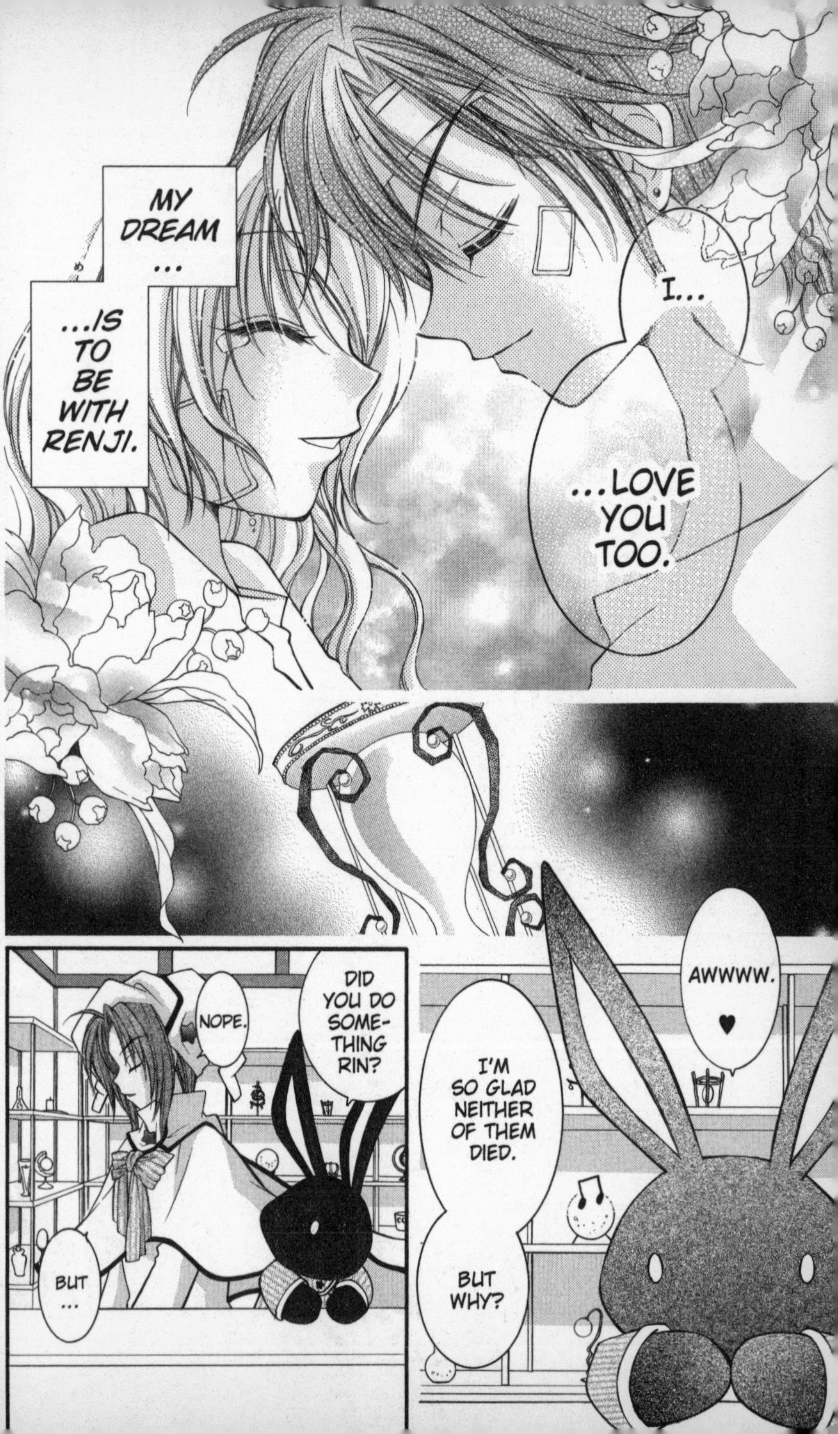
I...
...LOVE YOU TOO.
MY DREAM ...
...IS TO BE WITH RENJI.
AWWWW. ♥
I'M SO GLAD NEITHER OF THEM DIED.
BUT WHY?
DID YOU DO SOME-THING RIN?
NOPE.
BUT ...

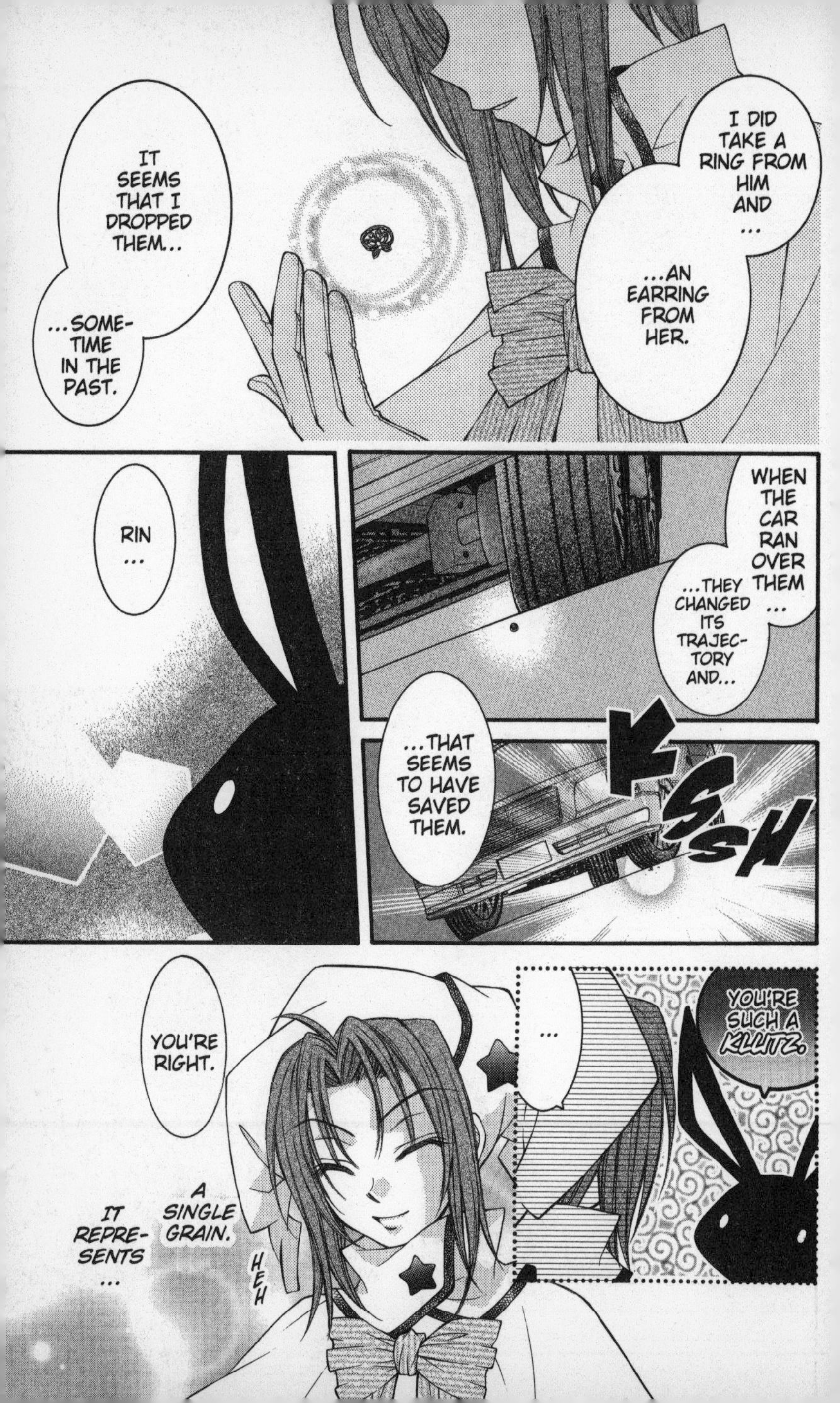
I DID TAKE A RING FROM HIM AND ...
...AN EARRING FROM HER.
IT SEEMS THAT I DROPPED THEM...
...SOME-TIME IN THE PAST.
WHEN THE CAR RAN OVER THEM ...
...THEY CHANGED ITS TRAJEC-TORY AND...
KSSH
...THAT SEEMS TO HAVE SAVED THEM.
RIN ...
YOU'RE SUCH A KLUTZ.
...
YOU'RE RIGHT.
A SINGLE GRAIN.
IT REPRE-SENTS ...
HEH

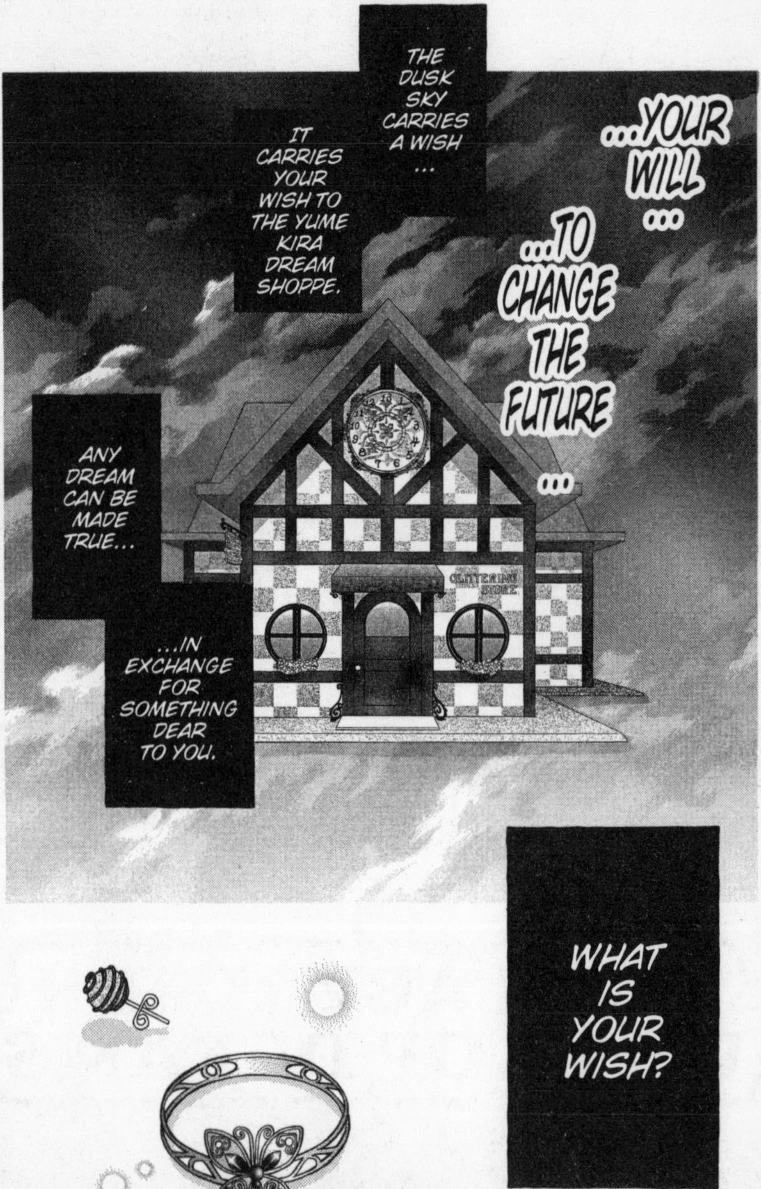
THE DUSK SKY CARRIES A WISH...
...YOUR WILL...
...TO CHANGE THE FUTURE...
IT CARRIES YOUR WISH TO THE YUME KIRA DREAM SHOPPE.
GLITTERING STORE
ANY DREAM CAN BE MADE TRUE...
...IN EXCHANGE FOR SOMETHING DEAR TO YOU.
WHAT IS YOUR WISH?

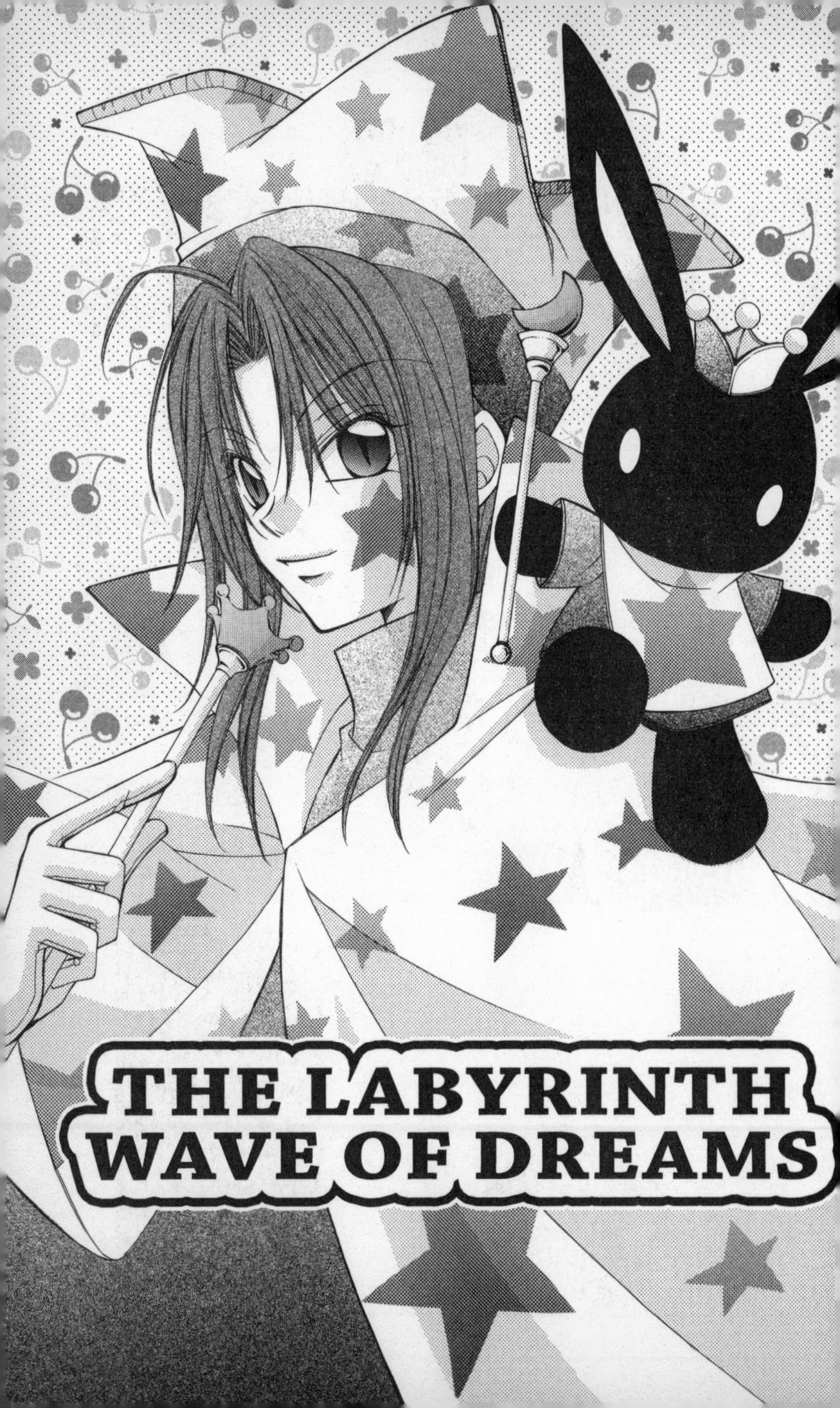
THE LABYRINTH
WAVE OF DREAMS

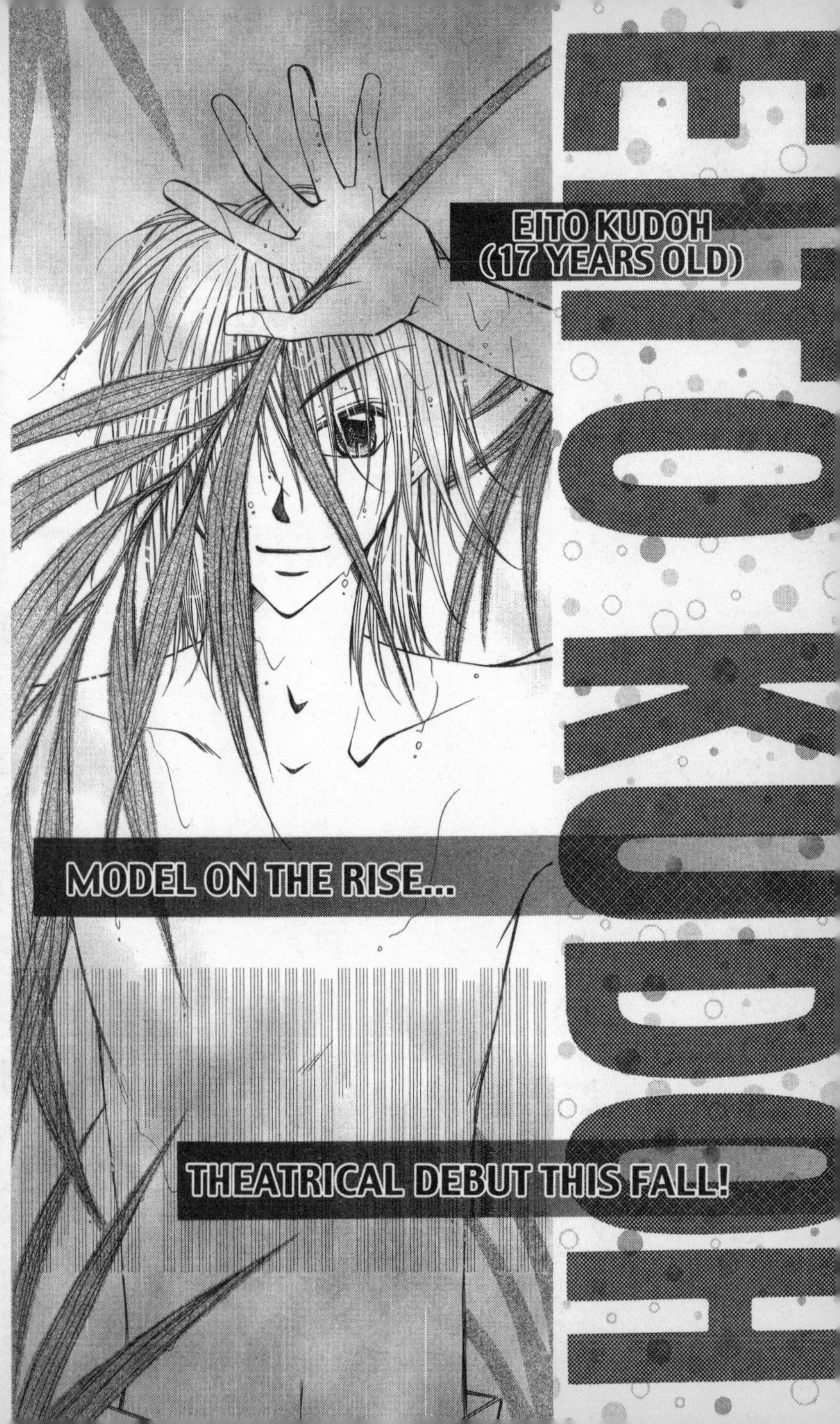
EITO KUDOH
EITO KUDOH
(17 YEARS OLD)
MODEL ON THE RISE...
THEATRICAL DEBUT THIS FALL!

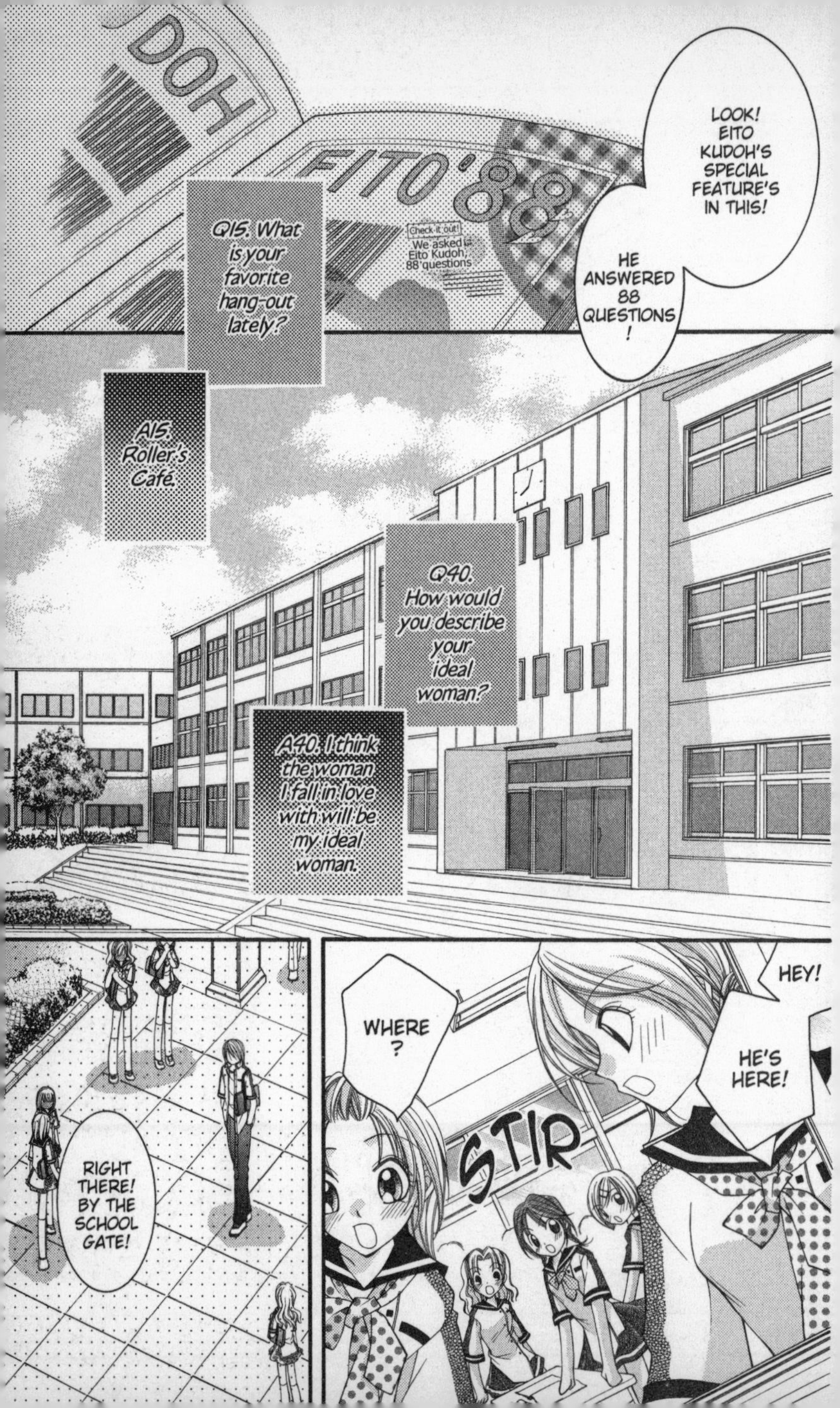
DOH
EITO '88
Check it out!
We asked Eito Kudoh 88 questions
LOOK! EITO KUDOH'S SPECIAL FEATURE'S IN THIS!
HE ANSWERED 88 QUESTIONS!
Q15. What is your favorite hang-out lately?
A15. Roller's Café.
Q40. How would you describe your ideal woman?
A40. I think the woman I fall in love with will be my ideal woman.
HEY!
HE'S HERE!
WHERE?
STIR
RIGHT THERE! BY THE SCHOOL GATE!

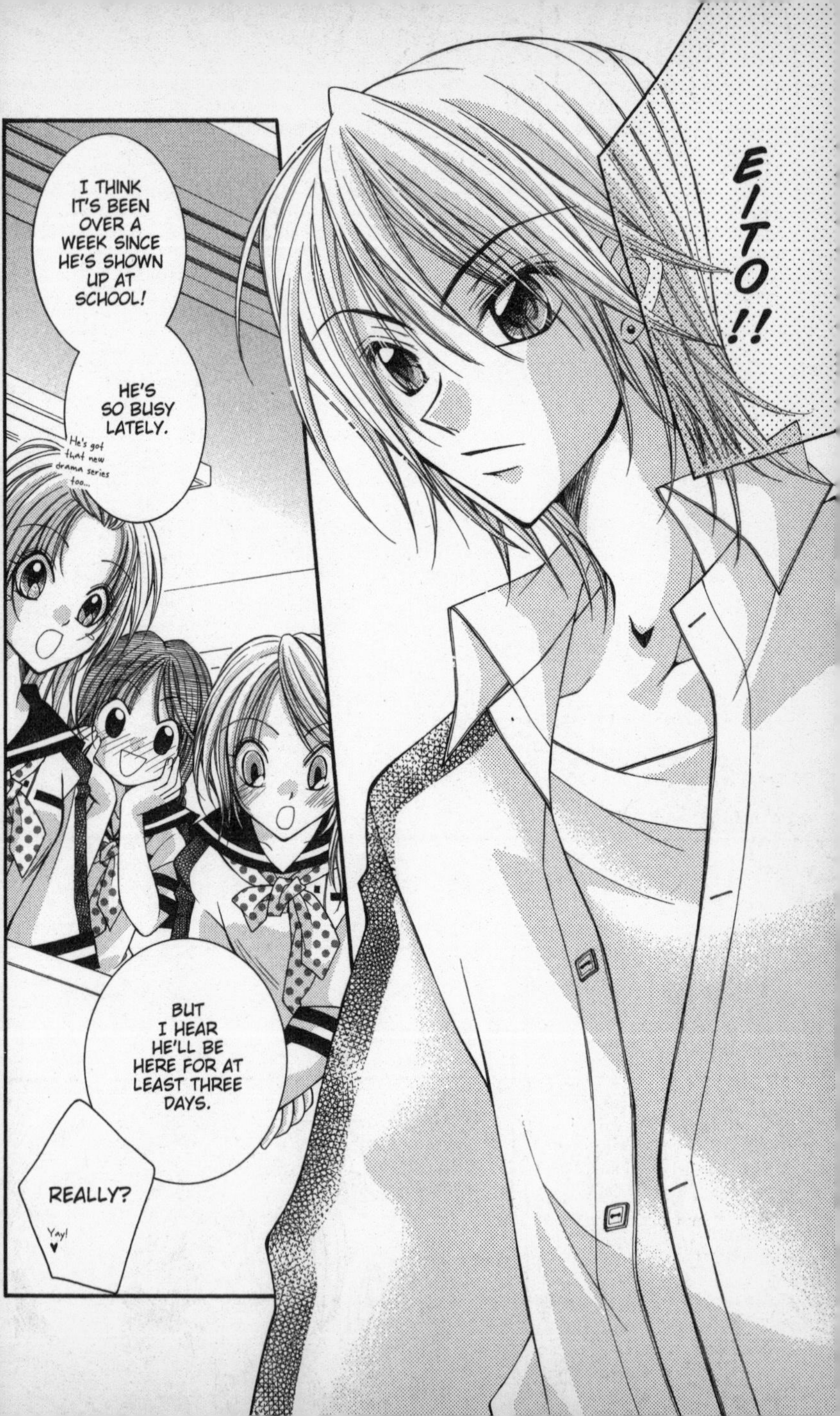
EITO!!
I THINK IT'S BEEN OVER A WEEK SINCE HE'S SHOWN UP AT SCHOOL!
HE'S SO BUSY LATELY.
He's got that new drama series too...
BUT I HEAR HE'LL BE HERE FOR AT LEAST THREE DAYS.
REALLY?
Yay! ♥

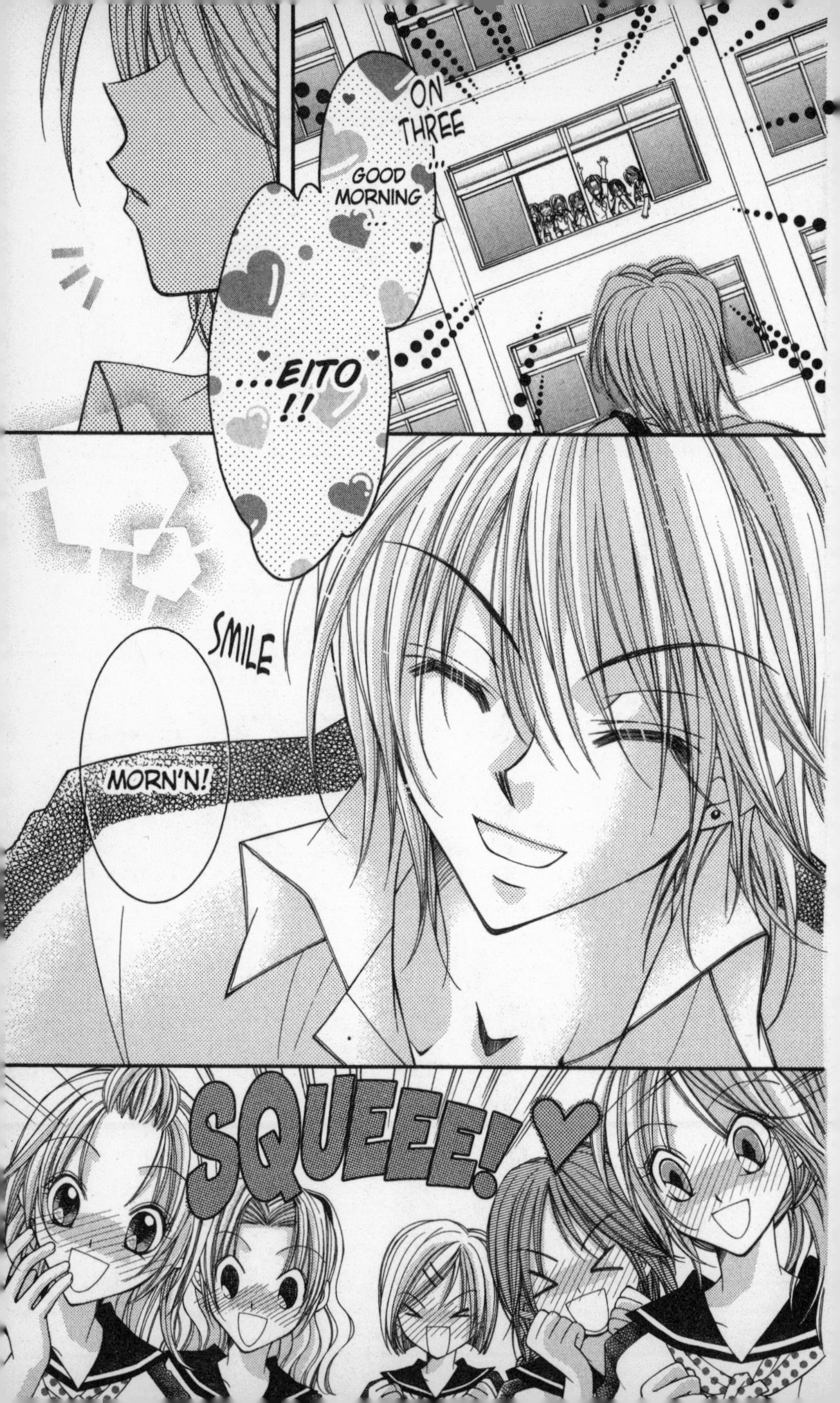
ON THREE ...
GOOD MORNING ...
...EITO !!
SMILE
MORN'N!
SQUEEE!

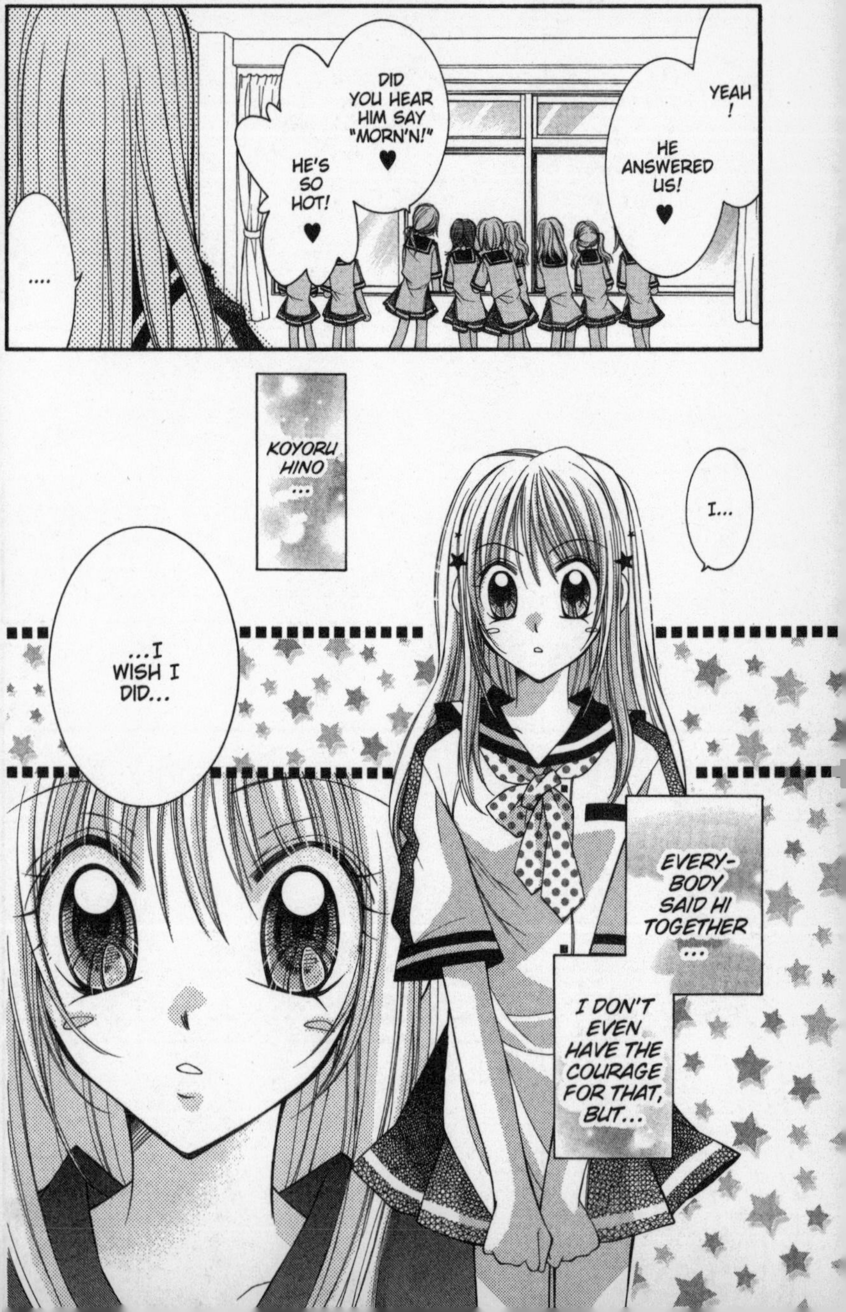
YEAH! HE ANSWERED US! ♥
DID YOU HEAR HIM SAY "MORN'N!" ♥
HE'S SO HOT! ♥
....
I...
KOYORU HINO ...
EVERY-BODY SAID HI TOGETHER ...
I DON'T EVEN HAVE THE COURAGE FOR THAT, BUT...
...I WISH I DID...

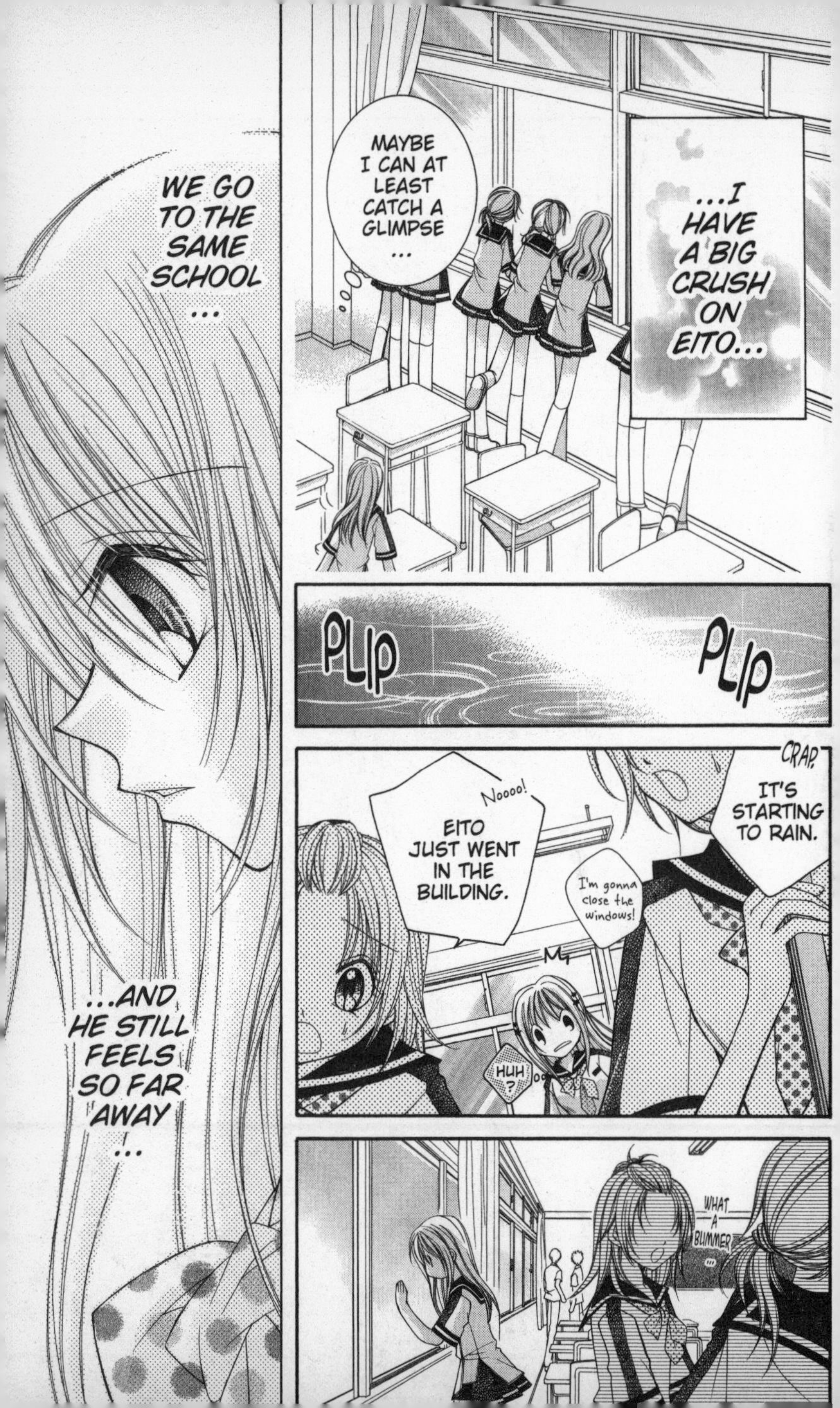

...I HAVE A BIG CRUSH ON EITO...
MAYBE I CAN AT LEAST CATCH A GLIMPSE ...
PLIP
PLIP
CRAP.
IT'S STARTING TO RAIN.
I'm gonna close the windows!
Noooo!
EITO JUST WENT IN THE BUILDING.
HUH?
WHAT A BUMMER ...
WE GO TO THE SAME SCHOOL ...
...AND HE STILL FEELS SO FAR AWAY ...

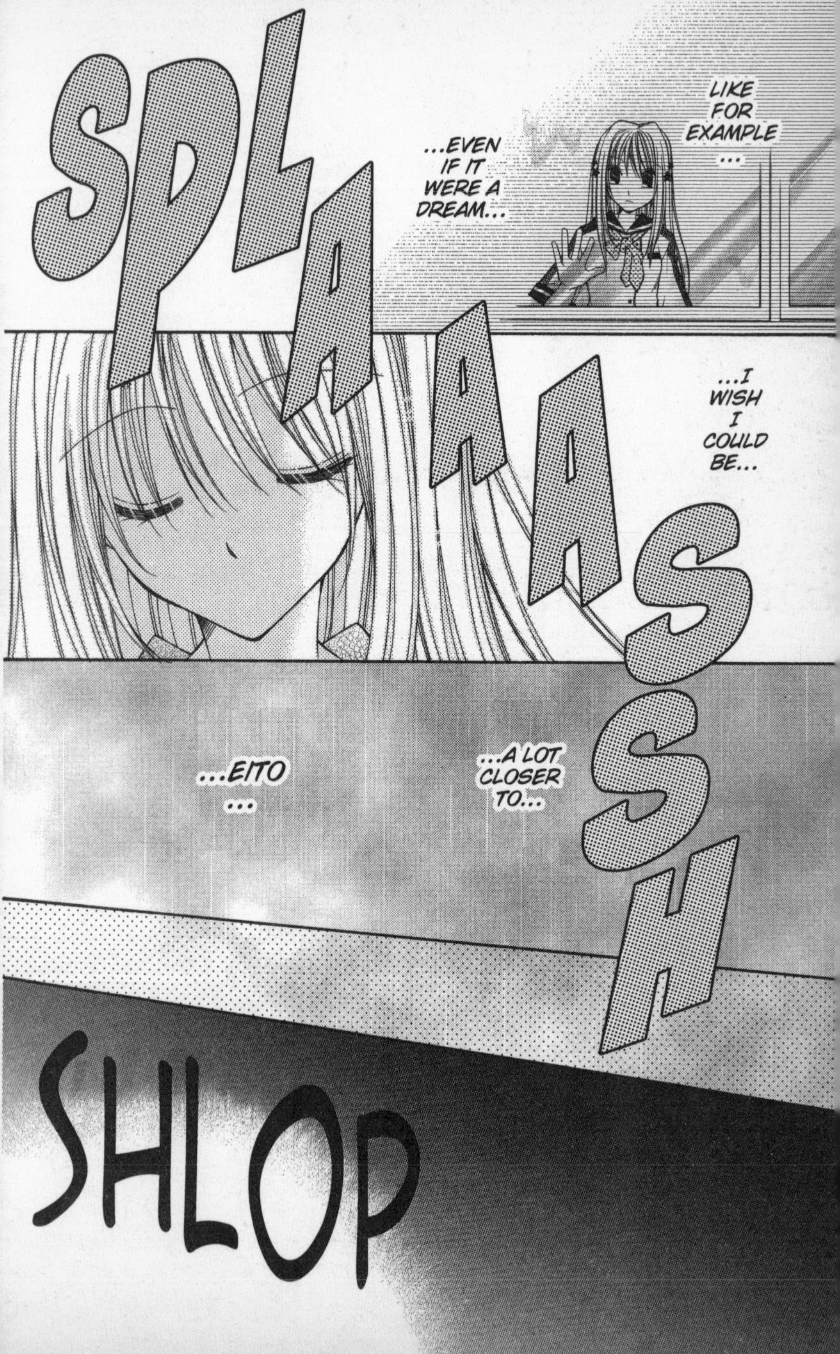
LIKE FOR EXAMPLE...
...EVEN IF IT WERE A DREAM...
SPLAAASH
...I WISH I COULD BE...
...A LOT CLOSER TO...
...EITO...
SHLOP

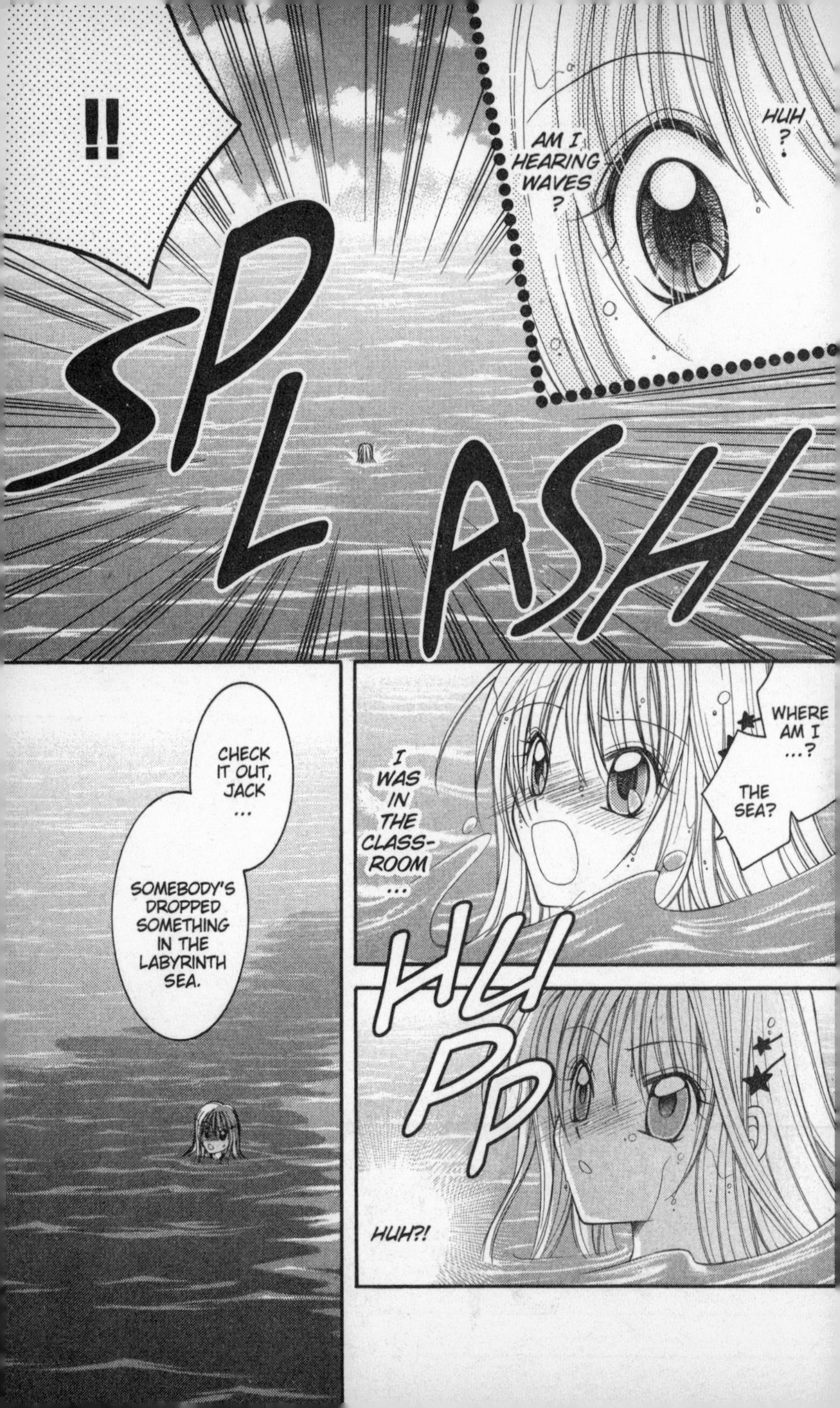
HUH?
AM I HEARING WAVES?
!!
SPLASH
WHERE AM I ...?
THE SEA?
I WAS IN THE CLASS-ROOM ...
HUPP
HUH?!
CHECK IT OUT, JACK ...
SOMEBODY'S DROPPED SOMETHING IN THE LABYRINTH SEA.

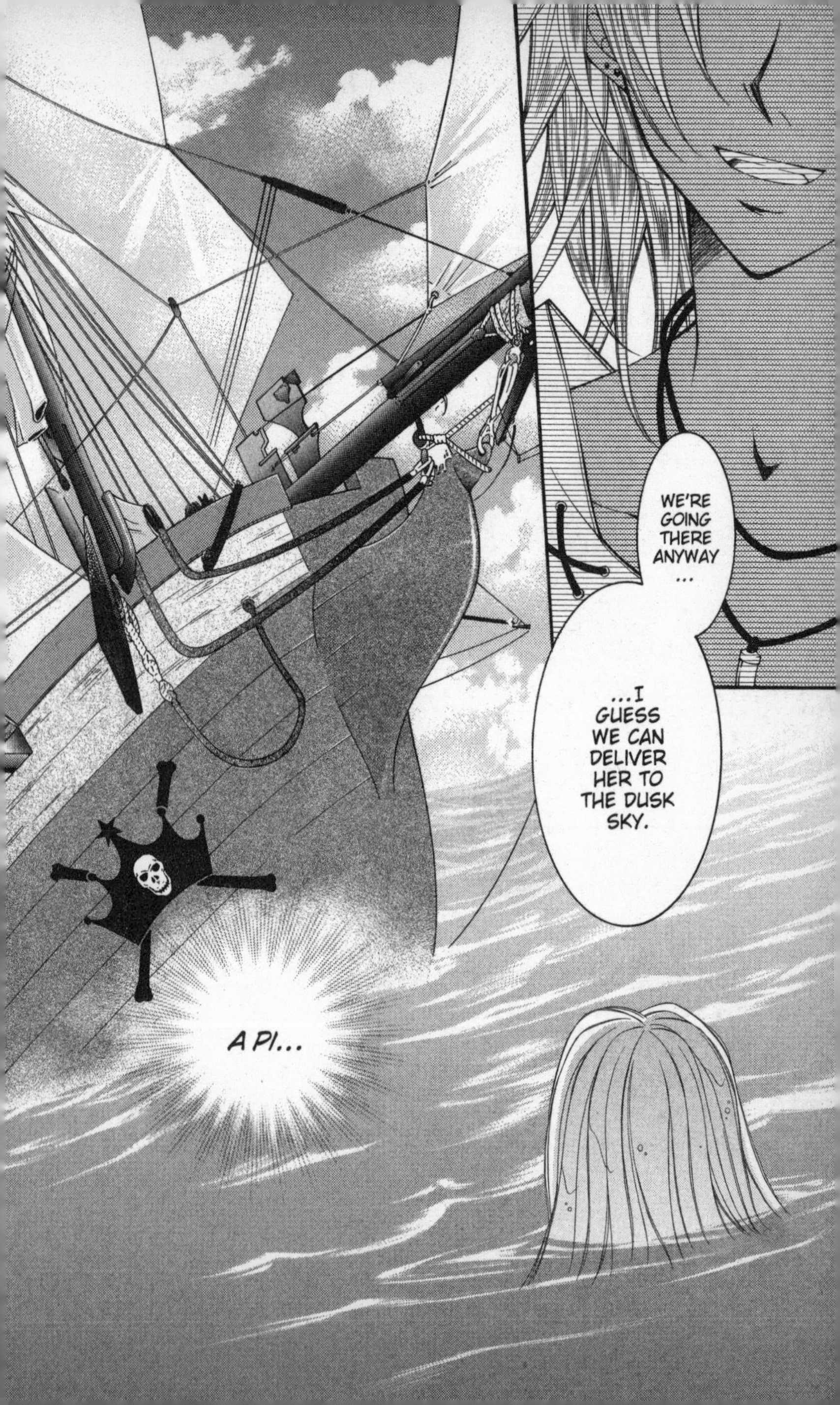
WE'RE GOING THERE ANYWAY ...
...I GUESS WE CAN DELIVER HER TO THE DUSK SKY.
A PI...

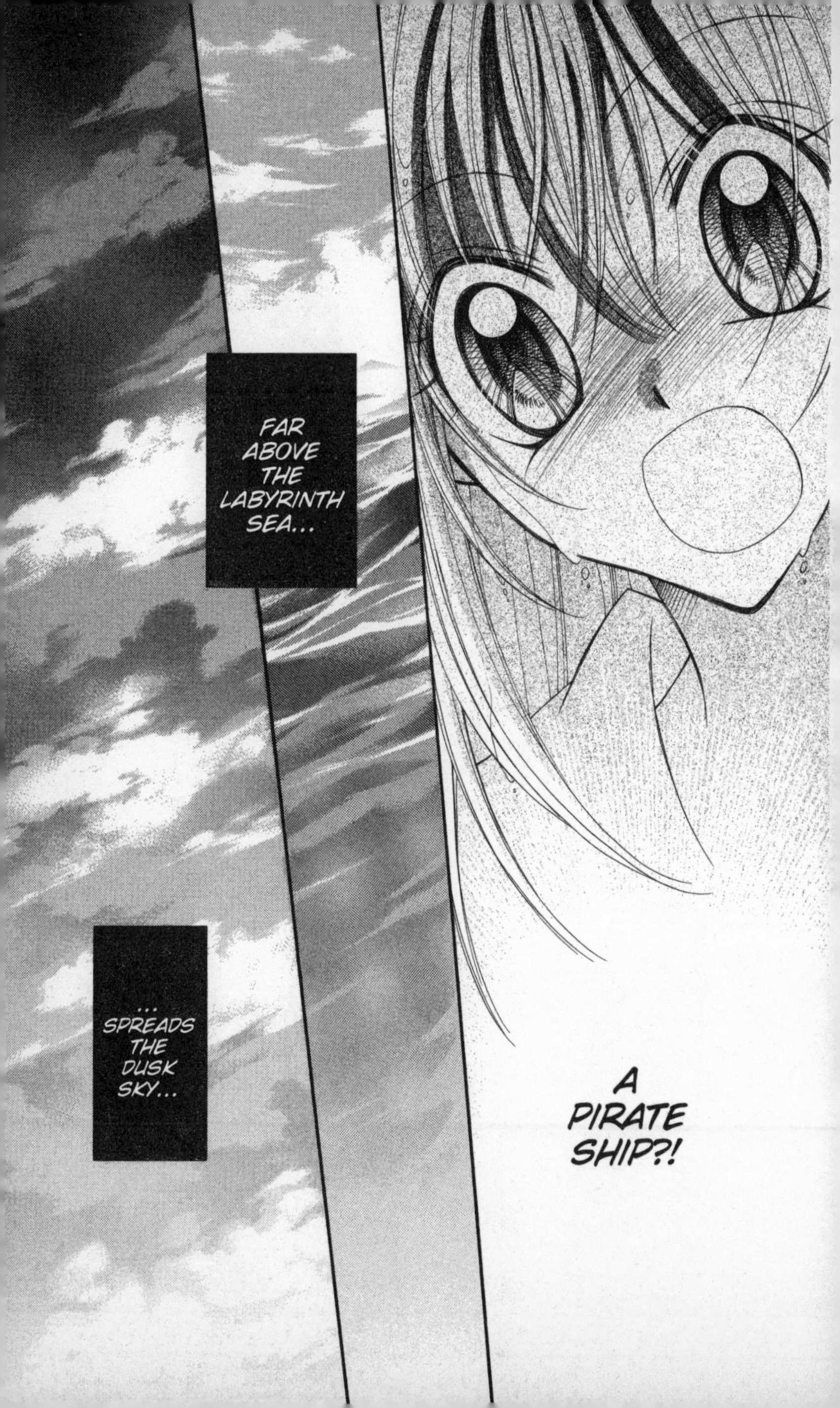
A PIRATE SHIP?!
FAR ABOVE THE LABYRINTH SEA...
...SPREADS THE DUSK SKY...

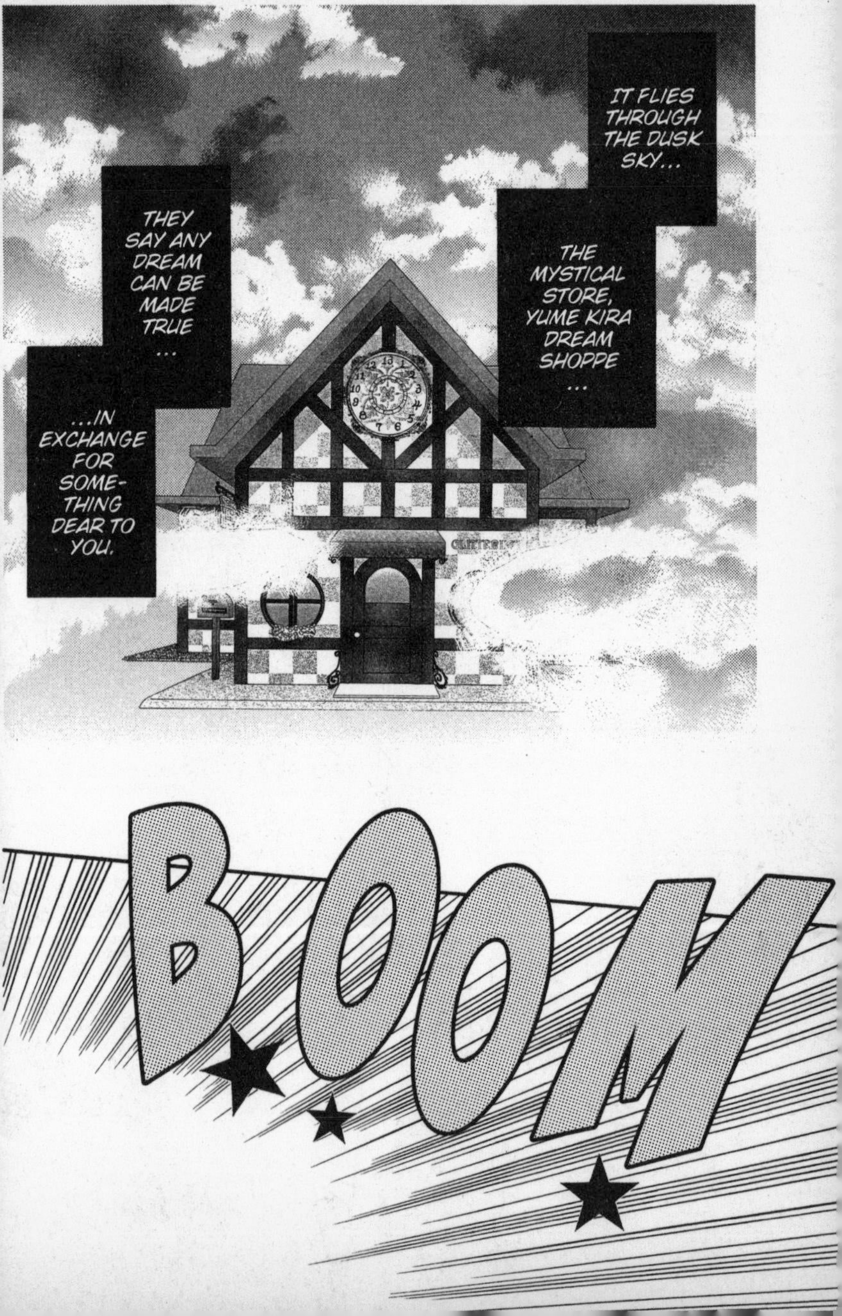
IT FLIES THROUGH THE DUSK SKY...
THE MYSTICAL STORE, YUME KIRA DREAM SHOPPE...
THEY SAY ANY DREAM CAN BE MADE TRUE...
...IN EXCHANGE FOR SOME-THING DEAR TO YOU.
BOOM

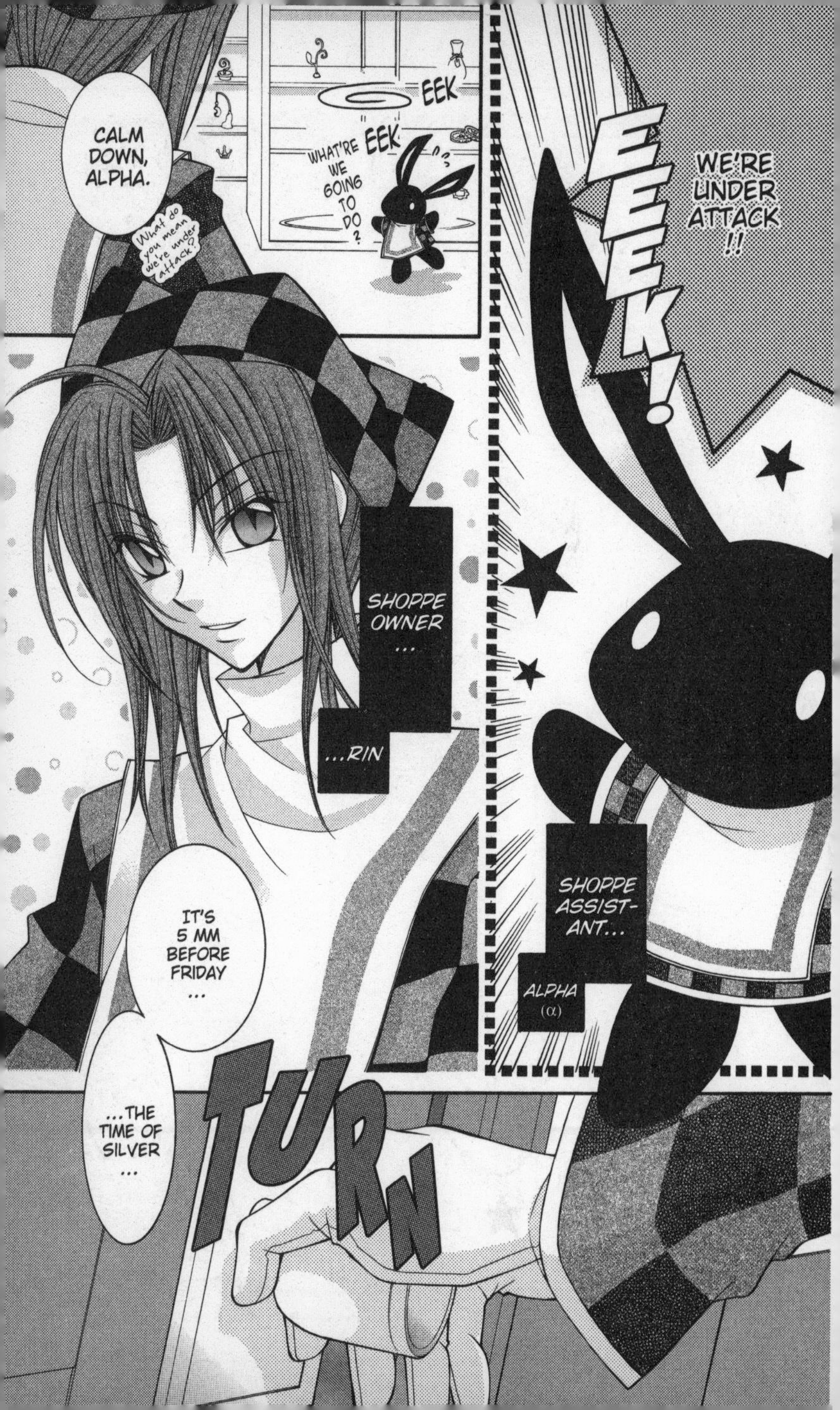
EEEK!
WE'RE UNDER ATTACK!!
SHOPPE ASSISTANT...
ALPHA (α)
EEK
EEK
WHAT'RE WE GOING TO DO?
What do you mean we're under attack?
CALM DOWN, ALPHA.
SHOPPE OWNER...
...RIN
IT'S 5 MM BEFORE FRIDAY...
...THE TIME OF SILVER...
TURN

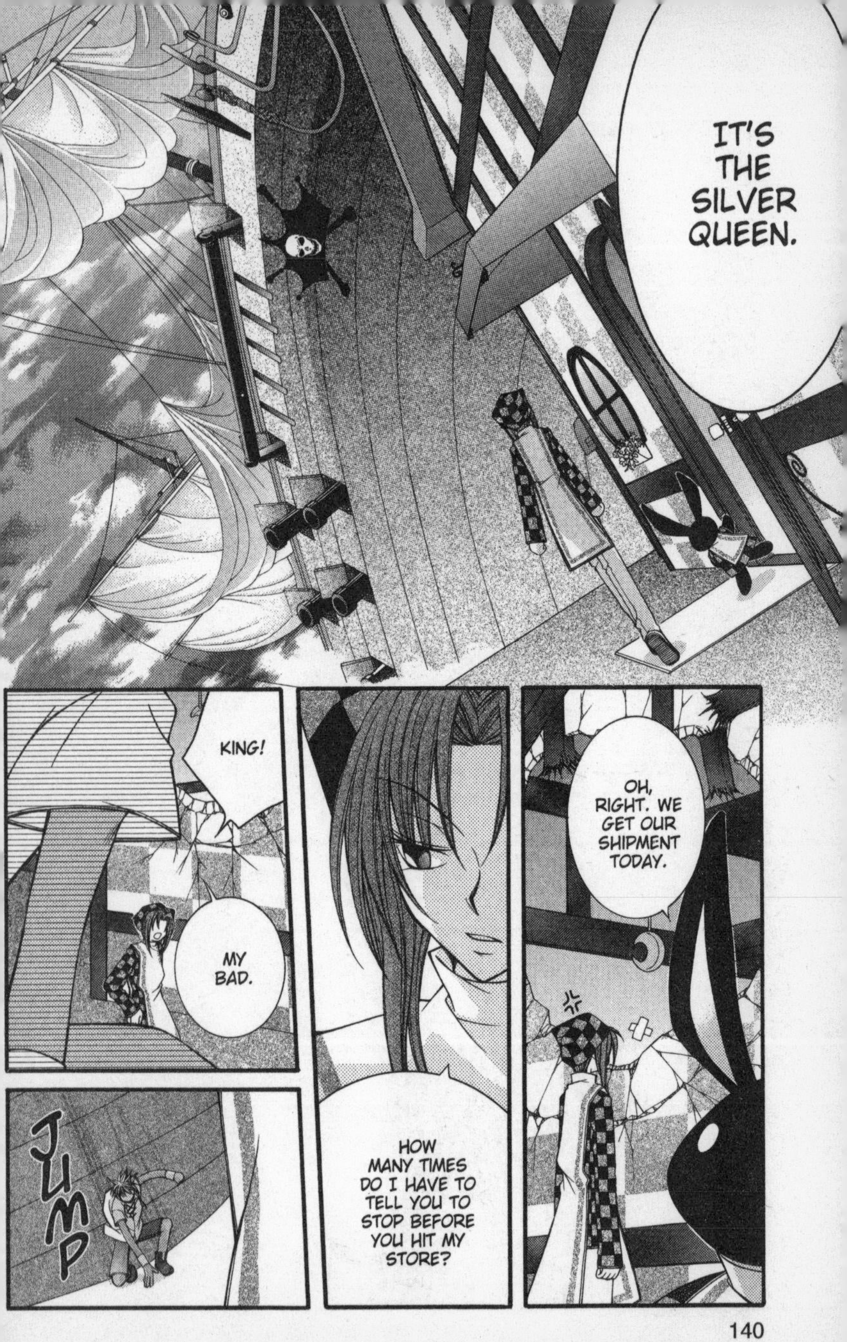
IT'S THE SILVER QUEEN.
OH, RIGHT. WE GET OUR SHIPMENT TODAY.
HOW MANY TIMES DO I HAVE TO TELL YOU TO STOP BEFORE YOU HIT MY STORE?
KING!
MY BAD.
JUMP

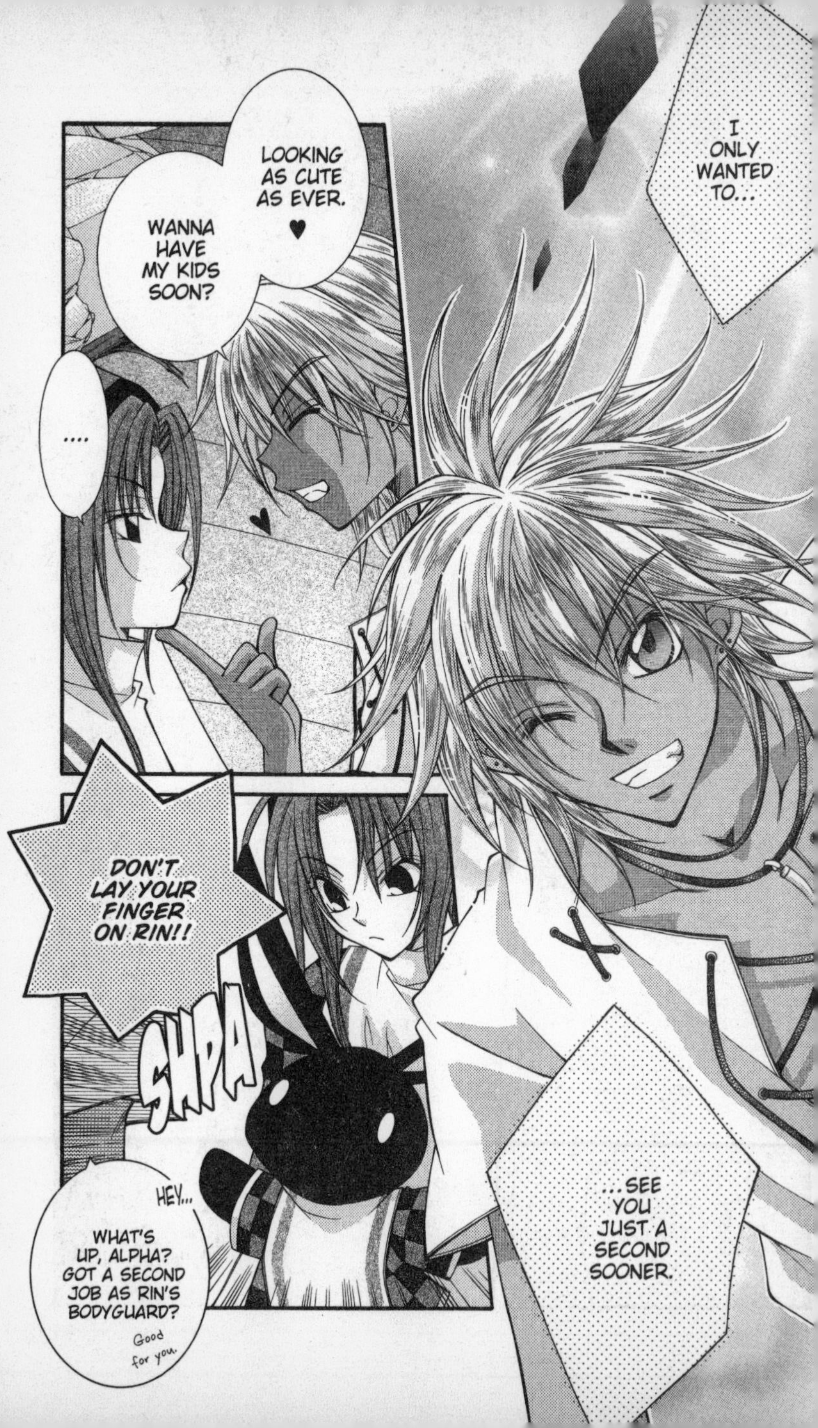

I ONLY WANTED TO...
...SEE YOU JUST A SECOND SOONER.
LOOKING AS CUTE AS EVER. ♥
WANNA HAVE MY KIDS SOON?
....
DON'T LAY YOUR FINGER ON RIN!!
SHPA
HEY...
WHAT'S UP, ALPHA? GOT A SECOND JOB AS RIN'S BODYGUARD?
Good for you.

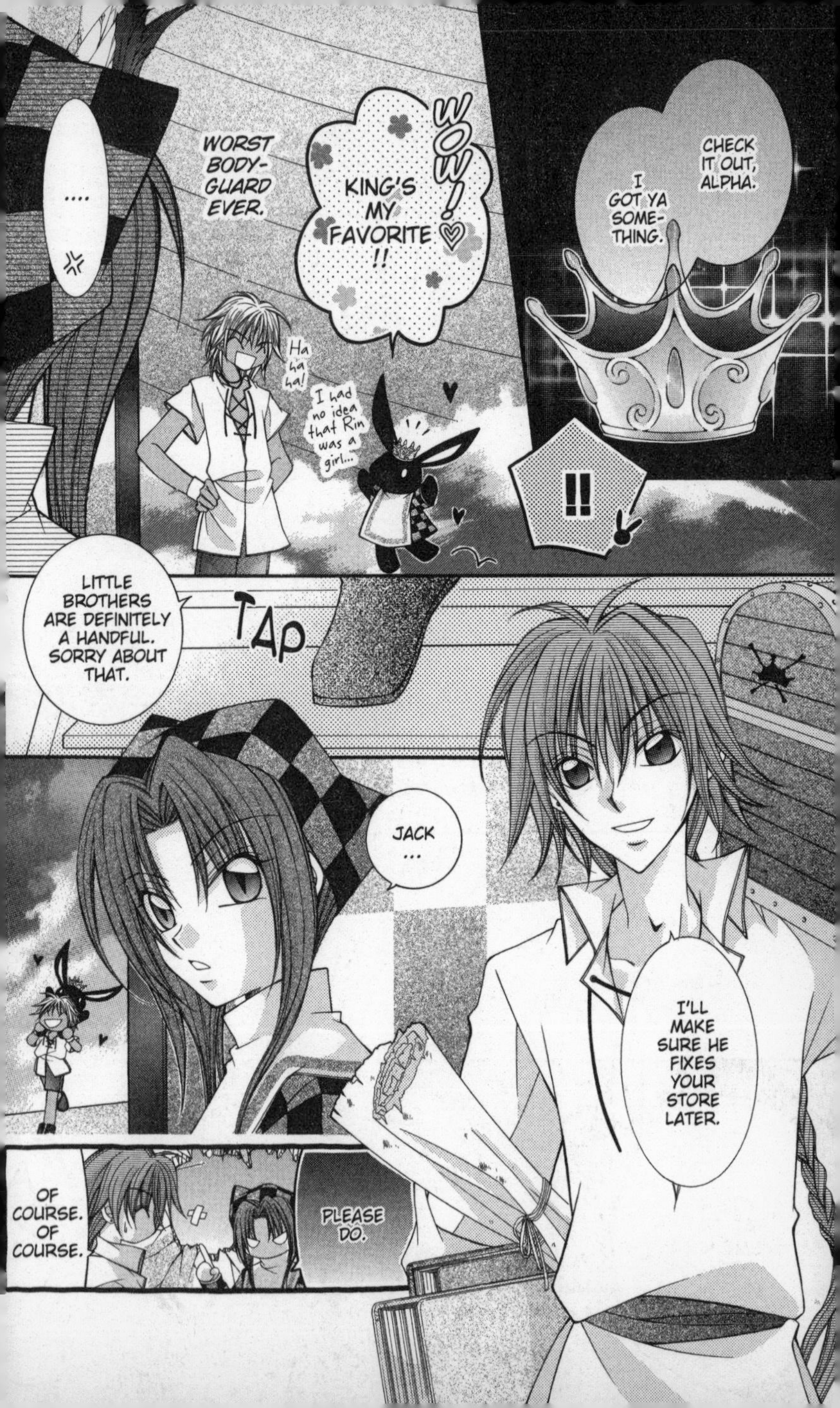
CHECK IT OUT, ALPHA.
I GOT YA SOME-THING.
!!
WOW!
KING'S MY FAVORITE!! ♡
WORST BODY-GUARD EVER.
Ha ha ha!
I had no idea that Rin was a girl...
....
TAP
LITTLE BROTHERS ARE DEFINITELY A HANDFUL. SORRY ABOUT THAT.
JACK ...
I'LL MAKE SURE HE FIXES YOUR STORE LATER.
PLEASE DO.
OF COURSE. OF COURSE.

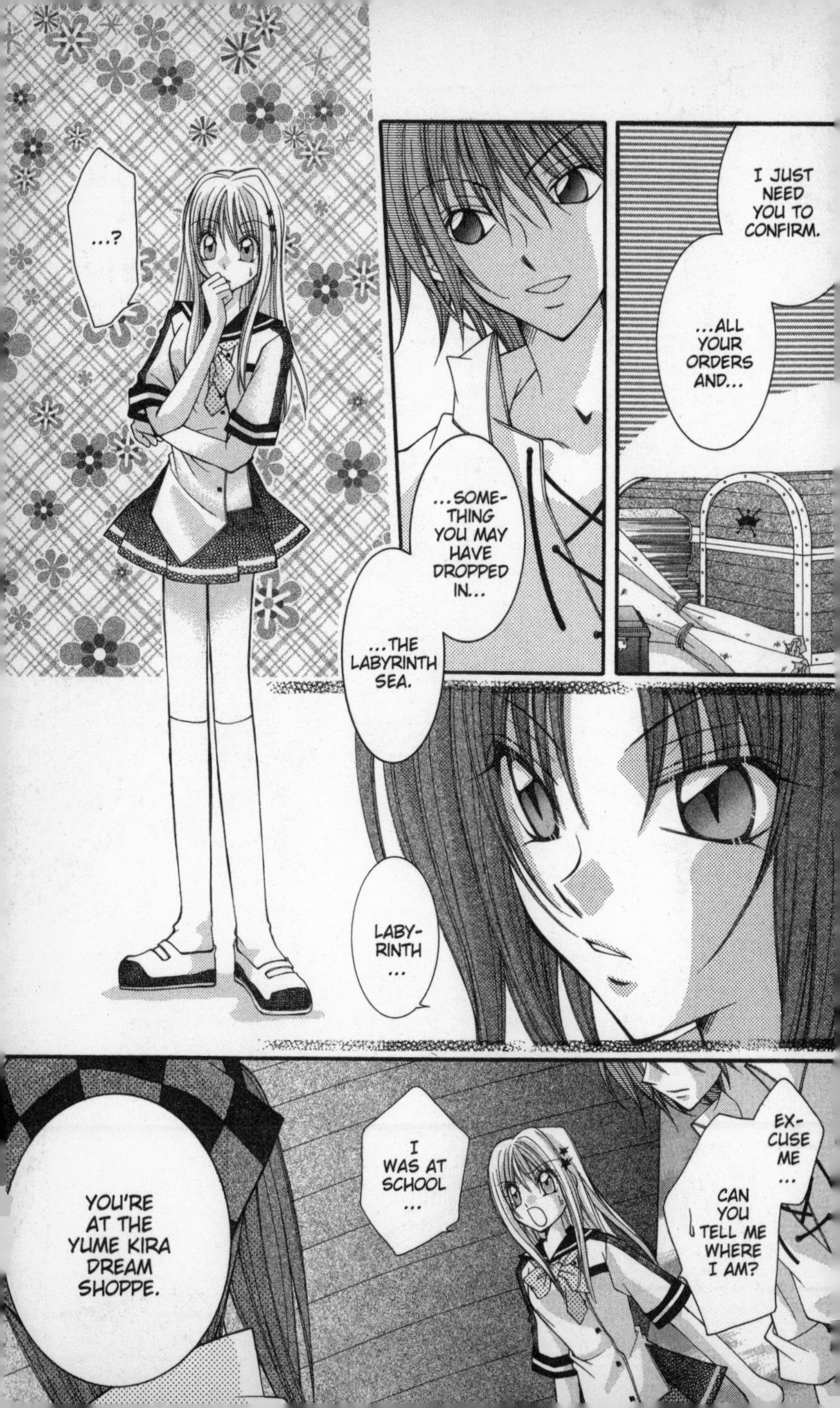
I JUST NEED YOU TO CONFIRM.
...ALL YOUR ORDERS AND...
...SOME-THING YOU MAY HAVE DROPPED IN...
...THE LABYRINTH SEA.
LABY-RINTH...
...?
EX-CUSE ME...
CAN YOU TELL ME WHERE I AM?
I WAS AT SCHOOL...
YOU'RE AT THE YUME KIRA DREAM SHOPPE.

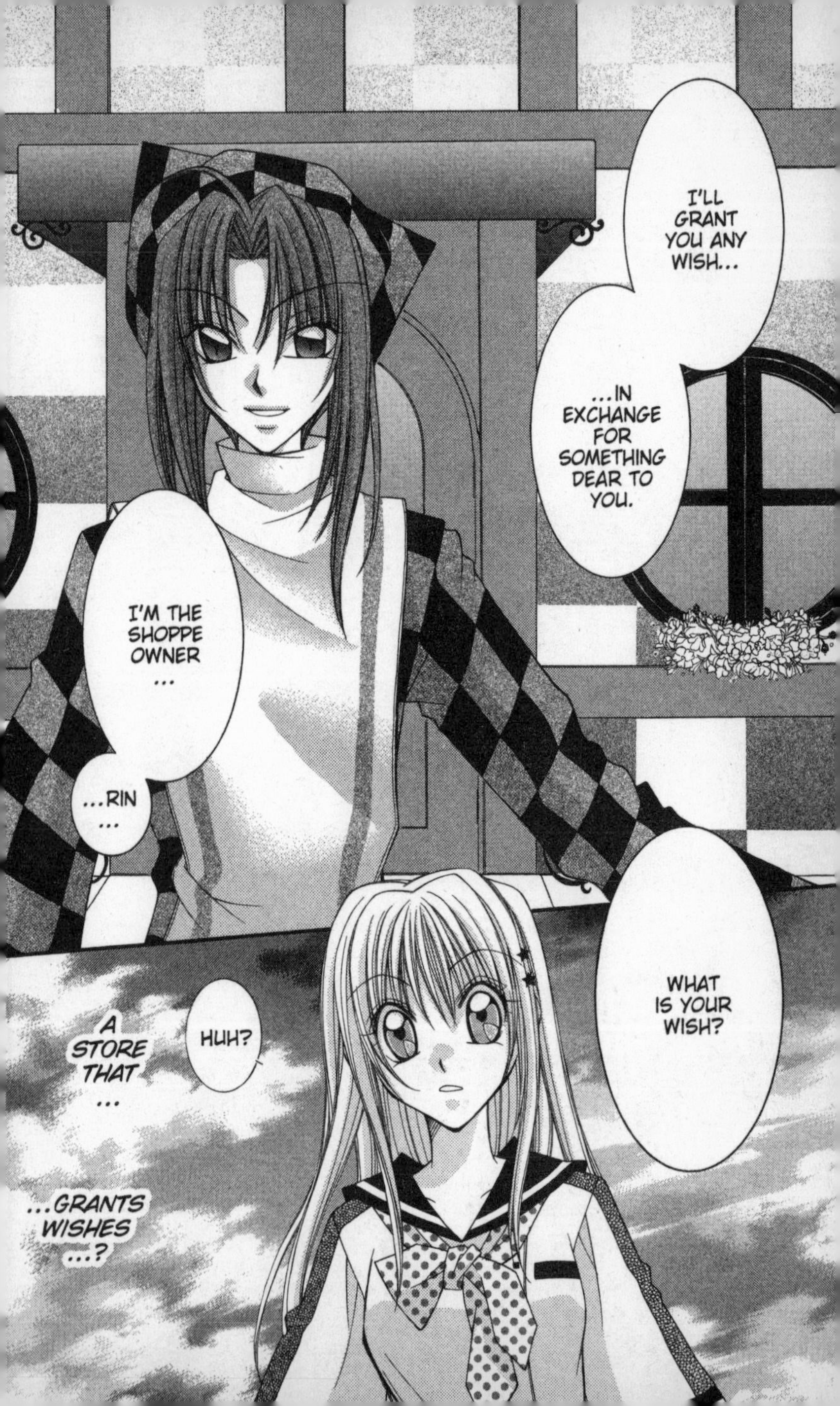
I'LL GRANT YOU ANY WISH...
...IN EXCHANGE FOR SOMETHING DEAR TO YOU.
I'M THE SHOPPE OWNER...
...RIN...
WHAT IS YOUR WISH?
HUH?
A STORE THAT...
...GRANTS WISHES...?

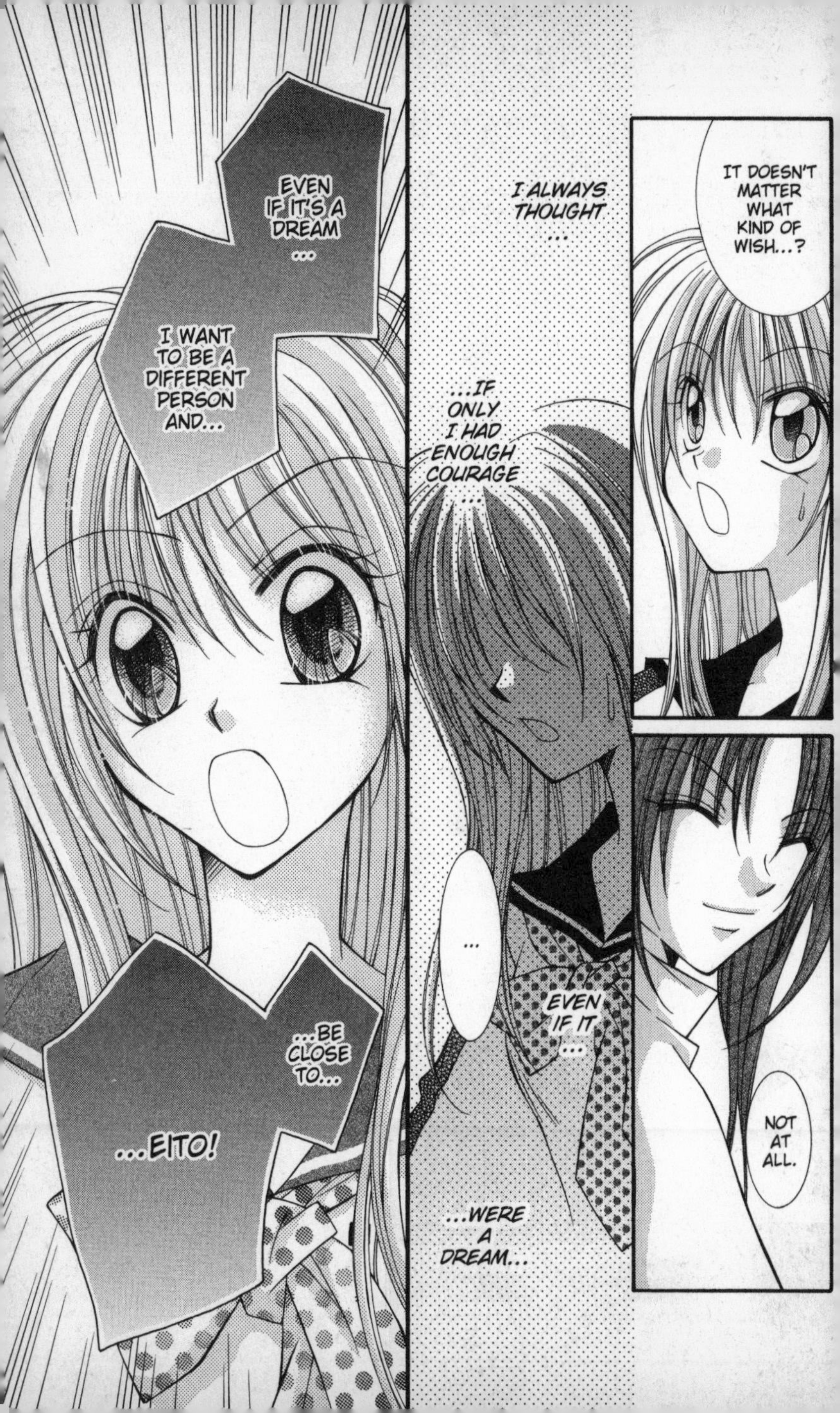
IT DOESN'T MATTER WHAT KIND OF WISH...?
NOT AT ALL.
I ALWAYS THOUGHT ...
...IF ONLY I HAD ENOUGH COURAGE ...
...
EVEN IF IT ...
...WERE A DREAM...
EVEN IF IT'S A DREAM ...
I WANT TO BE A DIFFERENT PERSON AND...
...BE CLOSE TO...
...EITO!

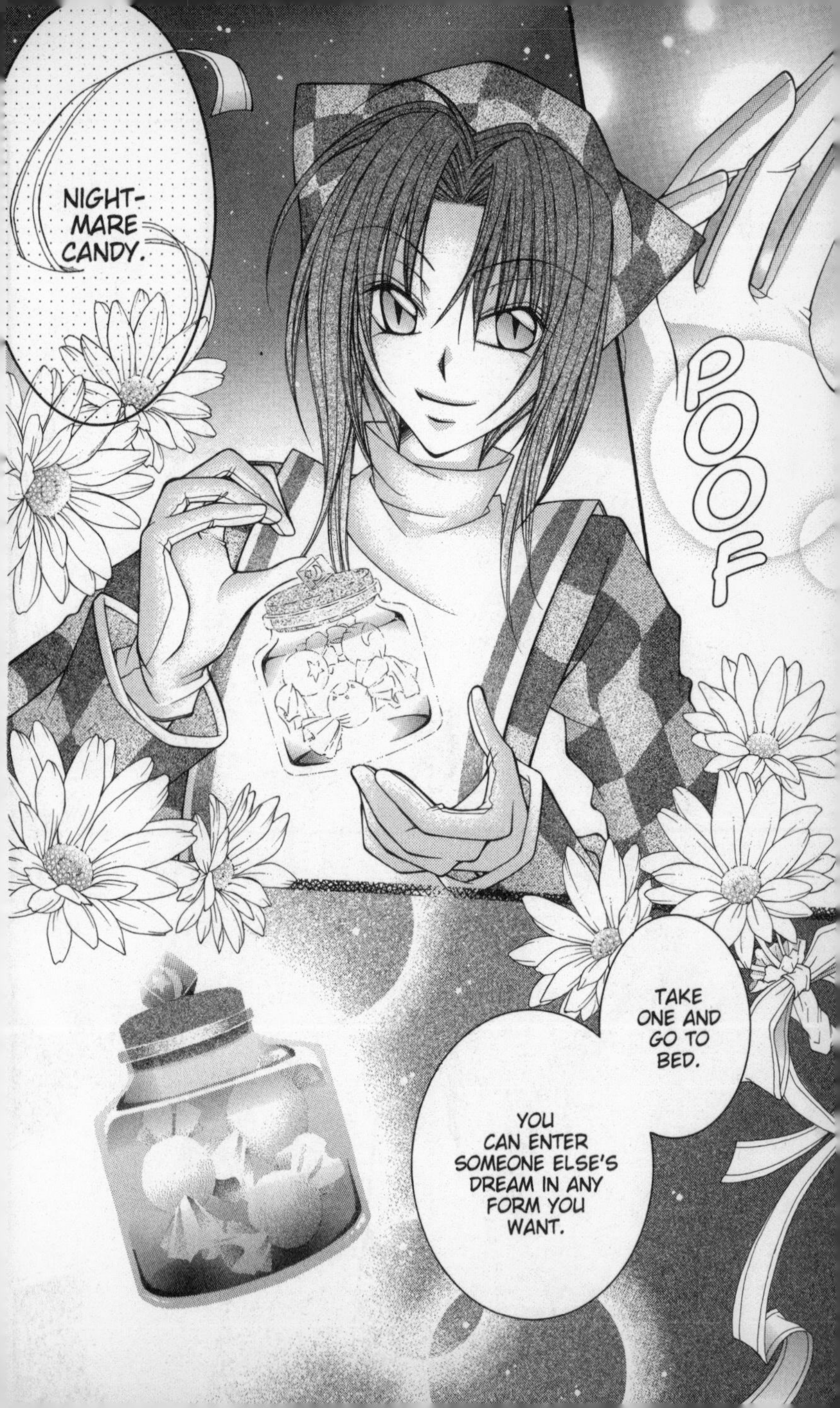
NIGHT-MARE CANDY.
POOF
TAKE ONE AND GO TO BED.
YOU CAN ENTER SOMEONE ELSE'S DREAM IN ANY FORM YOU WANT.

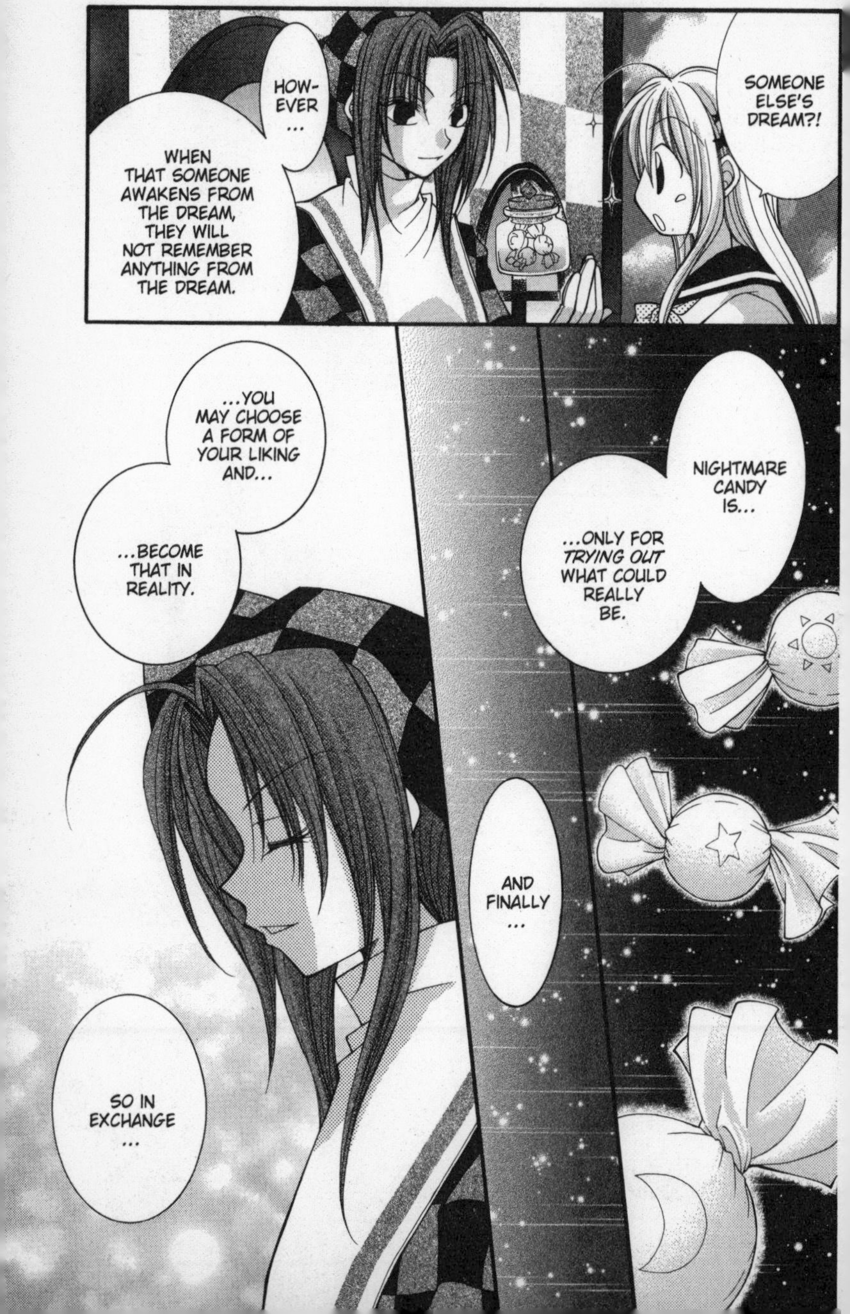
SOMEONE ELSE'S DREAM?!
HOW-EVER ...
WHEN THAT SOMEONE AWAKENS FROM THE DREAM, THEY WILL NOT REMEMBER ANYTHING FROM THE DREAM.
NIGHTMARE CANDY IS...
...ONLY FOR *TRYING OUT* WHAT COULD REALLY BE.
AND FINALLY ...
...YOU MAY CHOOSE A FORM OF YOUR LIKING AND...
...BECOME THAT IN REALITY.
SO IN EXCHANGE ...

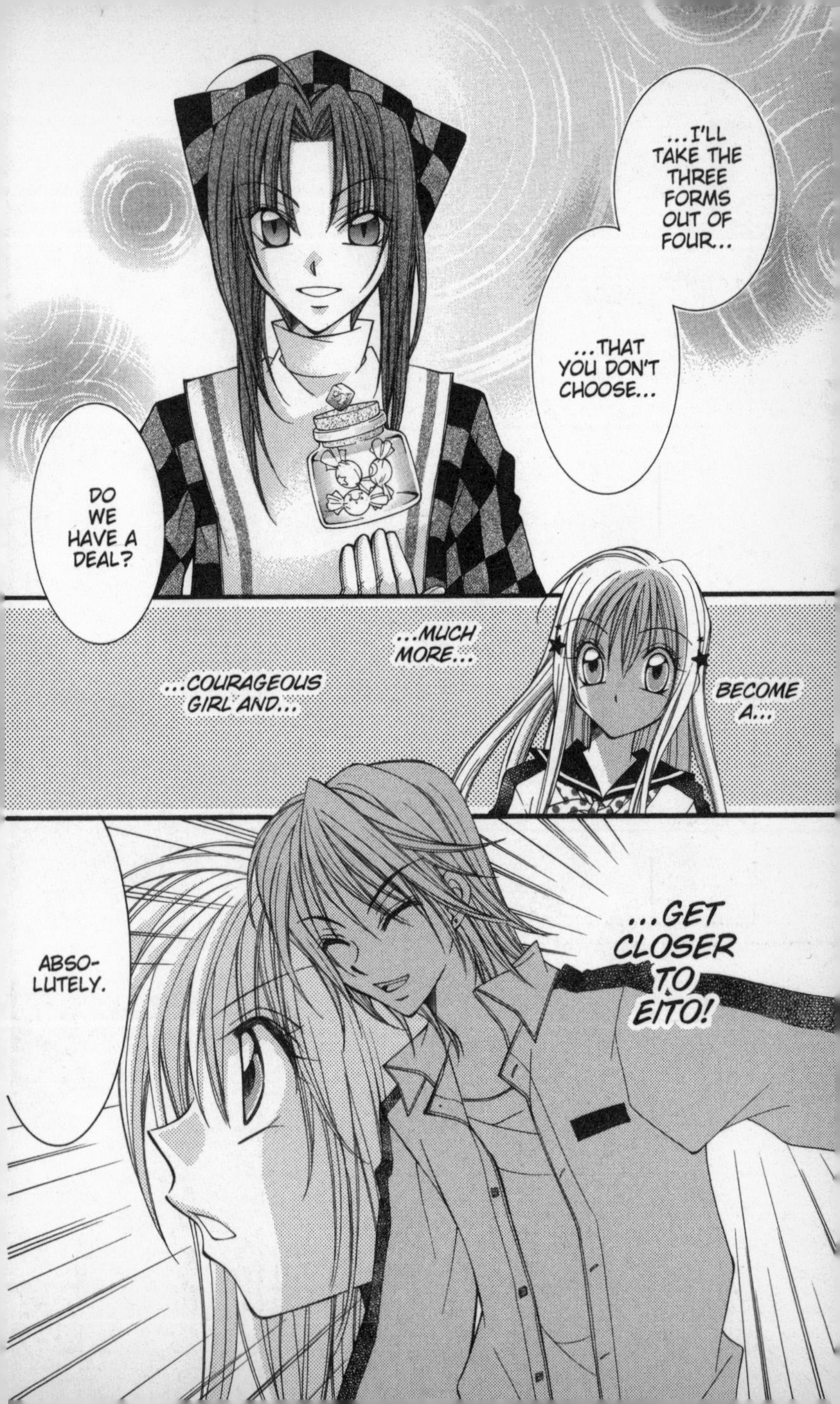
...I'LL TAKE THE THREE FORMS OUT OF FOUR...
...THAT YOU DON'T CHOOSE...
DO WE HAVE A DEAL?
BECOME A...
...MUCH MORE...
...COURAGEOUS GIRL AND...
...GET CLOSER TO EITO!
ABSO-LUTELY.

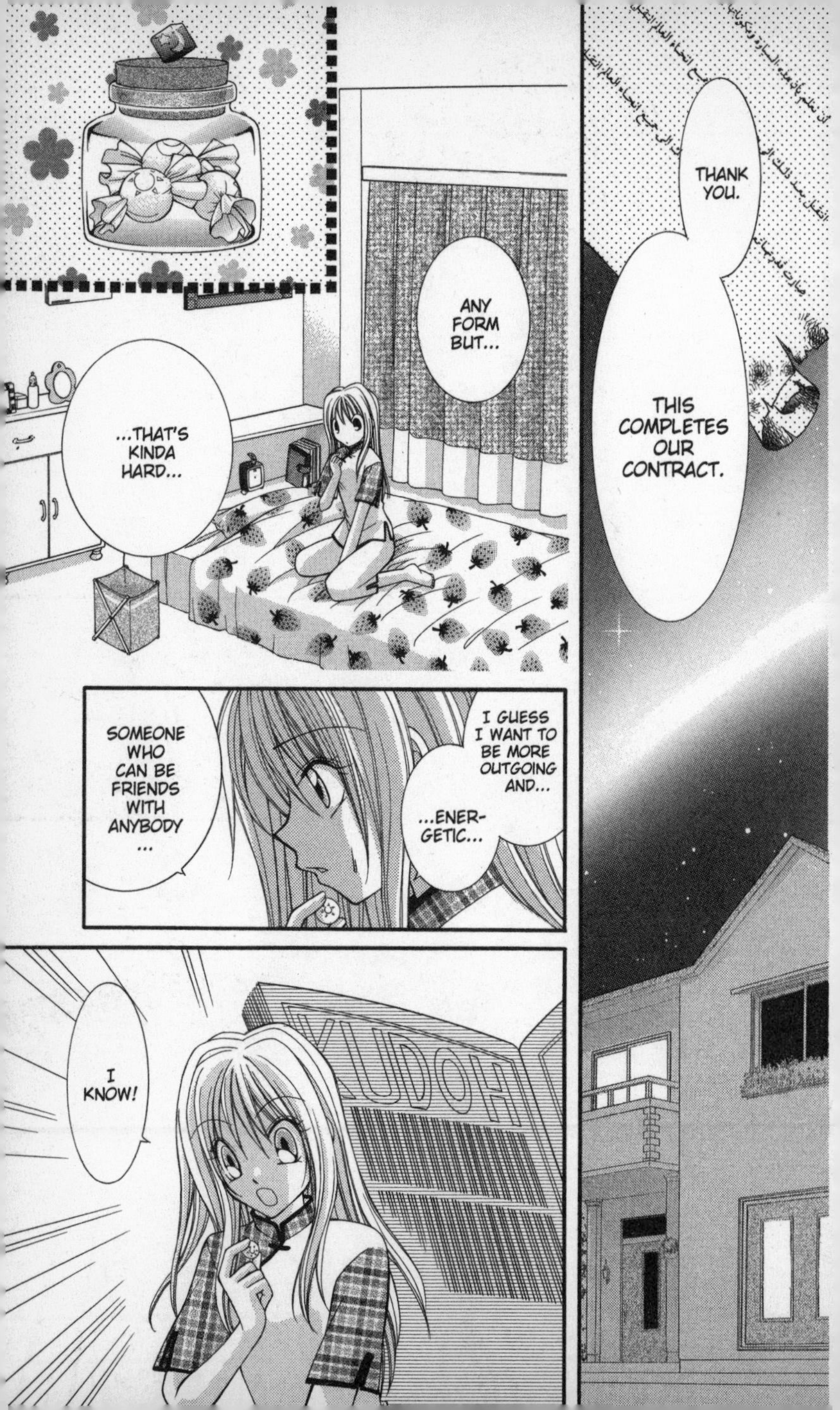
THANK YOU.
THIS COMPLETES OUR CONTRACT.
ANY FORM BUT...
...THAT'S KINDA HARD...
I GUESS I WANT TO BE MORE OUTGOING AND...
...ENER-GETIC...
SOMEONE WHO CAN BE FRIENDS WITH ANYBODY...
I KNOW!

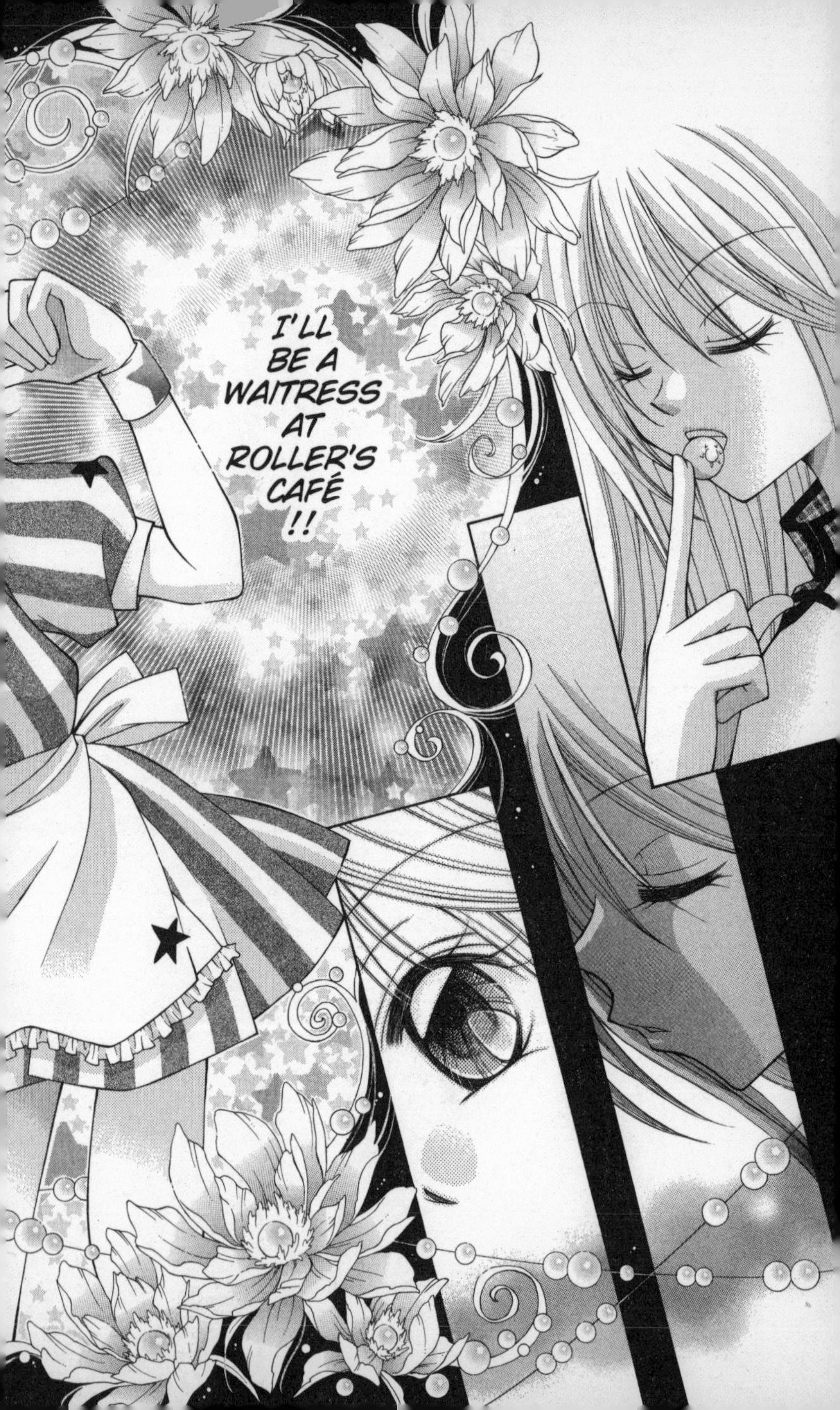
I'LL BE A WAITRESS AT ROLLER'S CAFÉ!!

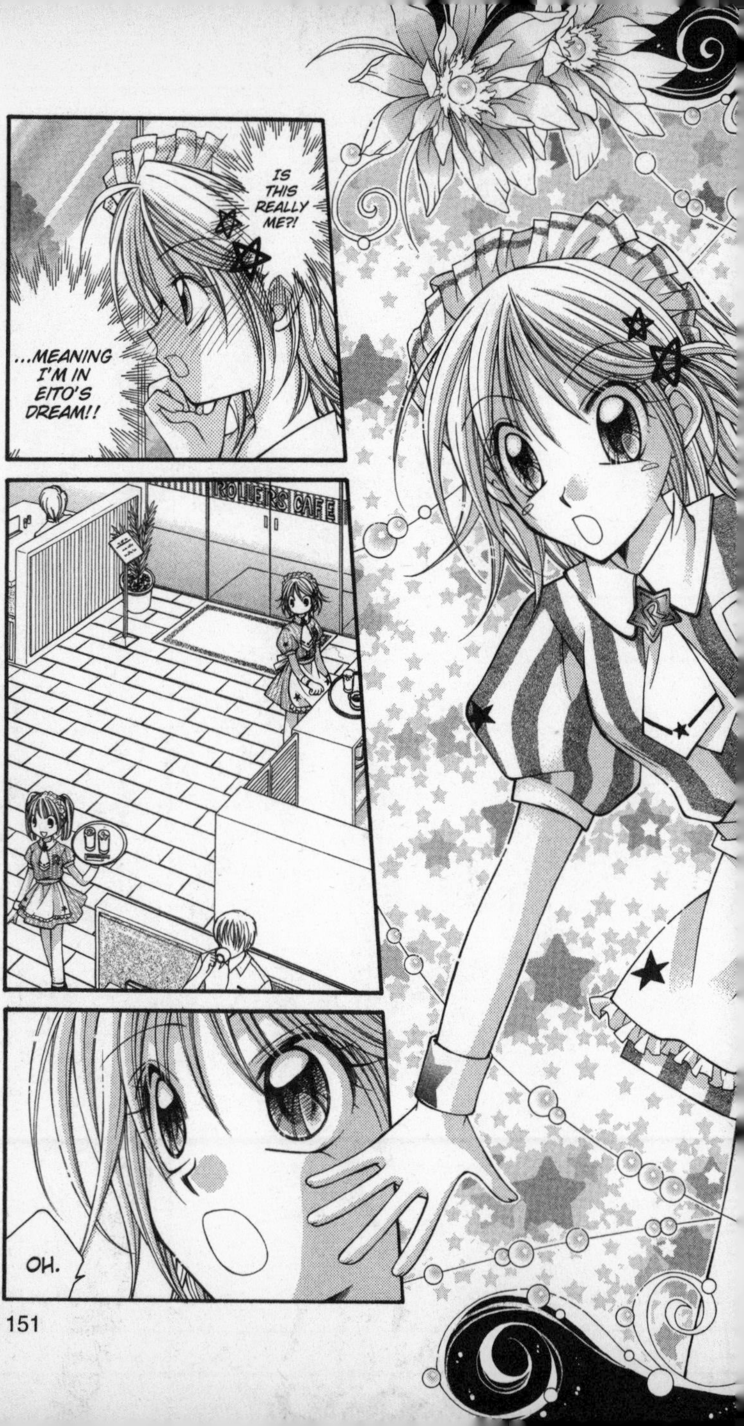
IS THIS REALLY ME?!
...MEANING I'M IN EITO'S DREAM!!
ROLLERS CAFE
OH.

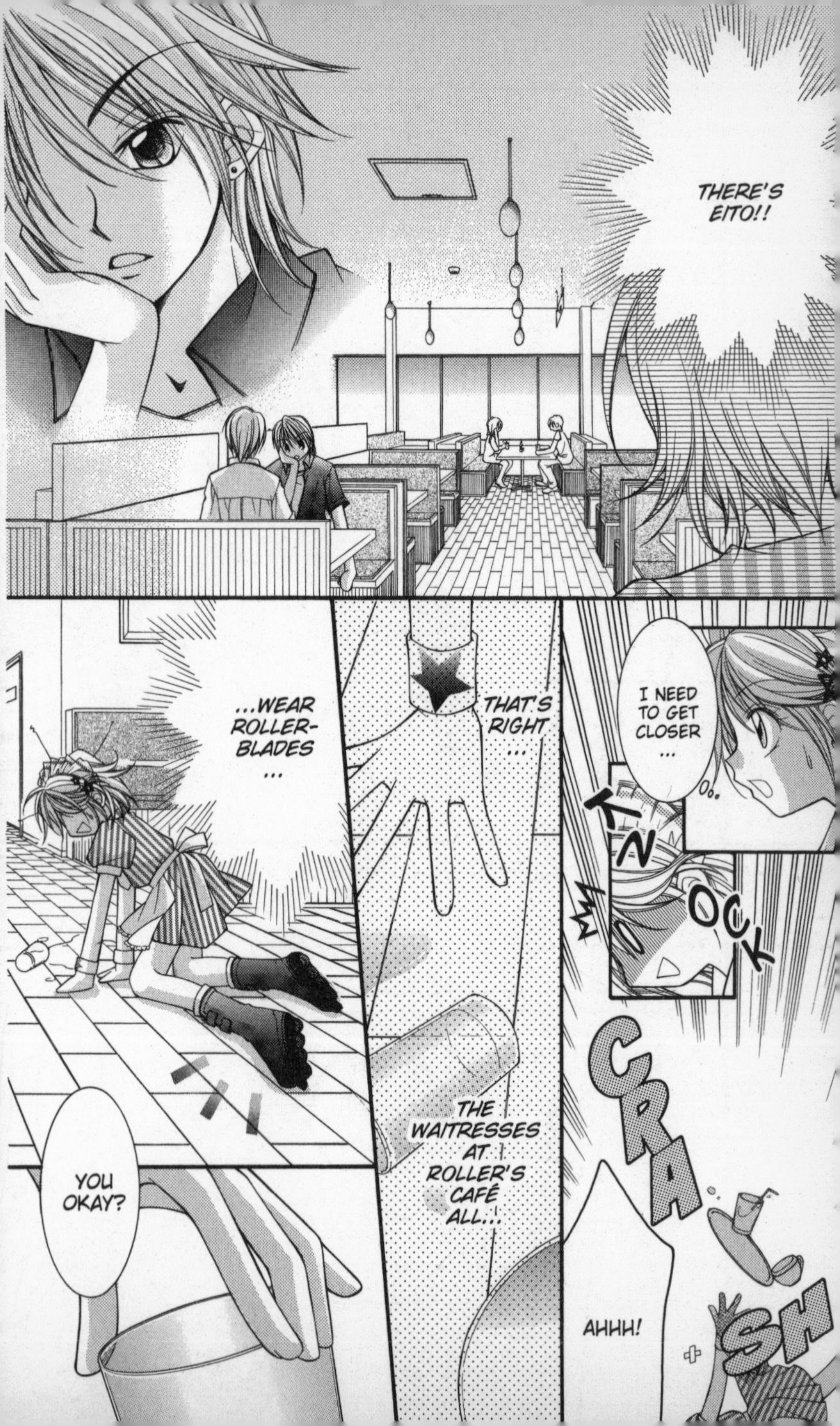
THERE'S EITO!!
I NEED TO GET CLOSER ...
KNOCK
CRASH
AHHH!
THAT'S RIGHT ...
THE WAITRESSES AT ROLLER'S CAFÉ ALL...
...WEAR ROLLER-BLADES ...
YOU OKAY?

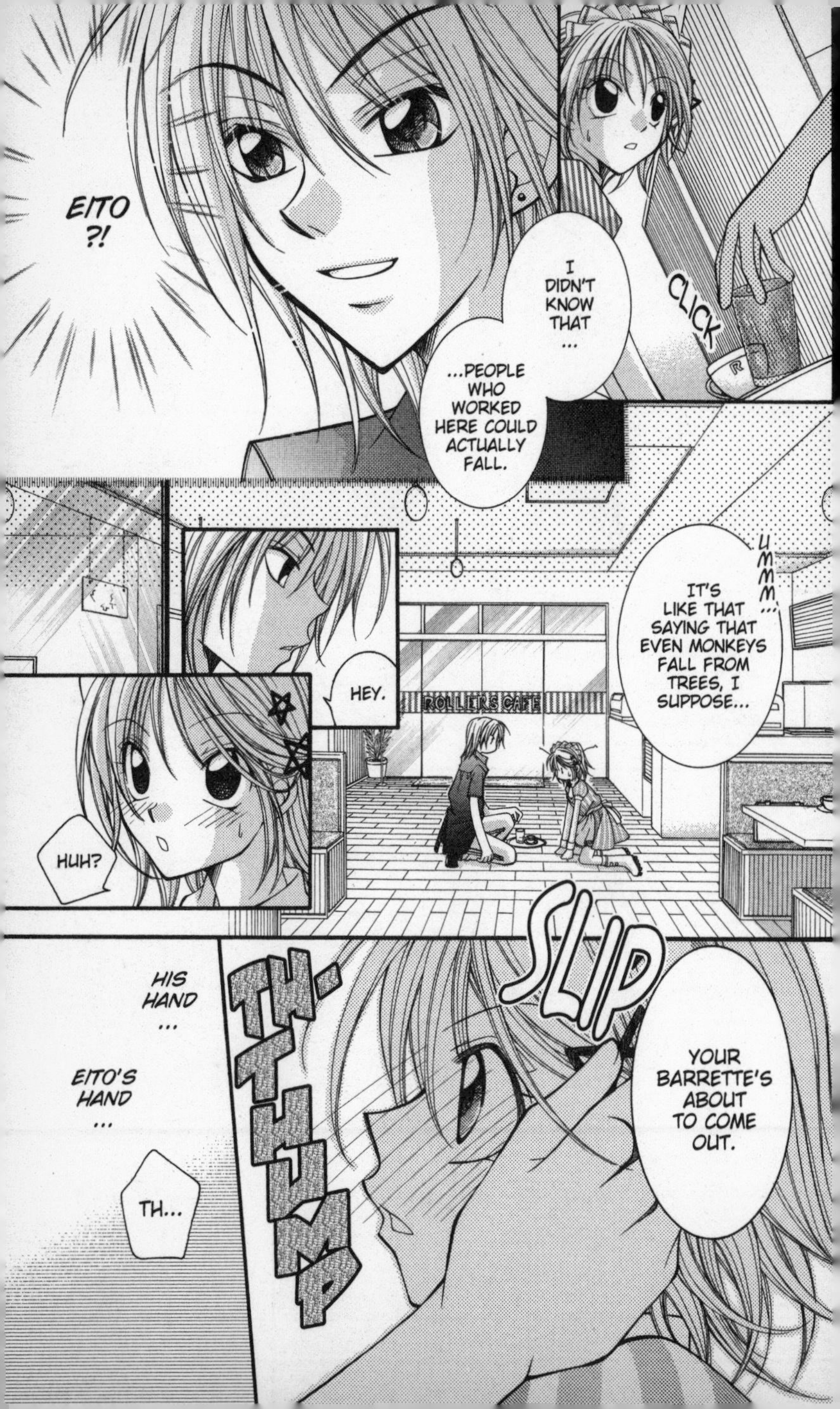

CLICK
I DIDN'T KNOW THAT ...
...PEOPLE WHO WORKED HERE COULD ACTUALLY FALL.
EITO ?!
UMMM...
IT'S LIKE THAT SAYING THAT EVEN MONKEYS FALL FROM TREES, I SUPPOSE...
ROLLER'S CAFE
HEY.
HUH?
SLIP
YOUR BARRETTE'S ABOUT TO COME OUT.
TH-THUMP
HIS HAND ...
EITO'S HAND ...
TH...

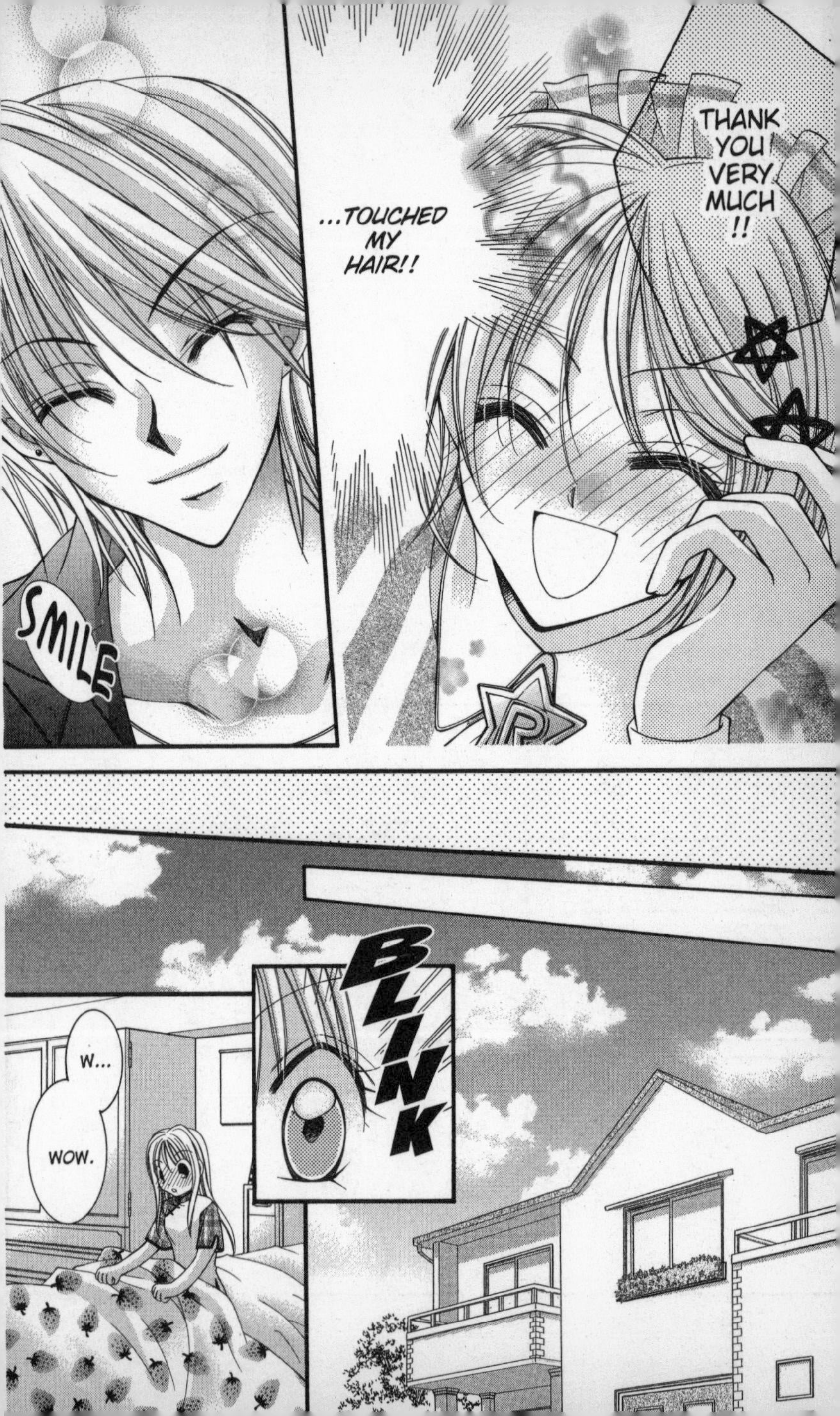
THANK YOU VERY MUCH!!
...TOUCHED MY HAIR!!
SMILE
BLINK
W...
WOW.

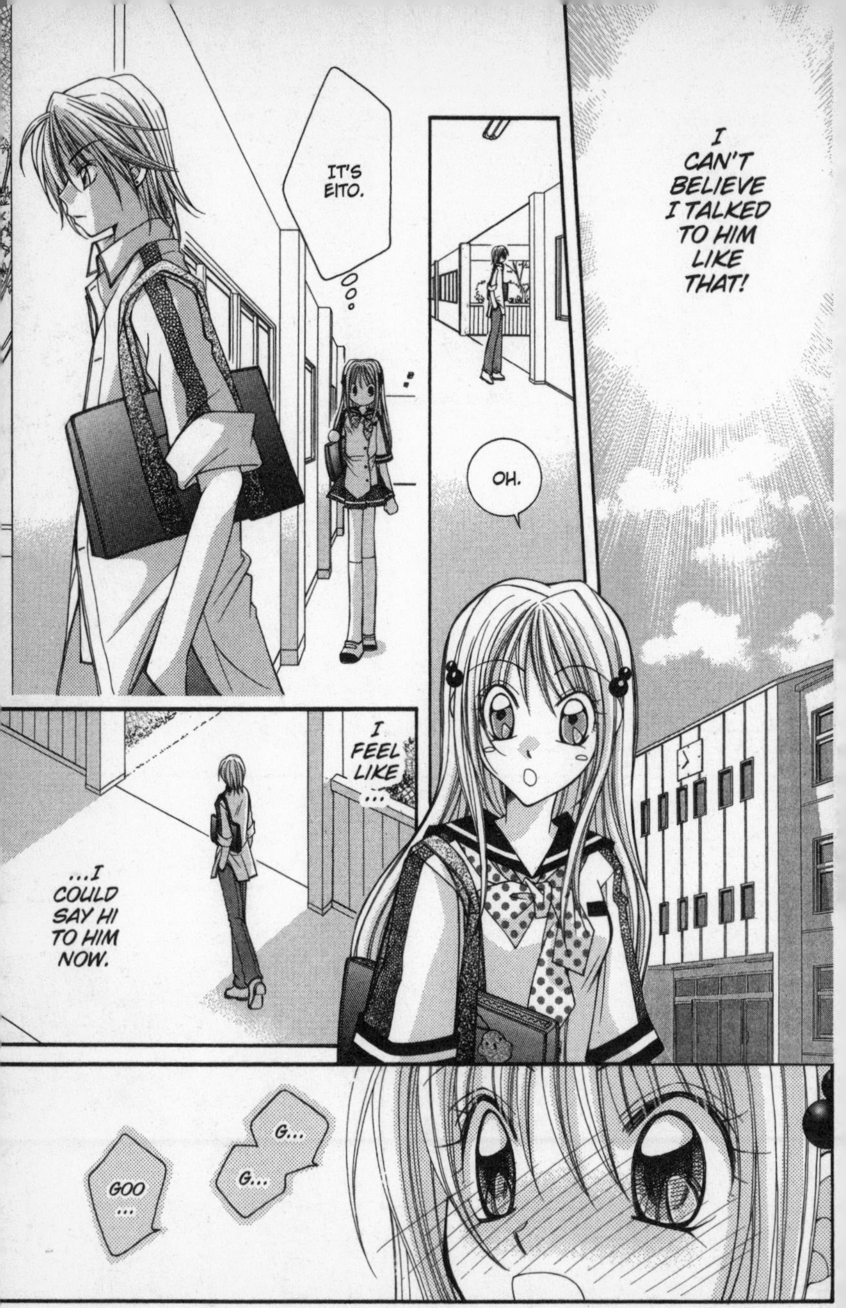

I CAN'T BELIEVE I TALKED TO HIM LIKE THAT!
OH.
IT'S EITO.
I FEEL LIKE...
...I COULD SAY HI TO HIM NOW.
G... G...
GOO...

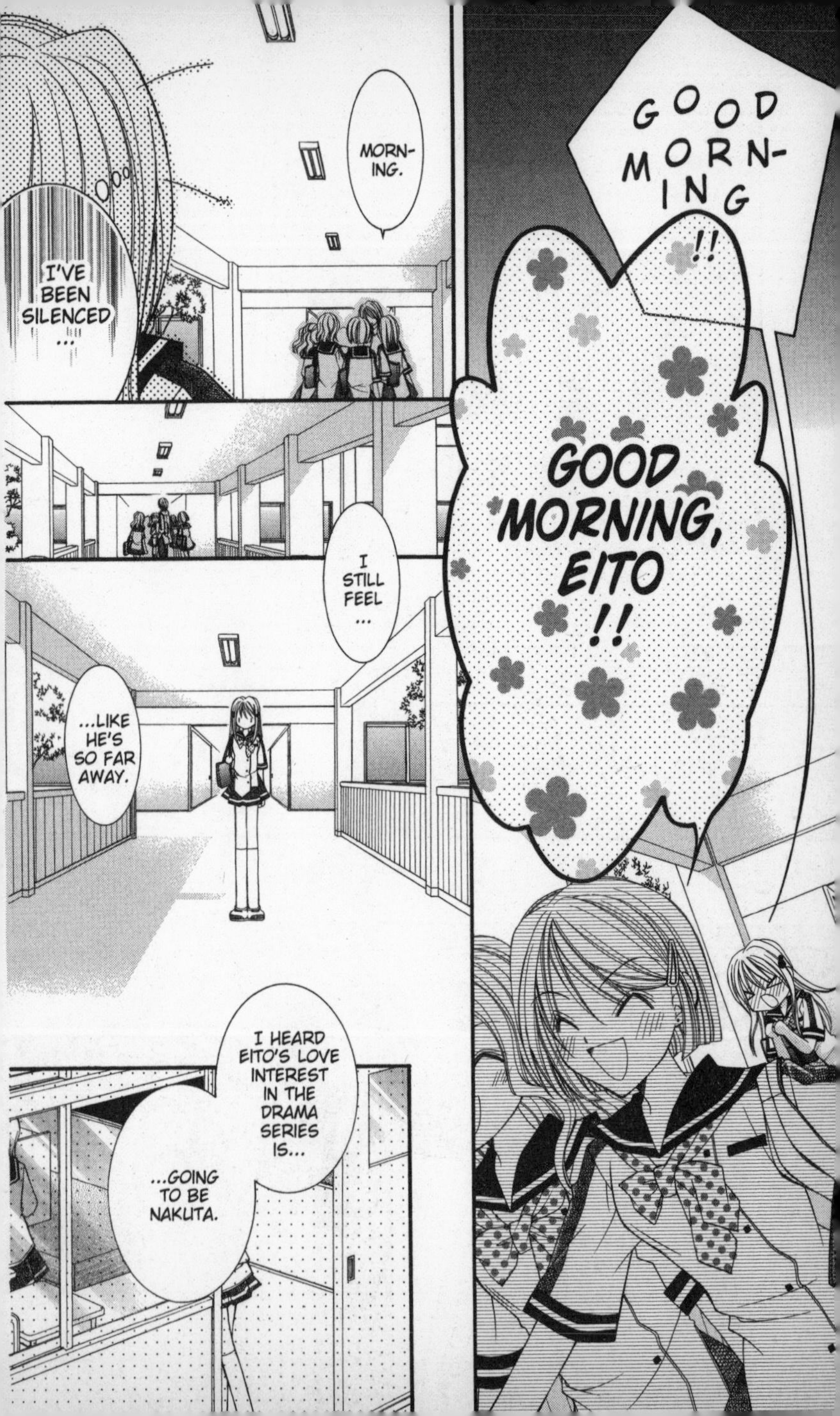
GOOD MORN-ING!!
GOOD MORNING, EITO!!
MORN-ING.
I'VE BEEN SILENCED...
I STILL FEEL...
...LIKE HE'S SO FAR AWAY.
I HEARD EITO'S LOVE INTEREST IN THE DRAMA SERIES IS...
...GOING TO BE NAKUTA.

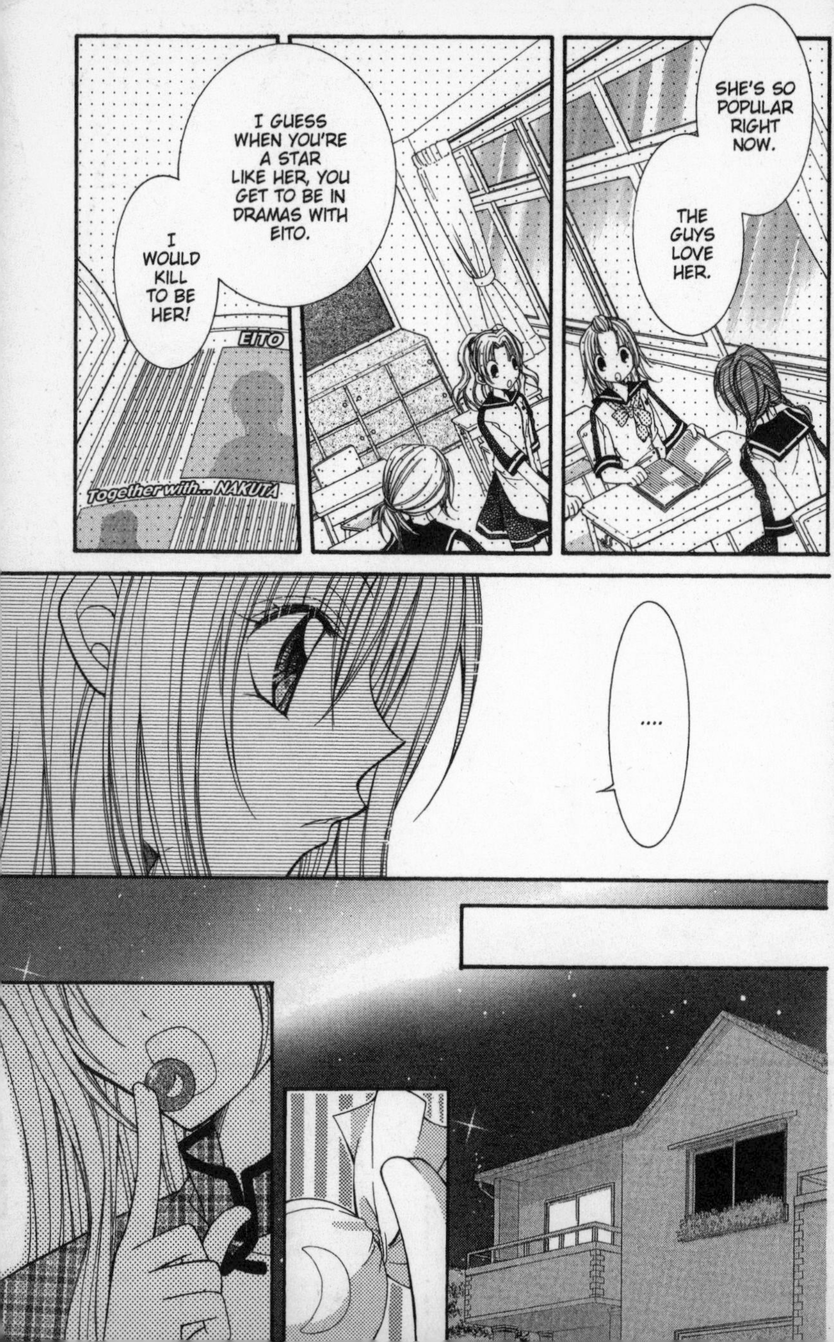
SHE'S SO POPULAR RIGHT NOW.
THE GUYS LOVE HER.
I GUESS WHEN YOU'RE A STAR LIKE HER, YOU GET TO BE IN DRAMAS WITH EITO.
I WOULD KILL TO BE HER!
EITO
Together with... NAKUTA
....

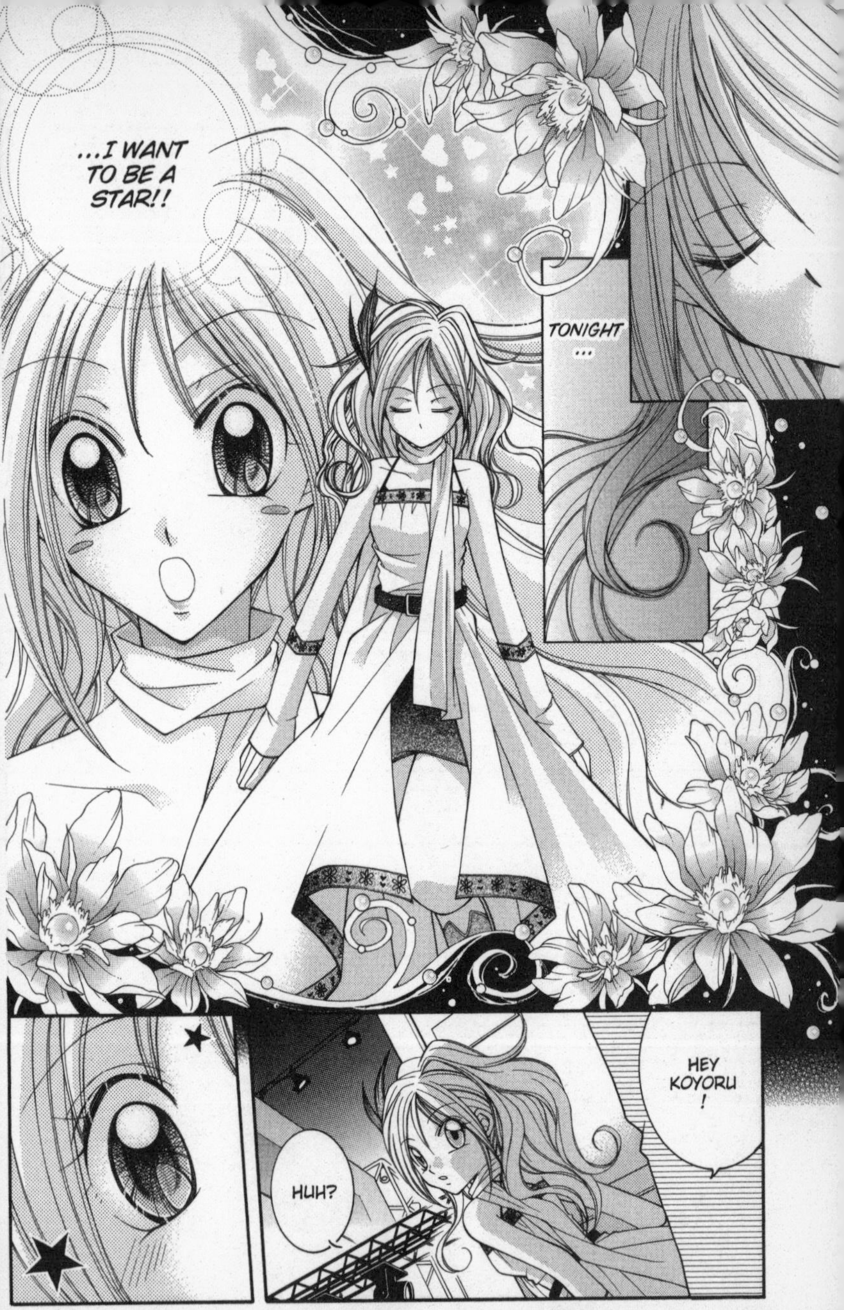
TONIGHT ...
...I WANT TO BE A STAR!!
HEY KOYORU!
HUH?

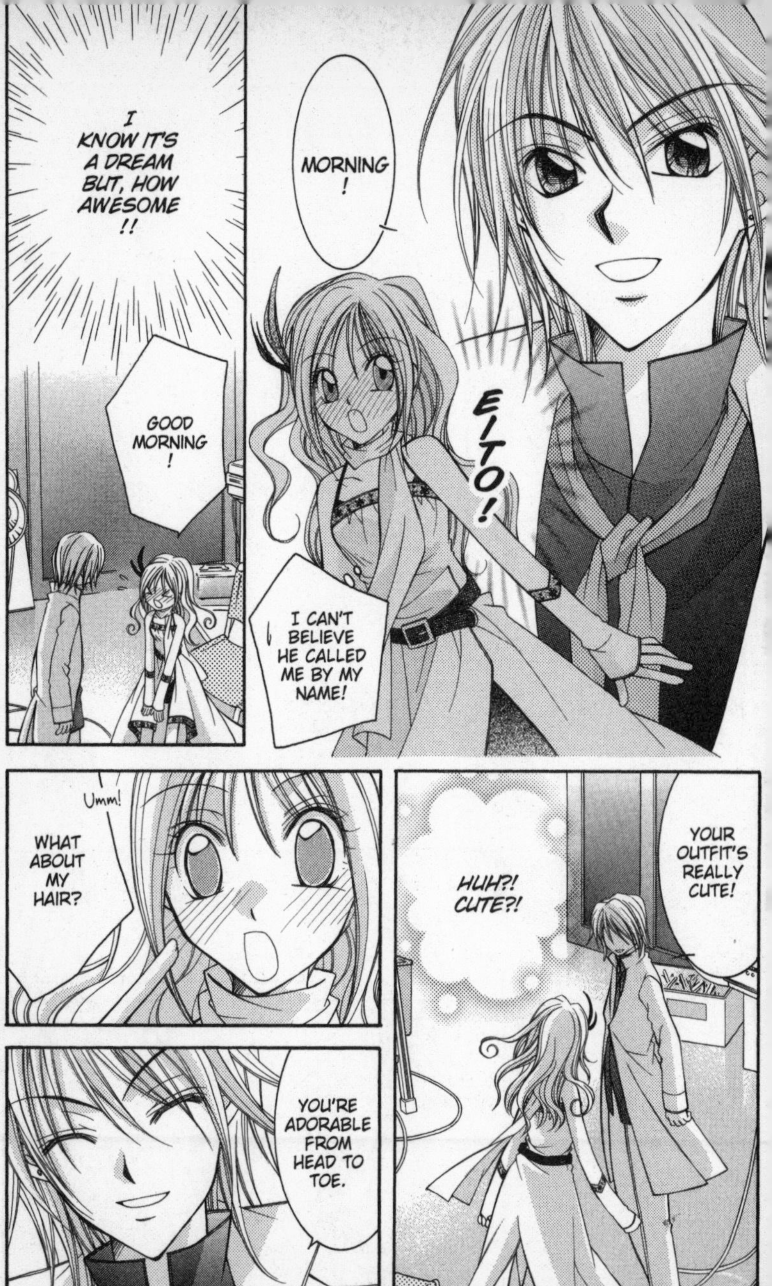
MORNING!
EITO!
I CAN'T BELIEVE HE CALLED ME BY MY NAME!
I KNOW IT'S A DREAM BUT, HOW AWESOME!!
GOOD MORNING!
YOUR OUTFIT'S REALLY CUTE!
HUH?! CUTE?!
Umm!
WHAT ABOUT MY HAIR?
YOU'RE ADORABLE FROM HEAD TO TOE.

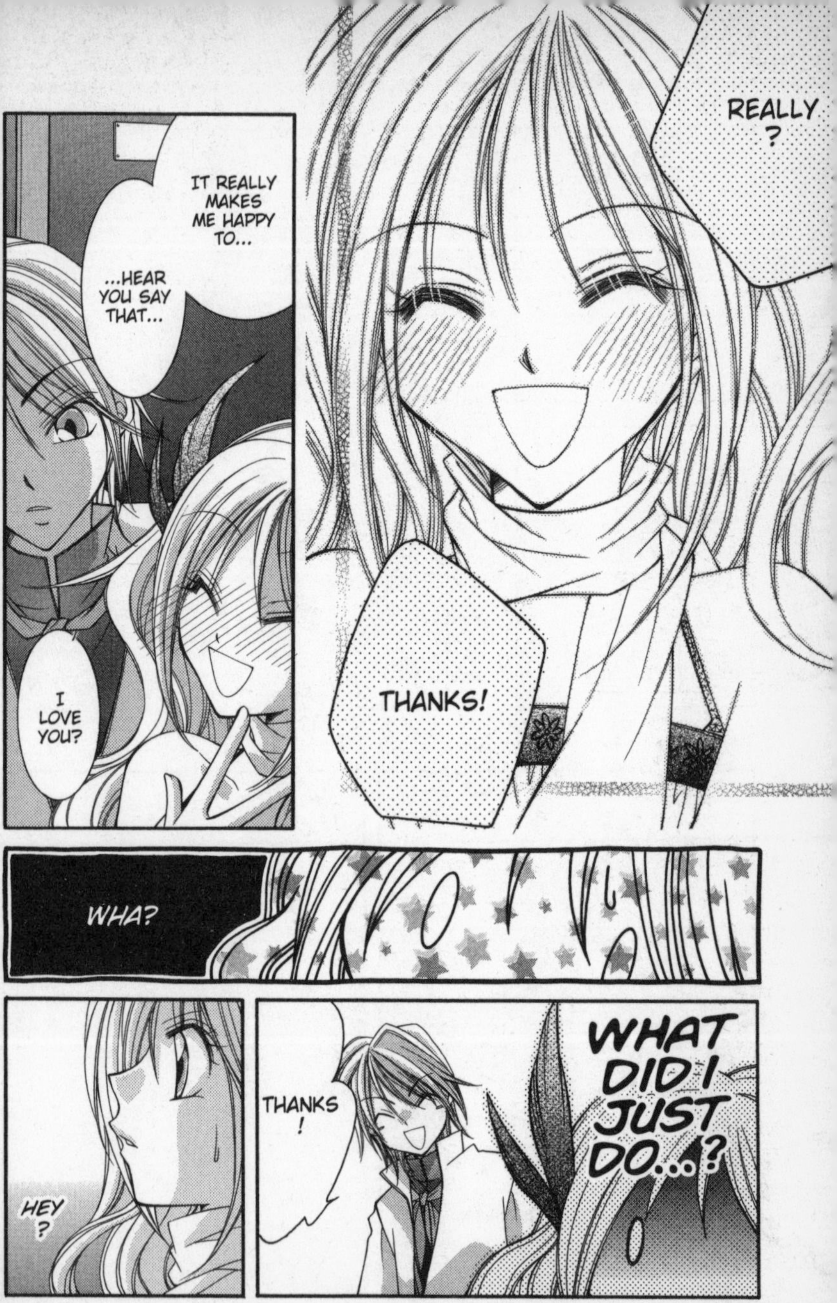
REALLY?
THANKS!
IT REALLY MAKES ME HAPPY TO...
...HEAR YOU SAY THAT...
I LOVE YOU?
WHA?
WHAT DID I JUST DO...?
THANKS!
HEY?

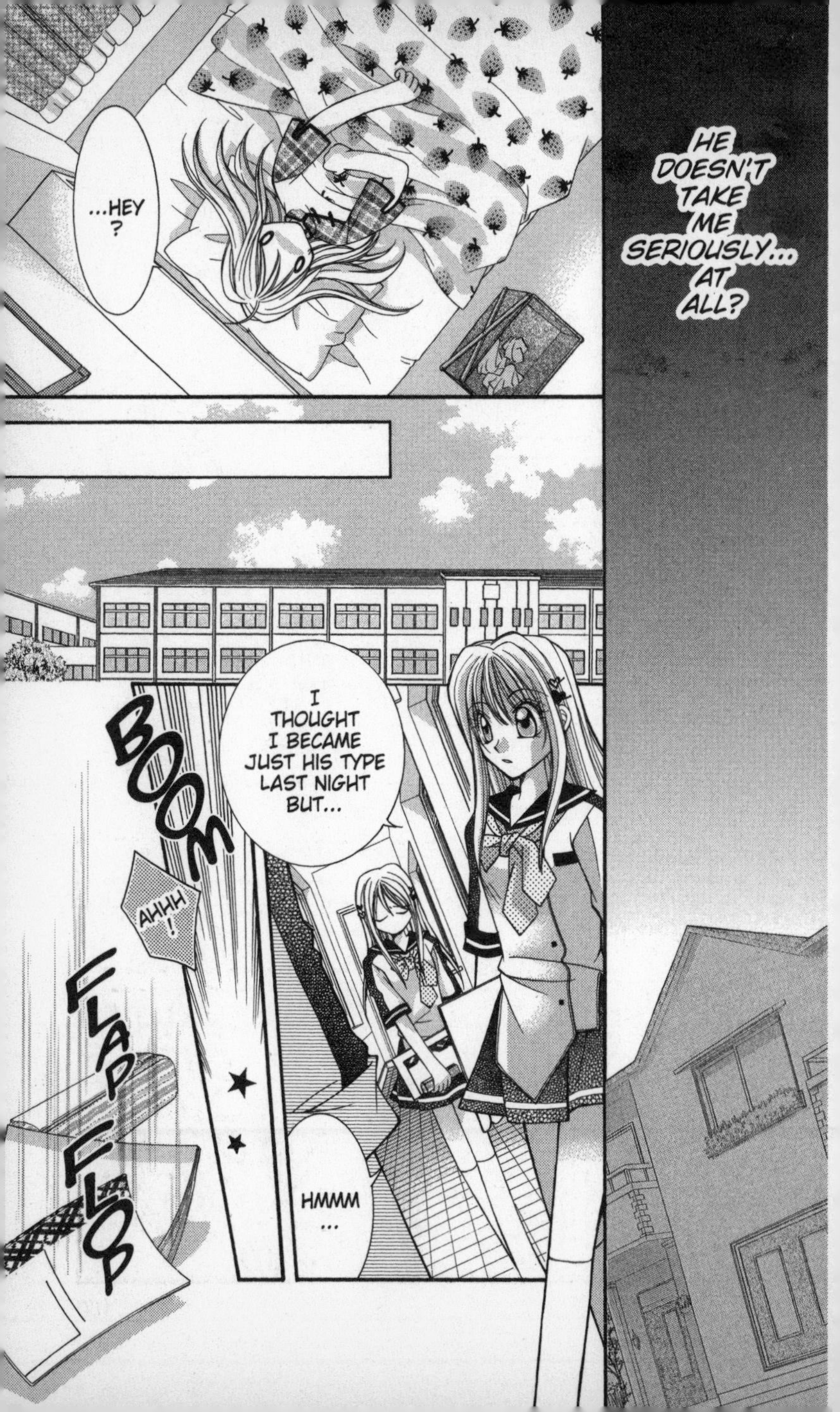
HE DOESN'T TAKE ME SERIOUSLY... AT ALL?
...HEY ?
I THOUGHT I BECAME JUST HIS TYPE LAST NIGHT BUT...
HMMM ...
BOOM
AHHH !
FLAP FLOP

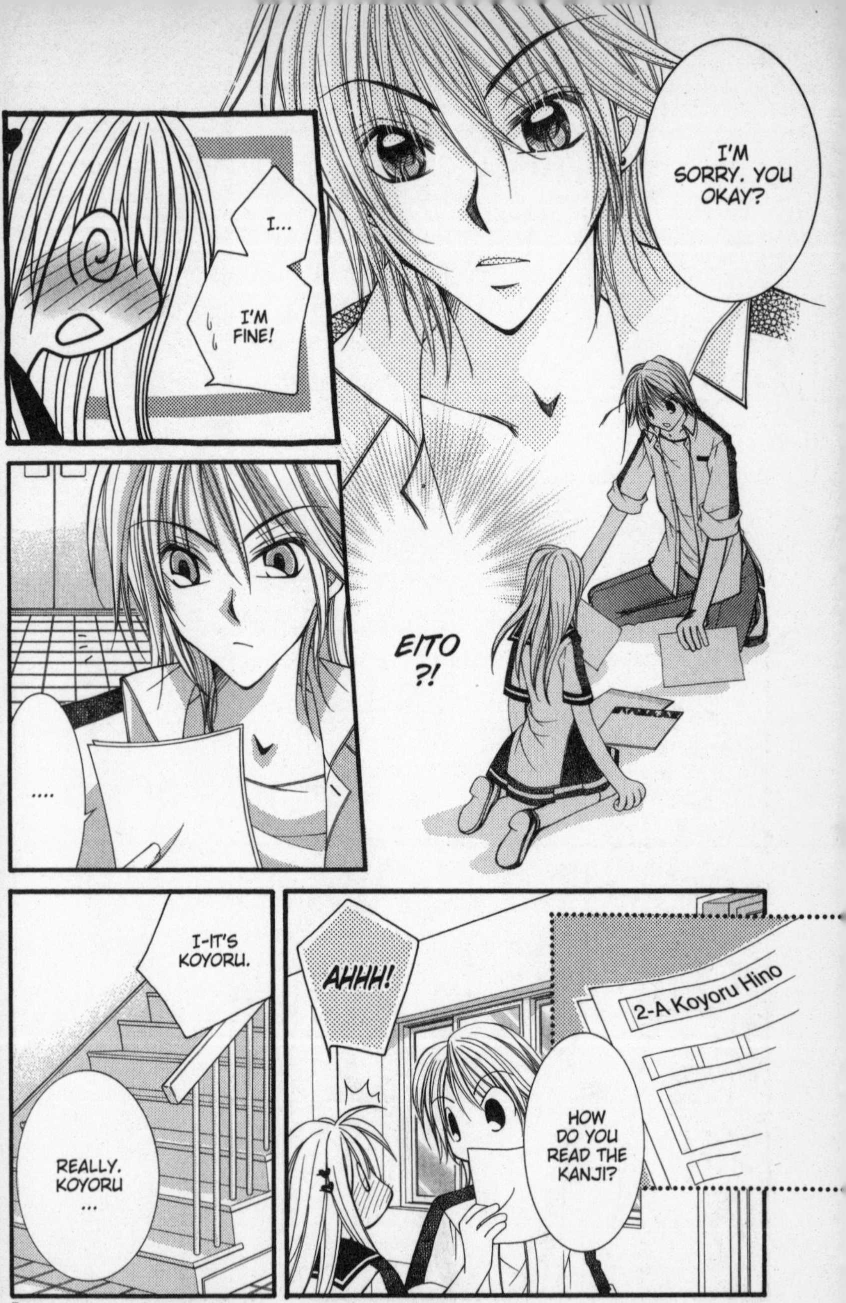
I'M SORRY. YOU OKAY?
EITO ?!
I...
I'M FINE!
....
2-A Koyoru Hino
AHHH!
HOW DO YOU READ THE KANJI?
I-IT'S KOYORU.
REALLY. KOYORU ...

Each kanji can have multiple pronunciations.

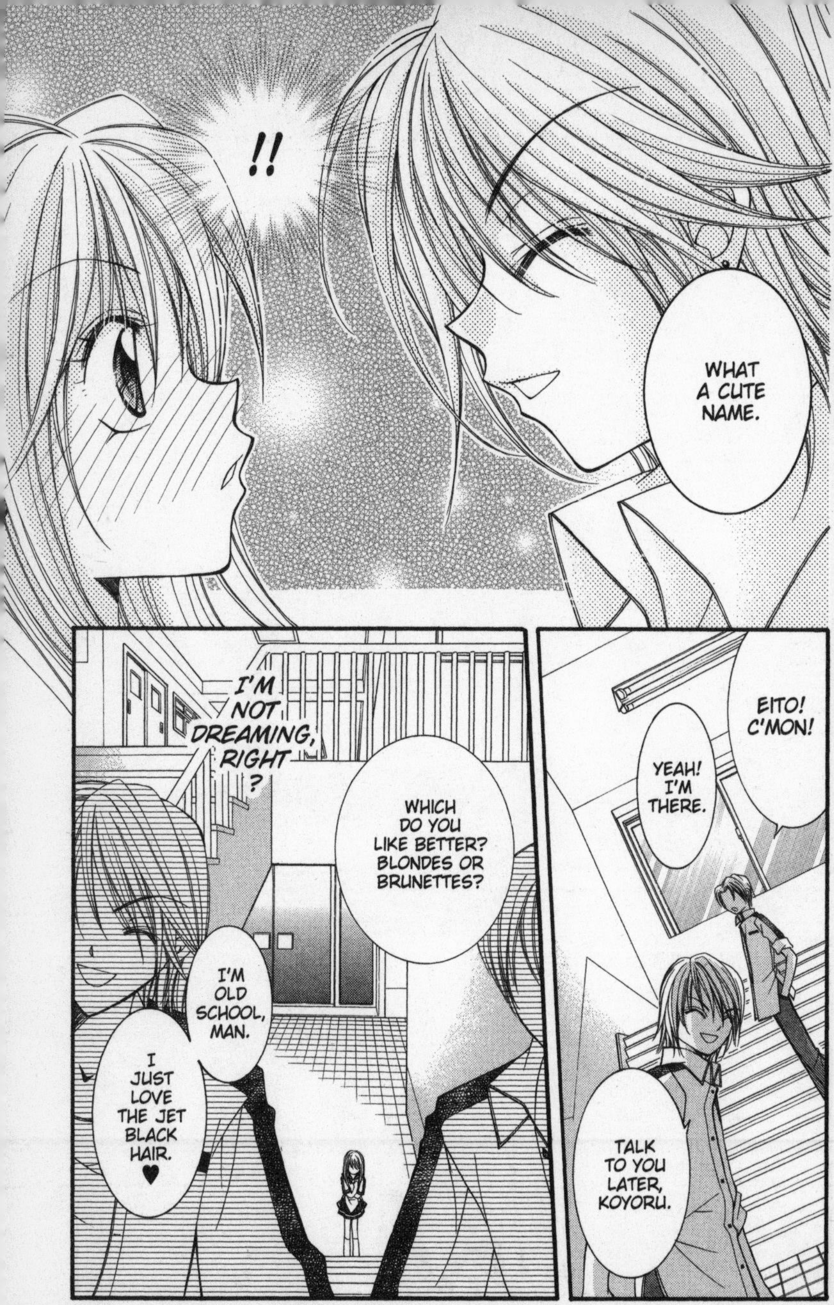
WHAT A CUTE NAME.
!!
EITO! C'MON!
YEAH! I'M THERE.
TALK TO YOU LATER, KOYORU.
I'M NOT DREAMING, RIGHT?
WHICH DO YOU LIKE BETTER? BLONDES OR BRUNETTES?
I'M OLD SCHOOL, MAN.
I JUST LOVE THE JET BLACK HAIR. ♥

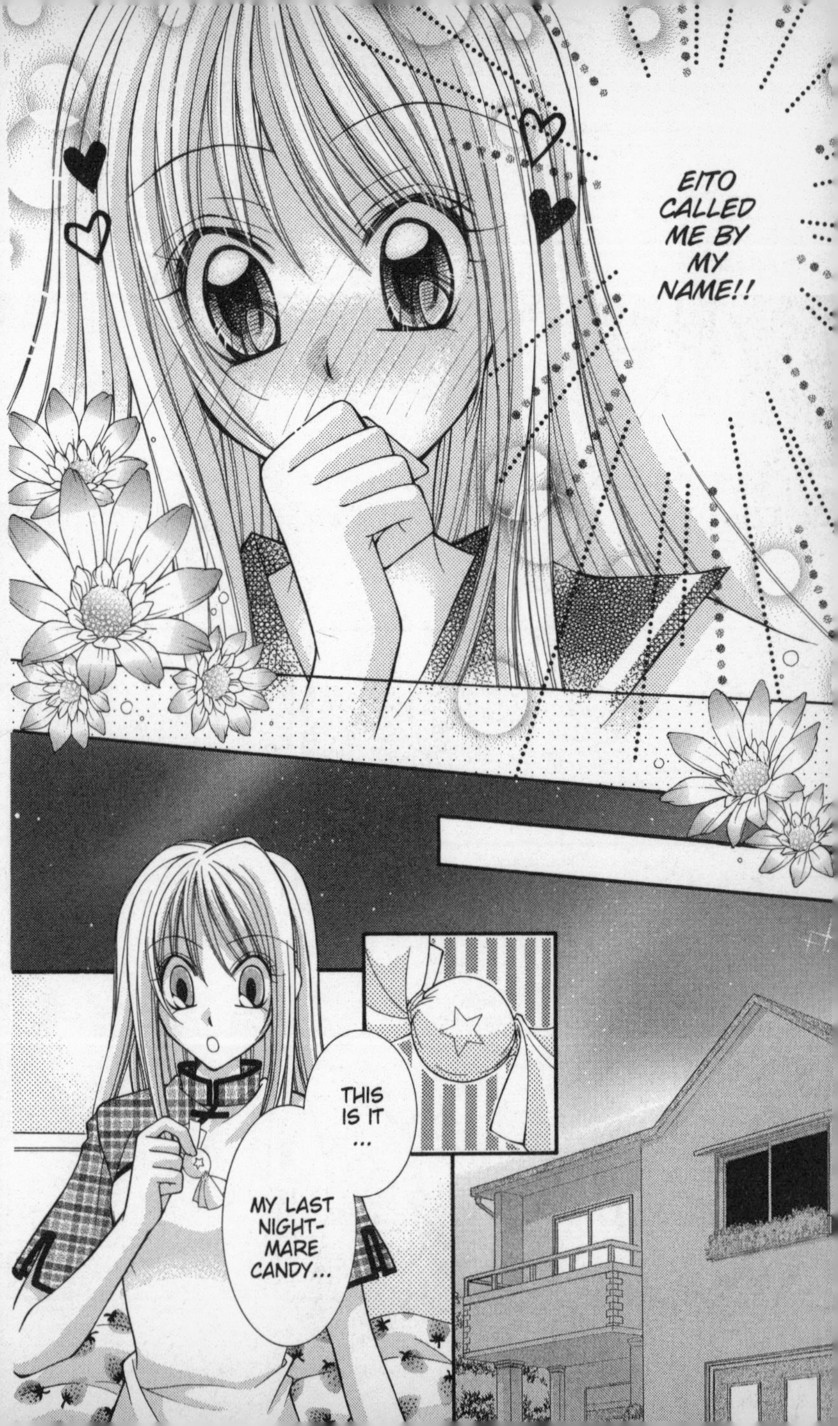
EITO CALLED ME BY MY NAME!!
THIS IS IT ...
MY LAST NIGHT-MARE CANDY...

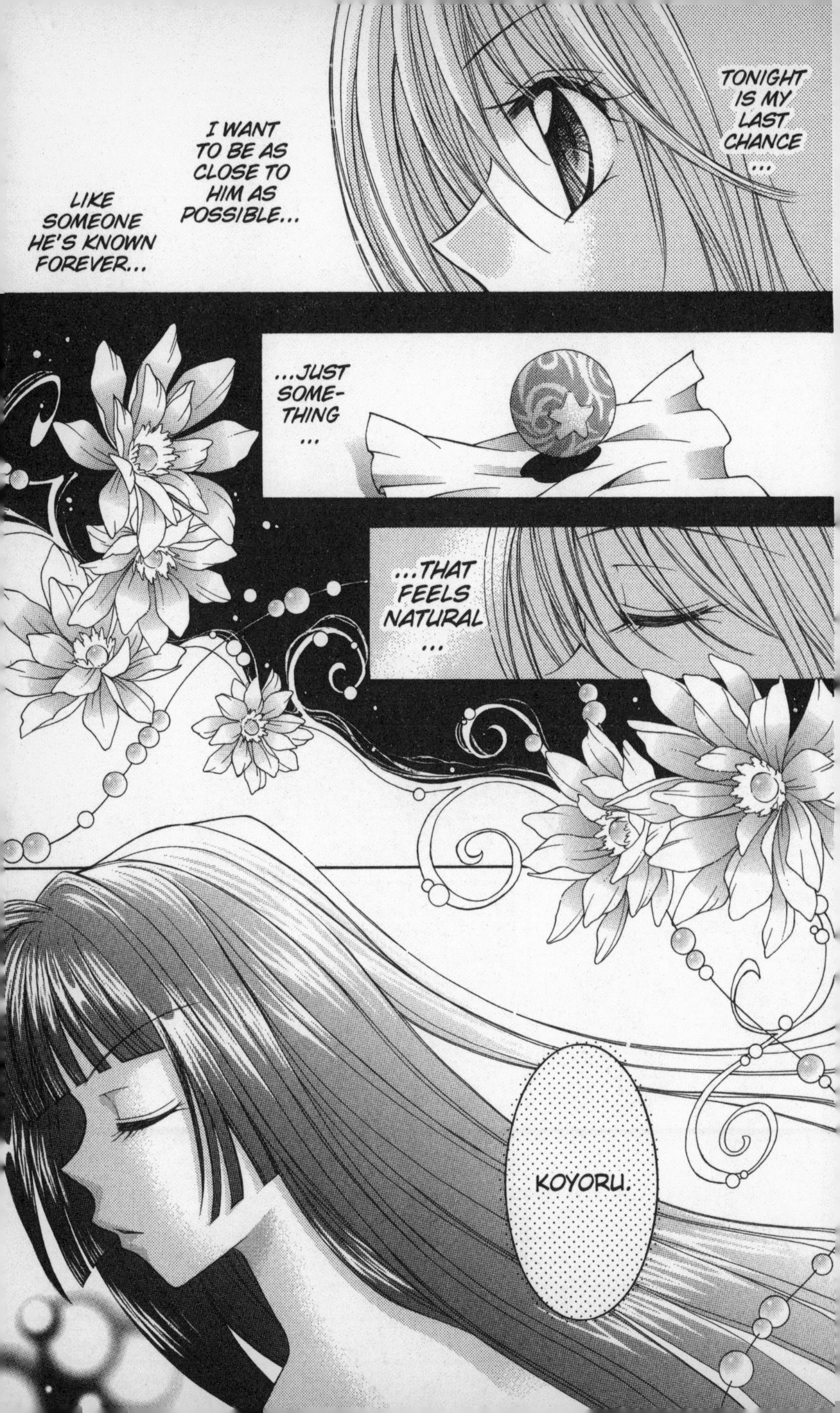
TONIGHT IS MY LAST CHANCE ...
I WANT TO BE AS CLOSE TO HIM AS POSSIBLE...
LIKE SOMEONE HE'S KNOWN FOREVER...
...JUST SOME-THING ...
...THAT FEELS NATURAL ...
KOYORU.

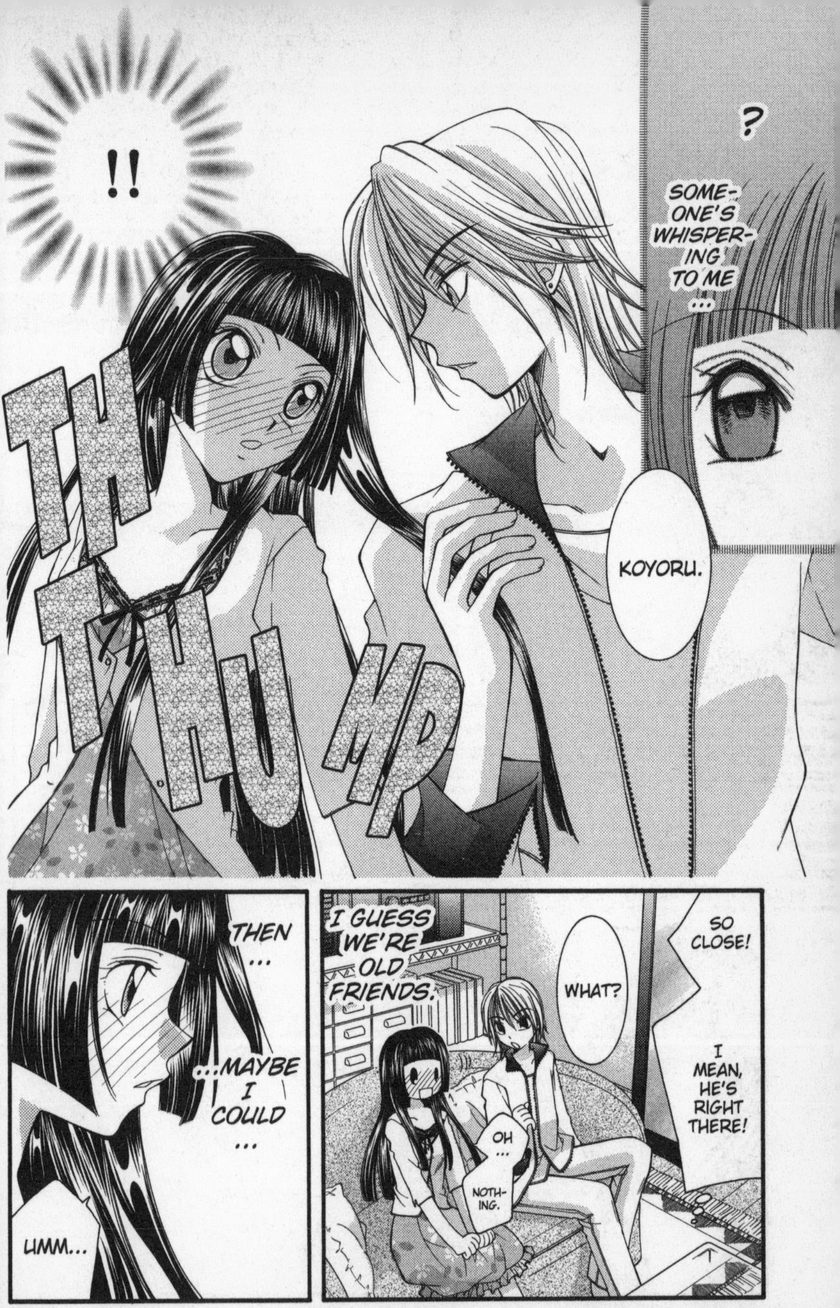
?
SOME-ONE'S WHISPER-ING TO ME ...
KOYORU.
!!
TH THTHUMP
SO CLOSE!
WHAT?
I GUESS WE'RE OLD FRIENDS.
I MEAN, HE'S RIGHT THERE!
OH ...
NOTH-ING.
THEN ...
...MAYBE I COULD ...
UMM...

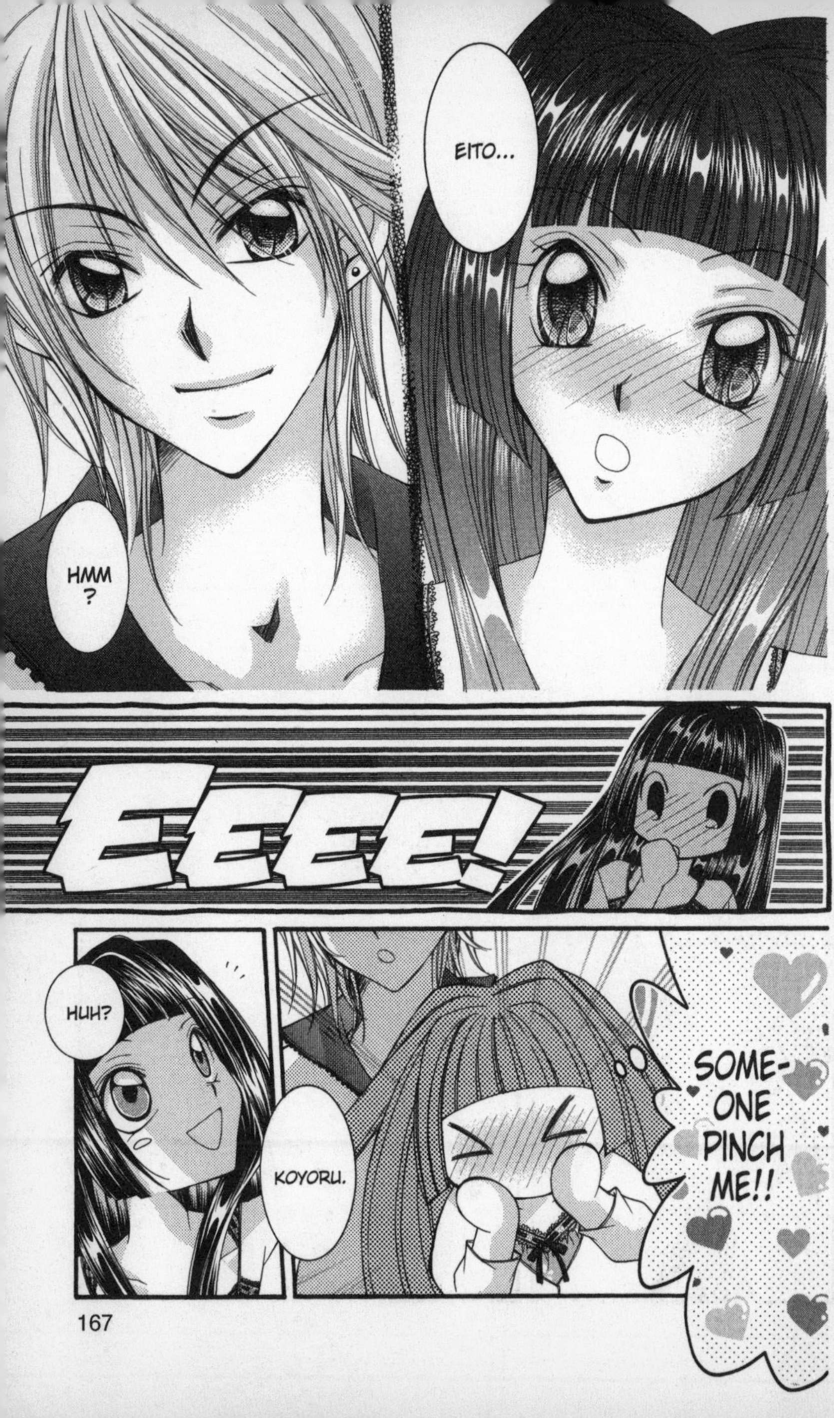
EITO...
HMM?
EEEE!
SOME-ONE PINCH ME!!
KOYORU.
HUH?

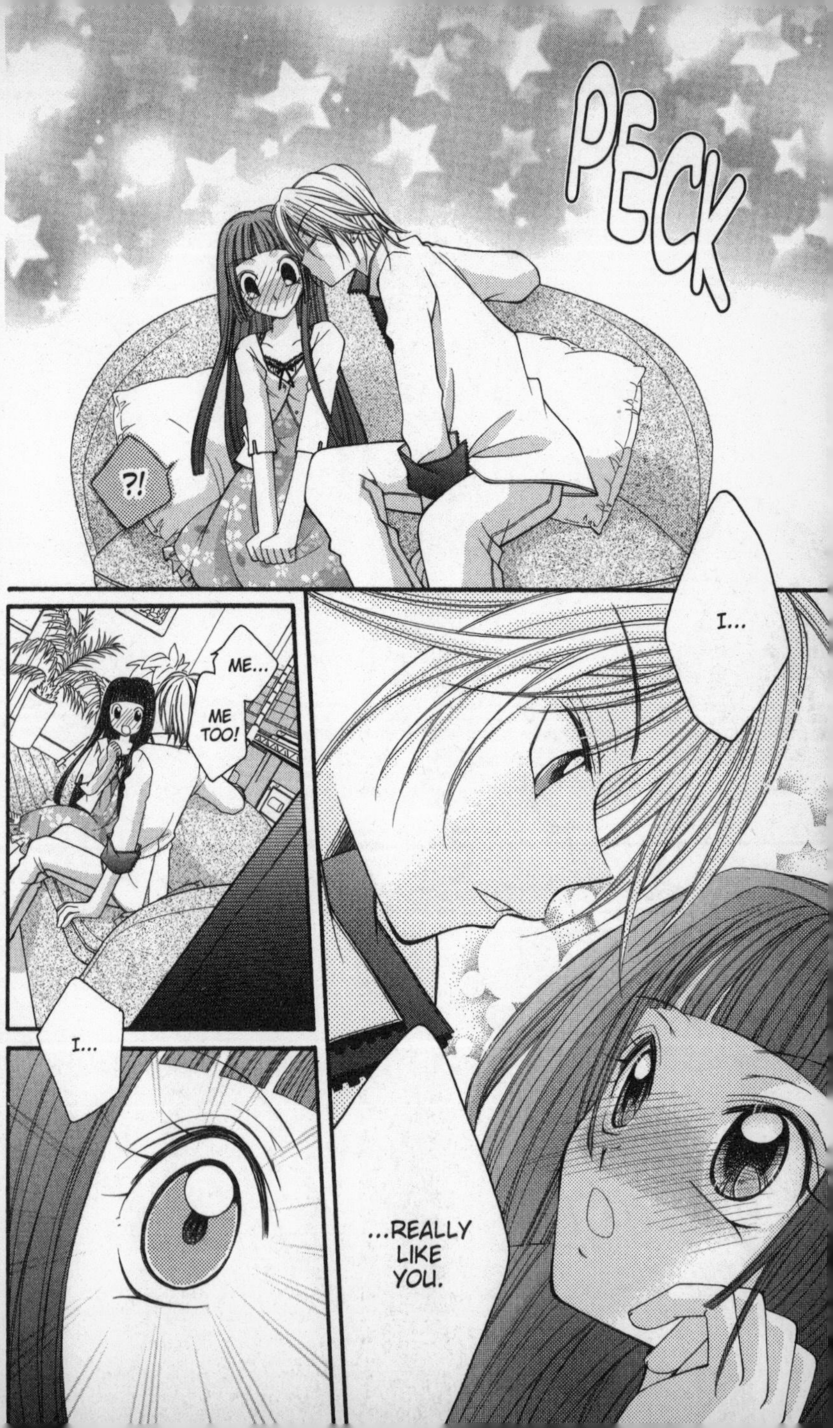
PECK
?!
I...
...REALLY LIKE YOU.
ME...
ME TOO!
I...

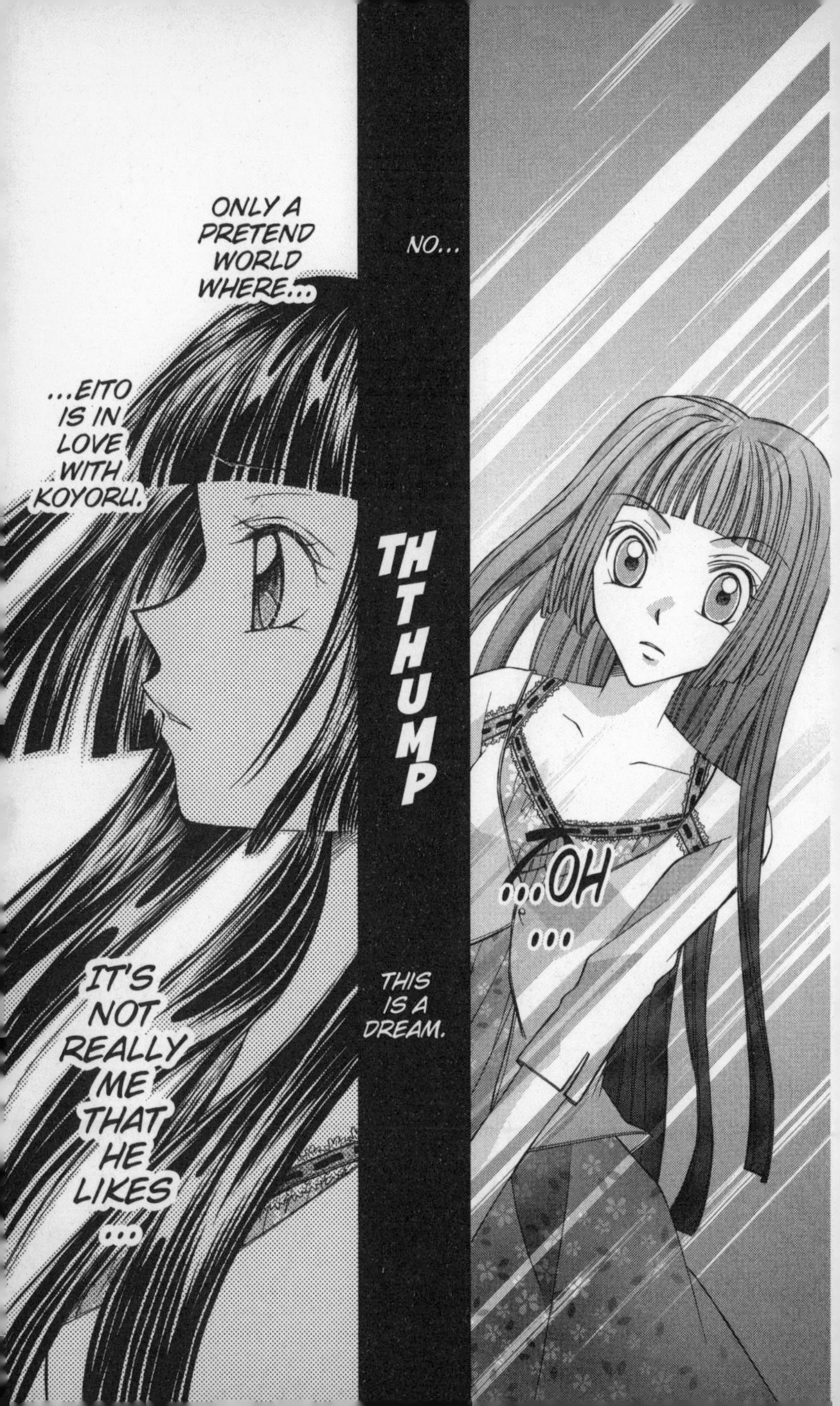

...OH...
NO...
THTHUMP
THIS IS A DREAM.
ONLY A PRETEND WORLD WHERE...
...EITO IS IN LOVE WITH KOYORU.
IT'S NOT REALLY ME THAT HE LIKES...

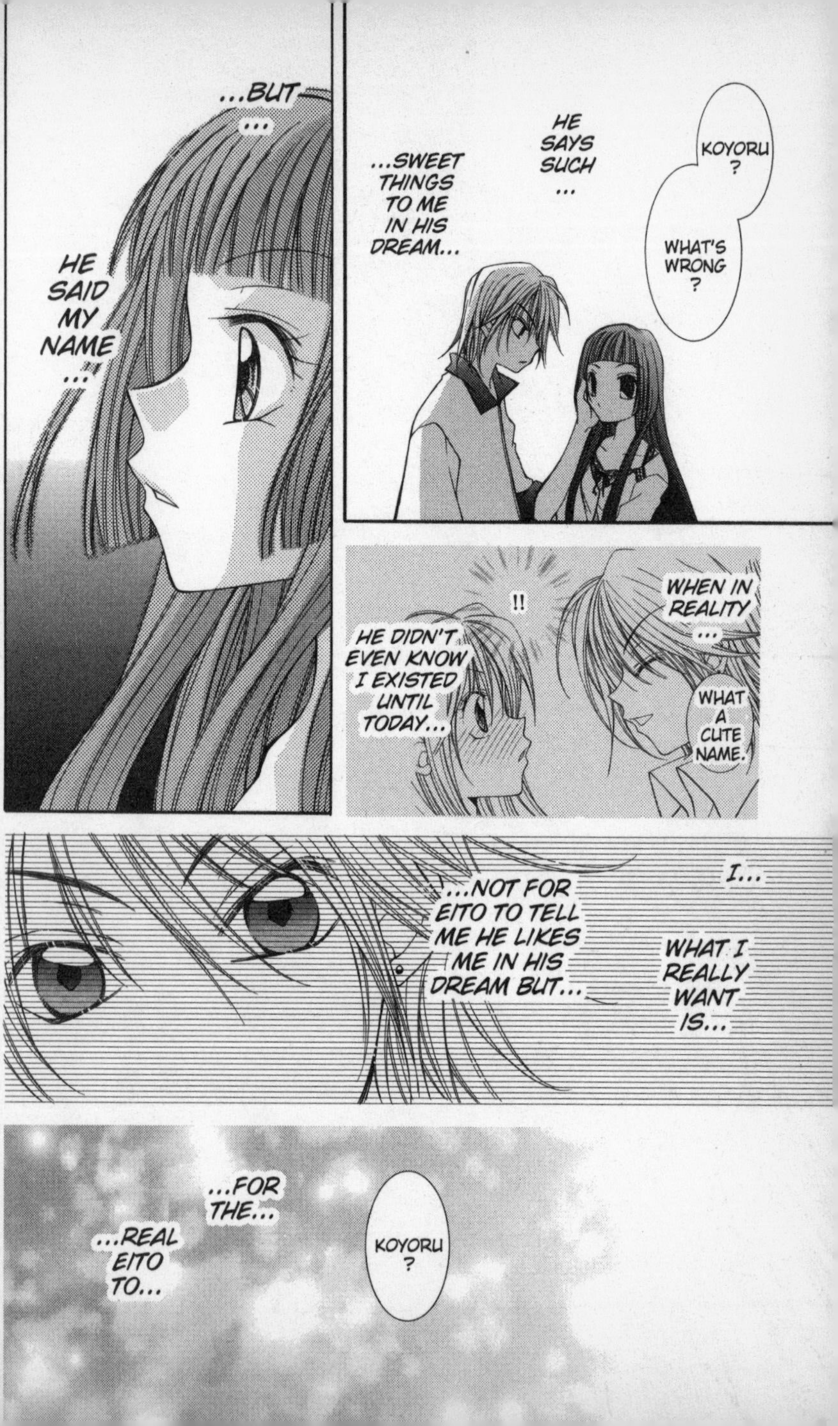
KOYORU?
WHAT'S WRONG?
HE SAYS SUCH...
...SWEET THINGS TO ME IN HIS DREAM...
WHEN IN REALITY...
WHAT A CUTE NAME.
!!
HE DIDN'T EVEN KNOW I EXISTED UNTIL TODAY...
...BUT...
HE SAID MY NAME...
I...
WHAT I REALLY WANT IS...
...NOT FOR EITO TO TELL ME HE LIKES ME IN HIS DREAM BUT...
KOYORU?
...FOR THE...
...REAL EITO TO...

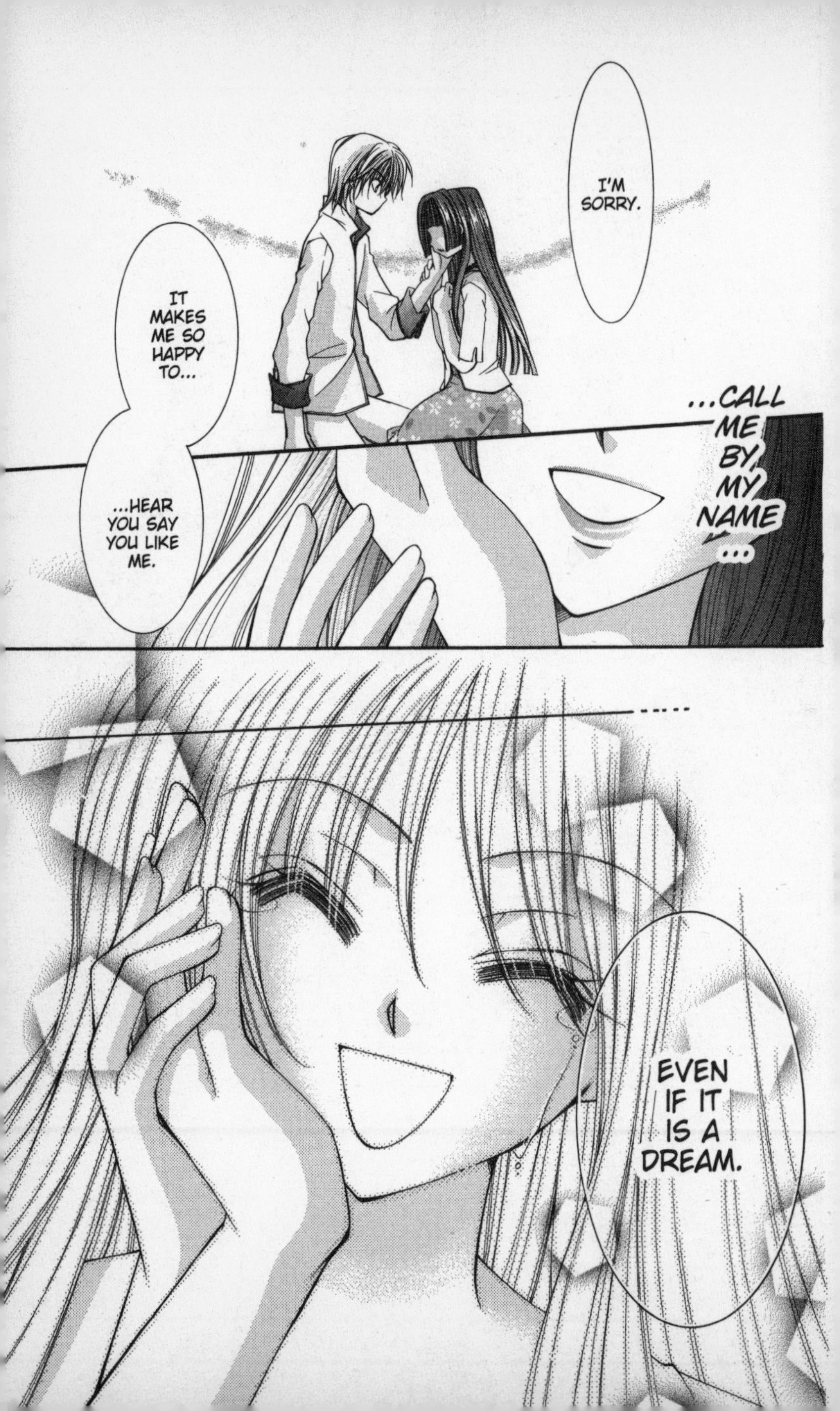
I'M SORRY.
IT MAKES ME SO HAPPY TO...
...CALL ME BY MY NAME...
...HEAR YOU SAY YOU LIKE ME.
EVEN IF IT IS A DREAM.

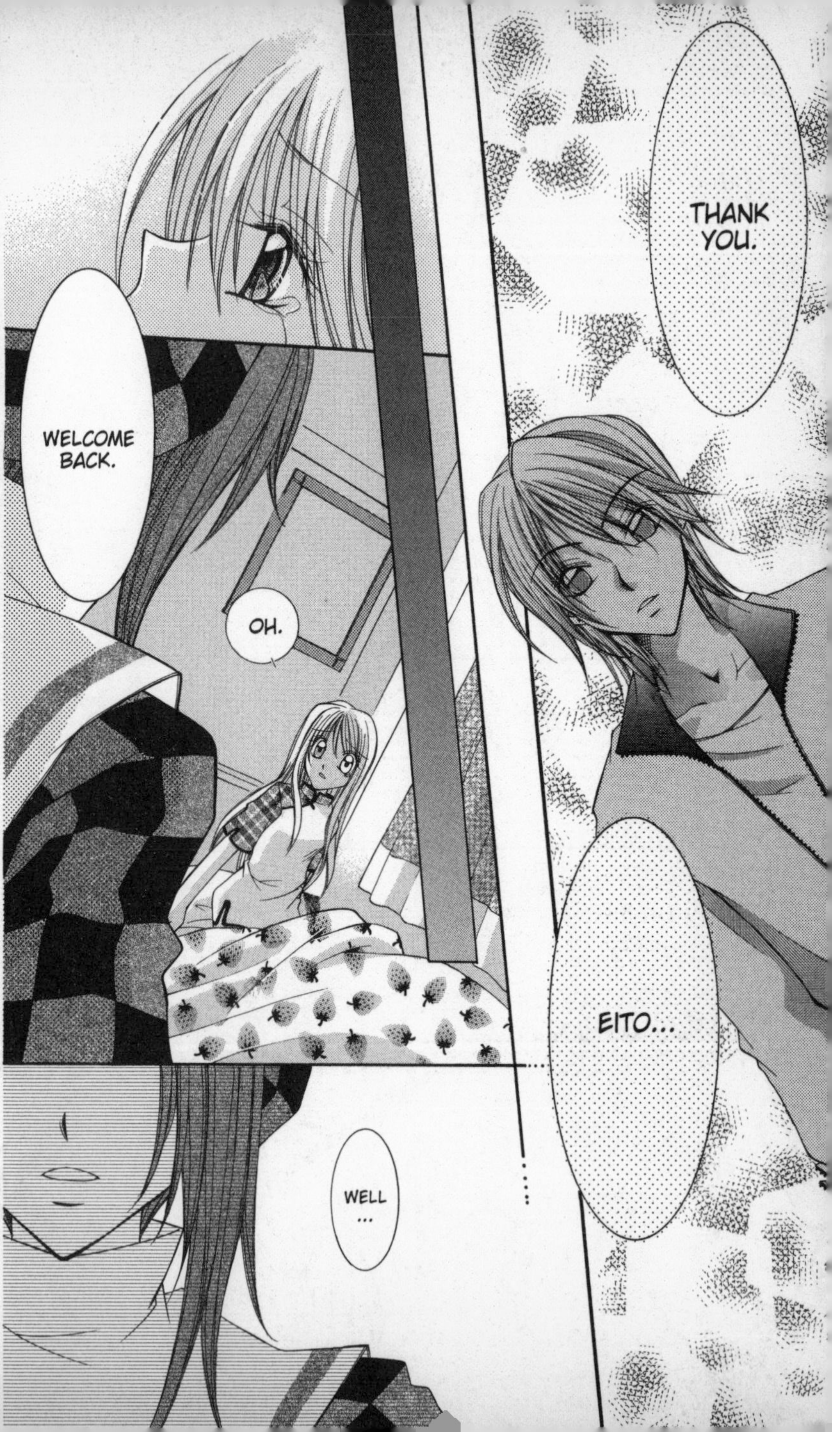
THANK YOU.
EITO...
WELCOME BACK.
OH.
WELL ...

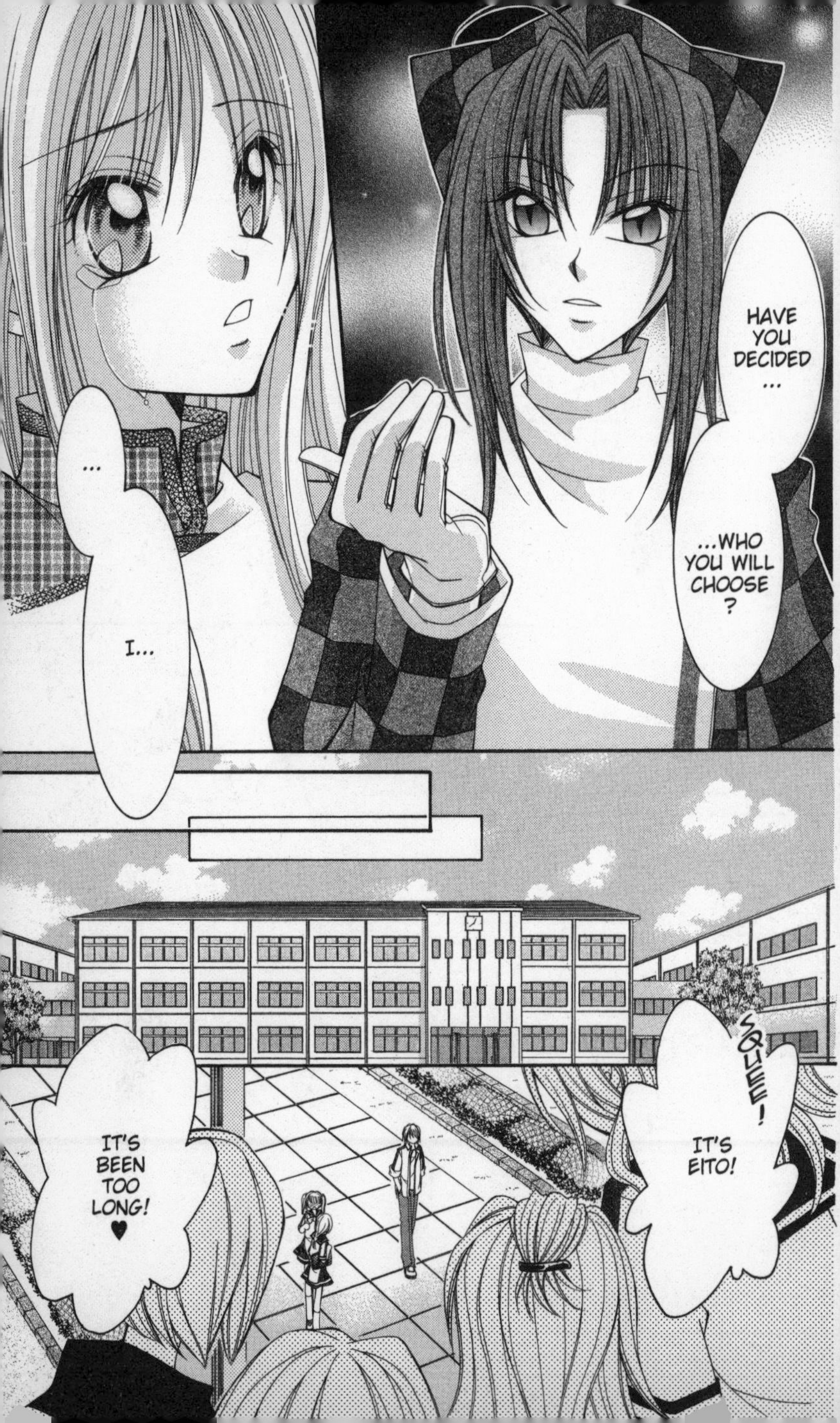
HAVE YOU DECIDED ...
...WHO YOU WILL CHOOSE?
... I...
SQUEE!
IT'S EITO!
IT'S BEEN TOO LONG! ♥

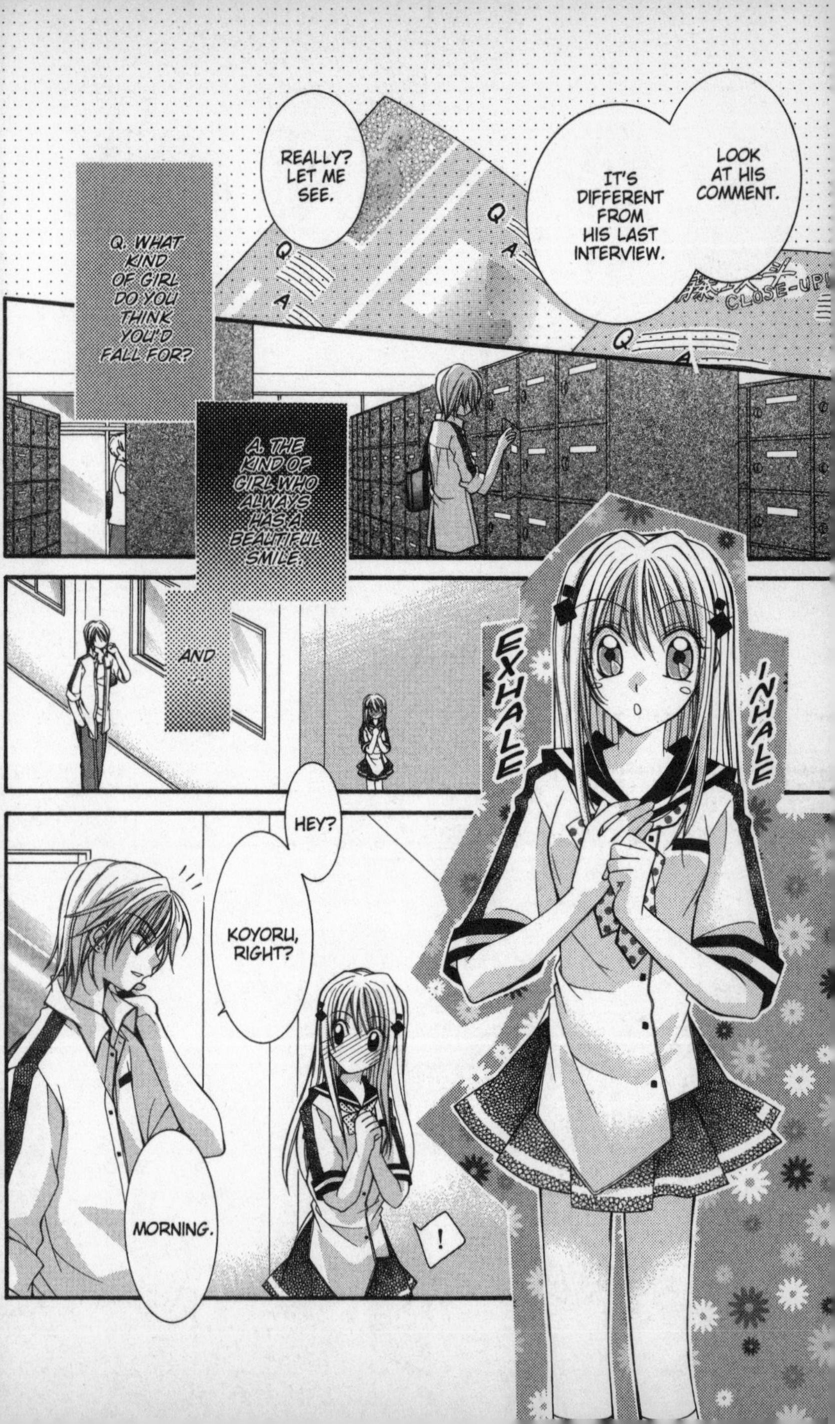
LOOK AT HIS COMMENT.
IT'S DIFFERENT FROM HIS LAST INTERVIEW.
REALLY? LET ME SEE.
CLOSE-UP
Q. WHAT KIND OF GIRL DO YOU THINK YOU'D FALL FOR?
A. THE KIND OF GIRL WHO ALWAYS HAS A BEAUTIFUL SMILE.
INHALE
EXHALE
AND ...
HEY?
KOYORU, RIGHT?
!
MORNING.

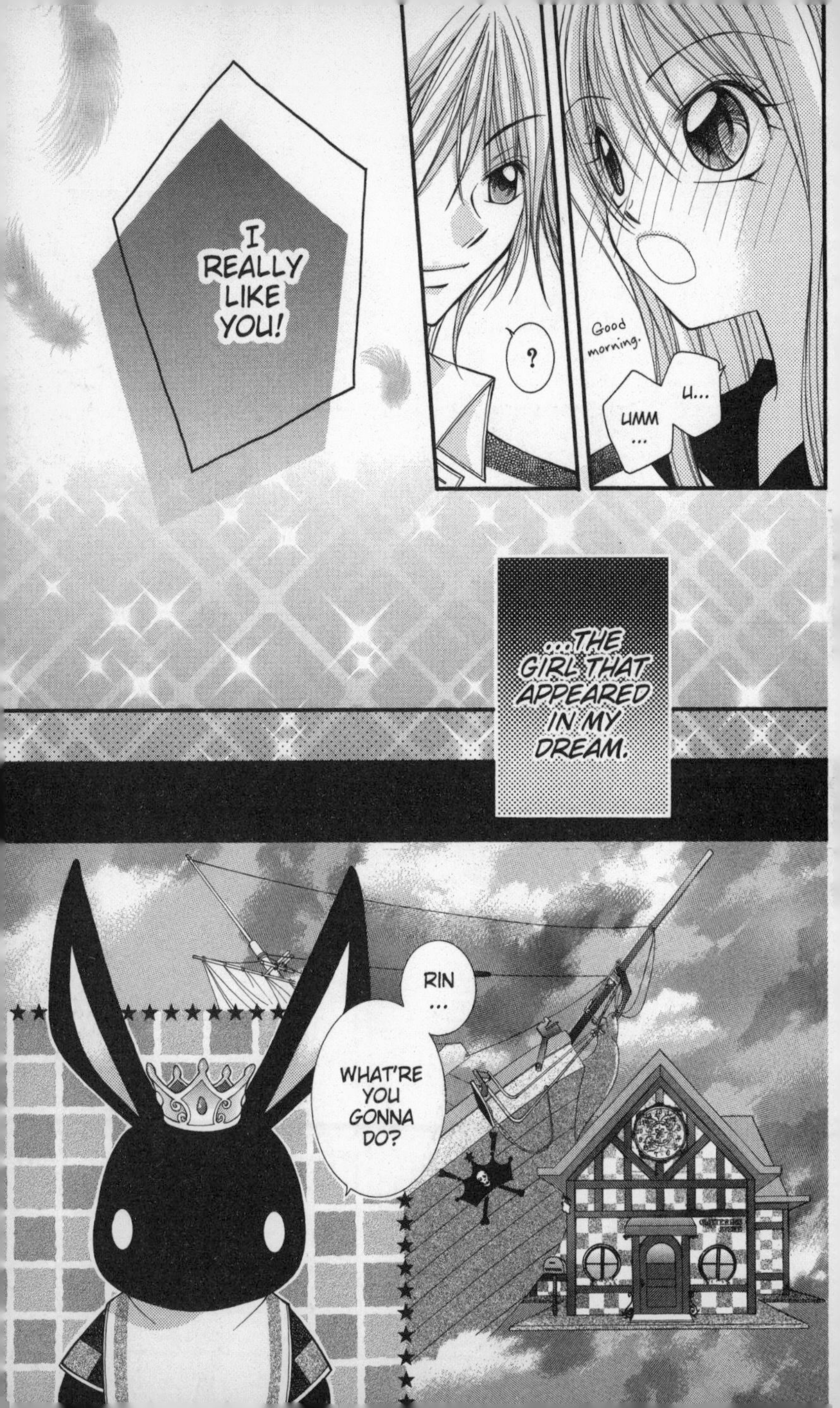
Good morning.
U...
UMM ...
?
I REALLY LIKE YOU!
...THE GIRL THAT APPEARED IN MY DREAM.
RIN ...
WHAT'RE YOU GONNA DO?

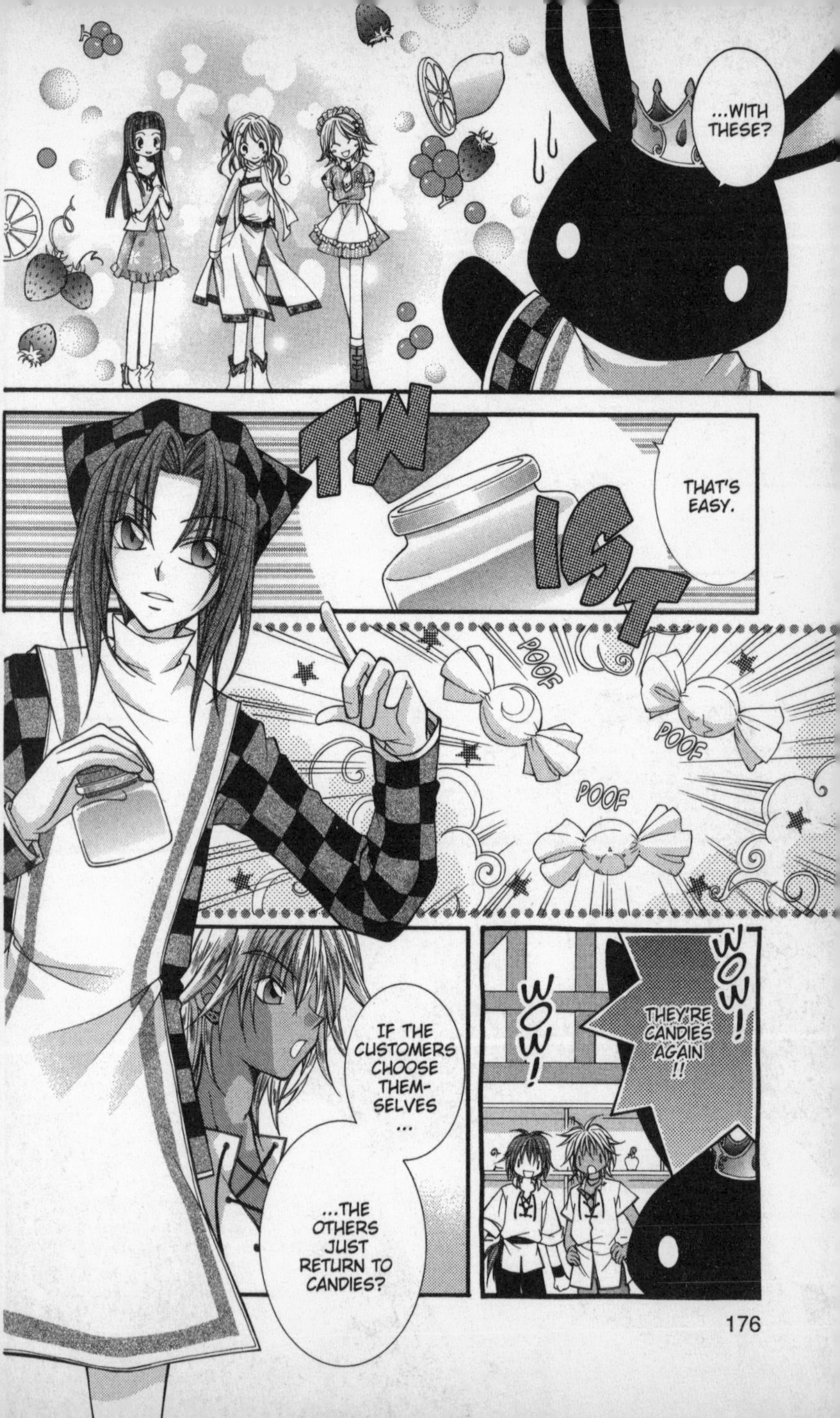
...WITH THESE?
TWIST
THAT'S EASY.
POOF
POOF
POOF
WOW!
THEY'RE CANDIES AGAIN!!
WOW!
IF THE CUSTOMERS CHOOSE THEM- SELVES ...
...THE OTHERS JUST RETURN TO CANDIES?

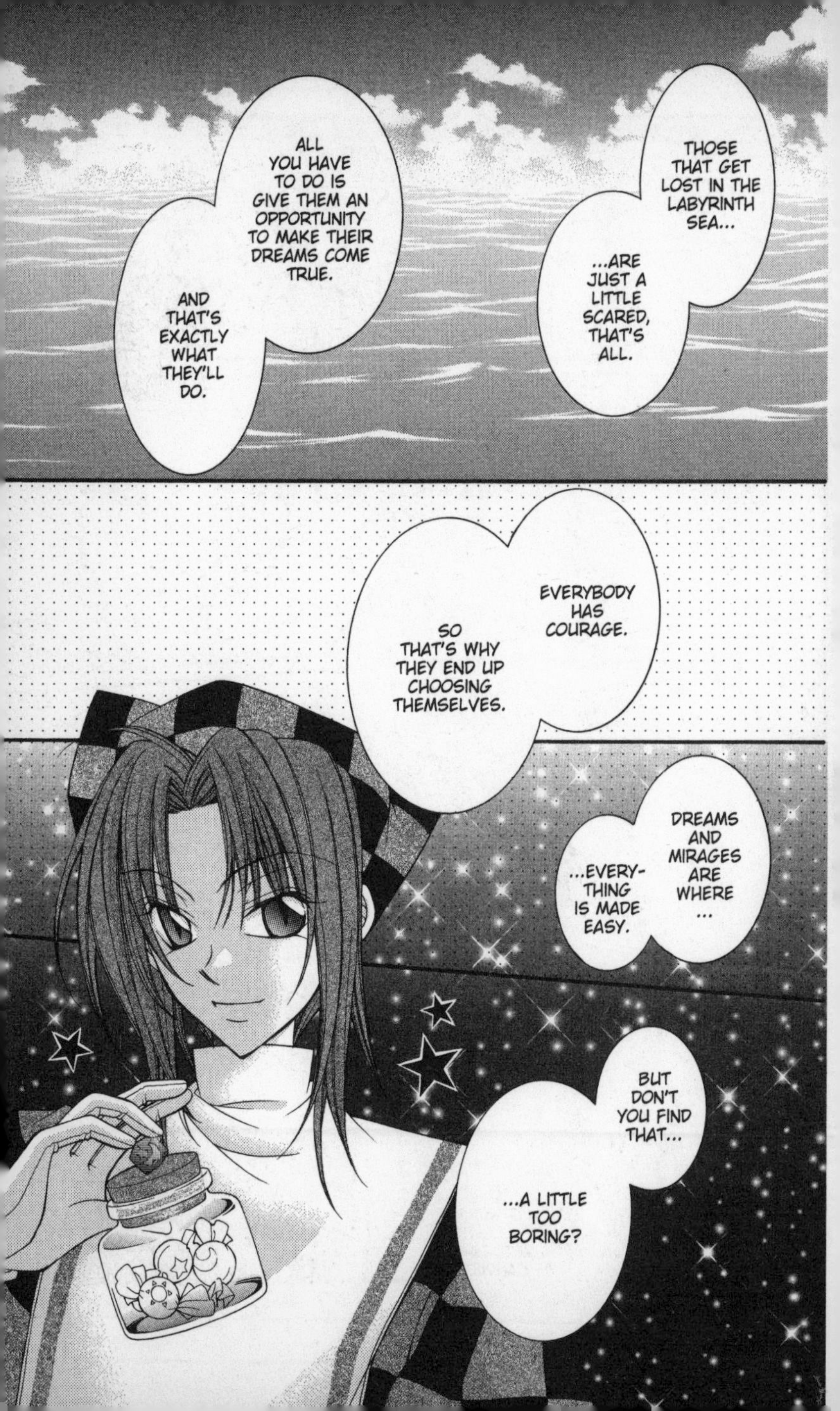
THOSE THAT GET LOST IN THE LABYRINTH SEA...
...ARE JUST A LITTLE SCARED, THAT'S ALL.
ALL YOU HAVE TO DO IS GIVE THEM AN OPPORTUNITY TO MAKE THEIR DREAMS COME TRUE.
AND THAT'S EXACTLY WHAT THEY'LL DO.
EVERYBODY HAS COURAGE.
SO THAT'S WHY THEY END UP CHOOSING THEMSELVES.
DREAMS AND MIRAGES ARE WHERE...
...EVERY-THING IS MADE EASY.
BUT DON'T YOU FIND THAT...
...A LITTLE TOO BORING?

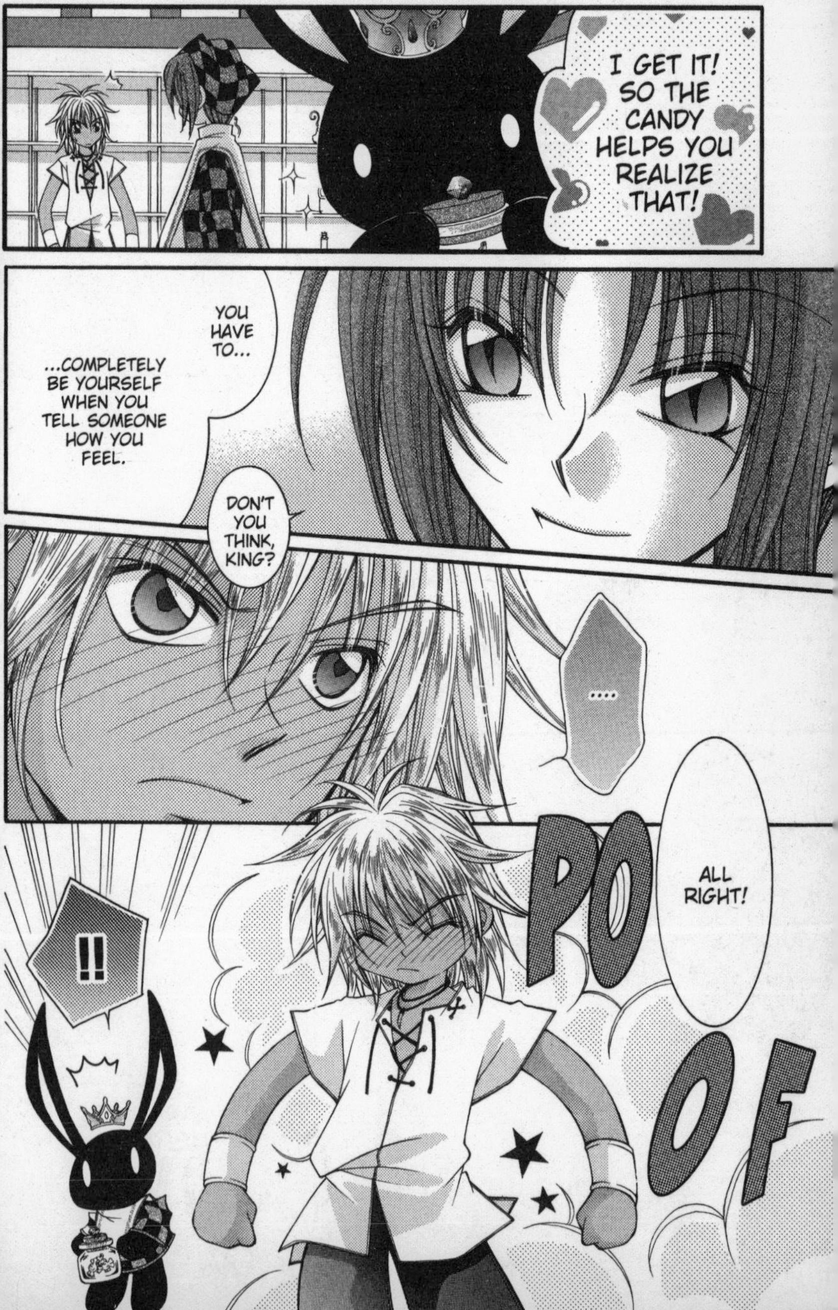
I GET IT! SO THE CANDY HELPS YOU REALIZE THAT!
YOU HAVE TO...
...COMPLETELY BE YOURSELF WHEN YOU TELL SOMEONE HOW YOU FEEL.
DON'T YOU THINK, KING?
....
ALL RIGHT!
POOF
!!

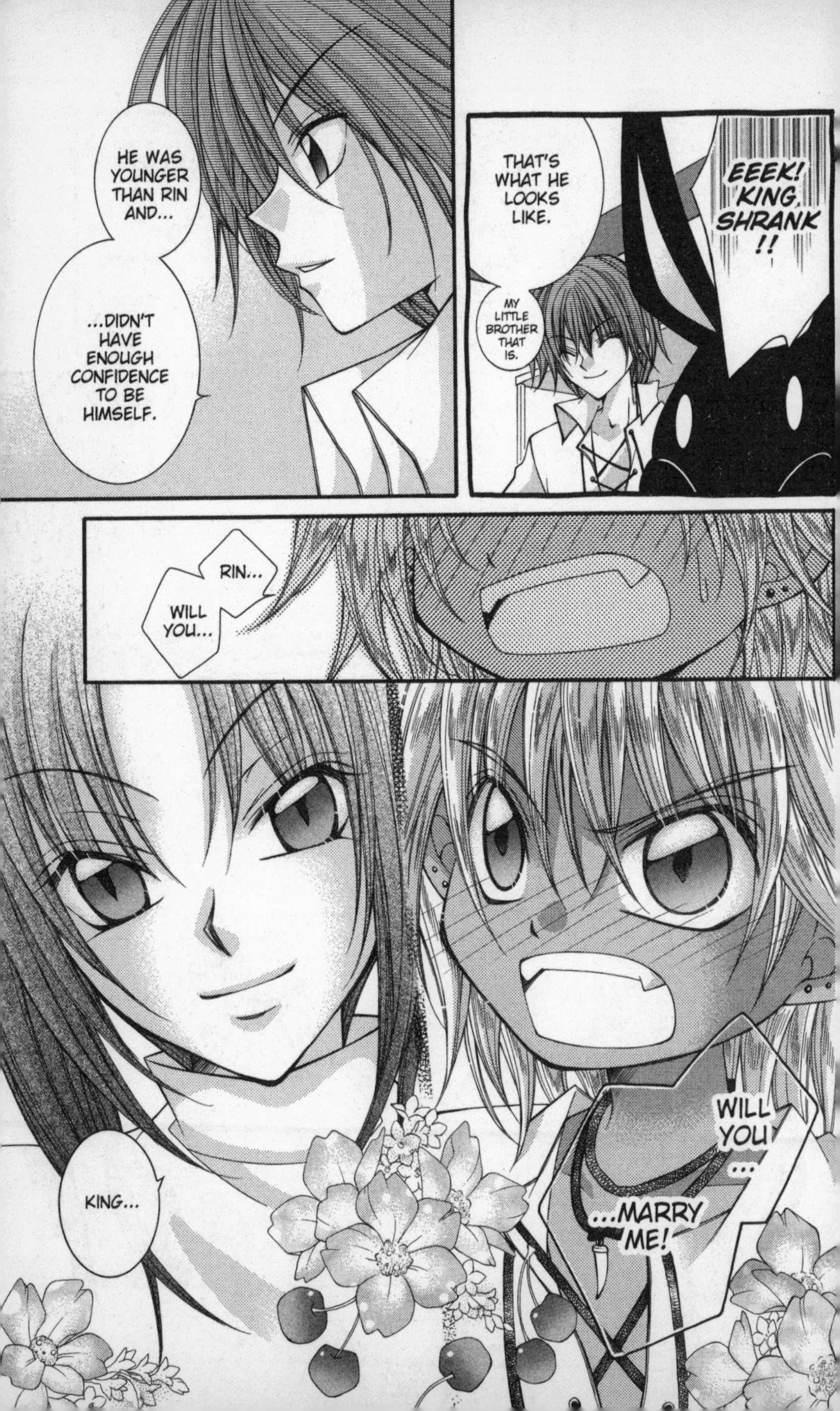
EEEK! KING SHRANK!!
THAT'S WHAT HE LOOKS LIKE.
MY LITTLE BROTHER THAT IS.
HE WAS YOUNGER THAN RIN AND...
...DIDN'T HAVE ENOUGH CONFIDENCE TO BE HIMSELF.
RIN...
WILL YOU...
WILL YOU ...
...MARRY ME!
KING...

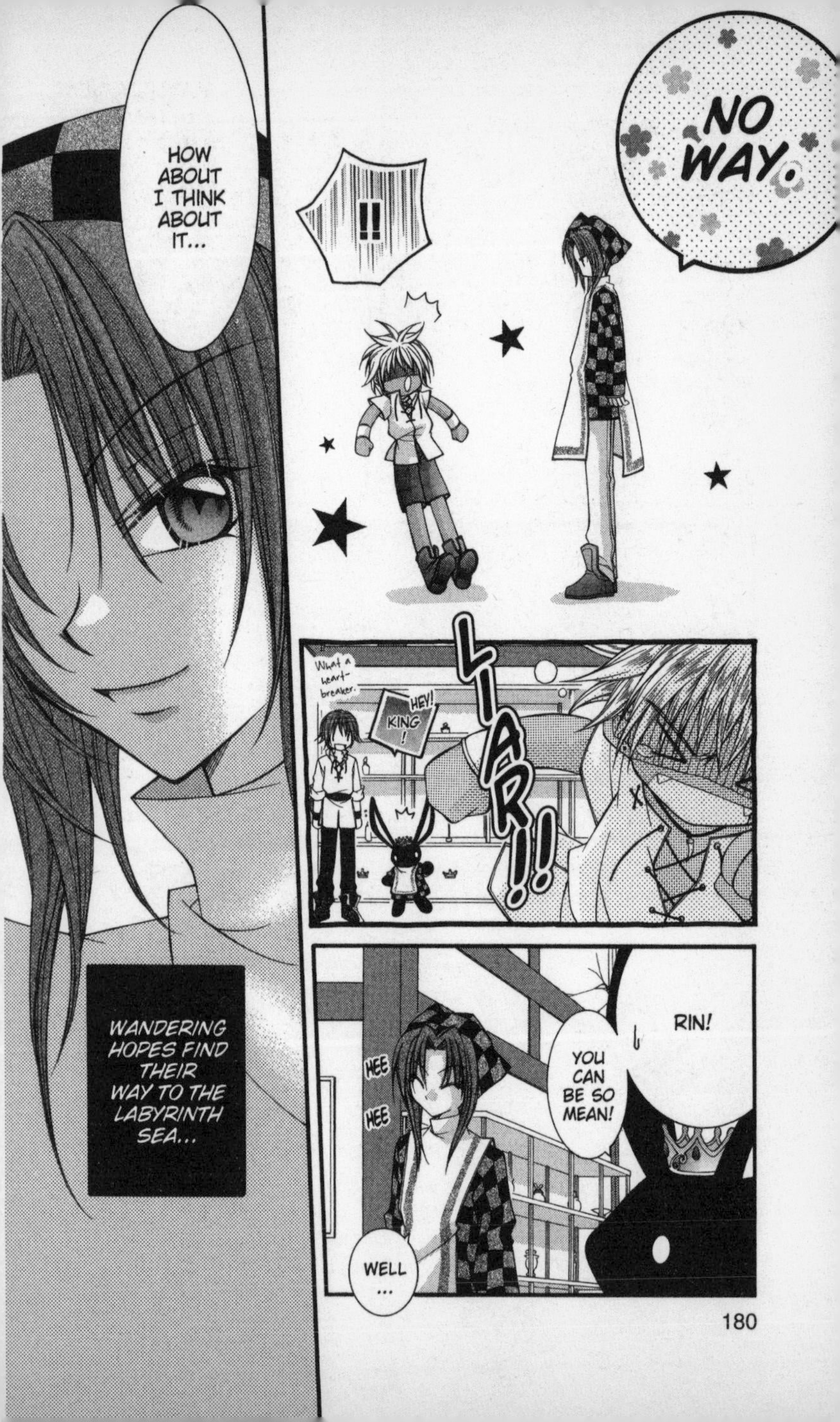
NO WAY.
!!
LIAR!!
HEY! KING!
What a heart-breaker.
RIN!
YOU CAN BE SO MEAN!
HEE HEE
WELL...
HOW ABOUT I THINK ABOUT IT...
WANDERING HOPES FIND THEIR WAY TO THE LABYRINTH SEA...

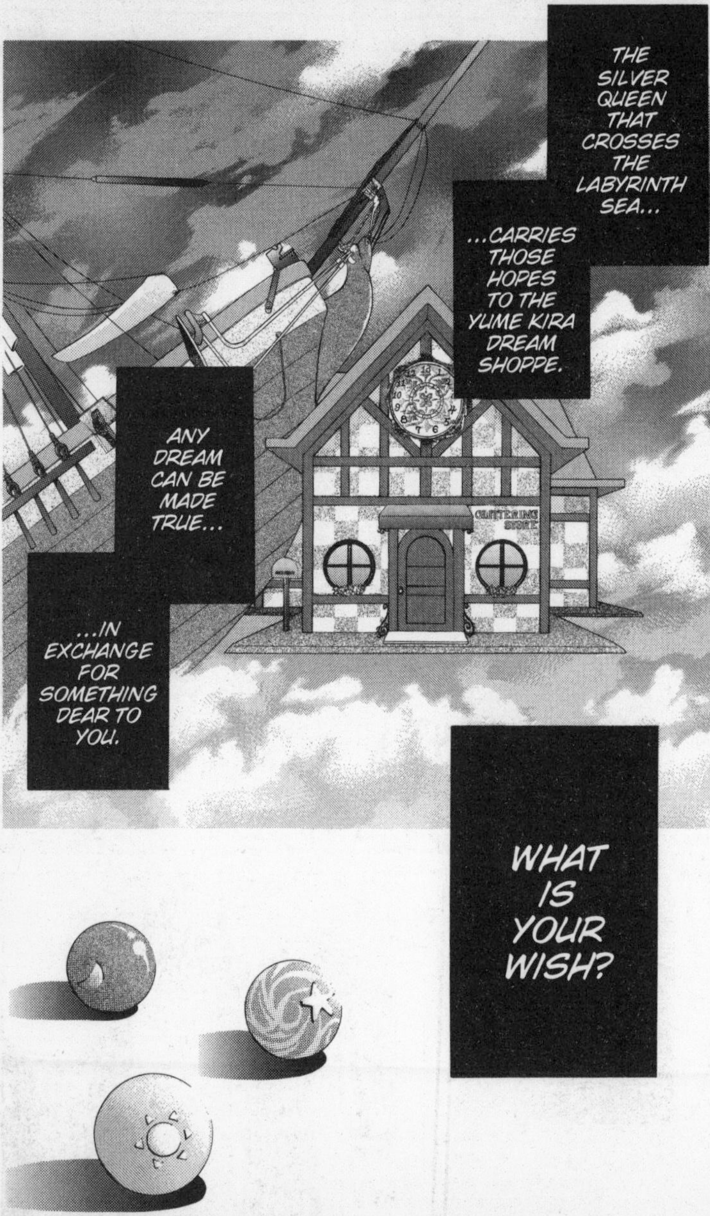
THE SILVER QUEEN THAT CROSSES THE LABYRINTH SEA...
...CARRIES THOSE HOPES TO THE YUME KIRA DREAM SHOPPE.
ANY DREAM CAN BE MADE TRUE...
...IN EXCHANGE FOR SOMETHING DEAR TO YOU.
WHAT IS YOUR WISH?

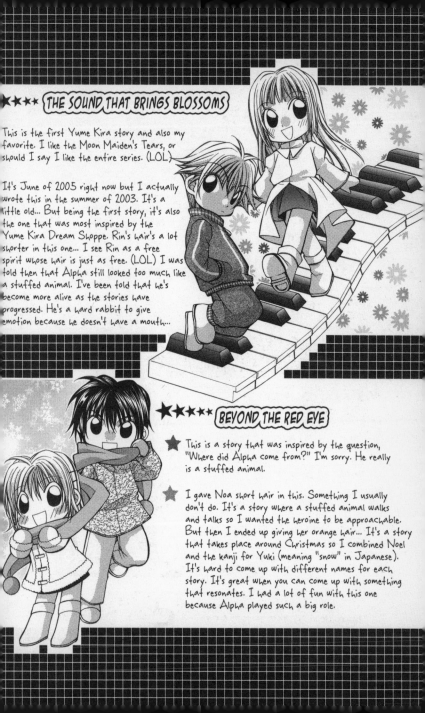

THE SOUND THAT BRINGS BLOSSOMS

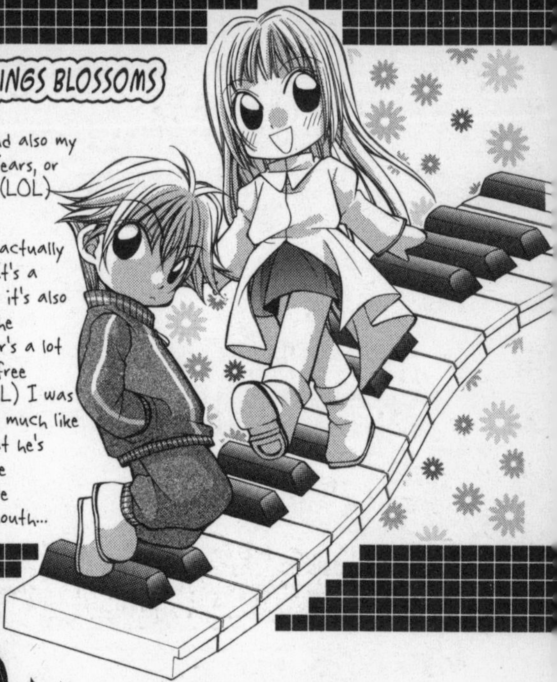

This is the first Yume Kira story and also my favorite. I like the Moon Maiden's Tears, or should I say I like the entire series. (LOL)

It's June of 2005 right now but I actually wrote this in the summer of 2003. It's a little old... But being the first story, it's also the one that was most inspired by the Yume Kira Dream Shoppe. Rin's hair's a lot shorter in this one... I see Rin as a free spirit whose hair is just as free. (LOL) I was told then that Alpha still looked too much like a stuffed animal. I've been told that he's become more alive as the stories have progressed. He's a hard rabbit to give emotion because he doesn't have a mouth...

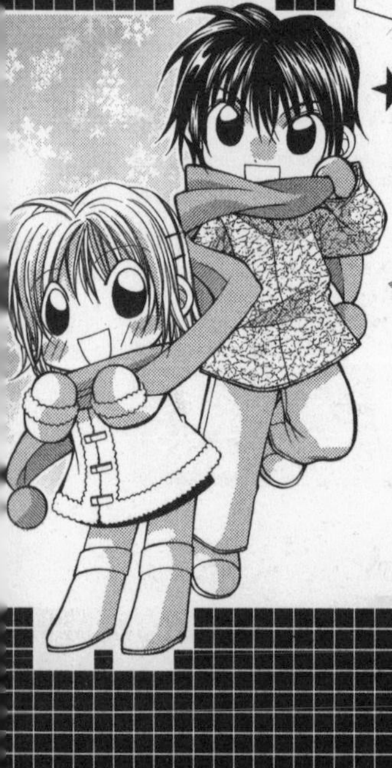

BEYOND THE RED EYE

This is a story that was inspired by the question, "Where did Alpha come from?" I'm sorry. He really is a stuffed animal.

I gave Noa short hair in this. Something I usually don't do. It's a story where a stuffed animal walks and talks so I wanted the heroine to be approachable. But then I ended up giving her orange hair... It's a story that takes place around Christmas so I combined Noel and the kanji for Yuki (meaning "snow" in Japanese). It's hard to come up with different names for each story. It's great when you can come up with something that resonates. I had a lot of fun with this one because Alpha played such a big role.

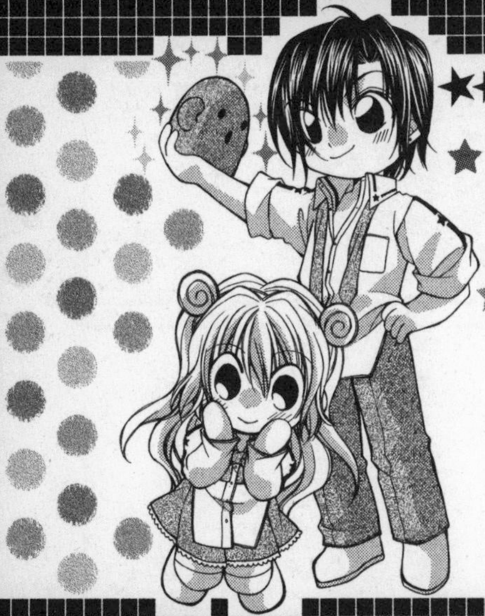

★★★★★ A PROMISE TO A GRAIN OF TIME

★ I had such a great time with the spread that I ended up using it for the cover. It was actually a toss-up to the end whether we were going to do this, but I wanted people to see the color version...

★ My editor actually suddenly sprang it on me. I drew a preview but my editor wanted the whole thing at the same time. I actually had to think of the story in an hour... which is a pretty scary memory. (LOL) I poured my heart into it but I regret not having more than 37 pages... But I swear I did my best!

I played around with Miki's hair quite a bit but my favorite ended up being the buns.

★★★★★ THE LABYRINTH WAVE OF DREAMS

★ I'm so happy I could incorporate the Silver Queen. King and Jack are my two favorite characters after Alpha. I like the dynamic of the clueless kid (Alpha) and the kid that gets teased (King).

★ I really like Koyoru's uniform. Not to toot my own horn. (LOL) My image for it in color (as seen on the back cover) was a sort of baby blue. I was able to enjoy drawing her in four different ways because she transforms three different times. I wanted Eito to be a little different but I ended up really liking what I came up with. Oh yes. And let's just keep Rin's sex a mystery. It's not like King has it figured out. Though I'm pretty sure his feelings wouldn't change even if Rin ended up being a boy...(LOL)

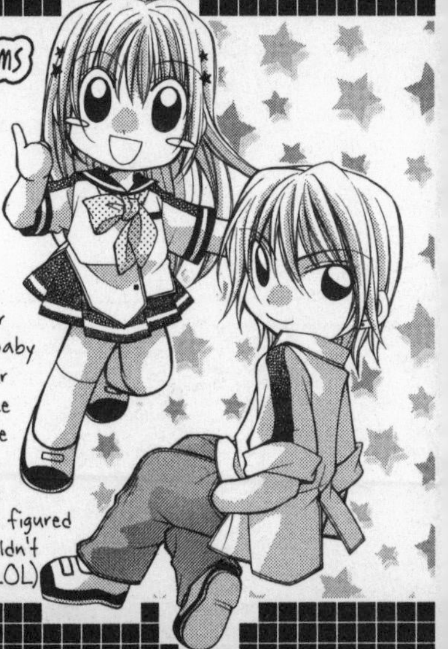

Alpha's Wish

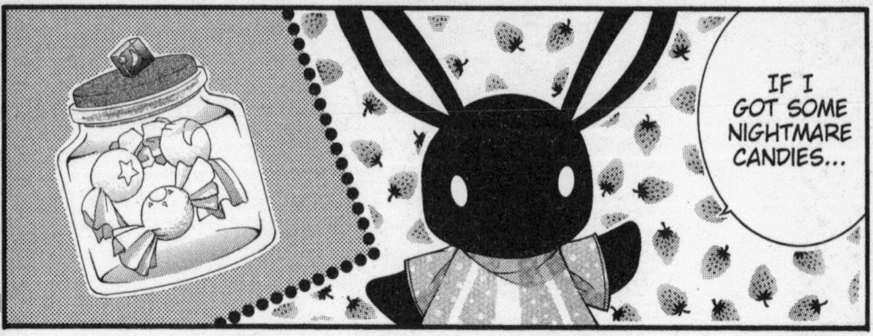
IF I GOT SOME NIGHTMARE CANDIES...

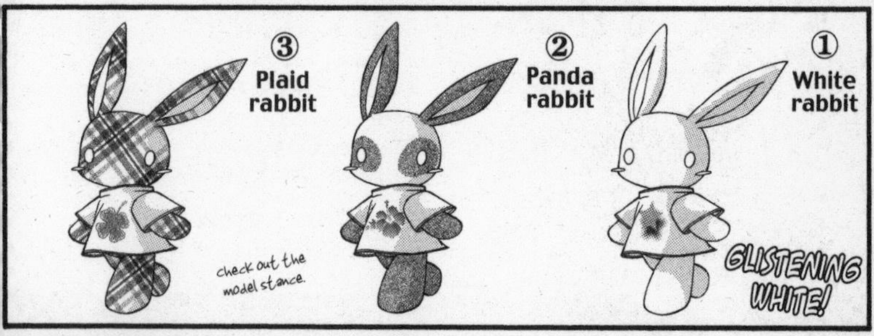
① White rabbit
GLISTENING WHITE!
② Panda rabbit
③ Plaid rabbit
check out the model stance.

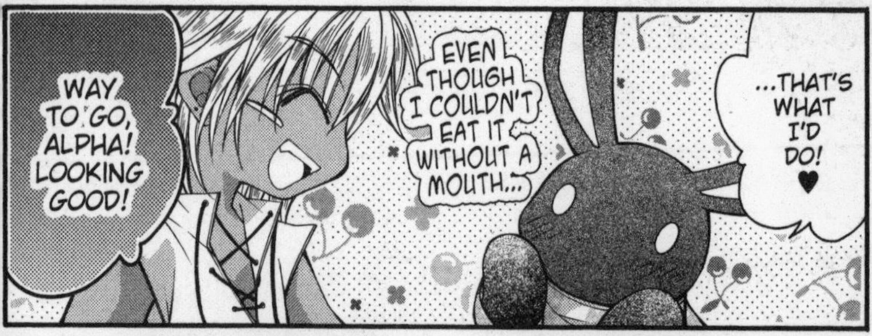
...THAT'S WHAT I'D DO! ♥
EVEN THOUGH I COULDN'T EAT IT WITHOUT A MOUTH...
WAY TO GO, ALPHA! LOOKING GOOD!

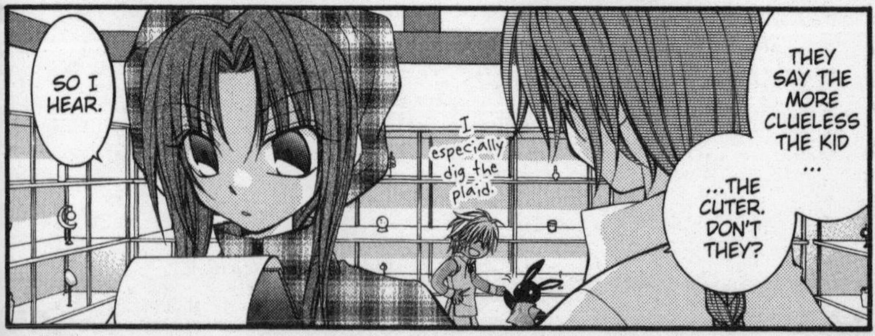
THEY SAY THE MORE CLUELESS THE KID ...
...THE CUTER. DON'T THEY?
I especially dig the plaid.
SO I HEAR.

★★★★★ Thank you so much for reading to the end. The underlying theme for Yume Kira Dream Shoppe is "hope." I tried to incorporate that in the titles as well. While the main characters are Rin and Alpha, I had "guest heroes/heroines" for each story and truly appreciate the difficulty of creating a one-time read. It was a lot of work but I had a great time. Especially thinking up the different products! I wanted to draw something that makes you feel warm and fuzzy inside once you finish. If you felt even a little "fuzz" or enjoyed yourself in the least bit, I couldn't ask for more. I'd like to continue drawing manga and would appreciate your continued support! I apologize in advance for not being able to answer you all, but I would love to hear any feedback you might have.

June, 2005 Aqua Mizuto

Aqua Mizuto c/o VIZ Media P.O. Box 77010 San Francisco, CA 94133

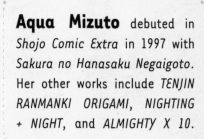

Aqua Mizuto debuted in *Shojo Comic Extra* in 1997 with *Sakura no Hanasaku Negaigoto*. Her other works include *TENJIN RANMANKI ORIGAMI*, *NIGHTING + NIGHT*, and *ALMIGHTY X 10*.

YUME KIRA DREAM SHOPPE
The Shojo Beat Manga Edition

This manga volume contains material that was originally published in English in *Shojo Beat* magazine, May–August 2007 issues.

STORY AND ART BY
AQUA MIZUTO

Translation & English Adaptation/Mai Ihara
Touch-up Art & Lettering/Rina Mapa
Additional Touch-up/Kam Li
Design/Amy Martin
Editor/Pancha Diaz

Editor in Chief, Books/Alvin Lu
Editor in Chief, Magazines/Marc Weidenbaum
VP of Publishing Licensing/Rika Inouye
VP of Sales/Gonzalo Ferreyra
Sr. VP of Marketing/Liza Coppola
Publisher/Hyoe Narita

Printed in Canada

Published by VIZ Media, LLC
P.O. Box 77010
San Francisco, CA 94107

Shojo Beat Manga Edition
10 9 8 7 6 5 4 3 2 1
First printing, September 2007

love ★ com

By Aya Nakahara

Lovely ★ Complex

Only $8⁹⁹

Love ★ com
Lovely ★ Complex
1
Aya Nakahara

Risa Koizumi is the tallest girl in class, and the last thing she wants is the humiliation of standing next to Atsushi Ôtani, the shortest guy. Fate and the whole school have other ideas, and the two find themselves cast as the unwilling stars of a bizarre romantic comedy!

Shojo Beat

Crimson Hero

By Mitsuba Takanashi

Only
$8.99

All that matters to 15-year-old Nobara Sumiyoshi is volleyball—she's an awesome player with big-time ambitions. But sometimes it seems like a girl just can't get a break in the competitive world of high school volleyball. When Nobara transfers to Crimson Field High School, known for its top-notch volleyball team, she decides to start playing offense!

Shojo Beat

MANGA from the H

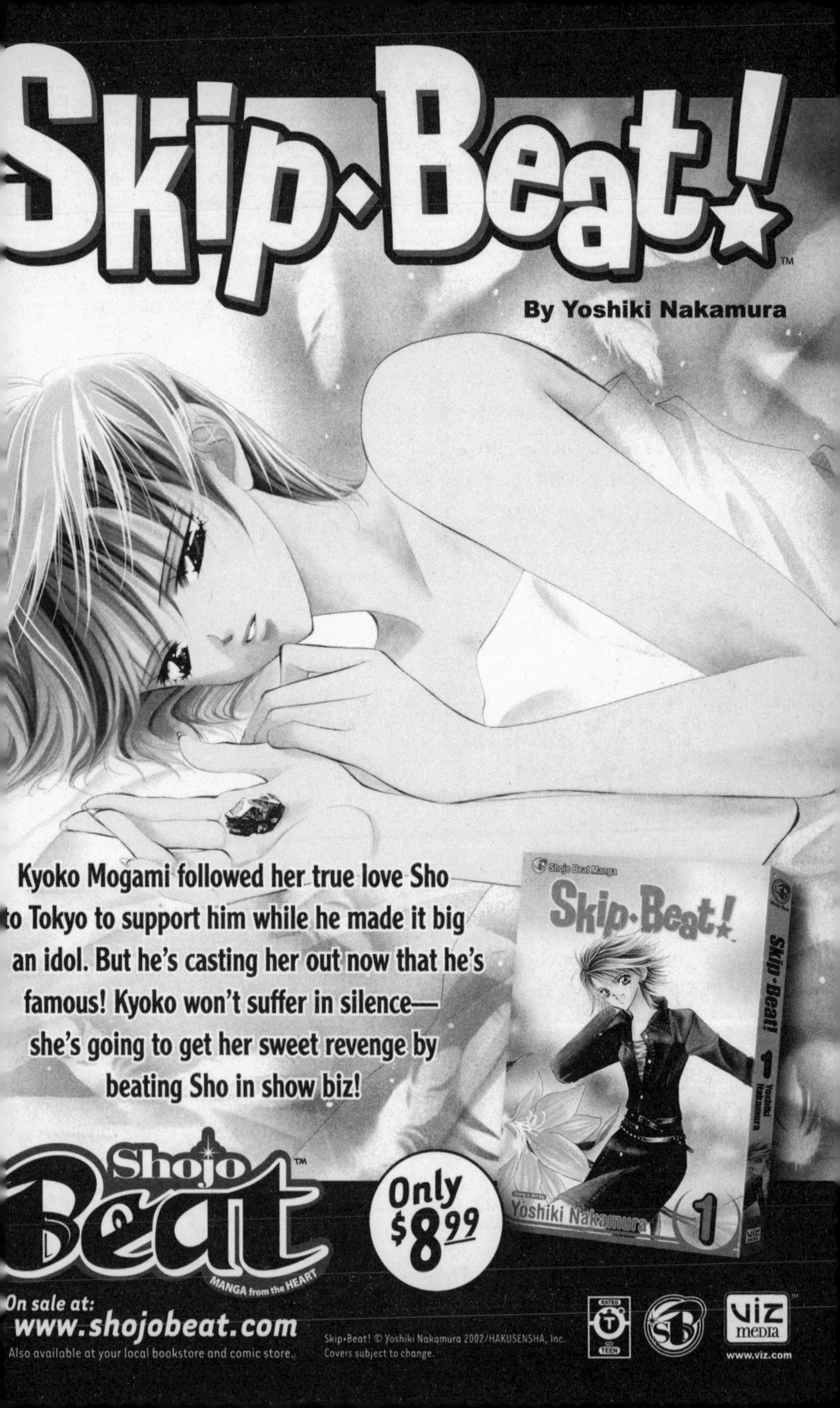

Skip·Beat!™
By Yoshiki Nakamura
Kyoko Mogami followed her true love Sho
to Tokyo to support him while he made it big
an idol. But he's casting her out now that he's
famous! Kyoko won't suffer in silence—
she's going to get her sweet revenge by
beating Sho in show biz!
Shojo Beat Manga
Skip·Beat!
Yoshiki Nakamura
1
Shojo Beat™
MANGA from the HEART
Only $8.99
On sale at:
www.shojobeat.com
Also available at your local bookstore and comic store.
Skip·Beat! © Yoshiki Nakamura 2002/HAKUSENSHA, Inc.
Covers subject to change.
RATED T TEEN
VIZ media
www.viz.com

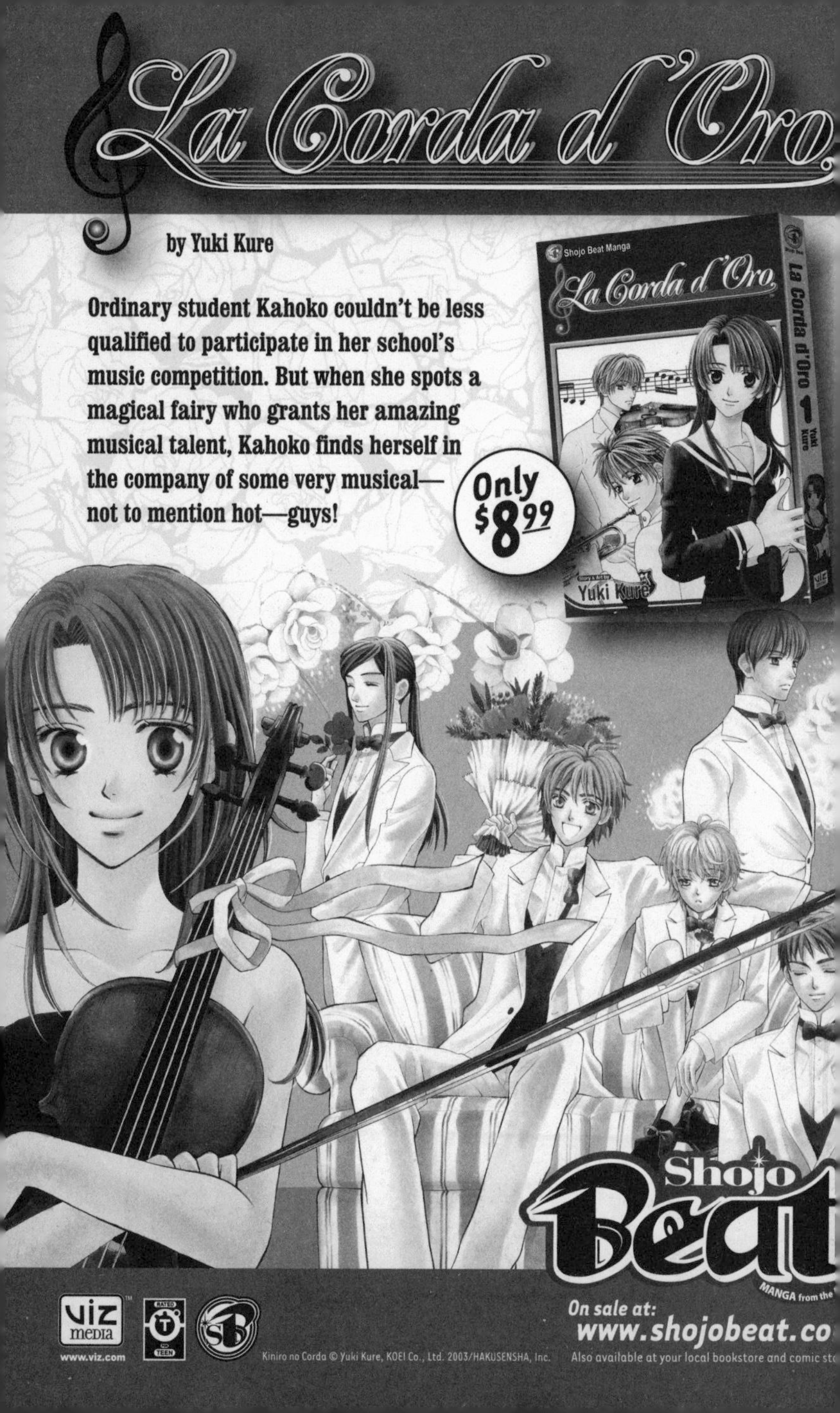
La Corda d'Oro
by Yuki Kure
Ordinary student Kahoko couldn't be less qualified to participate in her school's music competition. But when she spots a magical fairy who grants her amazing musical talent, Kahoko finds herself in the company of some very musical—not to mention hot—guys!
Only $8.99
Shojo Beat Manga
La Corda d'Oro
La Corda d'Oro 1 Yuki Kure
Story & Art by Yuki Kure
Shojo Beat
MANGA from the
On sale at:
www.shojobeat.co
Also available at your local bookstore and comic st
viz media
www.viz.com
RATED T TEEN
Kiniro no Corda © Yuki Kure, KOEI Co., Ltd. 2003/HAKUSENSHA, Inc.

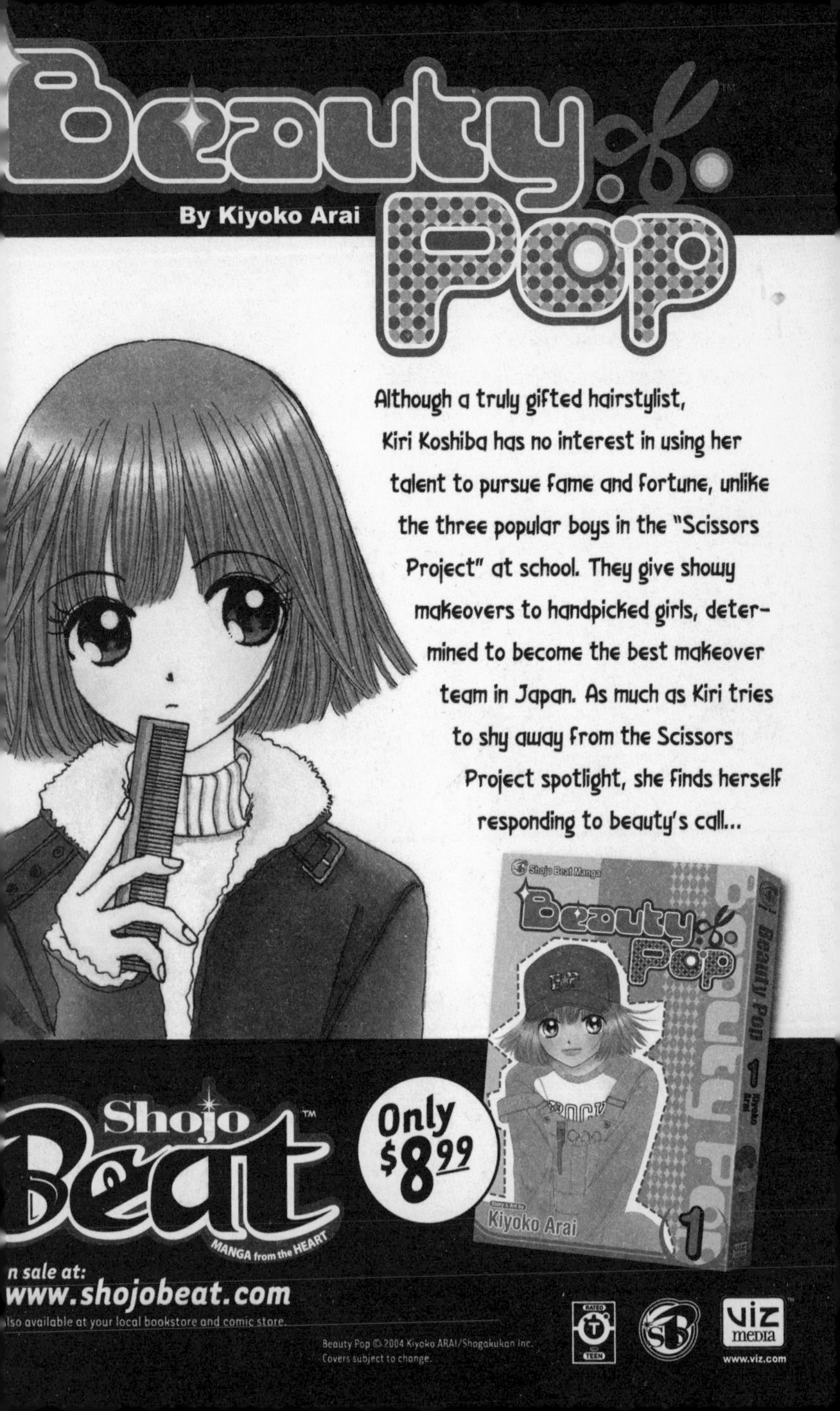

Beauty Pop
By Kiyoko Arai
Although a truly gifted hairstylist, Kiri Koshiba has no interest in using her talent to pursue fame and fortune, unlike the three popular boys in the "Scissors Project" at school. They give showy makeovers to handpicked girls, determined to become the best makeover team in Japan. As much as Kiri tries to shy away from the Scissors Project spotlight, she finds herself responding to beauty's call...
Shojo Beat Manga
Beauty Pop
Kiyoko Arai
1
Shojo Beat
MANGA from the HEART
Only $8.99
n sale at:
www.shojobeat.com
lso available at your local bookstore and comic store.
Beauty Pop © 2004 Kiyoko ARAI/Shogakukan Inc.
Covers subject to change.
RATED T TEEN
viz media
www.viz.com